The Business of Farm Anim

Globally, nearly 70 billion animals are farmed annually for meat, milk and eggs. Two-thirds of these are farmed intensively. The views held by food companies on animal stewardship, and the management practices and processes that they adopt are, therefore, of critical importance in determining the welfare of these animals.

Yet, despite the scale of the food industry's impact, farm animal welfare remains a relatively immature management issue. There is a lack of consensus around the specific responsibilities companies have for farm animal welfare, and around how companies should treat the animals in their or in their suppliers' care.

This book, *The Business of Farm Animal Welfare*, provides an extensive, authoritative analysis of current corporate practice on farm animal welfare. It critically reviews and assesses the ethical and business case for action. Through a series of practitioner case-studies, it describes how companies have addressed farm animal welfare in their operations and supply chains. It analyses the key barriers to companies adopting higher standards of farm animal welfare, and offers a series of practical recommendations to companies, consumers and policy makers on the role that they might play in raising farm animal welfare standards across the food industry.

As the first comprehensive account of business and farm animal welfare, this book is an essential resource for researchers, practitioners and general readers looking to understand and influence corporate practice on farm animal welfare.

Nicky Amos is the Executive Director of the Business Benchmark on Farm Animal Welfare.

Rory Sullivan is Expert Advisor to the Business Benchmark on Farm Animal Welfare.

The Business of Farm Animal Welfare

Edited by
Nicky Amos and Rory Sullivan

To Martin
Thank you for your
expertise and leadership
on farm animal welfare.
Nicky Amos
6 Sept 2017.

Martin
Many thanks for
everything
Rory
6/Sept/17

Routledge
Taylor & Francis Group
LONDON AND NEW YORK

First published 2018
by Routledge
2 Park Square, Milton Park, Abingdon, Oxon OX14 4RN

and by Routledge
711 Third Avenue, New York, NY 10017

Routledge is an imprint of the Taylor & Francis Group, an informa business

British Library Cataloguing-in-Publication Data
A catalogue record for this book is available from the British Library

Library of Congress Cataloging-in-Publication Data
A catalog record for this book has been requested

ISBN: 978-1-78353-412-8 (hbk)
ISBN: 978-1-78353-529-3 (pbk)
ISBN: 978-1-78353-411-1 (ebk)

Typeset in Goudy
by Saxon Graphics Ltd, Derby

To my family, David, James and Victoria

Nicky Amos

To my wife Melinda and our daughters, Claire and Laura

Rory Sullivan

Contents

Contributors

Inês Ajuda completed a BSc/MSc in veterinary medicine in 2012 at the Faculty of Veterinary Medicine, Technical University of Lisbon. Her master's thesis focused on comparing the comfort and adaptation of dairy cows to two different types of bedding (free stall and cubicles). After completing her degree she started working on the Animal Welfare Indicators (AWIN) Project as a PhD student, investigating pain assessment and means to mitigate pain in dairy goats. Inês attended several international conferences and meetings with stakeholders in order to raise awareness of the presence of pain in farm animals' lives and the importance of properly assessing that pain to help prevent or mitigate it. Inês joined Compassion in World Farming in 2015 as a research manager. She uses her experience in the field as well as knowledge of farm animal pain to support the team in its mission of placing farm animal welfare at the heart of the food industry, in addition to continuing to structure the scientific evidence base for Compassion's Food Business programme.

Nicky Amos is a recognized corporate responsibility professional with extensive experience in managing and directing corporate responsibility strategies in global organizations. Nicky advises multinational companies and leading non-governmental organizations on the development and implementation of sustainable development strategies and measurement frameworks, materiality assessments, stakeholder dialogue and disclosure practices. Together with Dr Rory Sullivan, Nicky developed the Business Benchmark on Farm Animal Welfare (BBFAW) and is Executive Director of the BBFAW. Rory and Nicky have also conducted a scoping study on the wildlife sourcing practices of the luxury goods, tourism and transportation sectors on behalf of an investor client and they have co-written a series of white papers on supply chain ethics. Nicky's other recent work includes preparing a group human rights policy and management framework for a multinational company, conducting a benchmark study on the reporting practices of pharmaceutical companies, drafting a series of international case studies on women in leadership, and writing multiple sustainability reports and integrated annual reports for market-leading companies.

Minna Autio is a senior lecturer in consumer economics in the Department of Economics and Management at the University of Helsinki. She specializes in the greening of consumer society, food and service consumption and consumer policy issues. She has recently studied consumers' viewpoints on local food and animal welfare, and is currently researching sustainable food networks and the consumption of wild food.

Jaakko Autio is a doctoral candidate in the Faculty of Social Sciences at the University of Helsinki. He is writing his doctoral dissertation on the management strategies of design companies. His recent research has focused on consumers' attitudes to animal welfare and meat consumption, service consumption and pet-related consumption.

Rosie Barraclough joined The Co-op in June 2015 as Agricultural Compliance Manager after graduating from Harper Adams University, where she studied bio-veterinary science. During her time at The Co-op, Rosie was responsible for monitoring and reporting on animal welfare data from The Co-op Farming Groups to the Farming & Food team. In June 2016, Rosie left The Co-op to begin studying for a PhD at the Royal (Dick) School of Veterinary Studies and the Roslin Institute, University of Edinburgh. Her PhD looks at the use of advanced technologies to enhance monitoring of dairy cow health.

Vicky Bond is now Managing Director, UK, at The Humane League. She has considerable experience of supporting companies in working towards more ethical and sustainable food supply chains. Vicky joined Compassion in World Farming in April 2011 as a research officer, before moving up to senior research manager and was part of the Food Business team between 2013 and 2016. In her role as EU Food Business Manager at Compassion in World Farming, Vicky worked in partnership with retailers, producers and manufacturers and covered all species of farmed animals as well as slaughter. Vicky qualified as a vet at Liverpool University in 2009. She obtained a master's degree at Sussex University in environment, development and policy, and graduated working part-time as a vet and researching for the Food Ethics Council *Food Justice* report. Vicky campaigned for better labelling of pig meat in the EU at a parliamentary level while working at Pig Business.

Martin Cooke is the International Head of Corporate Engagement at World Animal Protection. Martin leads on World Animal Protection's relationships with globally significant companies and helps colleagues to develop functional relationships with regionally and locally significant corporate partners aimed at protecting animals in farming, in disasters, in communities and in the wild. Martin is a member of the Royal College of Veterinary Surgeons and holds a master's degree in wild animal health from the Institute of Zoology. Martin has been a Trustee of the Zoological Society of London (ZSL) since 2012, and has a keen professional interest in wildlife conservation and conservation science.

Malcolm Copland started his career as a graduate recruit at Marks & Spencer, having completed a one-year business placement. Malcolm then invested a further 21 years in the business in a variety of roles within retail and purchasing category management. He joined Greggs Plc as the commercial director in 2014. He is a member of the Greggs Operating Board and has full accountability for category management, new product development, marketing and purchasing.

Jon Day is a biologist with broad experience in the agri-food sector, ranging from the livestock feed industry, pig production, nutrition, behaviour and welfare and consumer science. His consultancy connects businesses with relevant partners and formulates strategies to collaborate and exchange knowledge and expertise for mutual gain.

Kate Elliot is an ethical researcher at Rathbone Greenbank Investments, which she joined in 2007. She is a graduate of the University of Bristol with a master's in philosophy and mathematics. She has also completed a postgraduate qualification in environmental management, covering aspects of law, economics and corporate practices linked to social and environmental risks and opportunities. Kate is a member of Rathbone Greenbank's ethical research and engagement team, where she assesses the social and environmental performance of companies, in addition to monitoring and responding to emerging ethical and sustainability themes. Kate also helps co-ordinate Rathbone Greenbank's stewardship and engagement activities. Since 2014, she has been a member of the Admissions Panel for the Social Stock Exchange, helping to assess and identify companies that deliver social or environmental impact.

Ciara Gorst joined the Food Commercial Team at The Co-op in May 2008. Her roles have covered the technical responsibilities for The Co-op's meat, poultry and chilled categories and responsibility for livestock chains. Her role has grown further in the last 3 years with the development of The Co-op Farming Groups. She is now acting Senior Agricultural Manager, accountable for the delivery of the farming and food strategy, including fish sustainability, within The Co-op. She works closely within the supply chain building relationships with processors and farmers and ensuring a sustainable industry. Prior to joining The Co-op, Ciara spent 5 years working within the food supply chain.

Temple Grandin is a designer of livestock handling facilities and a Professor of Animal Science at Colorado State University. Facilities she has designed are located in countries such as the United States, Canada, Ireland, the UK, Mexico, Australia and New Zealand, among others. In North America, almost half of the cattle are handled in a centre track restrainer system that she designed for meat plants. Curved chute and race systems that Dr Grandin designed for cattle are used worldwide, and her writings on the flight zone and other principles of grazing animal behaviour have helped many people to reduce stress on their animals during handling. She has also developed an objective scoring system for assessing the handling of cattle and pigs at meat plants. This scoring system is used by many large corporations to improve animal welfare.

David Grumett is Chancellor's Fellow in Christian Ethics and Practical Theology at the University of Edinburgh, where he teaches courses in ethics and society, and theology and food. His books include *Theology on the Menu: Asceticism, Meat and Christian Diet* (Routledge, 2010). David is Associate Editor of *Brill Research Perspectives in Theology*, Assistant Editor of *Ecclesiology* and a Fellow of the Higher Education Academy. From 2008 to 2016 he served as Treasurer then Secretary of the Society for the Study of Theology. As an ethicist, he is a member of the Farm Animal Welfare Committee of the Department for Environment, Food and Rural Affairs.

Sally Healy earned her bachelor's degree in biology at Griffith University before completing her honours in environmental psychology. She is currently completing a doctorate degree in consumer behaviour and animal welfare at Griffith University. The focus of her thesis is on examining the connection between consumers and their attitudes towards animal welfare, specifically pertaining to laying hens, meat chickens and pigs. Sally hopes her research will identify ways consumers can engage in animal welfare issues and support higher welfare products through their purchasing decisions. In 2015 Sally completed an Endeavour Fellowship supported by the Australian Government to work alongside Compassion in World Farming's Food Business team.

Abigail Herron is Head of Responsible Investment Engagement at Aviva Investors. She leads responsible investment and corporate governance engagement across all asset classes and markets, and complements this work with public policy advocacy in the UK, EU, OECD and UN on a spectrum of issues from sustainable capital markets to antibiotic resistance and green bonds. She previously headed corporate governance at The Co-operative Asset Management (TCAM). Abigail sits on the leadership committee of the UK Sustainable Investment and Finance Association, the investor steering committee of the 30% Club, the corporate governance committee of the Institute of Chartered Accountants in England and Wales, and the non-executive environmental advisory panel of Travis Perkins. She is also a technical adviser to the Zoological Society of London's palm oil group and a trustee of the Chartered Secretaries' Charitable Trust. She is a fellow of the Institute of Chartered Secretaries and Administrators (ICSA), a chartered company secretary and a member of the Chartered Institute for Securities & Investment.

Jemima Jewell joined Compassion in World Farming as Head of Food Business in 2013. Her background is in corporate sustainability, and she has spent much of her career working with companies—from multinational corporations to start-ups—on how to harness the power of a business approach to address social and environmental challenges. Prior to joining Compassion, Jemima was Director of Partnerships at CSR Asia in Hong Kong. Jemima has a first-class degree in Human Sciences from Oxford University, is a Fellow of the On Purpose social enterprise leadership programme, and is a trustee for the international development charity Concern Worldwide (UK).

Cia Johnson earned her DVM and MS from the University of Missouri-Columbia. She is currently the Director of the Animal Welfare Division at the American Veterinary Medical Association and serves as an adjunct professor for the University of Florida Online Forensic Science Program.

Tracey Jones is Director of Food Business at Compassion in World Farming, the leading international farm animal welfare charity. The Food Business programme works with leading food companies and brands to raise the baseline standards of welfare for farm animals, and so effect change at scale. Since 2013, Tracey has overseen the development of supportive technical resources, the evolution of the programme tools and the introduction of the programme to the USA and China. Tracey has animal science and production degrees and an extensive background in applied farm animal welfare and behaviour research. Her focus while at Cambac Research and Oxford University centred on pig and poultry welfare, respectively, and included studies into handling systems for pigs at slaughter; tail-biting incidence and solutions in meat pigs and free-farrowing systems for sows; stocking density limits for broiler chickens; bathing water access for ducks; and breeding broilers for welfare traits.

Ari Kuismin is a doctoral candidate in the Department of Management Studies at Aalto University School of Business. His research focuses on changing work practices and organizational change, with his doctoral thesis focusing specifically on entrepreneurial work practices and the implications thereof, especially in terms of embodiment and space. He is also working on projects that focus on food and service consumption.

Géraldine Kutas is a senior expert in international trade regulations with an extensive knowledge in agriculture and bioenergy and a solid experience in advocacy work in the European Union, the United States and Brazil. She assists trade associations and companies in detecting and addressing regulatory risks in the European Union as well as in formulating strategies to adapt to new policy environment and promote best practices. Géraldine is the author and co-author of several international publications in the areas of bioenergy and agricultural policies as well as multilateral and regional trade negotiations in agriculture. She holds a PhD in international economics from the Institut d'Etudes Politiques de Paris (Sciences-Po).

Eliisa Kylkilahti is a doctoral candidate in consumer economics in the Department of Economics and Management at the University of Helsinki. She is writing her doctoral dissertation on everyday sense-making in the context of service consumption. Her research interests in the area of consumer studies include narrative and performative perspectives, especially on service and food consumption.

Steven McLean is Head of Agriculture & Fisheries Sourcing for the food business of Marks & Spencer (M&S). He joined M&S in 2008 as Agriculture Manager for red meat and dairy supply chains, and was appointed Head of Agriculture & Fisheries in 2012. Prior to joining M&S, Steven was Chief Executive of the British Texel Sheep Society and its subsidiaries, a manager with the ANM Lamb Marketing group, and a development officer with the Highlands & Islands Sheep Health Society. He is currently responsible for raw material sourcing across agriculture and wild caught fisheries for the M&S food business globally. This includes establishing and delivering sustainable agriculture and fish programmes and leading the development of global sourcing strategies for livestock and fish proteins, encompassing more than 10,000 individual farming and fishing businesses around the world.

Leonardo Mirone received a B.E. degree in chemistry from the University of Parma, Italy, in 1994, and a PhD in chemistry from the University of Catania, Italy, in 1998. In 1998, he joined Barilla as a scientist within the Research and Development team with a specialist focus on raw materials including meat, fish and tomatoes, as well as providing advice on chemical contamination in supply chains. In 1999, he became Buyer of Raw Materials and, from 1999 to 2016, held various roles within the Raw Materials Purchasing Department before assuming the role as Director of the Department with global responsibility for all raw materials. Mirone is a member of the Barilla Sustainability Steering Committee and of the Scientific Committee of the Barilla Center for Food and Nutrition Foundation (BCFN). He is also President of the Economic Affairs Committee of the Association of Chocolate, Biscuit and Confectionery Industries of Europe (CAOBISCO).

Emily Patterson-Kane is a New Zealand-born psychologist, former animal behaviour researcher and co-author of *The Sciences of Animal Welfare* (Wiley-Blackwell, 2009). She is currently employed as an animal welfare scientist at the American Veterinary Medical Association.

Heather Pickett, BSc MSc is a freelance researcher with 15 years' experience of research, analysis and writing in the fields of animal behaviour and welfare, agriculture and livestock production, environment and sustainability, human and animal health, nutrition, and food policy. Her clients include a number of high-profile organizations, primarily within the not-for-profit sector. Her work has been instrumental in achieving policy change at UK and European Union level and at major companies.

Richard Pike is Technical and Sustainability Director for COOK. He started life in the world of produce in the early 1980s, working for a number of family and multinational business in various quality, technical and operational management roles. Over time, Richard developed a deep distaste of the way that big business operated with particular regard to supply chain activities, and he began to search for a better way. In 2007, becoming increasingly disillusioned with the "volume at all costs" business model, and being "on the brink of becoming a beach bum", Richard joined COOK to shape the technical agenda with a focus on sourcing with collaboration and transparency throughout the supply chain.

Brigit Ramsingh is a Lecturer in Food Safety Management at the College of Health and Wellbeing, University of Central Lancashire. She specializes in international food safety standards, food labelling, policy, food law, and sustainability. She has previously studied the history of world food standards and systems, and worked in food policy for the Canadian government. She is currently investigating alternative food networks and sustainable food practices in the north-west of England.

Bronwen Reinhardt is Senior Food Business Manager at Compassion in World Farming, UK. Born in South Africa, Bronwen moved to the UK in 1998. She started her NGO career in 1999 with WWF-UK, account managing their corporate partnerships. She then moved to WSPA (now World Animal Protection) and, in 2015, joined Compassion in World Farming. Through her collaboration with high profile brands over the past 17 years, she has witnessed first-hand the impressive change that takes place when companies engage transparently with their CSR profile and how this engagement directly impacts their supply chain decisions for the long term. Working in partnership with these high impact businesses, she has advocated at the highest levels (including the UN and European Parliament). She has a wealth of commercial and NGO knowledge and experience, having worked across cultural global partnerships on a variety of activities including fundraising and advocacy.

Rory Sullivan is an internationally recognized expert on responsible investment. He works as an independent consultant, providing advice to investment managers and investment funds on how they can integrate environmental, social and governance issues into their investment processes. His recent projects include working with the Principles for Responsible Investment on its *Fiduciary Duty in the 21st Century* project, leading a major research project (Non-state Actors and the Low-carbon Economy) at the Centre for Climate Change Economics and Policy at the University of Leeds, and supporting the development of the Transition Pathway Initiative. Together with Nicky Amos he developed the Business Benchmark on Farm Animal Welfare (BBFAW), and he is currently expert advisor to BBFAW. Dr Sullivan is the author/editor of seven books and many papers and articles on responsible investment, corporate responsibility and related issues. His publications include *Valuing Corporate Responsibility:*

How Do Investors Really Use Corporate Responsibility Information? (Greenleaf Publishing, 2011) and *Corporate Responses to Climate Change* (editor, Greenleaf Publishing, 2008).

Anna Valros has an MSc in zoology (1998), and a PhD in animal behaviour and welfare (2003) from the University of Helsinki. She has been an associate member of the Animal Welfare Science, Ethics and Law sub-specialty of the European College of Animal Welfare and Behaviour Medicine since 2016. She works as Professor of Animal Welfare at the Department of Production Animal Medicine in the Faculty of Veterinary Medicine at the University of Helsinki. Her main research area is behaviour and welfare of pigs and poultry. She is responsible for teaching animal welfare, behaviour and management, and animal ethics, within the veterinary education at the University of Helsinki.

Helena Viñes Fiestas is the Head of Sustainability Research (ESG/SRI) at BNP Paribas Investment Partners (BNPP IP), where she leads a team that oversees and implements BNPP IP's responsible investment and ownership policies. She is BNPP IP's representative for the Principles for Responsible Investment and the Institutional Investors Group on Climate Change, a member of the advisory group for the FAO-OECD Guidelines on responsible agricultural supply chains and a member of the expert committee of the Access to Medicine Index. She joined the team in May 2011 after six years at Oxfam where she led Oxfam's advocacy work on responsible investment and its engagement with institutional investors in support of poverty reduction. She is the author of a book on corporate responsibility, and of many papers and articles on responsible investment.

Heleen van de Weerd is an animal welfare specialist who works with corporate, NGO and government clients, applying animal welfare knowledge to achieve improvements to animal's lives. Her consultancy includes applying practical knowledge on animal production to facilitate improvements in animal welfare, while never losing sight of business performance.

Foreword

Temple Grandin

PROFESSOR OF ANIMAL SCIENCE AT COLORADO STATE UNIVERSITY, USA

During a long career which started in the 1970s, I have observed huge improvements in both animal handling and housing. When I first started in the cattle industry, I mistakenly assumed that I could fix all welfare problems with the right system. It took me a number of years to learn that I could fix about half of the problems with an engineering approach; many people built new systems I had designed but only a few companies operated them correctly. I have a saying, "People want the thing more than the management". It is easy to specify that a farm has a certain type of housing system, but having improved production systems is no guarantee of better welfare for animals. For example, a cage-free hen house that is filthy with poor air quality provides low welfare conditions for laying hens. Similarly, a straw-bedded, group-housed sow farm where the sows are lying in muck because of a lack of sufficient straw, will compromise the health and welfare of the sows.

The manner in which companies manage farm animal welfare is of critical importance to the wellbeing of many billions of animals. Their management of farm animal welfare-related issues will be influenced by a number of factors, including company and employee attitudes, inclinations and knowledge. For example, in 1999, I was hired to train auditors for large restaurant companies to assess their meat suppliers. Using a simple outcome-based scoring system that I developed for assessing animal handling and stunning at beef and pork abattoirs (Grandin, 1998), the baseline data indicated that the primary cause of poor stunning was poorly maintained equipment (Grandin, 1998); that is, poor stunning was, essentially, a management rather than a technical issue. To improve their scores, companies were required to make a few simple changes such as strengthening management supervision of employees, attending to repairs and providing non-slip flooring. To remain a supplier to the restaurant group, supplier companies needed to meet minimum acceptable standards relating to animal vocalization and the number of animals falling. The use of this scoring system resulted in great improvements and also meant that most did not need to make significant capital investments (Grandin, 2001, 2005). In fact, out of 75 beef and pork slaughter plants, only three had to install expensive new equipment.

This is not an isolated example but illustrates a wider principle. Improving farm animal welfare requires enhanced knowledge of animal welfare by corporations, and it requires corporations to implement and monitor animal-based outcome measures.

The case studies and analysis in this book, *The Business of Farm Animal Welfare*, show that there has been significant progress in many areas. There is growing acknowledgement that it is important for animals to have positive emotions and a life worth living. There is a clear trend towards the use of animal-based outcome measures in animal welfare assessments (see also Wray *et al.*, 2003, 2007; Velarde and Dalmau, 2012; Grandin, 2015).[1] Some of the basic outcome measures that should be assessed are: lameness, body condition, sores and lesions, animal cleanliness, and air quality. These changes are being encouraged by consumers and clients interested in purchasing higher welfare products and by the greater attention being paid by investors to the management practices of the companies they invest in. Companies are now very aware that an undercover video highlighting filthy conditions or incidents of animal abuse would have serious negative effects on stock prices, sales and consumer trust. There must be an emphasis on direct observation of animal condition on supplier farms. Corporate management must avoid the situation where all the paperwork is in order, but the condition of the animals is poor.

Yet, as the editors of this book, Nicky Amos and Rory Sullivan, discuss in Chapter 13, there is still some considerable way to go before food corporations globally are effectively managing risks associated with animal welfare and driving performance. While many large companies have adopted policies that commit them to achieving high standards of farm animal welfare, there are many technical and practical challenges that still need to be addressed before farm animal welfare risks are managed as effectively as other risks associated with food production. It is here that this book is so important. It provides a practical bridge between high level corporate commitments and the tangible practical actions that need to be taken to ensure the effective delivery of these commitments. It emphasizes the importance of recognizing animals as sentient beings, of philosophies of continuous improvement, of allocating responsibilities and authorities, of internal and independent third party auditing, and of field observations as well as performance monitoring and reporting. Corporate representatives need to visit a few farms to make sure other auditors are doing their jobs.

It is my hope that the principles and practical advice outlined in this foreword and throughout this book will help corporations to efficiently implement effective animal welfare policies and ultimately drive higher welfare standards across the food industry.

References

Grandin, T. (1998). Objective scoring of animal handling and stunning practices at slaughter plants. *Journal of the American Veterinary Medical Association*, 212, 36-39.

Grandin, T. (2001). Cattle vocalizations are associated with handling and equipment problems in beef slaughter plants. *Applied Animal Behavior Science*, 7, 191-201.

1 See also Welfare Quality Network website: www.welfarequalitynetwork.net

Grandin, T. (2005). Special Report: Maintenance of good animal welfare standards in beef slaughter plants by use of auditing programs. *Journal of the American Veterinary Medical Association*, 226, 370-373.

Grandin, T. (2015). *Improving Animal Welfare: A Practical Approach*. Wallingford, UK: CABI Publishing.

Velarde, A., & Dalmau, A. (2012). Animal welfare assessments at slaughter in Europe: Moving from inputs to outputs. *Meat Sciences*, 92, 244-251.

Wray, H.R., Main, D.C.J., Green, L.E., & Webster, A.J.F. (2003). Assessment of welfare of dairy cattle using animal-based measurements, direct observations, and investigation of farm records. *Veterinary Record*, 153, 197-202.

Wray, H.R., Leeb, C., Main, D.C.J., Green, L.E., & Webster, A.J.F. (2007). Preliminary assessment of finishing pig welfare using animal-based measurements. *Animal Welfare*, 16, 209-211.

1 Introduction

Rory Sullivan

UNIVERSITY OF LEEDS AND BUSINESS BENCHMARK ON FARM ANIMAL WELFARE, UK

Nicky Amos

NICKY AMOS CSR SERVICES AND BUSINESS BENCHMARK ON FARM ANIMAL WELFARE, UK

Globally, nearly 70 billion animals are farmed annually for meat, milk, eggs and other products. Some two-thirds of these animals are farmed intensively. The gradual intensification of animal production systems over the past century, in response to market demands for higher production yields at lower cost, means that many of these systems are responsible for significant and widespread negative impacts on animal welfare. Practices such as the selection and manipulation of animals for rapid growth, and the use of confinement mechanisms, such as cages and crates, which severely restrict animal movement and behaviour, are pushing animals to their physical and mental limits. Moreover, these practices are starting to have a detrimental effect on the business case for intensive animal production, with many consumers unwilling to accept food that embodies poor welfare, and its association with poor quality.

Yet, animal welfare is just one of the many social and environmental challenges facing food companies. With the global population projected to reach 9 billion people by 2050, rising incomes in many regions, wider economic and climate-related issues affecting food pricing, security and supply, and changes in consumer preferences for more protein-rich diets, food companies have a critically important role to play in influencing what we eat, how that food is produced, and the social and environmental impacts of food production. Within the context of farm animal welfare, the views that food companies—producers, processors, retailers and other consumers of other animal-derived products—hold about the welfare of animals and the management practices and processes that these companies adopt are of vital significance in determining the welfare of billions of farm animals.

Farm animal welfare is not just about the ethics of using animals to provide food. Nor is it just about the responsibilities that humans owe to the animals used in this way. Farm animal welfare is increasingly recognized as an important commercial issue for companies across the food industry. Various factors have contributed to this, including: tightening farm animal welfare-related regulation (in particular within the European Union); growing consumer and, more recently, investor concern about animal welfare issues; high profile media stories (such as the 2013 European horsemeat scandal); the costs of product recalls; concerns about the human health effects of antibiotic use in food supply chains; and the damage to company brands and reputation as a result of allegations about poor farm animal welfare practices.

The reasons for food companies to be concerned about animal welfare are not just about reducing costs and avoiding or minimizing downside risks. There are many positive reasons for companies to take a proactive approach. These include the potential to improve efficiency, margins and profits through reduced wastage, the potential to access new markets and customers, the potential to produce higher quality products, and the ability to grow existing markets as a result of adopting higher welfare standards ahead of competitors. To take just one example, many retailers have made commitments to offer higher welfare products, such as cage-free eggs and antibiotic-free meat, creating market opportunities for producers that are able to meet or exceed these demands.

Despite the business, ethical and societal arguments for companies to engage with these issues, relatively little is known about how food companies, either individually or as a sector, manage farm animal welfare. For example, how do food companies define their responsibilities for the animals in their care? How do food companies define their responsibilities for the animals in their supply chains? What practices do food companies adopt to ensure the welfare of animals in their care or in their supply chains? How effective are these practices at protecting or enhancing the welfare of animals? What is the business case for action? What are the implications of farm animal welfare for capital expenditure, operating costs, profit margins, revenues, assets, brand or reputation? How large are the opportunities for companies that adopt higher standards of farm animal welfare? How quickly can companies expect to receive returns on their investments?

These questions are not just about the practices of today's food businesses but need to be analysed and interpreted in the context of the changing world within which food businesses operate. Food companies need to think about the implications of, for example: public and media scrutiny of corporate practices and activities in an increasingly transparent world; the pressure to keep prices low while ensuring that workers operate safely and are paid decent wages; competition for market share; the potential impact of technology and innovation; alternatives to animal proteins (protein diversification); changes to lifestyles and dietary preferences; the changing social, ethical and environmental expectations of customers and consumers, and the extent to which these influence purchasing practices and behaviours.

About *The Business of Farm Animal Welfare*

This book, *The Business of Farm Animal Welfare*, aims to provide a rounded account of current corporate practice on farm animal welfare in the context of the wider strategic and structural challenges faced by the food industry. It explains why animal welfare is, and will continue to be, an important commercial issue for food companies. It provides practical examples and analysis of how companies manage farm animal welfare in their own operations and in their supply chains, and of the practical challenges that they encounter. It offers suggestions on the actions—management processes, stakeholder engagement and communications, alternative production systems, new business models—that might be taken by companies to effectively manage the risks and opportunities associated with farm animal welfare.

We have divided the book into five parts. In the first, we set out some of the core principles that need to inform and structure thinking on how companies can and should manage farm animal welfare. In Chapter 2, Tracey Jones explains that the concept of good animal welfare requires us to pay attention to the individual animal, and to recognize that good welfare is not just about the absence of suffering but about allowing animals to satisfy both their functional and cognitive behavioural needs. David Grumett (Chapter 3) then sets out the ethical and the religious case for companies and other stakeholders to be concerned about farm animal welfare, and explains how ethical and religious traditions influence, or have the potential to influence, the treatment of animals in modern society.

Part II focuses on the reasons why companies need to be concerned about farm animal welfare. Heleen van de Weerd and Jon Day (Chapter 4) describe the evolution of animal welfare legislation, with a focus on the leadership role that has been played by the European Union (EU) in introducing legislation to address some of the most widely practised inhumane animal husbandry practices. They explain how EU legislation has evolved, why this evolution has been closely linked to changes in societal views and attitudes, and how this legislation has influenced global farm animal welfare standards and legislation.

In Chapter 5, Sally Healy discusses the role of consumer pressures, followed by Jemima Jewell (Chapter 6) discussing the role of civil society pressures. Both point to the influential roles played by the media and by non-governmental organizations in shaping and informing consumer views, and how this then manifests itself in purchasing decisions and in the pressures on companies to strengthen their approach to farm animal welfare.

Companies increasingly point to investor expectations as a key influence on their management of social and environmental issues. Chapter 7 (by Rory Sullivan, Kate Elliot, Abigail Herron, Helena Viñes Fiestas and Nicky Amos) provides a high-level overview of how investors analyse the business risks and opportunities associated with farm animal welfare. This is supplemented by three investor case studies, in which Kate Elliot (Rathbone Greenbank Investments) (Chapter 8), Abigail Herron (Aviva Investors) (Chapter 9) and Helena Viñes Fiestas (BNP Paribas Investment Partners) (Chapter 10) describe how they analyse farm animal welfare-related investment risks and opportunities, and how this analysis influences their investment decisions. These chapters point to growing investor interest in farm animal welfare, albeit with a greater focus on the risks associated with poor performance rather than on the opportunities associated with better performance.

We conclude Part II with two chapters focusing on strategies for changing understanding of and attitudes towards animal welfare. Chapter 11 (by Minna Autio, Jaakko Autio, Ari Kuismin, Brigit Ramsingh, Eliisa Kylkilahti and Anna Valros) discusses the potential role of product labelling, and how the success of such labels depends on factors such as consumer understanding of the relationship between animal welfare and meat, consumer views on the ethics of farming animals for food, and consumer ideas of place, location and landscape. Chapter 12 (by Emily Patterson-Kane and Cia Johnson) discusses the relationship between knowledge and humane agricultural practices. They argue that improved knowledge of the science of animal welfare is not, of itself, sufficient to change animal-based agriculture, and that there is a need to introduce the ideas and insights from other disciplines (e.g. relational psychology) if we are to "... continue to move agriculture towards providing conditions that honour the nature of the animal while allowing for its responsible use for human purposes such as the production of fibre, meat, milk and eggs".

Part III focuses on corporate practice. It starts with Chapter 13 (by Nicky Amos and Rory Sullivan) which presents a high-level assessment of how global food companies are managing farm animal welfare. It then presents seven corporate case studies (Chapters 14 to 20) from Barilla (Leonardo Mirone), BRF (Géraldine Kutas), COOK (Richard Pike), Greggs (Malcolm Copland), Marks & Spencer (Steven McLean), The Co-op (Rosemarie Barraclough and Ciara Gorst), and Unilever (Bronwen Reinhardt). In each case study the authors set out the reasons why farm animal welfare is an important business issue, describe how farm animal welfare issues have been addressed in operations and supply chains, and discuss some of the challenges encountered and how these were addressed. The case studies confirm that companies face multiple pressures—from consumers, from clients, from the media, from animal welfare organizations—to strengthen their approach to farm animal welfare. They also highlight the challenges of making an effective business case, in particular where significant capital investment is required. A recurring theme is that uncertainty about the future (e.g. customers' willingness to purchase higher welfare products, clients' willingness to pay a premium for higher welfare products, whether legislation will be adopted and enforced) is a major issue. Companies need to balance the certainty of capital investments with uncertainty about whether they will see some or all of the commercial and other benefits from developing higher standards of farm animal welfare.

In Part IV, we return to the specific question of the business case for action. The core theme of many of the chapters in this book is that the actions taken by companies are critically dependent on what is commonly referred to as the "business case for action". This is shaped by the external drivers for action (for example, legislation, consumer concerns, the media, industry and civil society pressures), the financial costs and benefits of taking action, and companies' views on the importance of farm animal welfare to their business over the short, medium and long term. In Chapter 21, we analyse each of these elements and, while we acknowledge the commercial and other pressures on companies, we conclude that there is much that can be done to drive higher standards of animal welfare across the food industry. We also argue that raising standards of farm animal welfare is clearly in the interests of companies that aspire to be successful and sustainable over the long term.

In Part V (Chapters 22 to 24), we present a series of short technical briefing notes on key animal welfare-related issues, namely those associated with different farm animal production systems (Heather Pickett and Inês Ajuda), the impacts of antibiotic use in animals on human health and animal welfare (Inês Ajuda, Vicky Bond and Jemima Jewell), and welfare issues in aquaculture (Martin Cooke). Each note describes the issue in question, explains the sources (or underlying causes) of the issue and discusses the actions that could be taken by companies to address or alleviate the issue. We also provide in Chapter 25 (by Rory Sullivan and Nicky Amos) practical guidance on corporate reporting on farm animal welfare, describing the information that companies are expected to provide on their policies, practices, processes and performance, and presenting examples of good corporate practices.

Part I

Core principles

2 The key issues in farm animal welfare

Tracey Jones

COMPASSION IN WORLD FARMING, UK

Introduction

The concept of animal welfare is still widely not understood in its holistic sense or catered for fully in modern agricultural systems. This chapter, therefore, has four objectives. The first is to provide a working definition of animal welfare, building on the widely cited Five Freedoms model. The second is to explain why farm animal welfare is important. The third is to identify the main welfare concerns in agriculture, and the fourth is to explain how to make meaningful improvements in animal welfare through changes in production system and husbandry practices.

What is animal welfare?

The apparent lack of a universal definition of animal welfare, the differing philosophical and religious viewpoints underpinning our ethical concerns in the use and treatment of animals, and the question of whether we can really measure animal welfare, all contribute to confusion in the definition of what animal welfare actually is. A practical starting point is that animal welfare is something that belongs to the individual animal and can range from very poor to very good.

The Five Freedoms and provisions

Awareness and concern for the welfare of intensively farmed animals, in confined and barren systems and dimly lit sheds, was raised as early as the mid-1960s by Ruth Harrison in her book *Animal Machines* (1964). In response, the British Government commissioned a report into the Welfare of Animals Kept under Intensive Livestock Husbandry Systems, commonly known as the Brambell Report (1965). Its definition of animal welfare embraced both the physical and mental wellbeing of the animal and recognized the need to take account of the feelings of animals derived from their behaviour as well as their structure and functions. The report stimulated the concept of the Five Freedoms (see Box 2.1) and, along with the setting up of the Farm Animal Welfare Council in 1979,[1] the beginning of the science of animal welfare.

The Five Freedoms outline an acceptable state (outcomes) for animal welfare. They apply to all stages of the animal's life-cycle—on-farm, transit and slaughter—and include elements of health, emotional state, and physical and behavioural functioning. The provisions, added later, indicate the sort of practical measures required to secure the freedoms, providing a logical framework for assessing the strengths and weaknesses of husbandry systems. While husbandry systems are clearly important, the Farm Animal Welfare Council was at pains to emphasize the importance of stockmanship to safeguarding welfare, laying "great stress on the need for better awareness of welfare needs, and for better training and supervision".[2]

Box 2.1 The Five Freedoms*

1 **Freedom from hunger and thirst**—by ready access to fresh water and a diet to maintain full health and vigour
2 **Freedom from discomfort**—by providing an appropriate environment including shelter and a comfortable resting area
3 **Freedom from pain, injury or disease**—by prevention or rapid diagnosis and treatment
4 **Freedom to express normal behaviour—**by providing sufficient space, proper facilities and company of the animal's own kind
5 **Freedom from fear and distress**—by ensuring conditions and treatment which avoid mental suffering

* See Note 1.

The Five Freedoms have been referenced as principles of animal welfare many hundreds of times. They have influenced the content of animal welfare legislation, codes of practice, commercial standards and schemes, and are increasingly referenced in food company policies on animal welfare. They are often presented in abbreviated format without the provisions, and each freedom seems straightforward, easy to grasp, and a simple ethical decision to say yes to.

Improving on the Five Freedoms

Meeting these Freedoms may be considered essential to avoid suffering and minimize poor welfare. However, there is increasing recognition that it is necessary for animals to experience positive emotions in order to have good welfare and a

1 See http://webarchive.nationalarchives.gov.uk/20121007104210/http:/www.fawc.org.uk/freedoms.htm, accessed December 2016.

2 See Note 1.

high quality of life. For example, Compassion in World Farming (2012) argues that there should be a sixth Freedom: Freedom to undergo positive experiences—by providing appropriate conditions to experience positive feelings, such as contentment, pleasure, being relaxed or excited.

More recently, John Webster, who first proposed the Five Freedoms, suggested the Fifth Freedom be more neatly expressed as the "Freedom of Choice" with regard to choice of diet, environment, social contact, comfort and security (Webster, 2016). He argues that "by assuming more or less total control of the physical and social environment [in factory farms], we deny animals the opportunity to make choices designed to promote their own quality of life".

The Five Freedoms have been criticized as being over-simplistic, predominantly for their lack of emphasis on positive welfare, but also for not being able to properly reflect the causes and stressors that lead to long-term problems, such as learned helplessness in sows due to long-term confinement in stalls and metabolic exhaustion in dairy cows (Webster, 2016). Broom (2014), for example, has argued that laws and guidelines for animal care should focus on providing for the needs of animals as evidenced from their study (of behaviour, motivation and preference), rather than freedoms.

A further criticism that could be made of the interpretation and implementation of the Five Freedoms, is that systems and practices that are hugely detrimental to welfare are still permitted by law, codes of practice, and by various assurance schemes and company policies that publicly sign up to the Five Freedoms. The most obvious failure is the confining of animals in largely barren cages and crates, where even the most basic of behaviours, such as being able to turn around, stretch limbs, and groom all parts of the body, let alone walk or perform instinctive behaviours such as foraging, rooting, and nest building, are denied or severely limited.

Moving away from the Five Freedoms: alternative models for animal welfare

The Five Domains

A major critique of the Five Freedoms has been presented by Mellor (2016), who argues that they "do not capture either in the specifics or generality of their expression, the breadth and depth of current knowledge of the biological processes that are germane to understanding animal welfare and to guiding its management". Mellor and Reid developed the Five Domains model to provide a more thorough, systematic and comprehensive means to assess negative welfare impacts. Its most recent update incorporates ways to grade both welfare compromise and welfare enhancement (Mellor and Beausoleil, 2015). The model incorporates four predominantly physical and biological functional domains (namely, nutrition, environment, health and behaviour) and a fifth mental domain focusing on the individual animal's negative and positive experiences. The net overall outcome in the mental domain represents the animal's overall welfare state.

The Five Domains model splits negative subjective feelings (affects[3]) between those that are linked to survival (e.g. breathlessness, hunger, thirst, pain, nausea, dizziness, debility, weakness and sickness) and those that are linked to cognition (e.g. fear, anxiety, pain, frustration, anger, helplessness, loneliness, boredom and depression). Negative survival affects can, at best, be neutralized or minimized by management factors related to the provision of food, water, thermal comfort and health, and the ability of the animal to motivate necessary life-sustaining behaviours, such as panting to cool down.

Negative cognitive emotions on the other hand may be elicited by extreme close confinement and isolation of animals in threatening or barren environments. As such, addressing these effects generally requires more fundamental changes in the manner in which animals are kept. For example, Mellor suggests

> Keeping animals in social groups in stimulus rich, safe environments, provide opportunities for engaging in behaviours that are rewarding for the animal, such as foraging, maternal care of young, play, sexual activity, and involve comfort, pleasure, interest, confidence, and a sense of control.
>
> (Mellor, 2016, p. 1)

He summarizes his argument by saying "For animals to have lives worth living, it is necessary, overall, to minimize their negative experience and at the same time to provide the animals with opportunities to have positive experiences" (Mellor, 2016, p. 1).

Quality of Life framework

The concept of Quality of Life (Kirkwood, 2007) recognizes that animals have both positive and negative experiences and that the balance between the two is of importance. In line with this, FAWC (2009) developed the notions of a "life not worth living", a "life worth living", and a "good life". In order to drive towards the upper levels—a life worth living and a good life—environments that satisfy both the functional and cognitive behavioural needs of animals would need to be provided. This framework was modified by Green and Mellor (2011) to include a "point of balance", where positive and negative experiences are equally balanced and is the best one may expect from full compliance with the codes of practice (directed more towards nutrition, health and environment) and a "life worth avoiding" whereby the balance may be restored by veterinary treatment or a change of husbandry practice.

While the Quality of Life framework is animal-focused and understandable, it is difficult to assess quality of life in objective terms. As such, the framework is considered to be more effective as a motivational tool than as a foundation for developing regulations.

3 That is, relating to affective states.

Welfare Quality

The Welfare Quality® project (see further Chapter 11 by Autio *et al.*) was funded by the European Commission (2004–2009) with the aim of developing European standards for on-farm welfare assessment and practical strategies for improving animal welfare in three main species: cattle (beef and dairy), pigs and poultry (broiler chickens and laying hens).

Welfare Quality® adapted and modified the Five Freedoms into four principles to safeguard welfare—good housing, feeding, health and appropriate behaviour—and highlighted 12 distinct but complementary criteria that underpin the assessment of welfare. Like the Five Freedoms and provisions, the affective (mental wellbeing) outcomes were not categorized separately, but were included in the list of criteria.

Towards a consensus model for animal welfare

Three schools of thought or orientations arose over the last 20 years in an attempt to describe an animal's welfare state: natural living-, feelings- (animal sentience) and biological functioning-based definitions (see Dwyer, 2008 for a more detailed explanation). The natural living-based definition suggests that good welfare is dependent on an animal's ability to perform a behavioural repertoire of importance to the individual species, and encompasses the wants and needs of animals and their integrity. The feelings-based definition acknowledges the role of subjective feelings and the emotional state of an animal as central to determining welfare. The biological functioning-based definition looks primarily at the animal's physiological response to stress, immune function, health and production.

Fraser *et al.* (1997) integrated these various definitions into a single model, as illustrated in Figure 2.1. The model suggests that an animal has good welfare and

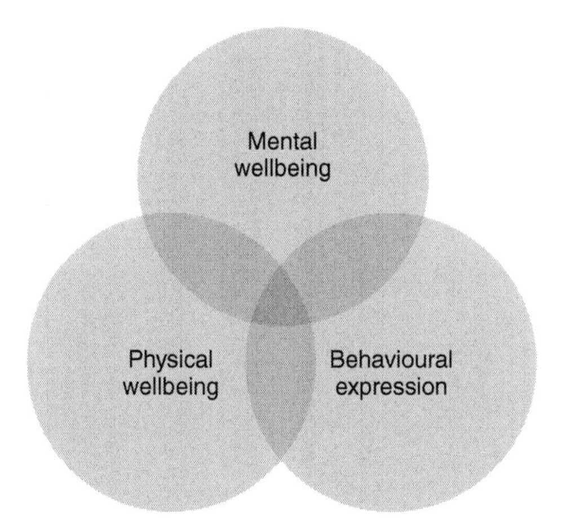

Figure 2.1 Consensus model of the three positive states required for good animal welfare
Source: This diagram originally appeared in Fraser et al. (1997). A scientific conception of animal welfare that reflects ethical concerns. Animal Welfare, 6, **187-205.** Reproduced with permission from the Universities Federation for Animal Welfare (UFAW).

a high quality of life when it is in good physical condition, is in a positive mental state and is able to express important species-specific behaviours. This is shown by the positive intersection of all three circles or states in Figure 2.1, and is adopted by the Food Business team at Compassion in World Farming in its working definition of animal welfare (see Box 2.2).

Different welfare concerns arise in each state, and invariably overlap with at least one of the other states if not both. For example, a lame animal can be said to have compromised physical condition, but may also experience pain and exhibit an altered behaviour pattern, such as reduced walking and fewer but longer feeding bouts. The latter demonstrates the animal's ability to cope with the lameness, while restriction of movement and pain relate to the welfare compromise.[4]

Box 2.2 Case study: compassion in World Farming's definition of farm animal welfare

Compassion in World Farming is the world's leading farm animal welfare charity. Since 2007, its Food Business team has worked with some of the world's biggest food companies—retailers, producers, manufacturers and food service companies—to place farm animal welfare at the forefront of their corporate social responsibility agendas.

Compassion in World Farming promotes the Five Freedoms along with a Sixth Freedom for animals to undergo positive experiences, and defines animal welfare according to the consensus model (see Figure 2.1). It acknowledges that good welfare and a high quality of life is underpinned by good housing, good feeding, good health, good stockmanship and management, and good breeding:

- Good housing refers to provisions such as, but not limited to, space allowance or stocking density, fixtures and fittings and their quality (feeders, drinkers, flooring and any species-specific items such as nest boxes for laying hens), ventilation systems and their effectiveness, and importantly a varied and stimulating environment for occupation and separate functional areas (for feeding, drinking, resting, activity).
- Good feeding refers to a diet appropriate in quantity and type for the species and age of animal concerned, and one that maintains the animal in good body condition and reproductive and/or production state.
- Good health not only refers to disease prevention and treatment through effective veterinary health plans and monitoring and recording systems, but also through maximizing the strength of the animals' own immune system.

4 For full descriptions of the welfare concerns by state for pigs, laying hens, broiler chickens and dairy cattle, see the Compassion in World Farming Resource Sheets No. 2–7 listed in the Supplementary resources section at the end of this chapter.

- Good stockmanship refers to husbandry skills and knowledge appropriate for the species being farmed, but also to the development of positive human–animal relations.
- Good breeding refers to selecting breeds for positive welfare traits balanced with moderate production traits, and the use of breeds adapted to the climatic and production conditions in which they are reared.

Why is animal welfare important?

Animals are sentient beings

The acknowledgement of animal sentience—that animals have feelings that matter to them—has occurred over time; the acknowledgement of sentience has gradually extended to all humans (instead of a subset of humans), to companion mammals, to primates, to large mammals, to all mammals, to all warm-blooded animals, to all vertebrates, and now to some invertebrates (Broom, 2014). It is likely to develop further as science is able to provide further evidence in invertebrate species.

According to Broom (2014), sentience implies a range of cognitive abilities, not just feelings, and includes some level of ability to evaluate the actions of others, remembering some of one's own actions and consequences, being able to assess risk and benefit, and possessing some degree of awareness. For example (Compassion in World Farming, 2012):

- Pigs have the ability to use deception and to understand knowledge held by other individuals when searching for food. They use vocal and olfactory cues to distinguish their home environment by one day old, they identify faces to distinguish between different people wearing the same clothes, and they understand what a mirror represents and can use it to find food.
- Chickens exert self-control and can show emotional frustration. When in pain, they choose to eat a more aversive food that contains analgesia. As adults, they solve mazes to be allowed access to dust-bathing material or a nest, and they communicate with representational noise signals, suggestive of "language".
- Cattle value social contact with other individuals and can remember up to 50–70 others. As calves, they can distinguish different people by their height and face. They show excitement in solving a problem, such as opening a gate, and they seem aware of others' emotions for example, by reducing their feeding if a companion is stressed.

In a landmark decision, the European Law recognized animals as sentient beings (as opposed to commodities) in a Protocol of the Treaty of Amsterdam (1997), and later as Article 13 in the Treaty of Lisbon (2009).[5] This paved the way for the development of the Strategy for the Protection and Welfare of Animals (2012 to 2015), designed to lay the foundations for improving welfare standards, their application and enforcement in all European Union countries (European Parliament, 2012).

People care about farm animals

How we, as a society, treat animals is largely dependent on what people judge to be acceptable, often driven by deep cultural beliefs and what science tells us. Animal welfare concerns largely fall into four areas (Dwyer, 2008): 1) ethical or moral concerns; 2) concern about human health and product quality and the link to animal welfare; 3) environmental and biodiversity concerns and the link to farming systems; and 4) trading and marketing concerns, either due to the impact of these issues on animal welfare or as a marketing tool to leverage higher prices or competitive advantage.

The various philosophical positions as to why we are or are not concerned about the welfare of animals are discussed further in Chapter 3 by David Grumett. For the purposes of this chapter, it is sufficient to say that on the whole people care about animals and how they are treated.

Animal welfare has been shown to be an important issue for the general public. In the most recent European survey (European Commission, 2016), 94% of EU citizens believe it is important to protect the welfare of farmed animals while 84% believe it should be better protected than it is now, and 64% want more information on the conditions in which farm animals are treated in their respective countries. More than half of all Europeans are prepared to pay more for products sourced from animal welfare-friendly production systems (59%). However, whereas, more than a third of respondents (35%) are prepared to pay up to 5% more, only a small minority (3%) are ready to pay more than 20%.

This willingness to pay more is mirrored in the price differential that applies to higher welfare products. For example, in one major UK supermarket at the end of 2016, the cost of a pack of six eggs ranged from 70p (12p/egg) for eggs from caged systems to 89p/box (15p/egg) for free-range eggs and £1.80/box (30p/egg) for organic eggs.[6] The price differential for chicken is greater; for example another UK supermarket in December 2016 offered a standard whole chicken for £2.95 (equivalent to £2.19/kg for a 1.35 kg chicken), compared with £7.95 for a free-range whole chicken (or £5.60/kg for a 1.33 kg chicken) and £8.91 for an organic chicken (or £6.70/kg for a 1.33 kg chicken).[7]

5 See, generally, https://ec.europa.eu/food/animals/welfare_en, accessed December 2016.

6 http://www.tesco.com/groceries/product/browse/default.aspx?N=4294697805&Ne=4294793660, accessed 14 December 2016.

7 http://www.sainsburys.co.uk/shop/gb/groceries/meat-fish/whole-bird#langId=44&storeId=10151&catalogId=10241&categoryId=276050&parent_category_rn=13343&top_category=13343&pageSize=30&orderBy=FAVOURITES_ONLY%7CTOP_SELLERS&searchTerm=&beginIndex=0, prices applied on 14 December 2016.

The need to encourage "alternative systems which are ethically acceptable to the concerned public, can be shown to improve the welfare of livestock and be economically competitive with existing systems of intensive production" was recognized by FAWC way back in 1979,[8] and is still a main driver of progress today. Public concern for animal welfare and a general demand for its improvement has over time been reflected in legislation (see further Chapter 4 by van de Weerd and Day) and more recently the private labels of food companies and standards-based assurance schemes (see FAO, 2014 for a comprehensive overview of legislation in European and non-European countries).

The law protects farm animals

The EU has among the world's highest standards for animal welfare. A core piece of EU legislation is Council Directive 98/58/EC of 20 July 1998 "concerning the protection of animals kept for farming purposes".[9] This lays down minimum standards for the protection of all farmed animals, ensuring owners "take all reasonable steps to ensure the welfare of animals under their care" and that "animals are not caused any unnecessary pain, suffering or injury".

Other EU legislation sets welfare standards for farmed animals during transport[10] and at the time of slaughter.[11] The transport requirements include additional provisions (such as bedding and improved ventilation) for journeys over eight hours, and maximum travel times after which animals must be unloaded and given food, water and a 24-hour rest period. In addition, the transportation of unfit animals is prohibited. The EU slaughter regulations require all animals, including poultry, to be stunned (rendered unconscious) before slaughter, although the legislation provides an exception in the case of animals slaughtered to provide food for religious communities.

The EU has also issued legislation setting minimum standards for the protection of calves, pigs, meat chickens and laying hens:

- The 2008 Pigs Directive[12] prohibits the use of sow stalls other than during the first four weeks of pregnancy, and prohibits the routine tail docking and teeth clipping of piglets. It also requires pigs to be given enrichment materials such as straw to fulfil their natural investigate behaviours, and sets minimum space allowances.
- The 1999 Laying Hens Directive[13] prohibits the use of barren battery cages, and sets minimum standards for barn and free-range systems, as well as for enriched cages.

8 http://webarchive.nationalarchives.gov.uk/20121007104210/http:/www.fawc.org.uk/pdf/fivefreedoms1979.pdf, accessed December 2016.

9 http://eur-lex.europa.eu/legal-content/EN/TXT/?uri=URISERV%3Al12100, accessed December 2016.

10 http://ec.europa.eu/food/animals/welfare/practice/transport_en, accessed December 2016.

11 http://ec.europa.eu/food/animals/welfare/practice/slaughter_en, accessed December 2016.

12 http://ec.europa.eu/food/animals/welfare/practice/farm/pigs_en, accessed December 2016.

13 http://ec.europa.eu/food/animals/welfare/practice/farm/laying_hens_en, accessed December 2016.

- The 2007 Broiler Directive lays down maximum stocking densities (33 kg/m^2 with two derogations to 39 and 42 kg/m^2), requires that all chickens have permanent access to litter which is dry and friable, and 6 hours of darkness.
- The 2008 Calf Directive[14] prohibits the use of "veal crates" but allows individual penning of calves for the first eight weeks of life, so long as they have visual, olfactory and tactile contact with other calves. The Directive also sets minimum provision for space and fibre in the diet.

Even though EU legislation is some of the most comprehensive in the world, it still permits certain practices and systems that restrict the expected improvements to animal welfare. In general, the minimum space requirements for animals are too low, and the maximum stocking densities set too high. For example: finishing pigs have barely enough room to lie down at the same time, especially heavy weight pigs reared for the cured meat market (space allowance for pigs reaching 170 kg is as little as 1 m^2 per animal), and typical stocking densities for broiler chickens mean they sit in a compressed state when near the end of their growing period (Bokkers *et al.*, 2011). Since fully slatted systems are legally permitted in pig systems, low space allowance and barren environments are commonplace in standard production, thwarting attempts to comply with legislation on enrichment provision and the non-routine use of tail docking. Slats do not allow for the provision of suitable manipulable materials, such as straw, in sufficient quantities in the pen, needed for meaningful occupation. Generally producers provide relatively meaningless chains or objects which occupy pigs for less than 2% of their time. Lack of stimulation and occupation leads to boredom and frustration and can (along with other factors) lead to pigs biting the tails of their penmates. Tail biting can cause serious welfare problems and so, in an attempt to reduce the incidence of tail biting, producers dock the tails of pigs; this leads to the circular problems of lack of a stimulating environment and tail docking being perpetuated. In an attempt to help producers meet the legislation regarding enrichment provision, the European Commission (2014) has produced a guidance document on suitable enrichment materials.

There is no species-specific legislation for other farmed animals. Of particular note are rabbits and quail (who are still predominantly reared in barren cages), dairy cows (who are still permanently tethered in some regions) and other meat poultry such as turkeys and ducks (who are reared at excessively high stocking densities in some countries, and without access to pecking substrates (turkeys) and bathing water (ducks), in most countries). See FAO (2014) for a comprehensive overview of legislation in European and non-European countries, as well as international organizations and private sector stakeholders.

What are the main welfare concerns?

The most obvious cases of animal cruelty and abuse are easy to recognize, such as poor treatment or neglect on farm, in transit and at slaughter. In most countries,

14 http://ec.europa.eu/food/animals/welfare/practice/farm/calves_en, accessed December 2016.

these would be dealt with under legislation such as the UK Protection of Animals Act, 1911. Intensive farming, commonly called factory farming, however, relies on systems and practices that at the minimum level do not meet the needs of animals, do not provide animal choice, do not promote positive welfare experiences mentally or behaviourally and require modification of the animal in an attempt to fit the animal to the surroundings rather the fitting the surroundings to the animal. The most obvious causes for concern are:

- **Confinement.** Examples of the most severe forms of confinement are cages for laying hens, rabbits, quail and even broiler chickens (in countries such as Russia, Turkey, China); sow stalls and farrowing crates; tethered systems for dairy cows; veal crates for calves. Confinement systems are associated with a lack of movement and opportunity to express even the most basic of behaviours, such as wing stretching and scratching (laying hens), sitting upright or hopping (rabbits), walking and turning around (sows), or having the comfort of one's own kind (calves). Severe confinement leads to stereotypic behaviours such as bar-biting and sham chewing, even depression (in sows), and is associated with muscular weakness.
- **Over-crowding.** High stocking densities and limited space allowance per animal in barns and pens, limit behaviour. Broiler chickens constantly bump into each other and disturb each other at commercial stocking densities (Dawkins *et al.*, 2004); are averse to sitting in such close proximity (Buijs *et al.*, 2010); sit in a compressed state (Bokkers *et al.*, 2011); and choose areas with more available space if given choice (Buijs *et al.*, 2011). Animals such as pigs have barely enough room to lie down simultaneously near slaughter weight and are unable to create functional areas (separate feeding, drinking, resting and activity zones) in their pens.
- **Barren environments.** These are usually associated with fully or partially slatted systems indoors or with feedlots outdoors. A lack of stimulation and meaningful occupation leads to boredom and frustration in pigs and laying hens, contributing to damaging behaviours such as tail biting in pigs and aggression and feather pecking in laying hens. It also leads to stereotypic behaviours such as tongue rolling in cattle and over-mating in broiler breeders.
- **Mutilations.** A range of mutilations are commonly performed in commercial practice. These include: beak trimming of hens and turkeys; tail docking of pigs, dairy cattle and sheep; mulesing of sheep; dehorning or disbudding of cattle; castration of male pigs, cattle and sheep; and spaying of female pigs and cattle in some regions of the world. Most mutilations are performed without anaesthesia or analgesia and so involve short- and long-term pain, neuroma formation, and associated depression of appetite and behaviour modification.
- **Breeding for high production traits.** Livestock are selected for ever higher growth rates in meat animals, milk yields for dairy animals, litter sizes in pigs and egg yields for laying hens. Rate of growth in the modern broiler is directly linked to lethargy, poor walking ability (Kestin *et al.*, 1992) and cardiac dysfunction (Olkowski, 2007). It is also associated with severe feed restriction

and chronic hunger in the parents of the meat chicken (D'Eath *et al.*, 2009). High production performance is correlated to high rates of lameness, mastitis and poor reproductive performance in dairy cows (Oltanecu and Broom, 2010), high rates of stillborn and low litter weights in pigs, and osteoporosis in laying hens.

- **Transport**. The concerns centre on handling stress during loading and unloading and space allocations that do not allow for normal standing postures or for animals to lie down without risk of being trampled. The duration of transport (i.e. transport time itself) is also of concern because of animal hunger, thirst and fatigue, and the occurrence of deaths in transit.
- **Slaughter**. The concerns at slaughter centre on the provision of rest in lairage, handling stress to the point of slaughter, whether the animals are effectively stunned before slaughter, and the distress associated with the slaughter method.
- **Animal health**. The prevention of disease and maintenance of healthy animals is a major topic in its own right. One aspect of this is ensuring that farm animals are fit and healthy. In addition, there are important public health concerns linked to the manner in which disease is prevented; examples include the overuse of antimicrobials in livestock production resulting in the development of antimicrobial resistance, and the food safety impacts that result from food contamination with bacteria such as *Salmonella*, *Campylobacter*, and *E. coli*.
- **Poor welfare outcomes**. Physical conditions that impair welfare are increasingly being measured. Examples include the incidence of lameness and mastitis in dairy cows, feather loss due to feather pecking in laying hens, poor walking ability in broiler chickens, and the incidence of tail biting in pigs. To date, most indicators of welfare are associated with the physical condition and production of animals (such as growth rate and mortality), while measures of behaviour are still in development (for a further discussion, see Broom (2014, Chapter 8) and the work of the Animal Welfare Indicators project,[15] Welfare Quality®[16] and the AssureWel project[17]).[18]

What does good welfare look like?

One of the key elements underpinning good welfare is the provision of good housing.[19] This is largely dictated by the type of production system in which

15 http://www.animal-welfare-indicators.net/site/, accessed December 2016.

16 http://www.welfarequality.net/everyone/41858/5/0/22, accessed December 2016.

17 http://assurewel.org/, accessed December 2016.

18 See Compassion in World Farming Factsheets 11–15 for species-specific lists of outcome measures, given in the Supplementary resources section at the end of this chapter.

19 In Chapter 22, Pickett and Ajuda provide a more detailed technical description of the production systems commonly used. This section focuses on the characteristics of the main species that are kept in these systems and the manner in which their natural behaviours can be compromised by these systems.

animals are reared. These systems vary in their potential to deliver holistic welfare (physical condition, mental wellbeing and behavioural expression); the outcomes that are achieved depend on their design and on factors such as sufficient living space and resources that meet the animal's needs—particularly in relation to behavioural expression. Good design and the provision of a stimulating environment can aid behavioural expression, reduce the incidence of problematic behaviours, provide choice and freedom of movement, increase cognitive ability and enhance performance, and should be undertaken with the animal's characteristics in mind. Successful delivery of the welfare potential of a system should be determined by assessing the animals themselves.

Caged or crated animals will always have a poor welfare potential because of the severity of confinement and behavioural limitations, irrespective of the animal being in good health and physical condition. Similarly animals reared in pens or sheds with low space allowances, high stocking densities and/or barren environments also have a poor welfare potential.

The following sections look at the characteristics of the main species confined in standard production, and discuss higher welfare alternatives.[20]

Laying hens

Laying hens are gregarious animals with elaborate social behaviours based on group structure in a flock, maintained in the wild by dominant males into harems. The ancestor to the laying hen is the jungle fowl, who lives on the jungle floor, searching for food via foraging and scratching, maintaining plumage condition through dustbathing and preening, and perching in trees at night to escape predators. The hen is a seasonal breeder, exhibiting an important nesting behavioural repertoire from careful nest selection (concealed in semi-darkness) and inspection, to settling and laying her egg followed by cackling and rejoining the flock. She lays 10–15 eggs before incubating them. After hatching the chicks imprint and stay close to the hen, who broods them frequently (every 40 minutes or so), teaches them what to eat and how to keep their feathers clean, and encourages behaviours such as roosting (at 6 weeks of age), and initiates "self-reliance" at 10–12 weeks of age. By 16–18 weeks the hen rejoins the harem and the chicks join the juvenile group.

Broodiness is largely selected out of the modern egg laying breeds, which range in temperaments from docile to highly strung. They are able to produce eggs throughout the year without the presence of males, controlled by lighting levels and patterns. Commercial hens are born in a hatchery, grown in a rearing house, and moved pre-lay to the laying house, where they produce 300—350 eggs in a year of production, after which they are slaughtered. Male chicks are currently killed at one day old, as they have little economic value due to their slow growth rate and slim conformation.

20 This section and the examples presented therein are based on the Compassion in World Farming Factsheets (8–10 and 16–35) listed in the Supplementary resources section at the end of this chapter.

Laying hens are highly adaptive to management practices but when their innate behaviour is thwarted, frustration and expression of non-adaptive behaviours such as feather pecking and cannibalism are evident. Other indicators of problems include a high percentage of floor eggs, smothering (caused by fear), keel bone fractures (from poor design or a lack of 3-dimensional training), and osteoporosis (from too high an egg output). Reducing fear by providing a complex environment, with learning opportunities and positive human–animal relationships is important for good welfare.

Different production systems have quite different welfare implications for laying hens. Standard systems are typically barren battery cages (prohibited in the EU) and enriched or colony cages. Both cage types deliver unacceptable levels of welfare largely because of the excessive behavioural restrictions imposed on the hen in barren systems and the inadequacy of the behavioural opportunities available in the enriched/colony cage.

Barn and free-range systems, if designed and managed properly, allow hens to express more of their natural behaviours and have the potential to deliver a higher level of welfare. It is important to rear the hens in housing systems that they will experience later in lay, so they have the opportunity to learn to navigate their 3-dimensional space without injury, particularly when using high perches and moving between multi-tiers. Likewise, the early provision of nest boxes and of outdoor access (if moving to free-range systems) allows the hens to learn and be confident before they move to the laying house.

Barn and free-range systems can have similar housing, characterized by single or multi-tiers. In the EU stocking density is limited to 9 hens/m^2, with the provision of nest boxes (1 per 7 hens), elevated perches (15 cm/hen) and a littered area that must occupy more than third of the floor area. Light control, ventilation and climate control are all important features, as is the quality of the litter to allow for dustbathing. The provision of enrichments such as brassicas, hay blocks, and string is essential to stimulate/satisfy foraging and pecking behaviour. Flocks are typically split into smaller colonies, to avoid/reduce the incidence of smothering (the bunching of hens on top of one another when fearful).

Free-range and organic systems permit access outdoors at a rate of 4 m^2 per hen. If the hens are to venture outside and be free-range, then the outdoor environment needs to be enriched with grass and herbs or shrubs to peck, dry earth or sand to dustbathe, trees and/or man-made covers for shade and shelter. The entrance to the house needs to be protected either by a porch or free draining gravel or sand to protect the litter from getting overly wet in the house.

Systems are considered to deliver good welfare if positive behaviours are observed, such as dustbathing, pecking, scratching, running, wing-flapping, and perching, and there is a low incidence of feather pecking (feather cover good at end of lay) and keel bone fractures. Operating flocks without beak trimming and maintaining good feather condition and coverage is indicative that the enrichment provision is adequate.[21]

21 See http://featherwel.org/ for further information.

Broiler chickens

Broiler chickens are young juvenile birds bred for fast growth, lean muscle deposition and high feed efficiency. The predominant global fast growth rate breeds are derived from a cross of the White Rock and Cornish chickens (breeds with larger breasts and wider stance). Broiler chicks hatch in a hatchery and are reared from day old to death in barn systems with or without access outdoors. They imprint on humans and objects in the house (in the first few days), then gradually flee from humans and develop aggressive behaviours in the form of play fights, but do not live long enough in commercial systems for aggressive fights to be real and harmful. Scratching, pecking, dustbathing, preening and perching are important aspects of behaviour as well as wing flapping, running and playing.

Standard systems are defined in EU legislation, while higher welfare systems are defined in the 2008 Regulation on Marketing Standards for Poultrymeat[22] and the 1999 Regulation on the Organic Production of Agricultural Products.[23] Caged systems are not permitted in the EU, but are used in countries such as Turkey, Russia and China.

Standard systems typically stock broilers at high densities, greater than 39 kg/m^2 (19 birds/m^2 for a 2.0 kg bird), and under relatively low light levels with short period of darkness, While EU legislation requires a minimum of 20 lux and 6 hours darkness, in many countries, broilers may be reared in light levels as low as 5 lux and with only 1 hour darkness. High stocking densities, low levels of light and fast growth rate leads to low levels of activity and high rates of poor walking ability in the modern broiler. Birds are slaughtered at a range of weights starting as early as 1.8 kg at 30–33 days, and may be thinned several times in the production cycle, to increase the number of birds reared per house over a range of final body weights.

Higher welfare and extensive systems indoors, if designed and managed properly, allow broilers to express more of their natural behaviours and have the potential to deliver a higher level of welfare. Higher welfare systems for fast growing birds are operated in the UK at reduced stocking density of 30 kg/m^2 (15 birds/m^2 for 2 kg birds) and the provision of natural light, straw bales for pecking and resting on and perches. Activity is increased and walking ability of the fast growth rate bird improved (Bailie *et al.*, 2013).

Extensive systems reduce stocking density further to 25 kg/m^2 (12.5 birds/m^2 for 2 kg birds) and use intermediate growth rate birds ($<$50 g/day growth rate averaged over the production cycle) that are more active and have fewer physical problems and are more robust than the fast growth rate birds. New systems designed with the bird in mind are starting to be developed. A good example is the Windstreek system in the Netherlands: the house is brilliantly lit by an 11 m tall window running the full length of the north-facing side of the house (equivalent to 50% of floor space), providing a gradient of light across the shed, allowing the birds choice

22 http://www.fsai.ie/uploadedFiles/Legislation/Legislation_Update/Reg543_2008.pdf, accessed December 2016.

23 http://eur-lex.europa.eu/LexUriServ/LexUriServ.do?uri=OJ:L:1999:222:0001:0028:EN:PDF, accessed December 2016.

of their preferred environment. Motherhoods are another distinctive feature, providing an area of refuge and warmth for the birds throughout their life; these areas contain infra-red heaters, LED lighting, a water line and perch, and manure belts remove litter regularly to maintain good litter and air quality. There is an 80% reduction in energy use compared to conventional housing.[24]

Free-range and organic systems require broilers to have outdoors access for half their life and from 6 weeks of age, respectively. They also require birds to be older at slaughter—56 days and 70–81 days, respectively, thereby encouraging the use of intermediate and slower growth rate breeds. Stocking density in the house is reduced to 27.5 kg/m^2 for free-range (or 13 birds/m^2) and 25 kg/m^2 (or 10 birds/m^2) for organic. Again, to ensure the broilers venture outside, the outdoor environment needs to be enriched.

Systems deliver good welfare if positive behaviours are observed, such as dustbathing, pecking, scratching, running, wing-flapping and perching, and birds have good walking ability and good physical outcomes (such as low mortality and low incidence of foot pad dermatitis, hock burn and breast blisters). Another positive outcome of higher welfare production systems is reduced antibiotic use.

Pigs

The domestic pig originates from the European wild boar. These are typically found in a range of habitats, often close to wooded areas and river valleys, containing separate areas for feeding and drinking, resting (in simple nests), cooling, rubbing and defecating. Pigs are very intelligent, highly sociable animals (they will lie and rest touching each other for companionship and for warmth), with a strong social hierarchy. They live in small family groups consisting of 2–4 sows and their young; boars are more solitary, joining the group to mate.

Pigs spend much of their time foraging for food which involves sniffing, rooting and chewing. They eat for several hours each day, and can range over hundreds of kilometres in search of a varied diet, which includes grass, roots, tubers, invertebrates, berries, nuts and small vertebrates. They do not have sweat glands, so use mud wallows to cool and condition the skin, which is enhanced by rubbing against trees. They urinate and defecate in separate areas, usually in corridors between trees and away from their lying areas.

One to two days prior to giving birth, sows go off alone to construct elaborate nests. They search for a suitable site, dig a hollow in the earth which they line with grass, leaves and twigs, and construct sides and an overhang from larger branches. This innate behaviour is hard-wired into the instincts of the sow. During farrowing and for a few days post farrowing the sow spends much of her time lying down on her side, initiating suckling through a series of grunts. She does not help her young or lick them. Young piglets are very active, standing within minutes of being born and test teats before selecting one for the duration of lactation. The sow avoids

24 http://www.compassioninfoodbusiness.com/awards/special-recognition-awards/best-innovation-award-2016/, accessed December 2016.

crushing her piglets in the nest by rooting and disturbing her piglets, and pushing them to one side, while she lies down with control and rolls to the other side away from her piglets. They suckle every hour or so then sleep. The sow encourages her young out of the nest at 7–14 days and slowly integrates them back into the family group after several weeks. Weaning is gradual starting at 3 weeks, when the piglets start to eat solid food, and can last until 13–17 weeks. Weaning age in commercial practice is typically 24–28 days. Piglets tend to stay in the family group until the sow is due to give birth again; they may return as daughters when they are due to farrow themselves.

Sows

Standard production systems typically involve the use of sow stalls either for the whole of the gestation period (outside the EU) or for 4 weeks following insemination (in some countries in EU), and all operate farrowing crates as standard. Sow stalls do not allow sows to turn around, or walk more than a few steps and lead to boredom and learnt helplessness, as well as muscular-skeletal problems and birthing difficulties. Farrowing crates were designed to prevent or reduce the mortality of piglets from overlaying by the sow. Both systems are typically barren. The strong urge to build a nest is thwarted in sows, interfering with the birthing process.

In Europe, following the partial ban on sow stalls and the complete ban on stalls in countries like the UK, group systems developed for pregnant sows. There are a wide range of systems in commercial practice, largely varying according to feeding system and group size/formation (stable or dynamic); some are enriched and some are barren. Higher welfare systems for dry sows incorporate key design features that help reduce aggression at mixing post weaning or insemination and during feeding. They also provide bedding for comfort and substrates for occupation and satiety.

Following many years of research and commercial development, there are increasing numbers of commercially available, indoor, free-farrowing systems that allow for varying degrees of freedom of movement, nest building and nurturing of young, as well as the sow's ability to get away from her piglets for periods of time. Higher welfare systems for farrowing and lactating sows provide nest-building substrates and separate functional areas in the pen for both the sow and piglets. Good stockperson ability and breeding for maternal ability and moderate litter size are key elements to successful free farrowing. Moderate litter size, producing good birth weight piglets (~1.5 kg), and good feeding, allows for the elimination of teeth-clipping practice.

Outdoor systems allow for the most freedom of movement. Typically, dry sows are kept in groups (either in small stable or larger dynamic groups) in paddocks with straw bedded arks or bale tents, and farrow in individual or small group paddocks with individual straw bedded arks or insulated huts. The paddocks are rotated to preserve the land and reseed the vegetation, as pigs actively root the soil and eat all vegetation. Outdoor units need to be situated on well drained land, and the best systems will provide shade and cooling wallows for the pigs. Using robust breeds is important for successful outdoor production.

Systems deliver good welfare if the sows exhibit positive behaviours such as rooting and manipulating substrates, are calm and non-aggressive with each other, and are able to conduct nest-building behaviour before farrowing. There should be low rates of lameness and fight damage, and the sows should demonstrate longevity, with good rates of fertility and body condition, and low levels of pre-wean piglet mortality.

Meat pigs

Standard systems for meat pigs typically provide low space allowance over the course of the growth cycle determined by legislation. Pigs at end of the growth period (0.65 m^2 for 100 kg pig) can just about lie down simultaneously, and there is no space for the development of functional areas in the pen. Standard systems are typically barren with full or part slatted flooring. Floor type, ventilation and manure handling systems preclude the use of bedding and manipulable substrates needed to occupy pigs; tail docking is therefore commonplace.

Higher welfare systems indoors provide more space (1.0 m^2 to 1.5 m^2 for 100 kg pigs) and straw bedding for comfort and manipulation. The better systems will allow for functional areas in the pen and lots of activity (15–20%) to reduce the risk of tail biting. Good ventilation, thermal comfort, plenty of feeding space, and good nutrition and health are all important for the reduction of tail bite incidence.

Outdoor systems for meat pigs provide most choice and freedom of movement. The more enriched the environment the better.

Systems deliver good welfare if the pigs exhibit positive behaviours such as rooting and manipulating substrates, and playing, and are able to rest in separate areas from where they feed and defecate. There should be low rates of lameness, fight damage and tail biting or ear biting.

Rabbits

The domestic rabbit originates from the wild European rabbit, found in a wide range of habitats including meadows, woods, forests, grasslands, deserts and wetlands. Rabbits are territorial, social animals, living in stable family groups of two to nine does, one to three adult bucks, a variable number of their offspring (under 3 months old) and some sub-adult males. They share a home range and live in a complex system of burrows (warren) used for rearing their progeny, resting and sheltering from intruding rabbits and predators. They are constantly aware of their surroundings, checking for predators by sitting or rearing up on their hind legs with ears upright; they escape predators by hopping away in a zig-zag motion, and, if captured, deliver powerful kicks with their hind legs; they will also bite to escape a struggle. They feed mainly during dusk and dawn on a variety of herbs particularly grass, lush leaves, fresh bark and roots, extracting most of their water requirements from fresh and dew-covered grass and herbs. They pass two distinct types of faeces: hard droppings and soft, black, viscous pellets; the latter are immediately eaten to digest their food further to maximize the nutrition derived from the food they eat. Hard faeces are defecated passively during feeding or actively at specific places within or at the boundary of the home range (as for urination). Rabbits rest intermittently for 12–18 hours a day, preferring to lie against trees or walls, with the company of other rabbits.

Pregnant does search for a suitable burrow to build a nest, constructing a concave "straw nest" from collected material before lining the nest with hair from her own body. After delivering and cleaning her offspring (kits), she plugs (closes) the nest entrance to protect from predators and temperature changes, returning to the nest to suckle her young for only 3 minutes per day. Does can be particularly aggressive when lactating and defending their litter. They abandon their young at 4 weeks of age in order to dig a new burrow in preparation for her next litter; by this time, the young are fully able to feed themselves.

The rabbit's behavioural repertoire has not changed greatly through domestication and breeding and they show many of the behaviours exhibited by wild rabbits, including their social hierarchy, mutual grooming (for group cohesion), grazing, hopping, gnawing (to prevent their teeth from overgrowing), and their maternal nesting and nursing behaviour.

Standard production systems typically involve the use of wire barren cages, often used in a dual-purpose capacity: the doe and her young are kept together (with access to a nest box) until weaning, after which the doe is transferred to another cage while the young growers remain in the same cage. Does are typically caged individually, while growers/fatteners are group housed (often as littermates) with a space allowance between 450 and 600 cm^2 per animal and a height restriction of 28 to 35 cm. Both space allowance and height are restrictive, limiting behaviours such as hopping, sitting upright, and lying stretched out. The wire flooring leads to lesions on the paws and the barren environment can lead to stereotypic fur pulling behaviour and aggression. Lack of gnawing opportunities leads to overgrowth of the incisor teeth, while lack of fibre leads to poor gut health. Some cages have platforms and gnawing blocks, but like the enriched cage for laying hens, these are considered inadequate to satisfy the behavioural needs of the rabbits.

Alternative systems to the cage have been developed commercially, particularly for growing/fattening rabbits. Indoor pen systems (also called Park or barn systems) have comfortable plastic flooring (slatted or slotted), provide an increased space allowance of between 800 and 1,500 cm^2 per rabbit, and enrichments such as raised platforms (for jumping onto and resting under), gnawing blocks, hiding tubes, hay racks/compressed straw tubes (for fibre provision), and natural light (usually with dawn/dusk dimming). In addition, there is no height restriction to the pen. Some systems may incorporate bedding materials.

Outdoor mobile systems tend to be used by small-scale farmers (often organic), and consist of a mobile outdoor cage (height greater than or equal to 50 cm) on grass with a covered area, moved daily to provide fresh grass. Space provision is usually between 2,000 and 4,000 cm^2 per animal. Rabbits are kept in groups and of robust cross breeds. Enrichments such as tubes (for hiding), a hay/straw rack (including *ad libitum* fibre and manipulable materials), and the wooden interior (for gnawing) are provided in the covered area.

Free-range (organic) systems are available at small scale, and offer rotational pastures with no height restriction for the rabbits. One doe is housed in a mobile run with her litter until weaning. The indoor section is used for a nest, where straw may be provided in the winter. Between litters, does are housed individually. An underground system has been developed in Italy. Does are kept individually; there is a concrete box built into the ground, providing a nest and enclosed hiding space which stays cool in hot climates. This is connected to an open-air cage by a tube. The outdoor cage has plastic slats, natural light and ventilation, and can be used by the doe to escape her young.

Aggression between does while lactating and on regrouping, and its negative effect on physical condition and reproduction, has been a major barrier to group housing does in commercial systems, but such systems are now being developed.[25]

Concluding remarks

Animal welfare is about the individual animal and meeting the needs and wants of the individual and providing a good quality of life. The quality of life of an individual animal depends not only on the animal being healthy and in good physical condition, but on the animal being in a positive mental state. The provision of good welfare is not limited to the absence of suffering. It requires that animals are provided with stimulating and rewarding experiences. This, in turn, is derived from fulfilling behaviours important to the animal from both a biological functioning perspective and from a cognitive perspective.

References

Bailie, C.L., Ball, M.E., & O'Connell, N.E. (2013). Influence of the provision of natural light and straw bales on activity levels and leg health in commercial broiler chickens. *Animal*, 7(4), 618-626.

Bokkers, E.A.M., de Boer, I.J.M., & Koene, P. (2011). Space needs of broilers. *Animal Welfare*, 20, 623-632.

Brambell, F.W.R. (1965). *Report of the Technical Committee to Enquire into the Welfare of Animals Kept under Intensive Livestock Husbandry Systems*. London, UK: HMSO.

Broom, D.M. (2014). *Sentience and Animal Welfare*. Wallingford, UK: CABI Publishing.

Buijs, S., Keeling, L.J., Vangestelc, C., Baertd, J., Vangeyted, J., & Tuyttens, F.A.M. (2010). Resting or hiding? Why broiler chickens stay near walls and how density affects this. *Applied Animal Behaviour Science*, 124, 97-103.

Buijs, S., Keeling, L.J., & Tuyttens, F.A.M. (2011). Using motivation to feed as a way to assess the importance of space for broiler chickens. *Animal Behaviour*, 81, 145-151.

Compassion in World Farming (2012). What is animal welfare? Godalming, UK: Compassion in World Farming. Retrieved from http://www.compassioninfoodbusiness.com/resources/animal-welfare/what-is-animal-welfare/, accessed December 2016.

Dawkins, M.S., Donnelly, C.A., & Jones, T.A. (2004). Chicken welfare is influenced more by housing conditions than by stocking density. *Nature*, 427, 342-344.

25 See Factsheet 35 in the Supplementary resources section.

D'Eath, R.B., Tolkamp, B.J., Kyriazakis, I., & Lawrence, A.B. (2009). "Freedom from hunger" and preventing obesity: the animal welfare implications of reducing food quantity or quality. *Animal Behaviour*, 77(2), 275-288.

Dwyer, C.M. (ed.) (2008). *The Welfare of Sheep*. Dordrecht, The Netherlands: Springer Sciences and Business Media.

European Commission (2014). Guidelines on the provision of enrichment material for pigs. Retrieved from http://ec.europa.eu/dgs/health_food-safety/information_sources/docs/ahw/20140701_guideline_enrichment_en.pdf, accessed December 2016.

European Commission (2016). *Special Eurobarometer 442* (November – December 2015). Attitudes of Europeans towards animal welfare. Retrieved from http://ec.europa.eu/COMMFrontOffice/publicopinion/index.cfm/Survey/getSurveyDetail/instruments/SPECIAL/surveyKy/2096, accessed December 2016.

European Parliament (2012). *Resolution of 4 July 2012 on the European Union Strategy for the Protection and Welfare of Animals 2012–2015* (2012/2043(INI)). Strasbourg, France: European Parliament. Retrieved from http://www.europarl.europa.eu/sides/getDoc.do?pubRef=-//EP//TEXT+TA+P7-TA-2012-0290+0+DOC+XML+V0//EN, accessed December 2016.

FAO (2014). *Review of Animal Welfare Legislation in the Beef, Pork and Poultry Industries*. Rome: FAO Investment Centre. Retrieved from http://www.fao.org/3/a-i4002e.pdf, accessed December 2016.

FAWC (2009). *Farm Animal Welfare in Great Britain: Past, Present, and Future*. London: Farm Animal Welfare Council. Retrieved from https://www.gov.uk/government/uploads/system/uploads/attachment_data/file/319292/Farm_Animal_Welfare_in_Great_Britain_-_Past__Present_and_Future.pdf, accessed December 2016.

Fraser, D., Weary, D.M., Pajor, E.A., & Milligan, B.N. (1997). A scientific conception of animal welfare that reflects ethical concerns. *Animal Welfare*, 6, 187-205.

Green, T.C., & Mellor, D.J. (2011). Extending ideas about animal welfare assessment to include "quality of life" and related concepts. *New Zealand Veterinary Journal*, 59, 316-324.

Harrison, R. (1964). *Animal Machines*. London: Vincent Stuart.

Kestin, S.C., Knowles, T.G., Tinch, A.E., & Gregory, N.G. (1992). Prevalence of leg weakness in broiler chickens and its relationship with genotype. *Veterinary Record*, 131, 190-194.

Kirkwood, J.K. (2007). Quality of life: The heart of the matter. *Animal Welfare*, 16, 3-7.

Mellor, D.J. (2016). Updating animal welfare thinking: Moving beyond the "Five Freedoms" towards a "Life worth Living". *Animals*, 6(3), 21. doi: 10.3390/ani6030021.

Mellor, D.J., & Beausoleil, N.J. (2015). Extending the "Five Domains" model for animal welfare assessment to incorporate positive welfare states. *Animal Welfare*, 24, 241-253.

Olkowski, A.A. (2007). Pathophysiology of heart failure in broiler chickens: structural, biochemical, and molecular characteristics. *Poultry Science*, 86(5), 999-1005.

Oltenacu, P.A., & Broom, D.M. (2010). The impact of genetic selection for increased milk yield on the welfare of dairy cows. *Animal Welfare*, 19(S), 39-49.

Webster, J. (2016). Animal welfare: Freedoms, domains and "A Life Worth Living". *Animals*, 6(35). doi: 10.3390/ani6060035.

Supplementary resources

Compassion in World Farming provides a series of fully referenced information sheets and best practice booklets and case studies on higher welfare farming systems and solutions.

1 What is Animal Welfare? At http://www.compassioninfoodbusiness.com/resources/animal-welfare/what-is-animal-welfare/
2 Welfare issues for sows. At http://www.compassioninfoodbusiness.com/resources/pigs/welfare-issues-table-sows/
3 Welfare issues for meat pigs. At http://www.compassioninfoodbusiness.com/resources/pigs/welfare-issues-table-meat-pigs/
4 Welfare issues for laying hens. At http://www.compassioninfoodbusiness.com/resources/laying-hens/welfare-issues-table-laying-hens/
5 Welfare issues for broiler chickens. At http://www.compassioninfoodbusiness.com/resources/broiler-chickens/welfare-issues-table-broiler-chickens/
6 Welfare issues of dairy cattle. At http://www.compassioninfoodbusiness.com/resources/dairy/welfare-issues-table-dairy-cows/
7 Welfare issue of dairy calves. At http://www.compassioninfoodbusiness.com/resources/dairy/welfare-issues-table-dairy-calves/
8 Tail docking and tail biting in pigs. At http://www.compassioninfoodbusiness.com/resources/pigs/tail-docking-and-tail-biting/
9 Tooth resection in pigs. At http://www.compassioninfoodbusiness.com/resources/pigs/tooth-resection/
10 Castration of male pigs. At http://www.compassioninfoodbusiness.com/resources/pigs/piglet-castration/
11 Laying hen welfare outcomes. At http://www.compassioninfoodbusiness.com/resources/laying-hens/welfare-outcome-summary-laying-hens/
12 Broiler chicken welfare outcomes. At http://www.compassioninfoodbusiness.com/resources/broiler-chickens/welfare-outcome-summary-broiler-chickens/
13 Sow welfare outcomes. At http://www.compassioninfoodbusiness.com/resources/pigs/welfare-outcome-summary-sows/
14 Meat pigs welfare outcomes. At http://www.compassioninfoodbusiness.com/resources/pigs/welfare-outcome-summary-pigs/
15 Measuring welfare in dairy cows. At http://www.compassioninfoodbusiness.com/resources/dairy/dairy-welfare-outcomes-booklet/
16 Hen welfare in alternative systems. At http://www.compassioninfoodbusiness.com/resources/laying-hens/hen-welfare-in-alternative-systems/
17 Welfare potential by production system for laying hens. At http://www.compassioninfoodbusiness.com/resources/laying-hens/welfare-potential-matrix-laying-hens/
18 The importance of appropriate pullet rearing. At http://www.compassioninfoodbusiness.com/media/7426400/case-study-the-importance-of-appropriate-pullet-rearing.pdf
19 Higher welfare systems for laying hens—practical options. At http://www.compassioninfoodbusiness.com/resources/laying-hens/higher-welfare-systems-for-laying-hens/
20 Rearing hens in a barn system without beak trimming: The Rondeel example. http://www.compassioninfoodbusiness.com/media/5817306/rondeel-case-study-july-2014.pdf
21 Welfare potential by production system for broiler chickens. At http://www.compassioninfoodbusiness.com/resources/broiler-chickens/welfare-potential-matrix-broilers/
22 Broiler welfare in commercial systems. At http://www.compassioninfoodbusiness.com/resources/broiler-chickens/broiler-welfare-in-commercial-systems/

23 The Windstreek broiler house. At http://www.compassioninfoodbusiness.com/media/7429131/windstreek-broiler-house-case-study.pdf and accompanying video at: http://www.compassioninfoodbusiness.com/awards/special-recognition-awards/best-innovation-award-2016/

24 Welfare potential by production system for sows and meat pigs. At http://www.compassioninfoodbusiness.com/resources/pigs/welfare-potential-matrix-sows-and-meat-pigs/

25 Group housing systems for dry sows. At http://www.compassioninfoodbusiness.com/resources/pigs/group-housing-systems-for-dry-sows/

26 Free farrowing systems for sows. At http://www.compassioninfoodbusiness.com/resources/pigs/free-farrowing-systems/

27 Indoor housing for dry sows—practical options. At http://www.compassioninfoodbusiness.com/resources/pigs/indoor-housing-for-dry-sows-practical-options/

28 Indoor free farrowing systems for sows—practical options. At http://www.compassioninfoodbusiness.com/media/7428869/indoor-free-farrowing-systems-for-sows.pdf

29 Welfare potential by production system for does and meat rabbits. At http://www.compassioninfoodbusiness.com/resources/rabbits/welfare-potential-matrix-meat-rabbits-and-does/

30 Production statistics and legislation for rabbit production in the EU. At http://www.compassioninfoodbusiness.com/resources/rabbits/rabbit-meat-production-in-the-eu/

31 Welfare potential by production system for does. At http://www.compassioninfoodbusiness.com/resources/rabbits/welfare-issues-table-breeding-does/

32 Welfare potential by production system for meat rabbits. At http://www.compassioninfoodbusiness.com/resources/rabbits/welfare-issues-table-growing-rabbits/

33 The welfare of breeding rabbits. At http://www.compassioninfoodbusiness.com/resources/rabbits/welfare-of-breeding-rabbits/

34 The welfare of meat rabbits. At http://www.compassioninfoodbusiness.com/resources/rabbits/welfare-of-growing-rabbits/

35 Group housing for does—the Kani-Swiss case study. At http://www.compassioninfoodbusiness.com/media/7427861/kani-swiss-case-study-on-group-housing-for-does.pdf

3 Ethics, religion and farm animal welfare

David Grumett

UNIVERSITY OF EDINBURGH, UK

Introduction

Farmed animals do not capture the ethical attention of most ordinary people. This is partly because, in the UK and other developed Western societies, the large majority of people do not live in close proximity to them. It is also because farmed animals are typically viewed at a group level rather than individually, and so do not have the personal attributes projected onto them that might suggest they are worthy of moral consideration. Nevertheless, animals that are farmed have a close relation to humans. This is shown by their vulnerability, especially their inability to defend themselves against predators and disease (Palmer, 2011). It is also shown by their dependency, with farmed animals having been reared to have their needs met principally by humans. Due to this close relation with humans, farmed animals deserve a high level of ethical consideration by humans.

This chapter focuses mostly on ethics, with particular reference to the UK, and then considers religious issues towards the end. This is because most people in the UK accept the validity of some kind of ethical principle to regulate human actions, whereas fewer people, at least where farm animal welfare is concerned, draw their principles from religion. Nevertheless, religion provides strong motivating principles for a minority of people and so cannot be altogether disregarded.

Ethics

Consumers are increasingly concerned about the welfare of the farmed animals whose meat and other products they buy (Mayfield *et al.*, 2007a), and food retailers of all sizes are well aware of this concern. In order to gain and preserve market share, meat and farm animal products will need to be ethically sustainable: that is, meet the rising ethical expectations of consumers. Although expectations will be higher among some individual consumers and consumer groups than others, ethics is an important business concern for all products and suppliers.

Nevertheless, ethics can never be a matter of mere business advantage. Going beyond purely instrumental concerns, such as maximizing sales or profit, ethics concerns the fundamental principles that shape how business decisions are made. Indeed, it may well call business priorities into question. Ethical action requires i) knowledge of relevant facts; ii) the acceptance of one or more ethical principles; and iii) the capacity to relate facts to ethical principles in practice. I shall now consider each of these in turn.

Knowledge

Consumers have different kinds of ethically relevant knowledge about the meat and farm animal products they buy, dependent on retailer type and size. Independent retailers, such as butchers, farm shops and delicatessens, are likely to have a short supply chain and a high level of knowledge about the conditions in which their animals have been reared and slaughtered, which may therefore be presumed to be relatively good (Mayfield *et al.*, 2007b). Information with ethical relevance, such as how animals have been housed or pastured, what they have been fed, and the distance of travel to the slaughterhouse, may be obtained via conversation with shop staff and as local knowledge. When obtaining information this way, a degree of trust is necessary. However, because of the possibility of direct consumer verification and the likely negative impact on a business of giving false information, it is reasonable to place trust in the claims made. Levels of consumer trust in these retailers are indeed generally high (Agricultural and Horticulture Development Board, 2015).

In contrast, there is a common perception among supermarket customers that little information is available to them about the meat and animal products they buy (Mayfield *et al.*, 2007b). This perception is not entirely true. Rather, the information to which such customers have access is differently presented, and its interpretation requires contextual knowledge. Meat and farm animal products purchased in supermarkets are obviously subject to extensive and complex legislative requirements, with compliance verified by Food Standards Agency inspectors and local authority trading standards officers. Indeed, the formal registration, monitoring and inspection processes required by law are, in some respects, more rigorous for the large producers that supply supermarkets than for the small producers who supply independent retailers. Moreover, the information needed to trace the origin of any piece of meat or farm animal product on sale is available on its packaging, with the oval approval identification mark either containing a local authority approval code and unique number, or indicating where on the packaging these may be found. The country of origin is also indicated and, for products sourced from overseas, a similar coding system permits equivalent traceability. This information enables the consumer, should they wish, to find the exact farm or slaughterhouse of origin. If a slaughterhouse, this will, like a farm, be subject to many legislative requirements, with compliance verified by veterinary oversight and periodic inspection. Moreover, in 2015 the Food Standards Agency completed a programme of unannounced inspections in the wake of public concern following some isolated but widely publicized abuses. When purchasing meat and animal products in supermarkets, consumers may reasonably have a high level of trust that the products on sale comply with the minimal animal welfare requirements that are defined in legislation.

However, as suggested above, one of the reasons consumers may shop at independent retailers is that they believe the products on sale are from animals that have enjoyed a welfare standard higher than the minimum required by law. In supermarkets, by contrast, it is generally not possible to obtain information about the conditions in which animals have been farmed by informal means. Because of this, formal mechanisms have been developed to present meat and farm animal products as ethically sourced. Third-party farm assurance schemes allow retailers to display a logo on those products that meet a specified set of animal welfare requirements for the sector in question, with compliance periodically checked, often annually, by the certification body. However, these schemes do not necessarily indicate anything more than mere compliance with the law. Even this is sometimes according to a minimalist interpretation (Compassion in World Farming, 2012), and consumer trust in assurance schemes is variable (Mayfield *et al.*, 2007b). In the UK, the application of an objectively high and detailed welfare standard is indicated by the "RSPCA Assured" logo, which is the certification mark of its Freedom Food programme, with the welfare standards for each animal species running to literally hundreds of requirements (RSPCA, n.d.). However, this standard is in practice met for laying hens and pigs far more frequently than for cattle, sheep or meat chickens (Pickett *et al.*, 2014).

Knowledge is an excellent and frequently underrated starting point for ethics, enabling principles to be applied to real-life situations, thereby often improving them. Regrettably, in public discussions about farm animal welfare it is often in short supply, with complex practical issues frequently misunderstood or oversimplified. Nonetheless, even when a person possesses a high degree of knowledge, this in itself does not generate an ethical decision because, with regard to choice, knowledge is strictly neutral. Something beyond simple facts is needed to provide a person with the principles to shape their response to those facts.

Principles

In modern Britain, a range of ethical principles have been articulated and deployed with reference to farm animal welfare. Although each is differently grounded, they are in practice complementary. The greater challenge is not which ethical principle to accept in preference to others, but promoting ethical reasoning in general as a means of improving welfare outcomes. In this section, I shall outline in turn three possible ethical principles and demonstrate the relevance of each to welfare.

Utility: considering the consequences for animals

In the revolutionary year of 1789, the philosopher and social reformer Jeremy Bentham asserted, in his *Introduction to the Principles of Morals and Legislation*: "the question is not, Can they *reason*? nor, Can they *talk*? but, Can they *suffer*?" (Bentham, 1996, p. 283). Bentham was discussing where the species boundaries of ethical consideration should be drawn, arguing that these extend beyond humans to encompass animals. By their exclusion from ethical consideration, animals have, he protests, been "degraded into the class of *things*". Although Bentham personally liked animals (Boralevi, 1984), he had no problem with killing them for meat. He reckoned that meat-eating, while benefitting humans, leaves animals no worse off, given their inability to experience the state of death. Indeed, Bentham contends that death at human hands "commonly is, and always may be, a speedier, and by that means a less painful one, than that which would await them in the inevitable course of nature". However, he argues passionately that animals should not be, in his words, "tormented", whether during life or at death.

The principle of utility is that the morality of actual and possible actions should be assessed with reference to consequences. For Bentham, utility may be measured in terms of impact on the interests of individuals. The fundamental interest of all sentient beings, he contends, is to seek pleasure and avoid pain, with each of these characterized by intensity, duration, certainty, closeness, the likelihood of continuation and how widely they extend (Bentham, 1996). From an animal welfare perspective, a great strength of Bentham's position is that humans and animals are viewed as comprising a single moral community, even if, as Bentham himself recognized, humans experience political, moral and religious pleasure and pain in addition to the physical pleasure and pain that animals feel.

John Stuart Mill developed Bentham's ideas, particularly his distinction between different kinds of pleasure and pain, by distinguishing higher pleasures from lower pleasures (Hauskeller, 2011). This could be assumed to mean that, in a trade-off between the interests of humans and the interests of farmed animals, the latter are likely to come off worse because their pleasures and pains count for less. However, in his *Utilitarianism*, which was first published in 1861 as a trio of magazine articles, Mill regarded humans as different from animals in only two ways: the greater extent of their sympathy, and their more highly developed intelligence. Unlike "other" animals, whose instinct is self-defence or self-protection, humans are, he writes, able to sympathize with all sentient beings (Mill, 1998, pp. 186-187). Furthermore, their superior intelligence, as well as giving a "wider range to the whole of their sentiments", enables them to apprehend a "community of interest" that extends far beyond their immediate circle. Mill calls into question moral decision-making that fails to take account of wider interests, including the interests of farmed animals.

Since Bentham and Mill, utility has become a major ethical principle in farm animal welfare, underlying much current effort to raise standards. In particular, the Five Freedoms—from hunger and thirst; from discomfort; from pain, injury or disease; to express normal behaviour; and from fear and distress—are grounded in the acceptance that farmed animals should not suffer, and provide a useful and widely accepted structure for appraising welfare (Webster, 2005). However, four of these five freedoms are expressed negatively. Only the fourth freedom, to express normal behaviour, defines interests positively. At least potentially, utility may promote not merely the avoidance of animal suffering but the maximization of positive welfare states through animal flourishing. This will be discussed further below, in the subsection on teleology.

Utility is sometimes critiqued on the grounds that it reduces all objects, and even all people, to their instrumental value within a system of unending consumption, with the items under consideration being assumed to possess no intrinsic value. However, Bentham and Mill each saw themselves as working for social improvement, including by increasing the degree of ethical sensibility in society. With regard to farm animal welfare, the greater difficulty with utilitarianism is the supposition that pain and pleasure may be compared. From a physiological viewpoint, pain is the experience associated with nociceptor stimulation, but there is no single equivalent physiological pathway for the experience of pleasure. This suggests that pleasure is a more diffuse and varied sensation than pain and that it is difficult to compare the two systematically.

For Bentham and Mill, utility was an ethical theory capable of motivating many practical welfare improvements. However, recent utilitarians such as Peter Singer (1998) have radicalized the classical utilitarian concern for animals by arguing that, according to the terms of the theory, the only consistent ethical position is, at the least, vegetarianism, and possibly veganism. From an animal welfare perspective, the difficulty with this position is that, by suggesting that utilitarianism requires the abolition of animal consumption, and possibly of all human use of animals, it calls into question the tremendous gains that the application of the principle of utility has brought, and continues to bring, to real life outcomes.

Deontology: a duty of care for animals

While Bentham was developing and deploying his ethical principle of utility, Immanuel Kant was setting out with great precision the alternative principle of deontology or duty. Kant respected the practical moral reasoning that Mill recognized in his discussion of sympathy. However, he believed that experience was, by itself, a shaky foundation for morality. For Kant, the only reliable grounding for morals is reason. Key to his project is the "categorical imperative", which is an overarching moral principle valid at all times and in all places, rather than one relative to particular situations. It is: "act only in accordance to that maxim through which you can at the same time will that it become a universal law" (Kant, 2012, p. 34).

Because of Kant's great emphasis on reason, many interpreters assume that his ethics is mostly, or even exclusively, concerned with human beings. For this reason, animal ethicists are often more interested in utility than in deontology. Indeed, Kant presents universal law in apparently anthropomorphic terms: "So act that you use humanity, in your own person as well as in the person of any other, always at the same time as an end, never merely as a means" (Kant, 2012, p. 41). Lecture notes report him stating that humans have no direct duties to animals. Nevertheless, he also considers that a "hard-heartedness towards animals is not in accordance with the law of reason, and is at least an unsuitable use of means" (Kant 1997, p. 434). He goes on to describe any human action that torments animals, or that causes them to suffer distress, as demeaning to humans. Any such action is a violation of the moral duty that humans have to themselves, because it stifles the humane instinct and feeling that are part of human moral integrity.

In *The Metaphysics of Morals*, Kant accepts that animals should be killed quickly and painlessly. Violent and cruel treatment, in contrast, "weakens and gradually uproots a natural predisposition that is very serviceable to morality in one's relations with other men" (Kant, 1991, pp. 237-238). Kant also expresses this idea systematically, drawing a distinction between "duty *with regard to* other beings" and "duty *to* those beings". Humans, he argues, have no direct duty *to* animals: in the matter of safeguarding their welfare, the only direct duty is to humans. Even so, humans unquestionably have duties *with regard to* animals. For Kant, from the fact that only humans may act morally it in no way follows that only humans are worthy of moral consideration (Korsgaard, 2004). He uses the idea of personhood, referred to above in the definition of the categorical imperative, not to restrict the boundaries of ethical consideration, but as figurative shorthand for the rational order that, he argues, exists everywhere in the world. This "personification" of nature (Wood, 1998) is Kant's way of presenting everything in the world as worthy of treatment as an end in itself. Moreover, the specific ethical rules—or, as he calls them, maxims—that are developed when universal law is applied in particular cases carry a force of obligation that means they must always be obeyed. For this reason, deontology is an important ethical principle in farm animal welfare that should not be overlooked.

Even if Kant ultimately views the obligation on humans to refrain from the cruel treatment of animals indirectly, he provides a robust understanding of this obligation that admits of no compromise. Moreover, his theory usefully demonstrates that to take the ethics of animal welfare seriously does not entail an acceptance that animals possess any intrinsic rights or entitlements in relation to humans. Furthermore, the notion of duty translates well into a legal context. In the UK, section 9 of the 2006 Animal Welfare Act lays upon the person responsible for an animal a duty to ensure its welfare by meeting its needs. These are taken to include a suitable environment and diet, the ability to exhibit normal behaviour, housing with or apart from other animals, and protection from pain, suffering, injury and disease. This suggests that, in practice, it is widely accepted that, in animal welfare, the deontological principle applies not only to humans, who may be demeaned by inflicting suffering on farmed animals, but also directly to the animals on which such suffering may be inflicted. Moreover, the duty as framed in the legislation imposes positive duties on stockpersons to provide their animals with the conditions and resources needed to sustain a basic dignified life.

Teleology: promoting animal flourishing

A third ethical principle that may promote the welfare of farmed animals is purpose—or, in Greek, *telos*. This principle is older than both utility and deontology, being traceable to Aristotle, the Athenian philosopher who lived in the 4th century BCE. However, in recent decades teleology has made a comeback, because it has been seen as promoting an holistic approach to ethics that is able to take account of more complex states than mere pain and pleasure (Rollin, 2012). Moreover, rather than viewing nature as a competitive arena in which the flourishing of one part requires the diminishment of another part, Aristotle regards the world as a single integrated system in which the flourishing of a part contributes to the flourishing of other parts and of the whole. According to Aristotle, each animal species exhibits a particular natural mode of flourishing that should be respected and promoted within this.

Although more than one-sixth of Aristotle's extant work concerns animals, ethicists have typically ignored it. This is unfortunate, because much is said of relevance to animal welfare in general, and to farm animal welfare in particular. As already explained, key to Aristotle's teleology is the belief that every living being exists for a purpose within an ordered whole. He values pastoral farming highly, arguing that animals that are farmed fulfil their purpose more completely than wild animals. This is because their entire life, from birth to death, is rationally ordered by humans, just as, in humans, the rational soul governs the bodily passions (Aristotle, 2000).

Teleology provides an ethical grounding for the concept of a "good life", which in farm animal welfare designates a condition of flourishing considerably higher than the legal minimum (Farm Animal Welfare Council, 2009). An animal that is said to have a good life will live free of avoidable suffering and enjoy a variety of positive, freely chosen environments and experiences. In the first book of his *Nicomachean Ethics*, Aristotle develops a rich understanding of the good life, which is readily applicable to farmed animals. In his terms, the good of an animal is that at which it aims. This aim is determined by function, which in the case of animals is sentience, which requires nourishment, which leads to growth, which contributes to the excellence with which the animal fulfils its function of sentient living (Aristotle, 2004). It is clear that Aristotle observed the behaviour of particular farmed species in detail. This included characteristics associated with herd and individual health, such as pregnancy, litter size, weight gain, milking cycles and yields. His observations extended further, however, encompassing self-chosen aspects such as feeding habits and dietary preferences, and even dreaming (Grumett, 2016). Aristotle observes each animal species exhibiting a range of freely chosen normal behaviours. This suggests that humans should not only permit these, but actively enable them, in order that individual animals may fulfil these behaviours, alongside others of their species, to the greatest extent possible (Harfeld, 2013).

As Martha Nussbaum points out, teleology means that species is an ethically relevant characteristic. Whereas the principle of utility, being grounded in the concept of sentience, may be used in support of the position that all sentient life (human, animal, microbial) is worthy of equal moral consideration, the ends and types of flourishing that are naturally sought by some species are evidently of a higher level than those pursued by others. To designate these higher modes of flourishing, Nussbaum uses the term "capabilities" (Nussbaum, 2007, pp. 360-407). Her discussion suggests that farmed animals, being more highly developed than many wild species, demand a relatively high level of ethical consideration. In any case, the concepts of flourishing and capability are well-suited to the task of promoting a welfare standard higher than one based on the provision of basic freedoms from harm.

Prudence: relating knowledge to principles

It is sometimes assumed that different ethical systems are in competition and that one must be preferred over others. In fact, the principles of utility (consequences), deontology (duty) and teleology (purpose) support each other. To be required to take utility seriously entails an obligation to consider the likely consequences of future actions. Deontology, which is based on the idea of making individual ethical rules comply with universal moral law, assumes some overall purpose for the world into which particular purposes fit. Teleology suggests that the consequences of actions have some significance, because they promote or hinder the flourishing of other living beings. Ethical theorists enjoy imagining extreme cases in which different principles commend sharply contrasting courses of action, but such conundrums are a long way from the daily lives of most farmers, stockpersons, food business operators, investors, retailers and consumers. In the practical context of promoting farm animal welfare, different ethical principles are likely to be mutually reinforcing.

The greater challenge in ethical decision-making about farmed animals is bringing facts and principles together and acting. A person might have a strong grasp of facts and a clear ethical conviction, but be unable to synthesize the two. Such a person is likely to behave inconsistently and attribute responsibility for situations to others, depending on whether, at any particular time, their focus is on facts or on principles. What is missing in such a person is a developed moral character, which would enable them to act effectively in real life situations. In book 6 of his *Nicomachean Ethics*, Aristotle defines the capacity of combining facts and principles effectively in deliberating about how to act as prudence (Aristotle, 2004, pp. 144-166).[1] Unlike animal welfare research, the kind of reasoning that prudence uses is unscientific, because it does not seek to prove any particular theory. Nevertheless, prudence is intellectual as well as practical, being concerned with what is good and bad rather than simply with what is the case, as are the purely practical tasks of observation and information gathering.

It might reasonably be claimed that ordinary description is never entirely separated from ethical principles. According to the theory of "thick" description, if, for example, I describe a laying hen as "thirsty", I am not only making a neutral statement about its desire for water but identifying this as a bad state of affairs that I or anyone else standing close by should take action to address. This is a fair and important point. Although it is useful for expository and critical purposes—such as this chapter—to keep knowledge and principles distinct, the concept of prudence suggests that the two are, in practice, interrelated. Ethical principles help shape how we perceive the world and structure the facts presented to us, just as we develop those principles in the context of our experience of the world around us.

Prudent individuals, whether they are farmers, stockpersons, food business operators, investors, retailers or consumers, will be able to negotiate the complexities of ethical action and act responsibly. Prudence is especially needed

1 This classical concept of prudence is very different from the modern popular understanding, which is typically associated with inaction or indecisive action.

when dealing with issues related to farm animals, because compromise is required. All producers, sellers and consumers of meat operate on the understanding that it is ethically acceptable for animals to be killed for human consumption. The principles of utility, deontology or teleology could each, if taken to an extreme, be deployed to refute this understanding, but the ethical conclusions reached would be of little use in an industry based on the assumption that animals may be reared, killed and eaten in huge numbers.

Prudence is also needed to handle uncertainty. On the farming side, the effects on animals of different feeding and slaughter methods are not known with complete certainty, being the object of ongoing research. A precautionary approach is therefore advisable, recognizing that, although some methods might not harm animals, knowledge of the facts is incomplete and further evidence is needed before a particular practice may be endorsed. On the consumer side, reliable knowledge of farming methods needs to be obtained from objective sources and subjected to rigorous, objective evaluation, rather than reliance being placed on uninterrogated assumptions that might be false. For example, images on packaging of green fields or a smiling farming family convey no reliable information about the welfare conditions in which animals have been kept, and may be used purely to boost sales. Meat from an independent butcher might be produced to a higher welfare standard than supermarket meat, although in many urban areas might also, unlike supermarket meat, be the product of non-stun slaughter. There are big legitimate questions about this slaughter method; it is likely to cause animals to experience greater pain than those slaughtered after mechanical, electrical or low atmospheric pressure stunning as appropriate to their species.

The practical imperatives to compromise and to acknowledge uncertainty are both contradicted by simplistic stances. A constructive response is often to employ language carefully. In public debate, critiques are frequently launched of "industrial" or "factory farming", even though these are meaningless terms in that they have no formal definition in law or welfare science. To determine whether a particular animal has been "industrially" farmed would require scoring against an accepted list of measures such as stocking density, natural light levels, feeding regime and the availability of outdoor space, and agreement on the point at which these scores, whether separately or in combination according to a formula about which there was consensus, defined a transition from one farming type to another. Moreover, because farmed animals live in relationship with humans and require human care, an animal housed indoors with its needs met will enjoy a higher quality of life than an animal living in a field that is, for instance, cold or has an inadequate food supply.

Religion

In the context of farm animal welfare, religion has become a contentious topic because of its primary association in the public mind with non-stun slaughter, which the UK Government permits for animals intended for Islamic halal and Jewish kosher consumption. The wide public concern about this slaughter method, although not always well informed (Grumett, 2015), is appropriate, given it is likely that cutting an animal's neck with a sharp knife does not render it immediately unconscious and that the animal therefore experiences significant pain before death (Johnson *et al.*, 2015). Advocates of non-stun slaughter who believe that it is no more painful, or even less painful, than slaughter with pre-stunning, need to engage with the scientific evidence that suggests this may be untrue. Moreover, considerably more meat is produced by non-stun slaughter than is required by Muslims and Jews, with the excess being sold in the wholesale market or by independent butchers.

Among Muslims, there is a diversity of views about the permissibility or otherwise of stunning, whereas the official Jewish position is that stunning is prohibited. Nevertheless, there are far more British Muslims (about 3 million) than British Jews (about 350,000), and stunning remains more of an issue in the halal sector than in the kosher sector mainly because it is far larger. During a sample week in 2013, 617,745 animals were slaughtered for halal consumption without stunning, whereas only 22,792 were slaughtered for kosher consumption. Furthermore, within the halal sector the proportion of animals slaughtered without stunning is increasing. Between 2011 and 2013, it rose from 15% to 25% for cattle, from 18% to 37% for sheep and goats, and from 12% to 16% for poultry (Food Standards Agency, 2012, p. 5, 2015, p. 4).

Nevertheless, it must be emphasized that religion is by no means entirely bad news for animals. In general, religious communities develop and transmit ethical systems, including in animal welfare. The slaughter method, although very important, is but one aspect of a larger picture. The halal and kosher designations may also indicate welfare gains above the secular legal minimum. From a theological standpoint, to describe a particular food as halal or kosher means that it is permissible, or fit for consumption, which indicates that it conforms to a series of welfare requirements. According to Islamic teaching, animals killed or used for their products must not be mistreated or mutilated at any point in their life (Masri, 2007). Taken seriously, the prohibition against mistreatment would certainly suggest that the Five Freedoms, which were discussed earlier, should be safeguarded. Moreover, when an animal is killed, this must be done quickly and professionally according to the applicable rules, which include a prayer spoken by the individual slaughterman that recognizes the value of the life of the individual animal as a gift of Allah (Masri, 2007). This should have the effect of preventing animals being seen in purely instrumental terms or as no more than production units to satisfy human wants. In addition, animals killed as a sacrifice, such as on the festival of Eid or for another family occasion, must not be blemished, that is, not be underfed, blind or lame (Masri, 2007). Comparable requirements and justifications exist in the far smaller kosher meat sector (Shechita UK, 2009).

These welfare requirements are far removed from the imagery conjured by the emotive and frequently used phrase "religious slaughter", and point to a shared understanding across Islam, Judaism and Christianity of animals as created by God and therefore as the property of God rather than of humankind. Indeed, within the halal sector the concept of *tayyib*, meaning wholesome, is available and increasingly in use to designate meat and farm animal products that do not simply conform to the minimum requirements of Islam but meet a high physical and moral food standard, which potentially includes a high standard of farm animal welfare.

In reality, religion is currently a significant source of division in farm animal welfare because food traditions and rules help to define community (Grumett and Muers, 2010). Animal farming requires the ownership, or at least the use, of rural land, and in the United Kingdom this is almost exclusively the preserve of people who are white and, at least nominally, Christian. A similar demography is apparent in allied occupations such as veterinary science. Muslim and Jewish people have very little involvement in animal farming, meaning that the full life-cycle of an animal farmed according to halal or kosher principles is not visible. Rather, halal and kosher meat is regulated by certification schemes that place an emphasis on the slaughter method, which is easily verifiable. In these schemes, similar matters of trust arise as in the secular contexts of knowledge described at the beginning of this chapter. Some halal retailers consider that their reputation in the local community and commendations from its leaders provide sufficient endorsement and consumer assurance, especially as some halal consumers are wary about taking formal endorsements on trust (Miele and Rucinska, 2015). Nevertheless, other consumers and community leaders prefer certification schemes.

With regard to Islam, attitudes to slaughter methods are often more conservative in diaspora religious communities than in states in which Islam is the largest religion or the officially recognized religion. In countries like Indonesia, Malaysia and Saudi Arabia, much of the meat consumed is imported from New Zealand, where stunning is mandated by law without exception (Salamano *et al.*, 2013). In the Muslim states in which this meat is consumed, it is widely accepted as halal. This suggest that, in countries such as the UK, better understanding needs to be gained of the views of believers about farm animal welfare in general and stunning in particular. These may differ from those promoted by their representative food authorities, which are not entirely consistent with the rules and practices in other parts of the Muslim world.

Conclusion

Being concerned with underlying commitments, beliefs and motivations, ethics and religion perform roles in farm animal welfare that are different from scientific investigation. They provide principles that may, in a person with prudence, shape the responses to facts about farm animal welfare, whether this person is a farmer, a stockperson, a food business operator, an investor, a retailer or a consumer. For this reason, ethics and religion each have significant and distinctive positive contributions to make to farm animal welfare.

References

Agricultural and Horticulture Development Board (2015). Butcher's a cut above the rest when it comes to consumer trust. Retrieved from http://pork.ahdb.org.uk/news/

news-releases/2015/april/butcher-s-a-cut-above-the-rest-when-it-comes-to-consumer-trust/ [accessed 15 March 2017].

Aristotle (2000). *The Politics* (T.A. Sinclair with Trevor J. Saunders, Trans.). Harmondsworth, UK: Penguin.

Aristotle (2004). *The Nicomachean Ethics* (J.A.K. Thomson with Hugh Tredennick, Trans.). Harmondsworth, UK: Penguin.

Bentham, J. (1996). *An Introduction to the Principles of Morals and Legislation*, J.H. Burns and H.L.A. Hart (Eds.). Oxford: Clarendon.

Boralevi, C. (1984). *Bentham and the Oppressed.* Berlin: de Gruyter.

Compassion in World Farming (2012). *Farm Assurance Schemes and Animal Welfare: How the Standards Compare.* Godalming: Compassion in World Farming.

Farm Animal Welfare Council (2009). *Farm Animal Welfare in Great Britain: Past, Present and Future.* London: Farm Animal Welfare Council.

Food Standards Agency (2012). Results of the 2011 FSA animal welfare survey in Great Britain. Retrieved from https://www.food.gov.uk/sites/default/files/multimedia/pdfs/board/fsa120508.pdf [accessed 15 March 2017].

Food Standards Agency (2015). Results of the 2013 animal welfare survey in Great Britain. Retrieved from https://www.food.gov.uk/sites/default/files/2013-animal-welfare-survey.pdf [accessed 15 March 2017].

Grumett, D. (2015). Animal welfare, morals and faith in the "religious slaughter" debate. In V.E. Cree, G. Clapton & M. Smith (Eds.). *Moral Panics for our Times?* (pp. 211-219). Bristol: Policy Press.

Grumett, D. (2016). Aristotelian ethics in farm animal welfare. Unpublished.

Grumett, D. & Muers, R. (2010). *Theology on the Menu: Asceticism, Meat and Christian Diet.* London: Routledge.

Harfeld, J. (2013). Telos and the ethics of animal farming. *Journal of Agricultural and Environmental Ethics*, 26, 691-713.

Hauskeller, M. (2011). No philosophy for swine: John Stuart Mill on the quality of pleasures. *Utilitas*, 23, 428-446.

Johnson, C., Mellor, D., Hemsworth, P. & Fisher, A. (2015). A scientific comment on the welfare of domesticated ruminants slaughtered without stunning. *New Zealand Veterinary Journal*, 63, 58-65.

Kant, I. (1991). *The Metaphysics of Morals* (Mary Gregor, Trans.). Cambridge, UK: Cambridge University Press.

Kant, I. (1997). *Lectures on Ethics* (Peter Heath, Trans.). Cambridge, UK: Cambridge University Press.

Kant, I. (2012). *Groundwork of the Metaphysics of Morals* (Mary J. Gregor with Jens Timmermann, Trans.) (2nd ed.). Cambridge, UK: Cambridge University Press.

Korsgaard, C. (2004). Fellow creatures: Kantian ethics and our duties to animals. In Grethe B. Peterson (Ed.). *The Tanner Lectures on Human Values* (ed. 25/26) (pp. 77-110). Salt Lake City, UT: University of Utah Press.

Masri, A. (2007). *Animal Welfare in Islam.* Markfield, UK: The Islamic Foundation.

Mayfield, L., Bennett, R., Tranter, R. & Wooldridge, M. (2007a). Consumption of welfare-friendly food products in Great Britain, Italy and Sweden, and how it may be influenced by consumer attitudes to, and behaviour towards, animal welfare attributes. *International Journal of Sociology of Food and Agriculture*, 15, 59-73.

Mayfield, L., Bennett, R. & Turner, R. (2007b). United Kingdom. In A. Evans & M. Miele (Eds.). *Consumers' Views about Farm Animal Welfare. Part I: National Reports based on Focus Group Research* (pp. 115-154). Cardiff, UK: Cardiff University Press.

Miele, M. & Rucinska, K. (2015). Producing halal meat: the case of Halal slaughter practices in Wales, UK. In J. Emel & H. Neo (Eds.). *Political Ecologies of Meat* (pp. 253-275). London: Routledge.

Mill, J. (1998). *On Liberty and Other Essays.* Oxford, UK: Oxford University Press.

Nussbaum, M. (2007). *Frontiers of Justice: Disability, Nationality, Species Membership.* Boston, MA: Harvard University Press.

Palmer, C. (2011). The moral relevance of the distinction between domesticated and wild animals. In T.L. Beauchamp & R.G. Frey (Eds.). *The Oxford Handbook of Animal Ethics* (pp. 701-725). New York: Oxford University Press.

Pickett, H., Crossley, D. & Sutton, C. (2014). *Farm Animal Welfare: Past, Present and Future.* London: Food Ethics Council.

Rollin, B. (2012). Telos. In C.M. Wathes, S. Corr, S. May, S. McCulloch & M. Whiting (Eds.). *Veterinary & Animal Ethics: Proceedings of the First International Conference on Veterinary and Animal Ethics, September 2011* (pp. 75-83). Oxford, UK: Wiley.

Royal Society for the Prevention of Cruelty to Animals (n.d.). RSPCA welfare standards: Helping to improve the lives of millions of farm animals. Retrieved from http://science.rspca.org.uk/sciencegroup/farmanimals/standards [accessed 15 March 2017].

Salamano, G., Cuccurese, A. Poeta, A., Santella, E., Sechi, P., Cambiotti, V. & Cenci-Goga, B.T. (2013). Acceptability of electrical stunning and post-cut stunning among Muslim Communities: A possible dialogue. *Society & Animals*, 21, 443-458.

Shechita UK (2009). *A Guide to Shechita.* Retrieved from http://www.shechitauk.org/wp-content/uploads/2016/02/A_Guide_to_Shechita_2009__01.pdf [accessed 15 March 2017].

Singer, P. (1998). A vegetarian philosophy. In S. Griffiths & J. Wallace (Eds.). *Consuming Passions: Food in the Age of Anxiety* (pp. 71-80). Manchester, UK: Manchester University Press.

Webster, J. (2005). *Animal Welfare Limping towards Eden: A Practical Approach to Redressing the Problem of our Dominion over the Animals.* Oxford, UK: Blackwell.

Wood, A. (1998). Kant on duties regarding nonrational nature. *Proceedings of the Aristotelian Society Supplement*, 72, 189-210.

Part II

Why should companies be concerned about farm animal welfare?

4 The legal journey to improved farm animal welfare

Heleen van de Weerd and Jon Day

CEREBRUS ASSOCIATES, UK

Introduction

The process by which societies adapt to increasing knowledge about farm animal welfare issues can be described as a journey (Mellor and Webster, 2014). Different drivers—regulation, consumer pressure, corporate responsibility, campaigns by non-governmental organizations, media coverage—have all played important roles in improving farm animal welfare.

In this chapter, we focus specifically on the role that can be played by legislation. We use the European Union to demonstrate the contribution that legislation can make and to highlight some of the challenges associated with relying exclusively on legislation to deliver change. The European Union is a relevant and important example for a number of reasons. First, many of its standards are the most stringent in the world. Second, because of its scale, it is one of the most important markets for animal producers around the world. In turn, this means that many of the European Union standards are now effectively minimum standards for companies that aspire to be global scale producers of meat and other animal-derived products. Third, the EU's approach to the design and development of legislation has changed significantly over the past 40 years, reflecting changes in scientific understanding, changes in animal management practices, and changes in public and consumer expectations. As such, it is an important case study of how animal welfare-related policy and legislation may change over time.

Animal welfare legislation in the EU

The European Union (EU) has been developing animal welfare laws for over 40 years, and farm animal welfare plays a prominent role in agricultural policy-making in the EU (Horgan and Gavinelli, 2006). This emphasis has strengthened in the face of growing demands from civil society that animal production systems need both to be sustainable and to take ethical factors into account in formulating policy (Appleby, 2005; Horgan and Gavinelli, 2006).

The EU's approach to animal welfare legislation is explicitly based on sound scientific knowledge and evolves as knowledge evolves. The EU takes the ethics of animal use as a starting point for framing the goals of legislation in this area, while also seeking to support the competitiveness of the EU agricultural industry. The emphasis on current scientific knowledge and on ethical considerations has led to the EU being widely recognized as a global leader for legislation it has developed and implemented in the field of animal welfare (Dalla Villa *et al.*, 2014). This legislation has helped to raise public awareness of farm animal welfare and has contributed to changes in the European public's attitudes to animal welfare (Pritchard, 2012). Such benefits are not readily expressed in economic terms.

History and scope

The basis of the European Union's animal welfare policy is the "Protocol on protection and welfare of animals", which was first introduced as an annex to the 1997 Treaty of Amsterdam (one of the founding treaties for the modern European Union). In 2009, the Treaty of Lisbon updated the Treaty on the Functioning of the European Union (TFEU). Following the adoption of the Treaty of Lisbon, Article 13 TFEU extended the concept of "sentience", reinforced the recognition of animals as being sentient (i.e. capable of feeling pleasure and pain), and requires the EU and its Member States to pay "full regard to the welfare requirements of animals" when formulating and implementing the Union's policies in certain key areas. This put animal welfare on an equal foundation with other issues (Stevenson, 2012). The Treaty of Lisbon has led to a process of building and expanding animal welfare-related regulation by the European Commission.

It is relevant to note that the EU operates under the principles of conferred competences and subsidiarity. That is, competences not conferred upon the EU remain with the Member States. In line with the principle of subsidiarity, the EU shall act only if and in so far as the objectives cannot be sufficiently achieved by the Member States. While the regulation of farm animal welfare has been conferred on the EU, other topics of animal protection (notably the use of animals as companions, the use of animals in competitions, shows, cultural or sporting events, and the welfare concerns relating to captive wild animals) have remained the responsibility of EU Member States.

Policy development

The development of animal welfare policies in the EU was influenced by the initial work of the (international) Council of Europe[1] (COE) in the 1960s, with the first European Convention on animal welfare (covering the protection of animals during international transport) being adopted in 1968. The EU has subsequently

1 The Council of Europe (COE) is an international organization comprising 47 European countries whose aims are to promote democracy and protect the rule of law in Europe. Conventions (and their secondary legal instruments such as Recommendations and Technical Protocols) adopted by the COE serve as guidelines for the European Parliament, national (member) governments and political parties within Europe. Once a state has signed and ratified a Convention, it should implement its provisions into national law (http://www.coe.int/en/web/conventions/about-treaties, accessed June 2016).

closely cooperated with the COE in the development and application of European Conventions and their secondary legal instruments such as Recommendations and Technical Protocols (Pritchard, 2012).

The EU policy development process is a deliberative process involving consideration of a mixture of elements including official information provided by agricultural organizations, the outcome of stakeholder consultations including animal protection organizations, the results of specific socioeconomic studies on possible impacts of new legislative initiatives, and the experience of the Member States in relation to the enforcement of existing animal welfare rules (Horgan and Gavinelli, 2006).

In 2006, the Commission adopted the first Community Action Plan on the Protection and Welfare of Animals (2006–2010). This was the first time that the "Protocol on protection and welfare of animals" had been translated into an approach for the development of the protection of animals in Europe. One of the Plan's primary objectives was to ensure a more consistent and coordinated approach across the EU's policy areas and to formulate strategic priorities and future actions.

The evaluation of the Animal Welfare Action Plan in 2010 showed that the welfare conditions for those groups of animals that were covered by targeted legislation (examples included pigs, calves, laying hens, and animals during transport) had improved. It also highlighted the need to strengthen the enforcement of existing legislation and acknowledged the associated costs of changing animal welfare standards for farmers (Paulsen, 2010; Rayment *et al.*, 2010). The plan that followed was the Strategy for the Protection and Welfare of Animals (covering 2012–2015).[2] The key focal points for this Strategy were to improve enforcement of current legal requirements, to boost existing international cooperation on animal welfare issues, to focus on information and education of consumers, and to stimulate more animal welfare research.

The European Commission's policy work is underpinned by scientific opinions given by the European Food Safety Agency (EFSA) and other scientific fora. EFSA's Animal Health and Welfare Panel (AHAW) provides scientific advice related to aspects of animal health and welfare (but not on ethical or cultural issues) to the European Commission, European Parliament and Member States. The panel focuses primarily on food-producing animals (pigs, chickens, dairy cows and fish) and examines a wide range of topics such as housing and husbandry systems, nutrition and feeding, transport, and stunning and killing methods.

Animal welfare policies are not always easy to enforce because of the complex nature of animal welfare and its assessment. These factors have led to the adaptation of a risk assessment approach to animal welfare by EFSA (Ribó and Serratosa, 2009; Algers, 2009). The assessment of risks related to animal welfare is a continuing process for EFSA's AHAW Panel. The Panel has delivered 38 scientific opinions on animal welfare between 2004 and 2012 (Berthe *et al.*, 2012).[3] The opinions have covered a wide variety of topics: housing, husbandry and

2 http://ec.europa.eu/food/animals/welfare/strategy/index_en.htm, accessed June 2016.
3 See also: http://ec.europa.eu/food/animals/welfare/efsa_opinions/index_en.htm, accessed June 2016.

welfare, transport, cloning, stunning and killing of animals, and animal species: sheep, pigs, dairy cows, calves, rabbits, laying hens, broiler chickens and farmed fish. These opinions are used to inform reviews of the implementation of existing legislation and to identify subjects for potential future legislation.

Current EU legislation that applies to farm animals

Legislation is the most commonly used type of policy instrument used by the EU to achieve minimum welfare standards for farm animals on farm, during transport and at slaughter and to prohibit some of the most inhumane aspects of intensive, industrial livestock production.

EU laws concerning the protection of farm animals are termed either Directives or Regulations. The difference between these two instruments is laid down in the Treaty on the Functioning of the European Union (TFEU), which states that "A directive shall be binding, as to the result to be achieved, upon each Member State to which it is addressed, but shall leave to the national authorities the choice of form and methods" and further states that an EU Regulation "shall be binding in its entirety and directly applicable in all Member States" (TFEU, 2007). That is, while a Directive is binding in relation to the result that is to be achieved, each Member State can decide what kind of legislative instrument it employs to achieve the result. However, on entry into force, EU Regulations automatically become (as written) part of the national law of each Member State. Member State governments may adopt more stringent rules provided they are compatible with the provisions in EU laws (Directives or Regulations).

The aim of EU policy is to spare animals all unnecessary suffering in three main areas of their lives: farming, transport and slaughter. To that end, minimum animal welfare standards have been established to ensure that animals are protected, while avoiding competition distortions between producers in various Member States. The most important standards are concerned with natural behaviour, space, feed and water supply, lighting, veterinary care and good stockperson skills.

Council Directive 98/58/EC forms the basis for protection of animals kept for farming purposes in the EU. It sets out general rules for the protection of animals of all species kept for the production of food, wool, skin or fur or for other farming purposes (including fish, reptiles or amphibians). Farming activities are also subject to specific Directives that define topics such as space allowances, as well as providing requirements on the management of the animals. Minimum standards for the protection of pigs, calves, laying hens and meat chickens are all defined in legislation (Table 4.1).

The welfare of animals being transported is addressed in a Regulation, while another Regulation covers the protection of animals at the time of slaughter or killing.

Another piece of EU legislation with animal welfare implications is the Regulation on organic production and labelling of organic products (Regulation (EC) No 834/2007) that includes high animal welfare standards as one of its principal objectives. These standards often exceed the requirements of the EU's animal welfare rules.

Table 4.1 Overview of animal welfare legislation in the European Union and the requirements that are most relevant for animal welfare[4]

Short name	*Full name (and reference)*	*Requirements most relevant for welfare*
All farm animals [Directive 98/58/EC]	Council Directive 98/58/EC of 20 July 1998 concerning the protection of animals kept for farming purposes Official Journal L 221, 8.8.1998 pp. 23-27	Applies to farmed animals (including fish) kept for the production of food, wool, skin or fur or for other farming purposes Specifies requirements for housing and husbandry, such as the provision of feed and water, together with inspection and record-keeping requirements Requires the prevention of unnecessary pain, suffering or injury, and requires animals to be allowed freedom of movement Prohibits the farming of animals selected for such high levels of productivity that the animals suffer from serious health and welfare problems
Pigs [Directive 2008/120/EC]	Council Directive 2008/120/EC of 18 December 2008 laying down minimum standards for the protection of pigs Official Journal L 47, 18.2.2009 pp. 5-13 (codified version, consolidating earlier Directives adopted in 1991 and 2001)	Prohibits the tethering of sows (from 2006) Prohibits the use of sow stalls except for first 4 weeks of pregnancy (from 2013) Prohibits routine tail-docking, teeth clipping and grinding Prohibits early weaning of piglets from the sow (less than 28 days) Specifies minimum space allowances as well as general conditions for inspection frequency, lighting, ventilation of buildings and quality of floor surfaces Specifies conditions for different types of pigs e.g. the provision of bulky or high-fibre feed for sows For the first time, behavioural needs were included by requiring some form of material to "satisfy the behavioural needs of all pigs"
Calves [Directive 2008/119/EC]	Council Directive 2008/119/EEC of 18 December 2008 laying down minimum standards for the protection of calves Official Journal L 10, 11.01.2009 pp. 7-13	Applies to calves (bovines), up to 6 months of age, that are confined for rearing and fattening Prohibits tethering of calves Prohibits veal crates (from 2007) Requires that calves must be kept in groups after 8 weeks of age, and before this, in individual pens that are large enough to allow turning around and lying down Prohibits all-liquid, iron-deficient diets (part of veal crate systems) and requires the provision of solid fibrous food and dietary iron

(Continued overleaf)

4 For a more detailed description of these laws and the implications for animal welfare, see Stevenson (2012).

Table 4.1 *(continued)*

Short name	*Full name (and reference)*	*Requirements most relevant for welfare*
Laying hens [Directive 1999/74/EC]	Council Directive 1999/74/EC of 19 July 1999 laying down minimum standards for the protection of laying hens Official Journal L 203, 3.8.1999 pp. 53-57	Prohibits barren battery cages (from 2012) Permits enriched cage systems so long as they meet minimum requirements for space and height, and provide litter for pecking and scratching, a nest area and appropriate perches Specifies minimum space allowances for barn and free-range systems Prohibits all mutilations, but beak trimming (to prevent feather pecking and cannibalism) may be authorized, provided it is carried out by qualified staff and on chickens less than 10 days old Prohibits forced moulting (that involves food deprivation)
Meat chickens (broilers) [Directive 2007/43/EC]	Council Directive 2007/43 of 28 June 2007 laying down minimum rules for the protection of chickens kept for meat production Official Journal L 182, 12.7.2007, pp. 19-28	Only applies to holdings with broilers, but not to holdings with broiler parent or grandparent, great grandparent or pedigree breeding chickens Specifies minimum standards for housing and husbandry such as permanent access to dry and friable litter Requires all chickens to be inspected twice a day and requires the training of persons in charge of chickens Prohibits stocking densities of more than 42 kg/m^2, thus limiting densities for broilers for the first time Permits higher stocking densities (between 33 and 42 kg/m^2) if additional criteria are met. These criteria relate to the performance (mortality) and welfare of previous flocks in the house, the maintenance of suitable documentation and the ability to properly control environmental parameters in a broiler house
Animals during transport [Regulation (EC) No 1/2005]	Council Regulation (EC) No 1/2005 of 22 December 2004, on the protection of animals during transport and related operations and amending Directives 64/432/EEC and 93/119/EC and Regulation (EC) No 1255/97 Official Journal L 3, 5.1.2005, pp. 1-44	Applies to the transport of live vertebrate animals in connection with an economic activity, and to markets, assembly centres and slaughter plants Prohibits the transport of an animal in a way which is likely to cause injury or undue suffering Prohibits the transport of animals that are not fit for the intended journey Requires that journeys shall not exceed 8 hours, after which the animals must be unloaded and given food, water and at least 24 hours rest, except in situations where additional requirements are met (e.g. provision of bedding, ventilation systems) Requires livestock hauliers to obtain a certificate of competence with additional requirements applied to those involved in long distance transport

Short name	*Full name (and reference)*	*Requirements most relevant for welfare*
Animals at the time of slaughter [Regulation (EC) 1099/2009]	Council Regulation (EC) No 1099/2009 of 24 September 2009 on the protection of animals at the time of killing Official Journal L 340, 31.12.1993, pp. 21-34	Applies to animals bred or kept for the production of food, wool, skin or fur, and to the killing of animals for disease control Requires that animals must be spared any avoidable pain, distress or suffering during killing and related operations Requires all animals, including poultry, to be stunned before slaughter, but allows religious slaughter without the animals being pre-stunned Requires that stunning must be followed as quickly as possible by a procedure causing death, such as bleeding Imposes specific requirements for the movement and lairage of animals in slaughterhouses, for the restraint of animals before stunning, slaughter or killing and for stunning and killing methods (specifying minimum currents) Requires certificates of competence for staff involved in killing and related operations Includes obligations for self-checking and for the presence of an animal welfare officer

Enforcement

Embedded in EU Directives and Regulations is the provision that Member State competent authorities check compliance with the legal requirements.

The Commission, in turn, is responsible for ensuring that EU legislation is properly implemented and enforced in Member States, assisted, *inter alia*, by inspections carried out by the Food and Veterinary Office (FVO). Within the present arrangements the FVO works only on the welfare of farmed animals.

The FVO reports on the level of compliance with animal welfare Directives and Regulations. Non-compliances and infringements are often found. For example in the period 2005–2010, a total of 82 FVO mission reports on animal welfare were produced across all Member States (Rayment *et al.*, 2010). Some of the most common non-compliances were:

- Pigs: the lack of material for manipulation
- During transport: overstocking, lack of equipment for long distance transport
- At slaughter: lack of effective stunning for poultry, excessive use of the derogation for stunning, inappropriate restraint of small ruminants

The FVO's role is clearly defined but its impact in enhancing welfare standards is limited by the frequency of inspections, the limited range of species that can be covered, and the difficulty of resolving cases of conflict with a Member State (Rayment *et al.*, 2010). Rayment *et al.* (2010) have argued that increasing the resources for inspection efforts would provide greater certainty of compliance with legislation across Member States.

A brief overview of global animal welfare legislation

Although there are no general global standards concerning animal welfare, the topic has increasingly become a global issue. This has partly resulted from the development and use of explicit animal welfare standards that has helped to integrate animal welfare as a component of national and international public policy, commerce and trade (Fraser, 2014). Despite the effort that has gone into developing animal welfare standards, the reality is that, while food safety and animal health are important issues in negotiating and establishing trade agreements, environmental, animal welfare and labour issues are of much less importance in these negotiations (van Wagenberg *et al.*, 2012).

The EU has promoted the inclusion of animal welfare via bilateral trade agreements with third (non-EU) country suppliers of animals and animal products. In the majority of non-EU countries, with the notable exception of Switzerland, only basic requirements have been laid down in legislation with regard to animal welfare. These countries mainly rely on standards from voluntary, industry-driven systems to regulate animal welfare.

To raise awareness of animal welfare at the global level, the European Commission has actively contributed to the development of standards for animal protection at an international level by contributing to the work of intergovernmental organizations such as the OIE (World Organisation for Animal Health), FAO (Food and Agriculture Organization of the United Nations) and the WTO (World Trade Organization) (Horgan and Gavinelli, 2006).

The OIE World Assembly (representing 178 countries) has adopted animal welfare standards for terrestrial animals (OIE, 2012a) and for farmed fish (OIE, 2012b). These standards are based on scientific knowledge which has both increased their credibility and facilitated their use in legislative and regulatory initiatives in those countries that are at an earlier stage of developing farm animal welfare legislation and policy (Mellor and Webster, 2014).

The OIE standards are not mandatory for Member Countries, but provide many countries with their first explicit and officially supported standards for animal welfare. At the very least, having such widely acknowledged standards gives authorities a basis for promoting improvements in animal welfare in their respective jurisdictions, and the opportunity to develop approaches to improving animal welfare (e.g. facilitating the provision of shelter, food, water and health care, by improving basic handling, transportation and slaughter) (Fraser, 2014).

The EconWelfare report (Schmid and Kilchsperger, 2010) describes the legal frameworks for animals and animal products in the main EU trading partner countries (i.e. Australia, Brazil, Canada, China, New Zealand and the USA). Most of these countries only have an animal protection law, but no detailed regulations for husbandry, transport and slaughter for the main types of farm animals (dairy cows, pigs, broiler chickens and laying hens). Some federal states (Australia,

Canada and the US) have left the animal welfare legislation under the jurisdiction of their member states/regions. Other trade partner countries make use of codes of practice.

In China, the level of animal welfare legislation is lower than in the EU. The legal framework is set by the "Animal Husbandry Law of the People's Republic of China" (2005). The focus of this law is more on health and veterinary aspects. There is no legislation for the transport and slaughter of animals, except for slaughter of pigs (*ibid.*).

In the USA, the level of animal welfare legislation is also lower than in the EU. Farm animal welfare has been a growing concern since the 1990s but the federal government remained relatively inactive for a long time. Legislation at the federal level is limited to the Humane Slaughter Act and the Twenty-Eight Hour Law for transport. Industry-driven, animal protection organization-driven, and retailer guidelines all exist; to provide just one example, the national chicken council (NCC) has established criteria for welfare of broilers. Some (but not all) of these guidelines are based on the work of third-party (independent) scientific committees with third-party audits.

In Brazil, the level of animal welfare legislation is slightly lower than in the EU. Animal welfare is predominantly regulated through legislation for non-organic and organic production. Legislation for the transport and slaughter of animals is in existence, although not for poultry (van Horne and Bondt, 2013).

The existing differences in levels of and approaches to welfare legislation and standards between EU countries and important international trade partners can affect the competitiveness of the animal production sectors within the EU (Schmid and Kilchsperger, 2010). It may affect the relative costs of producers in different regions, it may provide a competitive advantage for exporters from the EU and it may mean that producers outside the EU need to raise standards if they wish to sell their products within the EU. The international activities of the EU are widely recognized as having raised the profile and awareness of animal welfare in a global context. Research into Europeans' attitudes to animal welfare concluded that these activities are supported by EU citizens and recommended that they should continue to be a priority area for the EU (European Commission, 2015).

Different approaches to law making and how this achieves welfare improvements

EU welfare legislation has a long history and the approach to drafting welfare laws has changed over time. In this section, two examples of EU legislation will be discussed to illustrate different approaches, reflecting political and agricultural developments, as well as progress in animal welfare science.

Welfare has traditionally been assessed according to the housing and resources that have been provided to the animals (input- or resource-based measures). In recent years, however, the focus has shifted to outcome- or animal-based measures (e.g. lameness, feather cover) which focus on an animal's current welfare state, while also integrating long-term consequences of past husbandry (Webster *et al.*,

2004). Welfare is a characteristic of the individual animal, not just the system in which animals are farmed (Butterworth, 2009).

Assessment systems for animal welfare also increasingly use combined measures (including resource- and animal-based measures) to address welfare criteria, in order to assess whether animals are housed in a way that is meaningful for their species. Besides biological functioning and a focus on resources, welfare assessments now also include ways of assessing welfare outcomes in terms of animals' experiences (i.e. their affective states) (Mellor and Webster, 2014). When all these criteria are chosen carefully, relevant outcome- and input-based measures correlate with increased welfare (Webster *et al.*, 2004).

The first example of EU legislation concerns the protection of laying hens which used the "traditional" approach to animal protection by defining the (minimum) inputs of the farm environment and management to protect the animals (input- or resource-based measures). The second example is the case of meat chicken protection which has fewer prescriptive measures and places a greater focus on the effects of the farm environment and farm management on the animals themselves (outcome based-measures).

EU legislation for laying hens: the Laying Hen Directive 1999/74/EC

Directive 1999/74/EC or the "laying hen Directive" sets out a series of requirements for egg production systems. Laying hens may face a number of welfare problems when housed in a barren environment, including: disease risk, bone breakage, harmful pecking, behavioural problems and mortality (EFSA, 2005). Other welfare risks are high levels of fearfulness, acute and chronic pain caused by beak trimming, frustration and boredom and no access to appropriate substrates and perches (Janczak and Riber, 2015). These problems and risks led to EU legislation with the aim of protecting laying hens.[5]

The first version of EU laying hen legislation was one of the first Europe-wide statutes that actually specified how animals were to be kept (Appleby, 2003). The history of this legislation goes back to the Council of Europe's recommendations as laid down in the Convention on the Protection of Animals Kept for Farming Purposes (Council of Europe, 1976), which were subsequently developed into more specific requirements.

The EU became a party to the Convention on the Protection of Animals Kept for Farming in 1978 and following this, the Commission proposed its first set of standards for the keeping of hens in battery cages in 1986 (Directive 86/113/EEC). These standards were revised in 1988 (88/166/EEC) to provide more specific guidelines regarding space allowances, provisions for eating and drinking, and cage shape and design. The standards applied to all cages from 1995.

In 1996, the Scientific Veterinary Committee (SVC, 1996) of the European Commission evaluated the welfare benefits and deficiencies of cages and non-cage systems and concluded that battery cages have inherent severe disadvantages for

5 A detailed account of the history of laying hen legislation is provided in Appleby (2003).

the welfare of hens. Subsequently, a potential ban of the battery cage was discussed within the European parliament, against a backdrop of growing public concern, campaigns by various animal welfare organizations and political interest in a number of European countries including Germany, the UK and Sweden (Appleby, 2003).

In 1999, 13 of the then 15 EU Member States approved a new Directive (1999/74/EC) with a far-reaching ban on barren battery cage systems after 2012. From 2012, all cage systems were required to provide nest sites, appropriate perches, litter (scratch) facilities and claw shortening devices, and to increase cage space to 750 cm^2 per hen. Minimum space allowances and maximum stocking densities were also provided for non-cage alternative housing systems.

Farmers and operators were given a transitional period of 12 years to adjust to this measure. The battery cage ban was welcomed by the organizations that had campaigned for this, such as Eurogroup for Animal Welfare and Compassion in World Farming. While the egg industry campaigned to overturn the ban, these efforts were unsuccessful. Some countries, such as Sweden and Austria, banned cages ahead of the EU ban.

In the transition period before the cage ban came into force, independent scientific and socioeconomic studies lent support to the EU's legislative decision, by outlining the benefits of changing to so-called "enriched" cages or alternatives to cage systems (free-range or barn). For example, EFSA (2005) assessed the impact of the various housing systems on the health and welfare of laying hens, and concluded that keeping hens in unenriched cages increased the risk of disease, bone breakage, harmful pecking, behavioural problems and mortality. EU-funded research such as the LayWel project (Blokhuis *et al.*, 2007) also confirmed that unenriched cages presented serious welfare problems and that there were clear benefits associated with the adoption of enriched caging or alternative systems. Other research concluded that the welfare of hens in well-designed, modern, enriched cages was comparable to or better than in other systems (Elson and Tauson, 2012).

The European Commission also examined the economic implications of banning unenriched cages, taking into account the concerns expressed by egg producers. The socioeconomic consequences of the various systems for rearing hens were reviewed in model scenarios. While it was concluded that the variable cost of switching to enriched cage production (or any other alternative system) would increase (Agra-CEAS, 2004), the expectation was that the mandatory requirement to improve housing systems for laying hens offered EU producers a competitive advantage over third country producers by meeting a growing consumer demand for welfare-friendly eggs. This research also acknowledged that it was extremely difficult for European farmers to compete with their counterparts in certain third countries on production costs alone.

The battery cage ban took a long time to achieve. It was 48 years after the publication of *Animal Machines* (Harrison, 1964) that the protest calls to "Ban the Battery cage" had their impact (Appleby, 2003). One of the key factors that enabled change was the availability of enriched or furnished cages (containing perches, nest boxes and a litter/scratch area) as a viable alternative system

(Appleby, 2003). Some countries (e.g. Germany) moved beyond the requirements of the Directive to require even higher standards with greater space and height in so-called *kleingruppenhaltung* (Fröhlich *et al.*, 2012). In other EU countries, the egg industry has adopted cage-free systems (e.g. the UK egg market[6] in 2014 consisted of 49% non-cage eggs, and for retail this was 56%). Increasingly, global restaurant chains and retailers are sourcing cage-free eggs for their own-brand product lines (Amos and Sullivan, 2016), suggesting that some consumers do not regard enriched cages as acceptable alternatives for the conventional battery cage.

Some egg producers who were active both before and after the transition, argued that while alternative egg systems might be better for hen welfare and might address consumer concerns, such systems were similar or worse to conventional battery cages for other aspects, especially labour (Stadig *et al.*, 2016). Interestingly, despite this, these egg producers were not overly concerned about the general consequences of the cage ban for their businesses (*ibid.*).

Despite the fact that the Laying Hen Directive is input-based legislation (i.e. its focus is on the systems within which hens are kept), there is still a lack of clarity with regard to certain requirements. This is compounded by the fact that enriched cages have only been in commercial use for a relatively short period of time, with most industry R&D being conducted in the years immediately preceding the ban in 2012. More research and development is required to optimize cage and group size, the type and amount of litter, lighting and light intensity, and the catching and handling of hens during depopulation (Elson and Tauson, 2012; Janczak and Riber, 2015).

EU legislation for broiler meat chickens: the Broiler Directive 2007/43/EC

Chickens kept or reared for meat production (also called broilers) present welfare problems that have many causes, including the conditions under which these animals are reared. Genetic selection and environmental factors (accommodation, temperature, lighting programmes, feeding systems) have led to animal welfare issues such as foot pad dermatitis, breast lesions, joint lesions/lameness, hock burn, cellulitis, ascites, respiratory problems, wing fractures and emaciation (Butterworth *et al.*, 2016). This prompted the development of EU Directive 2007/43/EC which aims to protect meat broilers.

The main goal of Directive EC/2007/43 was to reduce the high industry stocking density, viewed by many as the main contributor to poor welfare (Estevez, 2007). The Directive, which was developed following a long period of difficult discussion (*Veterinary Record*, 2006) between the EU Member States, had two unique features: it was the first EU welfare law that focused on broilers, and it was the first time that outcome-based indicators, such as mortality, were included in EU animal welfare legislation as a means of measuring compliance with the legislation.

There had, previously, been no regulation protecting broiler welfare, although Denmark and Sweden had imposed maximum stocking densities of 40 kg/m^2 and

6 www.egginfo.co.uk/egg-facts-and-figures/industry-information/data, accessed June 2016.

36 kg/m^2 respectively, and monitored foot pad dermatitis in abattoirs linked to farm performance (Berg and Algers, 2004). A number of other countries (e.g. Germany) controlled stocking densities through voluntary guidelines.

The Directive sets out minimum standards for housing and husbandry issues, with the aim of providing chickens with a good level of welfare and health under indoor climate conditions. The Directive limits the maximum stocking density to 33 kg/m^2. However, under certain conditions, with good ventilation and temperature control, the maximum can be raised to 39 kg/m^2. Under high welfare conditions, the density can be increased by a further 3 kg to 42 kg/m^2. This has to be justified through low mortality rates. These criteria relate to the performance and welfare of previous flocks in the house, the maintenance of suitable documentation, and the ability of each house to properly control environmental parameters (lighting, litter, feeding and ventilation requirements). Proven records of good animal welfare (e.g. low daily mortality rates), in addition to the breed of the chickens and the number of broilers dead on arrival, need to be recorded and provided at the slaughterhouse.

Where poor animal welfare conditions are detected either by inspecting the data on the accompanying flock documents or during the post-mortem inspections of the animals (e.g. abnormal levels of contact dermatitis or systemic illness), the official veterinarian of the slaughterhouse must communicate these findings to the owner or keeper of the animals and to the competent authorities for them to take appropriate measures.

Sweden and Denmark have adopted additional legislative requirements, specifically that the prevalence of foot pad lesions must not exceed a certain level for maximum stocking densities to be approved (Berg and Algers, 2004). Similarly, in the Netherlands, producers may not exceed a maximum agreed level of hock burns in order to be permitted to keep birds at 42 kg/m^2.

The Broiler Directive's biggest potential to improve welfare is through altering housing conditions with increased attention to lighting, ventilation, and record-keeping and management practices, coupled with effective feedback on the quality of management to the producer.

The sampling and data collection requirements of the Directive offer great potential for welfare improvements through analysis and use of the post-mortem pathology measures taken in the slaughterhouse. There is agreement between Member States on a common range of welfare measures (foot pad dermatitis, hock burn, dead on arrival), which can already be practically assessed to fulfil the requirements of the Directive (Butterworth *et al.*, 2016). Post-mortem inspections of the whole carcass and the bird's feet contribute the most to the detection of welfare problems, and data on these animal-based indicators are more easily collected at slaughter than on farm (Huneau-Salaün *et al.*, 2015).

The impact of the Directive on the broiler industry was greatest in those countries where high stocking densities used to be applied (e.g. Netherlands, Eastern and Central European countries), and has less effect on countries such as Sweden, Germany and Denmark where the advised densities were already in practice (Pritchard, 2012).

The Directive has increased costs due to the need to regulate the additional stocking density with additional surveillance and inspection (Van Horne and Bondt, 2013), although it has been argued that it is unlikely that the global competiveness of the EU industry has significantly changed as a result (Pritchard, 2012).

It is too early to determine the long-term impact of the Directive on broiler welfare throughout the EU as Member States are at different stages of implementation of the Directive and have apportioned varying levels of resources and personnel to the activities required by the Directive (Butterworth *et al.*, 2016). However, increased harmonization of the implementation of the Directive across the EU could be achieved through sharing of methods and technical information between Member States. This process could eventually lead to improved animal welfare through increased consistency in the application of welfare control measures (*ibid.*).

Wider reflections on legislation as a driver of change

The EU legal framework has supported the adoption of optimal housing systems for farmed animals. This process has been assisted by translating scientific research into best practice, education, development of stock people's skills and the enforcement of legislation by Member State competent authorities. EU animal welfare legislation has led to the banning of veal crates, the banning of barren battery cages for laying hens, and severe restrictions on the use of stalls (gestation crates) for pregnant sows. Overall, this legislation has directly improved the welfare of billions of animals that are farmed in the EU.

However, there are limits to what has been achieved. It could be argued that EU legislation is "piecemeal" as there are groups of animals outside the scope of the current legislation that would also benefit from harmonized policies to achieve higher welfare standards (Rayment *et al.*, 2010). This applies especially to those species without specific legislation, such as cattle (beef and dairy cows), sheep, turkeys, ducks, rabbits and farmed fish. The case has also been made to include horses (Peli *et al.*, 2012). There is also a lot of potential in the existing legislation to advance welfare further; this is particularly the case if enforcement was intensified, for example with regard to routine mutilations such as tail docking for pigs and beak trimming for poultry. Finally, while EU animal welfare legislation has, thus far, focused on food-producing animals, there is debate on whether to extend legislation to all animals in captivity, by drafting an overarching EU legislative framework which consolidates the established general principles in order to simplify all the legal acts on animal welfare and ultimately facilitate their enforcement (EU Strategy on Animal Welfare 2012–2015).[7]

Legislation is a powerful tool as it allows standards to be enforced by law. However, legislation also has important limits: enforcement can be costly, it is difficult to monitor and oversee all producers, and the legislative process is slow (especially given the current number of EU Member States, their diversity of cultures and religions and their different levels of socioeconomic development).

7 http://ec.europa.eu/food/animals/welfare/strategy/index_en.htm, accessed June 2016.

But the impact of legislation is not confined to those entities covered by legislation or to those actors that are subject to monitoring and enforcement. A bigger impact of animal welfare legislation may be through awareness-raising, through the setting of precedents, and through showing what can be achieved. This is particularly the case with the EU, given that it is such an important market for many producers. To take just one example, the ban on sow stalls is being replicated by businesses (e.g. several global food companies, including Smithfield Foods, have committed to ban pork from gestation crates).[8] Expressed another way, legislation in combination with other drivers for change—companies' corporate social responsibility policies, consumer/citizen pressure, private animal welfare initiatives, innovation from agri-businesses—can, albeit sometimes relatively slowly, be a real driver for improving the welfare of farmed animals around the globe.

References

Agra CEAS Consulting Ltd. (2004). Study on the socio-economic implications of the various systems to keep laying hens. Report for the European Commission. Retrieved from http://www.ceasc.com/Images/Content/2120%20final%20report.pdf, accessed June 2016.

Algers, B. (2009). A risk assessment approach to animal welfare. In F. Smulders and B. Algers (Eds.). *Welfare of Production Animals: Assessment and Management of Risks* (pp. 223-235). Wageningen: Wageningen Academic Publishers.

Amos, N. & Sullivan, R. (2016). *The Business Benchmark on Farm Animal Welfare: 2015 Report*. London: Business Benchmark on Farm Animal Welfare. Retrieved from www.bbfaw.com/media/1338/bbfaw-2015-report.pdf, accessed June 2016.

Appleby, M.C. (2003). The EU ban on battery cages: history and prospects. In D.J. Salem & A.N. Rowan (Eds.). *The State of the Animals II: 2003* (159-174). Washington, DC: Humane Society Press. Retrieved from http://animalstudiesrepository.org/cgi/viewcontent.cgi?article=1008&context=sota_2003, accessed June 2016:

Appleby, M.C. (2005). Sustainable agriculture is humane, humane agriculture is sustainable. *Journal of Agricultural and Environmental Ethics*, 18, 293-303.

Berg, C. & Algers, B. (2004). Using welfare outcomes to control intensification: the Swedish model. In C.A. Weeks & A. Butterworth (Eds.). *Measuring and Auditing Broiler Welfare* (pp. 223-229). Wallingford: CABI.

Berthe, F., Vannier, P., Have, P., Serratosa, J., Bastino, E., Broom, D.M., Hartung, J. & Sharp, J.M. (2012). The role of EFSA in assessing and promoting animal health and welfare. *EFSA Journal*, 10(10), s1002. Retrieved from http://www.efsa.europa.eu/sites/default/files/scientific_output/files/main_documents/as1002.pdf, accessed June 2016.

Blokhuis, H.J., Fiks van Niekerk, T., Bessei, W., Elson, A., Guemene, D., Kjaer, J.B., Maria Levrino, G.A., Nicol, C.J., Tauson, R., Weeks, C.A. & van de Weerd, H.A. (2007). The LayWel Project: welfare implications of changes in production systems for laying hens. *World's Poultry Science Journal*, 63, 101-114.

Butterworth, A. (2009). Animal welfare indicators and their use in society. In F. Smulders & B. Algers (Eds.). *Welfare of Production Animals: Assessment and Management of Risks* (371-390). Wageningen: Wageningen Academic Publishers.

8 www.smithfieldfoods.com/responsible-operations/animal-care, accessed June 2016.

Butterworth, A., de Jong, I.C., Keppler, C., Knierim, U., Stadig L. & Lambton, S. (2016). What is being measured, and by whom? Facilitation of communication on technical measures amongst competent authorities in the implementation of the European Union Broiler Directive (2007/43/EC). *Animal*, 10(2), 302-308.

Council of Europe (1976). The European Convention for the Protection of Animals kept for Farming Purposes (ETS 87). Retrieved from www.coe.int/en/web/conventions/full-list/-/conventions/rms/0900001680076da6, accessed June 2016.

Dalla Villa, P., Matthews, L.R., Alessandrini, B., Messori, S. & Migliorati, G. (2014). Drivers for animal welfare policies in Europe. *OIE Scientific and Technical Review*, 33(1), 39-46. Retrieved from http://web.oie.int/boutique/extrait/04dallavilla3946.pdf

EFSA (2005) Opinion of the Scientific Panel on Animal Health and Welfare (AHAW) on the welfare aspects of various systems of keeping laying hens. EFSA. Retrieved from http://www.efsa.europa.eu/en/efsajournal/pub/197, accessed June 2016.

Elson, H.A. & Tauson, R. (2012). Furnished cages for laying hens. In V. Sandilands and P.M. Hocking (Eds.). *Alternative Systems for Poultry Health, Welfare and Productivity* (190-209). Wallingford, UK: CABI.

Estevez, I. (2007). Density allowances for broilers: where to set the limits? *Poultry Science*, 86(6), 1265-1272.

European Commission (2015). *Attitudes of Europeans towards Animal Welfare*. Special Eurobarometer 442. Retrieved from https://thepositiveanimal.com/wp-content/uploads/2016/04/Eurobarometer-2016-Animal-Welfare.pdf, accessed June 2016.

Fraser, D. (2014). The globalisation of farm animal welfare. *OIE Scientific and Technical Review*, 33(1), 33-38. Retrieved from http://web.oie.int/boutique/extrait/03fraser3338.pdf

Fröhlich, E.K.F., Niebuhr, K., Schrader, L. & Oester, H. (2012). What are alternative systems for poultry? In V. Sandilands and P.M. Hocking (Eds.). *Alternative Systems for Poultry Health, Welfare and Productivity* (pp. 1-22). Wallingford, UK: CABI.

Harrison, R. (1964). *Animal Machines the New Factory Farming Industry*. London: Vincent Stuart.

Horgan, R. & Gavinelli, A. (2006). The expanding role of animal welfare within EU legislation and beyond. *Livestock Science*, 103(3), 303-307.

Huneau-Salaün, A., Stärk, K.D.C., Mateus, A., Lupo, C., Lindberg, A. & Le Bouquin-Leneveu, S. (2015) Contribution of meat inspection to the surveillance of poultry health and welfare in the European Union. *Epidemiology and Infection*,143, 2459-2472.

Janczak, A.M. & Riber, A.B. (2015). Review of rearing-related factors affecting the welfare of laying hens. *Poultry Science*, 94(7), 1454-1469.

Mellor, D.J. & Webster, J.R. (2014). Development of animal welfare understanding drives change in minimum welfare standards. *Scientific and Technical Review*, 33(1) 121-130. Retrieved from http://web.oie.int/boutique/extrait/14mellor121130_0.pdf, accessed June 2016.

OIE - World Organisation for Animal Health (2012a). Introduction to the recommendations for animal welfare. Terrestrial Animal Health Code, Chapter 7.1. Paris: OIE. Retrieved from www.oie.int/index.php?id=169&L=0&htmfile=titre_1.7.htm, accessed June 2016.

OIE - World Organisation for Animal Health (2012b). Welfare of farmed fish. Aquatic Animal Health Code, Section 7. Paris: OIE. Retrieved from www.oie.int/index.php?id=171&L=0&htmfile=titre_1.7.htm, accessed June 2016.

Paulsen, M. (2010). *Report on Evaluation and Assessment of the Animal Welfare Action Plan 2006-2010*. European Parliament: Committee on Agriculture and Rural Development. Retrieved from http://ec.europa.eu/food/animals/docs/aw_arch_032010_eu_parliament_report_en.pdf, accessed June 2016.

Peli, A., Scagliarini, L., Calbucci, S. & Diegoli, G. (2012). Considerations on the sphere of application of European Union animal protection legislation for horses. *Veterinaria Italiana*, 48(4), 453-461.

Pritchard, D.G. (2012). The impact of legislation and assurance schemes on alternative systems for poultry welfare. In V. Sandilands & P.M. Hocking (Eds.). *Alternative Systems for Poultry Health, Welfare and Productivity* (pp. 23-52). Wallingford, UK: CABI.

Rayment, M., Asthana, P., van de Weerd, H.A., Gittins, J. & Talling, J. (2010). *Evaluation of the EU Policy on Animal Welfare and Possible Options for the Future.* GHK Consulting Ltd and ADAS report for DG SANCO. Retrieved from www.eupaw.eu, accessed June 2016.

Ribó, O. & Serratosa, J. (2009). History and procedural aspects of the animal welfare risk assessment at EFSA. In F. Smulders & B. Algers (Eds.). *Welfare of Production Animals: Assessment and Management of Risks* (305-335). Wageningen: Wageningen Academic Publishers.

Schmid, O. & Kilchsperger, R. (2010). *Report Containing Overview of Animal Welfare Standards and Initiatives in Selected EU and Third Countries.* EconWelfare project report D1.2.Retrievedfromhttp://www.econwelfare.eu/publications/EconWelfareD1.2Report_update_Nov2010.pdf, accessed June 2016.

Scientific Veterinary Committee (SVC), Animal Welfare Section (1996). *The Welfare of Laying Hens*. European Commission Report nr Doc VI/B/II.2.

Stadig, L.M., Ampe, B.A., Van Gansbeke, S., Van den Bogaert T., D'Haenens, E., Heerkens, J.L.T., & Tuyttens, F.A.M. (2016). Survey of egg farmers regarding the ban on conventional cages in the EU and their opinion of alternative layer housing systems in Flanders, Belgium. *Poultry Science*, 95(3), 715-725.

Stevenson, P. (2012). *European Union Legislation on the Welfare of Farm Animals.* Compassion in World Farming. Retrieved from http://www.ciwf.org.uk/media/3818623/eu-law-on-the-welfare-of-farm-animals.pdf, accessed June 2016.

TFEU (2007) Treaty on the Functioning of the European Union, art 288. Retrieved from http://eur-lex.europa.eu/legal-content/EN/TXT/?uri=CELEX:12012E/TXT, accessed June 2016.

van Horne, P. & Bondt, N. (2013). *Competitiveness of the EU Poultry Meat Sector.* The Hague: LEI Wageningen UR. Retrieved from http://edepot.wur.nl/292607, accessed June 2016.

van Wagenberg, C.P.A., Brouwer, F.M., Hoste, R. & Rau, M.L. (2012). *Comparative Analysis of EU Standards in Food Safety, Environment, Animal Welfare and Other Non-trade Concerns With Some Selected Countries.* LEI Wageningen UR. Retrieved from http://www.europarl.europa.eu/RegData/etudes/etudes/join/2012/474542/IPOL-AGRI_ET(2012)474542_EN.pdf, accessed June 2016.

Veterinary Record (2006). Broiler welfare talks collapse. *Veterinary Record*, 159(December 2006), 864.

Webster, A.J.F., Main, D.C.J. & Whay, H.R. (2004). Welfare assessment: indices from clinical observation. *Animal Welfare*, 13, S93-S98.

5 Consumers, corporate policy and animal welfare

How societal demands are shaping the food industry's approach to farm animal welfare

Sally Healy

ENVIRONMENTAL FUTURES RESEARCH INSTITUTE, GRIFFITH UNIVERSITY, AUSTRALIA

Introduction

Farm animal welfare is more important to consumers and to food businesses than ever before. Consumer surveys consistently indicate that consumers would prefer to have more information on farm animal welfare and be able to identify companies which take animal welfare seriously. The areas that consumers are concerned about include the close confinement of animals, routine mutilations such as tail docking, castration and beak-trimming, long-distance transport, the genetic modification of livestock, and pre-slaughter stunning. Consumers are becoming more vocal about their preference for higher welfare foods, and this is correlated with a surge in food marketing and product development that contains animal-friendly messages. Consumers are also communicating a desire for information about animal welfare, and want assurance that animals have been afforded the best possible conditions during their life and leading up to slaughter. Finally, there is strong evidence that consumers have started to move towards higher welfare food products, as evidenced by increases in the sales of higher welfare pork, eggs and chicken.

These trends are creating opportunities for food businesses to engage with customers on how they are improving animal welfare across their production lines. Food businesses of all sizes—from small companies to large multinational corporations—are starting to see the commercial benefits (e.g. increased consumer loyalty, recruitment of new customers, sales of higher value products) that can be achieved by focusing on animal welfare as a core facet of their social responsibility strategy.

This chapter analyses the implications of this growth in consumer interest for food companies. It begins by discussing the context within which consumer concerns have emerged, specifically the automation, mechanization and industrialization of food production and its implications for farm animal welfare. It then discusses why and how consumer views have changed, and how this manifests itself in consumer purchasing decisions and in pressure on food companies to improve their management of farm animal welfare. Finally, the chapter discusses the contribution that food companies can make to raising standards of farm animal welfare.

Changing systems, changing practices

Farm animal welfare has become an important ethical issue for one primary reason—animal farming is now dramatically different from what it once was. Driven by innovations in breeding and management practice, by scientific research and by technology, agriculture, especially animal production, has become more efficient than ever before, albeit at a considerable cost to animal welfare as well as the environment. It is important to understand how the farming industry has changed in order to appreciate why animal welfare is becoming so important to certain consumers and, in turn, why this increased consumer concern introduces new issues for the food industry to consider.

The starting point is to understand the changing patterns of meat consumption. Between 1960 and 2000 global meat, milk and egg production increased approximately threefold, twofold and fourfold, respectively (Speedy, 2003). According to the *OECD-FAO Agricultural Outlook 2015* (OECD and FAO, 2015), the surge in demand for agricultural products over the last decade is likely to continue, driven by the growing populations of developing countries who are experiencing increases in incomes and rates of urbanization. Protein consumption is predicted to increase on a global scale, with meat consumption expected to increase by an annual average of 1.4% between 2014 and 2024. Half of this increase will be due to growth in demand for poultry (OECD and FAO, 2015).

The modern animal production industry—which includes meat production, as well as the production of products such as eggs and milk—is overwhelmingly intensive in nature. In order to deliver the required financial returns for their owners, these farming facilities generally rely on close confinement (or high stocking densities), routine mutilations (e.g. beak trimming, tail docking) and high levels of antibiotic usage. The consequence is that animals frequently experience pain, have their ability to exhibit natural behaviours constrained and have their welfare and wellbeing compromised.

Intensive production facilities have been the subject of much consumer concern (De Jonge and van Trijp, 2013). The cramped conditions that laying hens are subjected to in cages is probably the most well-known animal welfare issue. In addition to laying hens, the treatment of farmed meat chickens and pigs has also been controversial. In fact, the welfare concerns surrounding the production of laying hens, meat chickens (broilers) and pigs have been consistently identified as concerns by European consumers for well over a decade (see, for example, the European Commission's Eurobarometer surveys (European Commission, 2007, 2016)).

Consumer views on farm animal welfare and the manner in which they respond have also been influenced by changes in wider society. The growth in urban populations has meant that fewer people know farming from a personal perspective (Grandin, 2014; Miele *et al.*, 2013). While our grandparents and great grandparents are likely to have lived in or around farming communities, the knowledge people have of farming is now based on the information they receive from the mainstream media, from online sources, from animal welfare organizations (such as Compassion in World Farming, World Animal Protection and the RSPCA in the UK) and from food advertising. Social media in particular allows consumers to share their concerns with one another about key welfare issues. It also acts as a platform in which food companies can promote their animal welfare policies and can market the improvements they are making within their supply chain. When the US McDonald's promised to switch to cage-free eggs in the US and Canada within the next 10 years it made global headlines and was shared extensively over social media (Kowitt, 2016).

Furthermore, due to differences in lifestyle, traditions and other sociocultural factors, consumers vary in the importance they ascribe to the treatment of farm animals, and whether they make efforts to modify their shopping behaviours in accordance with their values (Ohl and van der Staay, 2012).

Consumer expectations

In order for food businesses to manage changing expectations, they first need to understand why consumers are more concerned about animal welfare. Within the UK, Europe and many Western countries, there has been a gradual yet vital shift in the collective consumer awareness and concern about farm animal welfare. Current research suggests some consumers experience concern about animal welfare as part of a general discomfort about intensive farming practices. Other segments of consumers are able to cite specific concerns regarding animal-based foods; concern about access to the outdoors for laying hens is an example of a specific issue that is generally well known among Western consumers. Increasing consumer concern—together with pressure from animal welfare organizations and regulatory changes—is one of the primary reasons why food companies are starting to take notice of animal welfare. Consumer research consistently points to a growing awareness among consumers about the negative animal welfare impacts associated with intensive farming and the form of production system is therefore an important product attribute for many consumers (Kjaernes, 2012). Several major food scandals have heightened the public's interest in the traceability of the food supply chain. The ethics of how food is produced is now a key social concern among the world's consumers (Ingenbleek *et al.*, 2013).

Some might question why it is important to understand how consumers perceive animal welfare. After all, we know that food purchases are largely based on habit, price and convenience. The ethics of particular choices in supermarkets, restaurants or brands of egg may not be a priority for many shoppers. Nevertheless, it is important for businesses to understand the changing priorities of consumers and to reflect on how the food sector can take the initiative in improving farm animal welfare. An overwhelming majority of consumers subscribe to the belief that it is important to maintain the welfare of farmed animals. In the latest Eurobarometer research (European Commission, 2016), 94% of surveyed Europeans agree with this view; 82% of those surveyed believed that farm animal welfare needs to be improved; and 64% indicated that they were interested in receiving further information about farm animal welfare. This is a potentially significant opportunity for those food businesses that can advance positive attitudes about farm animal welfare through policies, marketing and information campaigns centred on the issue.

Studies show that over 70% of UK consumers are concerned about animal welfare, and the Eurobarometer surveys paint a similar picture across the European Union. In fact, animal welfare has been rated as the most important sustainability-related food issue by British shoppers (Clonan *et al.*, 2010; IGD, 2011), and has been identified as an important concern in, among others, the US (Grimshaw *et al.*, 2014; McKendree *et al.*, 2014) and Australia (Humane Research Council, 2014; Taylor and Signal, 2009). China, one of the world's biggest producers of pork, is also starting to pay attention to animal welfare. In 2015 one of China's major pork producers was recognized at the Compassion in World Farming Good Animal Welfare Awards for its vast improvements to animal welfare. A study by Wu *et al.* (2012) showed that Chinese consumers are becoming more aware of animal welfare issues. While the motivation behind this is largely health and safety, Chinese citizens are experiencing an awakening in awareness of animal welfare and animal rights within the context of wildlife, laboratory and companion animal treatment which, in turn, creates fertile ground for a preference for higher welfare foods (Lu *et al.*, 2013).

As stated previously, many consumers have reported specific concerns over animal welfare issues particularly relating to laying hens, meat chickens and pigs. Other species have also started to receive attention, and there are more species whose farming practices are receiving more public criticism such as dairy cows. The excruciatingly cramped farming conditions of laying hens can be viewed as one of the original iconic animal welfare issues. For example, in their surveys on Italian consumers, Vecchino and Annunziata (2012) found that 44% believed that the welfare of laying hens needed to be improved and a study by the UK Department for Environment, Food and Rural Affairs (2011) found that over 70% of households rated the animal welfare of chickens and laying hens as important. In both cases, the rationale behind supporting higher welfare products was simply related to emphasizing the importance of treating animals humanely. While knowledge of caged egg production is relatively established in the UK and its EU counterparts, awareness and concern about animal welfare is also emerging in China. In a study of Chinese consumers, Heng *et al.* (2013) reported that over half of respondents understood caged systems as being fraught with negative welfare impacts. Moreover, 85% of the consumers surveyed stated they would be willing to pay more for higher welfare egg systems that promoted outdoor access and cage-free housing.

Clearly, this consumer awareness and willingness to pay has direct implications for the poultry industry. The fact that this demand is consumer-driven rather than producer-driven means that the poultry industry needs to offer the higher welfare products that are being demanded by consumers, demonstrate it is managing welfare issues appropriately and strengthen its communications on these issues (Neeteson-Van Nieuwenhoven *et al.*, 2016).

In pig farming, the confinement of sows during pregnancy and farrowing has elicited strong opposition from consumers. McDonald's UK is an example of a company which reacted to consumer concern by stating it would move away from confined pork products and instead stock the RSPCA's Freedom Food pork (Pickett *et al.*, 2014). Dairy cows are emerging as another species associated with welfare concerns. Painful health conditions arising from intensive breeding cycles, limited access to pasture, tail docking and separation from calves are all areas where consumers have expressed discomfort with current farming practices (Schuppli *et al.*, 2014; Weary *et al.*, 2011; Ventura *et al.*, 2013).

Consumers' willingness to act on farm animal welfare concerns depends on a range of factors, including attitudes, values, lifestyle and socio-demographics to name just a few (Vecchio and Annunziata, 2012; Font-i-Furnols and Guerrero, 2014; Nijland *et al.*, 2013). A critical step in creating demand for higher welfare animal products comes from raising awareness on the treatment of farm animals. Consumers want to know more about farming and farm animal welfare (Frewer *et al.*, 2005; Zander and Hamm, 2010; Vanhonacker and Verbeke, 2009), and studies by Toma *et al.* (2012) and Lagerkvist and Hess (2011) have highlighted the connection between information provision and willingness to pay for higher welfare products. Many food businesses have recognized the business value to be gained from taking a proactive approach to farm animal welfare and providing consumers with the information they require. However, business-led disclosures such as product labels are not without their problems for consumers. It is frequently difficult to assess the differences between labels, certification schemes and standards, particularly when animal welfare is just one of a range of issues that consumers consider in their purchasing decisions. Currently, many consumers feel that they are exposed to disjointed and confusing animal welfare information through quality labels and marketing messages (Miele and Evans, 2010; Parker *et al.*, 2013; Smith and Brower, 2012; Vanhonacker and Verbeke, 2014). Food companies are in a unique position to encourage dialogue about farm animal welfare among the general public. Vecchio and Annunziata's (2012) study highlighted the link between consumer concern for animal welfare and their lack of understanding regarding welfare issues. Allowing consumers to voice their concerns and question the actions of food companies can help alleviate the negative perceptions of farming as a whole and contribute to restoring trust to certain players in the food system. Miele and Evans (2010) examined animal welfare concerns and awareness through 48 focus group discussions involving European citizens. They found that consumers generally had a low level of understanding of farming practices. Negative perceptions of "factory farming" were prevalent, yet these beliefs were not supported by knowledge of the scale to which such systems operated in the food industry. The focus groups indicated a disconnect between consumers and farming; while many were aware of the negative impacts of intensive farming it was assumed that it was not an issue in their country and so these consumers were therefore not actively engaged in the issue. It also meant that they saw less need to purchase higher welfare foods.

The importance of information on animal welfare is bidirectional; food companies that require superior animal welfare outcomes from their suppliers are motivated to educate consumers. Producers who implement and maintain animal welfare above legislative standards should have the capacity to communicate their practices to the general public (Grandin, 2014). Some farmers perceive the public's lack of knowledge of farming is a barrier to promoting their products. They also worry that consumers are not willing to pay the higher prices that are required to support improvements to welfare systems.

Company responses

Food companies can respond to consumer concerns in a number of ways. They can offer differentiated products that cater to those shoppers concerned about farm animal welfare. Eggs are a prime example; some brands provide options based on the cheapest and lowest welfare measure all the way up to organic, which is usually the dearest option yet often comes with higher welfare assurances.

Food companies can also remove products that are deemed to be socially unacceptable by consumers: for example, some restaurants and retailers have removed foie gras from their offerings to avoid unwanted media attention. Companies can also look to improve their standards and policies when it comes to how they source their products. Many major retailers such as Waitrose, Marks & Spencer and Tesco have made changes to their policies and made a point to actively communicate improvements with the general public. When food businesses do this they often open up a public dialogue about what constitutes best practice when it comes to animal welfare. Interestingly, while companies have been concerned about the reputational and brand risks associated with talking about farm animal welfare, their experiences have been generally positive. They have found that, more often than not, consumers appreciate transparency and honesty more than they worry about whether their specific expectations are currently met by the company's offerings (Egels-Zandén and Hansson, 2016; Luhmann and Theuvsen, 2016).

While food companies have widely mastered policies relating to environmental and social outcomes, it is probably fair to say that animal welfare is still an emerging tenet of best corporate practice. However, for some of the world's largest food companies, animal welfare is now regarded as a fundamental aspect of their social responsibility agenda, and this has allowed these companies to engage in valuable dialogue with their customers. It appears that this dialogue can provide real benefits to companies, as marketing strategies and company policies rely heavily on an acute understanding of consumer interest and expectations (Vanhonacker and Verbeke, 2014). The depth of this dialogue also suggests that companies do place significant emphasis on consumer attitudes to social and ethical issues.

This is being reflected in the growth in the number of companies developing and communicating animal welfare policies, and in the number of products boasting claims of improved welfare measures (examples include products labelled free-range, bred organic, and sow stall free). Higher welfare products can fulfil consumers' preferences to purchase in accordance with their values while also supporting product attributes such as health, safety and overall quality. Higher welfare food—when sold alongside its more intensively produced counterparts—caters to a niche market in which animal welfare is a desired product attribute. This is not just about product shifting; it is also about the ability of retailers and producers to attract new customers and to encourage customers to purchase higher value and higher margin products. In Europe, in particular, there has been an increase in the market-share of higher welfare foods. For example, free-range egg sales now account for more than half of total sales in the UK retail sector[1] (see, more generally Clonan *et al.*, 2010; Pickett *et al.*, 2014).

Farm animal welfare is just one aspect of sustainability that food companies are expected to communicate. In recent years mainstream media has brought to light a number of scandals concerning animal welfare. In that context, food companies can benefit enormously from initiating communication about what they are doing to improve animal welfare with their consumers.

Concluding reflections

It is clear that farm animal welfare is an important issue for many consumers. Research suggests there is a clear demand for foods that are sustainable, high quality and produced with high welfare standards.

Companies have started to respond to the risks and to the opportunities presented by this growing consumer interest in farm animal welfare. They have developed policies, they have started to offer higher welfare products and they have indicated that animal welfare is a priority for their business operations. Societal interest in farm animal welfare is likely to continue to support companies that produce animal products that are safe, healthy and produced with the highest possible animal welfare standards. This consumer interest suggests that food companies need to do more, that they need to act as a credible source of information, assurance and leadership regarding farm animal welfare issues. Food companies have many options for responding to changing consumer expectations. What is most important is that they take consumer concerns seriously and develop ways to provide credible, accurate and clear information about how they are going to improve animal welfare within their supply chains.

References

Clonan, A., Holdsworth, M., Swift, J., & Wilson, P. (2010). UK consumers' priorities for sustainable food purchases. In *84th Annual Conference of the Agricultural Economics Society, Edinburgh, 29–31 March 2010* (pp. 29-31). Banbury, UK: AES.

de Jonge, J., & van Trijp, H.C. (2013). The impact of broiler production system practices on consumer perceptions of animal welfare. *Poultry Science*, 92(12), 3080-3095.

Department for Environment, Food, and Rural Affairs (2011). *Attitudes and Behaviours around Sustainable Food Purchasing*. Report SERP 1011/10. Retrieved from http://www.defra.gov.uk/statistics/foodfarm/food/

Egels-Zandén, N., & Hansson, N. (2016). Supply chain transparency as a consumer or corporate tool: The case of Nudie Jeans Co. *Journal of Consumer Policy*, 39(4), 377-395. doi: 10.1007/s10603-015-9283-7

1 www.egginfo.co.uk/egg-facts-and-figures/industry-information/data

European Commission (2007). *Attitudes of EU Citizens towards Animal Welfare*. European Commission. Retrieved from http://www.vuzv.sk/DB-Welfare/vseob/sp_barometer_aw_en.pdf

European Commission (2016). Attitudes of Europeans towards Animal Welfare: Special Eurobarometer 442. Retrieved from http://ec.europa.eu/COMMFrontOffice/publicopinion/index.cfm/Survey/getSurveyDetail/instruments/SPECIAL/surveyKy/2096

Font-i-Furnols, M., & Guerrero, L. (2014). Consumer preference, behavior and perception about meat and meat products: An overview. *Meat Science*, 98(3), 361-371. doi: 10.1016/j.meatsci.2014.06.025

Frewer, L.J., Kole, A., Kroon, S.M.A.V.d., & Lauwere, C.d. (2005). Consumer attitudes towards the development of animal-friendly husbandry systems. *Journal of Agricultural and Environmental Ethics*, 18(4), 345-367. doi: 10.1007/s10806-005-1489-2

Grandin, T. (2014). Animal welfare and society concerns finding the missing link. *Meat Science*, 98(3), 461-469.

Grimshaw, K., Miller, R., Palma, M., & Kerth, C. (2014). Consumer perception of beef, pork, lamb, chicken, and fish. *Meat Science*, 96(1), 443-444.

Heng, Y., Peterson, H. H., & Li, X. (2013). Consumer attitudes toward farm-animal welfare: The case of laying hens. *Journal of Agricultural and Resource Economics*, 38(3), 418-434.

Humane Research Council (2014). *Animal Tracker Australia: Baseline Survey results - June 2014*. Voiceless. Retrieved from https://www.voiceless.org.au/content/animal-tracker-australia-0

IGD (2011). *Shopper Attitudes to Animal Welfare: A Report for Freedom Food by IGD*. Watford, UK: Institute of Grocery Distribution.

Ingenbleek, P., Harvey, D., Ilieski, V., Immink, V., de Roest, K., & Schmid, O. (2013). The European Market for Animal-Friendly Products in a Societal Context. *Animals*, 3(3), 808.

Kjærnes, U. (2012). Ethics and action: A relational perspective on consumer choice in the European politics of food. *Journal of Agricultural and Environmental Ethics*, 25(2), 145-162.

Kowitt, B. (2016, September 1). Inside McDonald's bold decision to go cage free. *Fortune*. Retrieved from http://fortune.com/mcdonalds-cage-free/

Lagerkvist, C.J., & Hess, S. (2011). A meta-analysis of consumer willingness to pay for farm animal welfare. *European Review of Agricultural Economics*, 38(1), 55-78.

Lu, J., Bayne, K., & Wang, J. (2013). Current status of animal welfare and animal rights in China. *Alternatives to Laboratory Animals*, 41, 351-357.

Luhmann, H., & Theuvsen, L. (2016). Corporate social responsibility in agribusiness: Literature review and future research directions. *Journal of Agricultural and Environmental Ethics*, 29(4), 673-696. doi: 10.1007/s10806-016-9620-0

McKendree, M., Croney, C., & Widmar, N. (2014). Effects of demographic factors and information sources on United States consumer perceptions of animal welfare. *Journal of Animal Science*, 92(7), 3161-3173.

Miele, M., & Evans, A. (2010). When foods become animals: Ruminations on ethics and responsibility in care-full practices of consumption. *Ethics, Place and Environment*, 13(2), 171-190.

Miele, M., Blokhuis, H., Bennett, R., & Bock, B. (2013). Changes in farming and in stakeholder concern for animal welfare. In H.J. Blokhuis, M. Miele, I. Veissier & B.

Jones (Eds.). *Improving Farm Animal Welfare* (pp. 19-47). Wageningen: Wageningen Academic Publishers.

Neeteson-Van Nieuwenhoven, A.-M., Appleby, M.C., & Hogarth, G. (2016). Making a resilient poultry industry in Europe. In E. Burton, J. Gatcliffe, H.M. O'Neill & D. Scholey (Eds.). *Sustainable Poultry Production in Europe*. Oxford: CABI.

Nijland, H.J., Aarts, N.M., & Renes, R.J. (2013). Frames and ambivalence in context: An analysis of hands-on experts' perception of the welfare of animals in traveling circuses in the Netherlands. *Journal of Agricultural and Environmental Ethics*, 26(3), 523-535.

OECD & Food and Agriculture Organization of the United Nations (2015). *OECD-FAO Agricultural Outlook 2015*. Paris: OECD Publishing. Retrieved from http://dx.doi.org/10.1787/agr_outlook-2015-en

Ohl, F., & Van der Staay, F.J. (2012). Animal welfare: At the interface between science and society. *The Veterinary Journal*, 192(1), 13-19.

Parker, C., Brunswick, C., & Kotey, J. (2013). The Happy Hen on Your Supermarket Shelf. *Journal of Bioethical Inquiry*, 10(2), 165-186.

Pickett, H., Crossley, D., & Sutton, C. (2014). *Farm Animal Welfare: Past, Present, and Future*. RSPCA.

Schuppli, C., von Keyserlingk, M., & Weary, D. (2014). Access to pasture for dairy cows: Responses from an online engagement. *Journal of Animal Science*, 92(11), 5185-5192.

Smith, K.T., & Brower, T.R. (2012). Longitudinal study of green marketing strategies that influence Millennials. *Journal of Strategic Marketing*, 20(6), 535-551.

Speedy, A. (2003). Global production and consumption of animal source foods. *The Journal of Nutrition*, 133(11), 4048S-4053S.

Taylor, N., & Signal, T.D. (2009). Willingness to pay: Australian consumers and "on the farm" welfare. *Journal of Applied Animal Welfare Science*, 12(4), 345-359. doi: 10.1080/10888700903163658

Toma, L., Stott, A.W., Revoredo-Giha, C., & Kupiec-Teahan, B. (2012). Consumers and animal welfare. A comparison between European Union countries. *Appetite*, 58(2), 597-607.

Vanhonacker, F., & Verbeke, W. (2009). Buying higher welfare poultry products? Profiling Flemish consumers who do and do not. *Poultry Science*, 88(12), 2702-2711.

Vanhonacker, F., & Verbeke, W. (2014). Public and consumer policies for higher welfare food products: Challenges and opportunities. *Journal of Agricultural and Environmental Ethics*, 27(1), 153-171. doi: 10.1007/s10806-013-9479-2

Vecchio, R., & Annunziata, A. (2012). Italian consumer awareness of layer hens' welfare standards: a cluster analysis. *International Journal of Consumer Studies*, 36(6), 647-655.

Ventura, B., Von Keyserlingk, M., Schuppli, C., & Weary, D. (2013). Views on contentious practices in dairy farming: The case of early cow-calf separation. *Journal of Dairy Science*, 96(9), 6105-6116.

Weary, D., Schuppli, C., & von Keyserlingk, M. (2011). Tail docking dairy cattle: Responses from an online engagement. *Journal of Animal Science*, 89(11), 3831-3837.

Wu, L., Xu, L., Zhu, D., & Wang, X. (2012). Factors affecting consumer willingness to pay for certified traceable food in Jiangsu Province of China. *Canadian Journal of Agricultural Economics/Revue canadienne d'agroeconomie*, 60(3), 317-333. doi: 10.1111/j.1744-7976.2011.01236.x

Zander, K., & Hamm, U. (2010). Consumer preferences for additional ethical attributes of organic food. *Food Quality and Preference*, 21(5), 495-503.

6 The power of partnership

The role of NGO–corporate engagement in setting food industry farm animal welfare standards[1]

Jemima Jewell

COMPASSION IN WORLD FARMING, UK

Big business: friend or foe?

"You mean you're going to take them down from the inside?" So said a friend when I described my new job at Compassion in World Farming, working on the "Food Business" team, aiming to influence huge food companies who produce and sell millions of animals for food each year.

Well, no, not quite.

Big business has often been seen as the enemy, particularly by those working in non-governmental organizations (NGOs) or the third sector more generally. There's no doubt "industry" has much to answer for, with multi-million pound businesses propelled by hefty marketing budgets ensuring that shrink-wrapped products (bearing little resemblance to their animal origins) fly off the shelves while the vast majority of the 70 billion animals raised for food each year suffer hugely inadequate standards of welfare. The influence of these businesses is immense. And therein, of course, lies the opportunity: the chance not to fight against this influence, but to harness it, and use it to create a more sustainable, humane food system fit for the 21st century.

Whether you see business as a blot on society's copybook, or as our only hope of salvation, there's little doubt it's here to stay. From an animal welfare perspective (i.e. that we can, and should, give animals reared for food lives worth living before they are humanely killed) then it surely makes sense to work with business rather than expect them to experience an ethical epiphany and declare that the world would be better off if they didn't exist.

Personally, I firmly and passionately believe in the potential for business to be a force for good in the world—and that includes their influence on animal welfare. Working with (rather than against) businesses is a very different approach from the purely placard and protest-based approach of many animal welfare organizations in decades past. Trail-blazed by a small number of leading environmental and sustainability organizations in the 1990s, many (though by no means all) NGOs now have some form of corporate partnership built into their approach.

1 The views expressed in this chapter are those of the author and do not necessarily represent the views of Compassion in World Farming.

Relationships between businesses and NGOs can fuse a potent combination of skills, expertise and agendas. Potentially powerful, they often also represent an uneasy alliance. They can be exhilarating and frustrating in equal measure. In this chapter I give my personal perspective on how Compassion in World Farming ("Compassion") approaches corporate partnerships on farm animal welfare, share some of the highs and lows of working with food businesses, and offer some thoughts on what the future might hold.

Combining campaigning and corporate engagement

In 1967, a British dairy farmer called Peter Roberts became concerned by the development of intensive, industrial agriculture which paid little or no regard to animal welfare. As a farmer, he felt that we all have a responsibility to give the animals we raise for food a "life worth living". Appalled by the cages and crates that had started to become commonplace, Peter took his concerns to the established animal charities of the day. When he saw how reluctant these organizations were to act, he called a small meeting around his kitchen table. At that meeting, with a few visionary friends, he decided to take matters into his own hands, and so Compassion in World Farming was born.

Compassion's campaigning history is rich and, since its inception, the organization has been a driving force in some of the most significant legislative animal welfare victories the world has seen.[2] In 1990, veal crates (truly awful, barren, isolated pens for raising calves for veal, which are so small that calves cannot even turn around) were banned in the UK, a ban which was extended to Europe in 2007. In 2005, the export subsidies for farmers transporting live cattle to countries outside the EU were eliminated. In 2012 barren battery cages for egg-laying hens (cramped, wire cages with barely the size of an A4 sheet of paper for each hen) were also banned in Europe. Keeping pregnant sows in narrow stalls has been banned in the UK since 1999 and (after the first four weeks of pregnancy) in the EU since 2013. Perhaps most significantly of all, in 1997, animals were legally recognized as sentient beings by the EU, following a ten-year campaign by Compassion in World Farming alongside a host of other organizations. Sentient beings are individuals with feelings that matter to them; they are capable of experiencing positive emotions such as joy as well as negative emotions such as fear. As such this legal recognition provides the backbone for all measures to protect farm animals.

Back in 2007, while I was still working in advertising (becoming increasingly disillusioned dreaming up questionable slogans for unnecessary products), the leadership team at Compassion started putting in place the building blocks for a ground-breaking corporate engagement programme. This programme was designed to work in collaboration with businesses, challenging and supporting them to source from higher welfare farming systems, rewarding progress publicly. It might have been easier for Compassion to have continued with a sole focus on public

2 See more at www.ciwf.org.uk/our-impact

campaigning and lobbying. But as a farmer himself, I hope our founder Peter would be proud of the fact that we now work directly with the food industry.

Working directly and collaboratively with companies brings a wealth of opportunity. The speed with which a motivated business can alter its operating model far outstrips the pace of change normally seen with legislative shift. But "getting into bed" with big business doesn't come without its challenges, not least moving from a black and white world into one where nuance, pragmatism and continuous improvement replace a backdrop of clear-cut protest.

Pushing for progress: a toolkit for working with business

Compassion's Food Business team has a clear mandate: everything we do must have a positive impact for animals, must enable a market shift towards higher welfare products, and must raise awareness of the importance of farm animal welfare in the food industry. Based on a collaborative approach, we have a "toolkit" of products and services designed to drive change as quickly and sustainably as possible.[3]

There are thousands of food companies, and billions of animals raised for food. As a corporate engagement team of around 13 people, we cannot work everywhere. So we focus our efforts on working with the biggest and most influential food companies in the world. Our relationships are mostly in Europe, the USA and increasingly in China, with ambitions to increase our global presence over time. A tailored "target" list of around 250 of the most significant food companies in the world guides our efforts. This list considers the company's size, its "animal footprint" (the number of animals in or directly influenced by the company's supply chain) and its influence or leadership in the global or regional market. Sometimes companies come to us, seeking partnership or ad hoc advice. More often, we approach them, and make the case for why the strategic, technical and communications guidance we can offer on farm animal welfare is something they should be interested in and can benefit from.

In doing so, we aim to raise the industry baseline for farm animal welfare. In practice, this means that we focus our efforts on improving the worst, not perfecting the best. As a team, we could easily fill our time working with small and medium sized enterprises (SMEs) who already have free-range, well-managed systems, helping them to further tweak their rearing, transport and slaughter of animals to become models of best practice. However, our "bottom line" is the number of animals who are set to benefit in a meaningful way from the policies and practices of our corporate partners. This bottom line currently stands at over 342 million animals who are set to benefit each year from our award winners' work, or at 719 million animals if we include those with the potential to benefit from joint project work. Working with a global retailer or restaurant to get the hens who supply their eggs out of cages, and into well-managed, cage-free systems (be they barn, free-range or organic) has the potential to transform many more animals' lives than

3 See www.compassioninfoodbusiness.com for more information on Compassion's Food Business programme.

focusing solely on niche operations, and to truly raise the baseline of what is seen as acceptable practice. It also has the potential to start a domino effect in industry. Nowhere has this been more evident than in the USA where, following McDonald's announcement in September 2015 that they would be transitioning to cage-free eggs by 2025, over 200 companies made similar pledges.

The "Good Farm Animal Welfare Awards" programme sits at the heart of our work with food companies. These awards recognize companies who achieve, or who commit to achieving within a five-year timeframe, certain standards of animal welfare for key species. These include hens, broiler (meat) chickens, dairy cows and calves, sows and meat pigs, does and meat rabbits. The criteria for the awards are based on a scientific platform of evidence for what constitutes "better" welfare. We emphasize "better" rather than "best" because the awards are not a welfare pinnacle, but a meaningful point along a journey of continuous improvement, one that is both challenging and achievable within a commercial setting. For example, to achieve the "Good Egg Award" for egg-laying hens, companies must produce or source eggs only from cage-free systems. For pigs, the criteria are more detailed. To achieve the "Good Sow Commendation", sows must be raised without close confinement. This means no sow stalls (or "gestation crates") are permitted during the "dry period" (i.e. pre or during pregnancy) and no farrowing crates are allowed for those giving birth and nursing piglets. Furthermore, sows must be provided with adequate manipulable material (such as straw) to satisfy their natural nest-building behavioural instincts and their desire to chew and investigate. Adequate bedding must also be provided throughout life. To achieve the "Good Pig Commendation" for meat pigs, adequate manipulable material and bedding is also required throughout life. In addition, the award addresses the routine mutilations that are sadly common in the pig industry; castration, teeth clipping or grinding, and tail docking are all prohibited.

Those companies which achieve both sow and meat pig commendations receive a full "Good Pig Award". This is often no easy task, particularly in countries where outdoor breeding and rearing operations are not possible or not well-developed. Indoor higher welfare production requires excellent management in order to be able to avoid the worst features (close confinement, routine mutilations, barren environments) of intensive systems. To take just one example, pigs normally have their tails docked because, as naturally curious animals in overcrowded environments with little stimulation, they resort to investigating one of the only points of interest, i.e. their neighbours' tails. Tail biting is painful and dangerous, and infection is common. It is so much easier to simply slice off the piglet's tail with a hot iron when it is young, taking away the curly temptation from its neighbours. Operating with pig tails intact requires a commitment to not only providing sufficient space and manipulable material, but also careful monitoring and management of countless other influencing factors, from diet to ventilation. In 2016, after years of collaboration, we were delighted to be able to recognize two leading producers in Italy (Fumagalli and Primavera) with a Good Pig Award.[4] In

4 See www.compassioninfoodbusiness.com/awards/ for details on all the Good Farm Animal Welfare Award winners.

contrast, investigative footage from Compassion has highlighted the overcrowding, barren conditions and extremely poor welfare common in typical Italian production systems. The difference is difficult to exaggerate, and the achievements and commitments of leading companies such as Fumagalli deserve recognition.

The Good Farm Animal Welfare Awards celebrate progress. They provide a goal for the often extensive negotiations that sourcing managers in companies must undertake to convince their business of the merits of giving animals better lives and people a better food product. They offer companies committing to better welfare a marketing tool, one that can support the values they want to stand for. As such, working towards an award forms a central part of our work programme with many food companies. For complex multinational companies, the awards provide a yardstick by which they can transform their welfare standards brand by brand. Unilever and Barilla are two such examples, and case studies of our long-standing relationships with both of these companies are available online.[5]

Beyond the Awards, our work with companies is diverse. Work on welfare policies constitutes a big chunk. We help companies to articulate their ambitions for farm animal welfare in a meaningful, honest way, from basic brand positioning statements to detailed species-specific commitments. Increasingly, especially for global companies with complex supply chains, detailed roadmapping and project work is required to fulfil these policies in a sensible timeframe.

Our in-depth project work often focuses on one particular welfare issue. For example, the aforementioned piglet castration is often a stated policy goal for companies, but it can be particularly tricky to address in countries such as Italy where rearing male pigs entire (i.e. with testicles intact) to heavier weights can lead to challenges of aggression and a changing body (and therefore product) composition. One alternative is the use of a vaccination to delay puberty, which avoids those problems entirely. Our team has worked closely with a leading retailer on their Italian meat supply for speciality cured hams and charcuterie. We have helped them to establish an exact protocol for administering the vaccine and addressing any associated management and welfare issues to ensure both a quality product and a life for male pigs free from the pain of surgical castration. This kind of work is detailed and time-consuming. But working with industry leaders in this way can provide a practical blueprint for others to follow, and signal a positive tipping point for a pervasive welfare issue.

For major retailers, our Food Business team offers a "Supermarket Survey", a confidential survey of retailer standards, which provides each participating supermarket with a tailored gap analysis of their welfare practices, and practical short- and long-term recommendations for improvement.

Last but not least in the team's "toolkit" is the Business Benchmark on Farm Animal Welfare[6] (see Chapter 13 by Nicky Amos and Rory Sullivan), a public ranking of how the world's leading food companies are managing and reporting on farm animal welfare. Conducted by an independent secretariat, the Benchmark is

5 http://www.compassioninfoodbusiness.com/case-studies/partnership-case-studies/

6 http://www.bbfaw.com/

supported by Compassion, fellow NGO World Animal Protection and investment firm Coller Capital. The Benchmark is published each year, and ranks companies in one of six tiers according to how well their publicly available information and reporting on animal welfare performs against a series of questions. Its transparent scoring system and clear expectations provide an excellent framework and shared starting point for us to work with companies on their approach to welfare. Because the Benchmark is designed as a tool to enable investors to assess how well companies are managing the risks and opportunities posed by farm animal welfare, and because the results are public, it has been an incredibly powerful accelerator for companies to sit up and pay attention to farm animal welfare as a business issue.

Placards vs. persuasion: what's the best route to change?

Apart from in exceptional circumstances, Compassion in World Farming does not campaign against individual companies. For our campaigning colleagues at Compassion, whose jobs demand that they harness public emotion and take practical action to raise awareness of animal welfare, I know there are times when this policy can be extremely frustrating. I'm sure there's nothing they would like better than to regularly organize protests outside an underperforming retailer's flagship store; and after particularly fruitless meetings, I find that very tempting too! But protesting one day, and expecting to sit at the board table the next, usually doesn't make for a productive and trusted relationship.

Other NGOs take a myriad of approaches ranging from pure corporate consultancy (i.e. working with companies) through to much more hard-line approaches (campaigning to boycott companies). For some, a hard-line approach emerges from an animal rights agenda: a belief that animals have rights that cannot be traded away, that they are not ours to raise for food (or to use for entertainment, clothes or experimentation). As such, these NGOs campaign for an end to both specific farming practices and the use of any animals in the food industry. People for the Ethical Treatment of Animals (PETA), famous for its shocking videos and headline-grabbing stunts, is one such example.

Animal *welfare* organizations, in contrast, believe that it *can* be acceptable to raise animals for food, providing that this is done in a manner which respects their physiological, mental and behavioural needs, and gives them a life worth living. Many animal welfare NGOs still publicly campaign vigorously and successfully against individual companies and industry as a whole, given the prevalence of extremely poor animal welfare practices. For example, Wakker Dier, an animal welfare organization in the Netherlands, ran a highly visible and effective campaign against all Dutch retailers selling "Plofkip" ("exploding" broiler chickens, bred to grow so fast that they can barely stand up in the days before slaughter).

Public pressure on companies is a vital part of the mix; keeping issues in the public spotlight makes them much harder for companies to ignore, and traditional campaigning remains an absolutely vital part of the recipe for industry change. Campaigners can be well complemented, however, by NGOs that offer support and strategic engagement. Without this willingness to engage, there is danger of either reaching a stalemate with business or of empty public promises that are not fulfilled once the headlines fade away.

At Compassion, it is testament to the will and creativity of our campaigning colleagues that they maintain hard-hitting public campaigning without undermining the industry relationships developed by the Food Business team. I believe Compassion is all the more effective for its ability to combine both campaigning and corporate collaboration. We will still call out industry where needed; we won't defend unacceptable practices; and we certainly don't pretend that the food industry is without fault. But we appreciate the trust that food businesses put in us and we take it very seriously, working hard to build and maintain relationships that we believe represent a vital route to change.

There's a clear case for us as an NGO to engage with companies: successful engagement is a powerful route to achieving our mission. But why do companies engage with us? I believe that many companies recognize the deep expertise NGOs offer, and the value that a collaborative but challenging partnership can bring. What form the engagement takes depends on what stage a business has reached in its animal welfare journey.

As a business issue, there are myriad different drivers for why companies choose to address farm animal welfare. There's no set business journey. Even within one company, asking the quality control manager, the sustainability director and the CEO why farm animal welfare is on their agenda might well produce strikingly different answers.

For many individuals working in food companies including, importantly, those who have the closest contact with the animals themselves, there is a deep conviction and desire to simply "do the right thing". Tireless work by these individuals often sits at the heart of progress for a company. Often though, a stronger "business case" is also needed to secure capital investment and top-level commitment to improving welfare.

To crudely over-simplify, companies tend to move through at least some of the following stages in their thinking about animal welfare issues:

1 **Resistance**. To begin with, there's often a wilful lack of acknowledgement of the issue. At this stage any approaches from NGOs are often met with the kind of corporate response that is tantamount to swatting away an annoying fly.
2 **Acknowledgement**. Farm animal welfare creeps onto the corporate agenda, perhaps driven by reluctant necessity (impending legislation) or a top down "tick box" exercise in response to a peer company's exposure in the media. Attempts to achieve a "quick fix" or greenwash are common. To move beyond this stage requires a changed, and longer-term, mind-set.
3 **Business risk**. A company recognizes the risks that may result from leaving farm animal welfare unaddressed. Exposure in the media is still a key driver. Clearly no company wants its consumers to be horrified by where their food comes from, particularly if said consumers have previously been presented with an idyllic-looking but utterly misleading picture of farming by the

marketing team. Although not an animal welfare scandal *per se*, the horsemeat scandal of 2013 also exposed the shocking ignorance many companies had of their supply chains. To be unable to guarantee what country, what farming system and indeed even what animal was associated with their products was a serious reality check and highlighted their exposure to risk.

4 **Strategic opportunity**. The potential for competitive advantage, for meeting market demand, and for commanding a price premium often comes into play at this stage. Higher welfare products are frequently associated in consumers' minds with higher quality, healthier products; indeed, higher welfare products often *are* healthier. For companies, what might start as a premium or specialist offering has the potential to become the norm, a hygiene factor within a certain product category. As more and more companies embrace the "strategic opportunity" stage, there is potential for higher welfare meat to follow a similar path to Fairtrade coffee; once considered a specialist or indulgent purchase by many, the pertinent question is no longer "why Fairtrade?" but "why not"?

5 **Enlightened self-interest.**[7] Self-interest here doesn't imply a lack of ethical value. Rather, animal welfare is seen as a linchpin for delivering high quality products in a future-proofed way, for developing farming systems that also deliver on wider sustainability issues and that don't rely on the routine use of antibiotics to be viable. Welfare is no longer a "nice to have" but a strategic necessity for a successful food business.

6 **Collective necessity**. This is perhaps best (if not catchily) understood as community-based enlightened self-interest. Companies often speak of the need for a level playing field for ethical issues. Without this, there is always a danger of the tragedy of the commons, where the positive actions of the few do not outweigh or compensate for the actions of the many, resulting in the trashing of the ecosystems on which we all depend. There is precedent here if we look at the case of climate change. Who would have anticipated a coalition of companies actively asking for stronger climate legislation, to protect the system on which their business depends? Yet that is exactly what happened when the Consumer Goods Forum, spearheaded by M&S and Unilever, called on governments for a binding two degrees deal (see Barry and Seabright, 2014). Will we see food companies demanding similar regulation for farm animal welfare in the future?

Barriers to progress—and how to break them down

Companies early in their journey (and indeed those with a more mature approach) can see animal welfare as a cost, rather than as an investment with a potential return. Upfront capital cost is often the key hurdle to overcome, particularly when "payback" is judged on short-term, narrowly defined financial returns rather than on the longer-term wider business benefits that may result.

7 A term the sustainable development NGO Forum for the Future has been using for many years (see Bent, 2008).

I believe that companies who are willing to invest in animal welfare should be able to benefit from this investment in terms of sales. One of the most frustrating scenarios that we, and companies, face all too often, is that positive changes to welfare remain invisible to (or misunderstood by) the end consumer. Sadly, many consumers across the globe are fundamentally disconnected from where their food comes from. For some, animal welfare may never be part of their purchasing decision. But for so many, there is a desire to buy meat, eggs and dairy from animals who have experienced a decent standard of living. Unfortunately, making an informed decision is not as easy as it should be. For most animal products, brands and retailers are not obliged to label the system in which the animal was raised. Of all the injustices in the food system, this is truly the one that I find most frustrating.

When "method of production" labelling is mandatory, it can have real and lasting impact on consumer purchasing patterns. In the EU, labelling is currently only a legal requirement for shell "whole" eggs, as opposed to "ingredient" eggs in other products such as cakes or quiches. Shell eggs must be labelled with one of four options: from hens reared in caged (3), barn (2), free-range (1) or organic systems (0). This clarity has driven up the volume of cage-free eggs produced and purchased in the UK, which has rocketed from 12% in 1994 to 49% in 2015, with a peak in 2012 of 51% (Defra, 2016).

The same labelling requirements do not apply to meat from broiler chickens. Here, a chicken raised in cramped, dark conditions, without any kind of environmental enrichment, is indistinguishable on the shelf from a chicken raised in a higher welfare indoor system, with more space to move around, natural light, perches and pecking substrates. These differences make a meaningful impact on a chicken's life, but the consumer is effectively prevented from supporting them. Free-range and organic chickens are easy for consumers to spot on the shelves—but there is a much greater price differential for free-range meat than eggs, which is a significant barrier to widespread adoption. I wish that companies making the investment in better *indoor* systems could benefit from increased sales to those consumers happy to invest just a little more in a higher welfare purchase from a decent indoor system. Of course, companies are free to label their products as "higher welfare". However, without standardized, widely recognized and credible criteria, such labelling can often go unnoticed on the shelf. The fact that intensively reared products are able to put misleading images on packs only adds to consumer confusion. Compassion is part of the Labelling Matters coalition and, as such, is one of a number of animal welfare NGOs campaigning for "method of production" labelling to be mandatory for all animal products.

I have no doubt that, despite opposition from more intensive producers, proper, credible labelling will become mandatory. To ensure good welfare, higher welfare systems need to be underpinned by robust management and animal-based welfare indicators. In the meantime, commercially switched-on businesses will continue to connect customers with their higher animal welfare food offerings, letting consumers draw their own conclusions about the other businesses who fail to communicate on these issues. Waitrose recently launched an advertising campaign with live-feed, on-farm cameras at their free-range laying hen farms and pasture-based dairy farms. McDonald's has invited bloggers onto its farms as part of its "Good to Know" marketing campaign. In time, every company will be forced to ask itself the question: "when my consumers open the farm doors will they be happy with what they see?"

Farm animal welfare and sustainability: a look to the future

Twenty, even ten years ago, sustainability issues were far more niche in the business world than they are today. Trailblazing companies, from The Body Shop to Ben & Jerry's, recognized the importance of sustainability, but they were very much in the minority. Today, issues such as climate change and water scarcity loom much larger on the corporate agenda, and their importance as business issues will only increase. What does this mean for farming and farm animal welfare?

In an era of growing population, few would argue against the need to use precious natural resources such as soil and water efficiently. This argument is often advanced in support of the intensification of livestock systems. But the true cost of cheap meat (and dairy) is far higher than the price paid by the end consumer. Even putting animal welfare to one side for a moment, the superficial "efficiency" of intensive farming systems only exists because we have been notoriously bad at valuing the true social and environmental costs (or the negative externalities) of our activities. The more we understand and account for these externalities, the more strongly the case for a different food and farming system is made. For example, the external costs (associated with global warming, air pollution from ammonia emissions and eutrophication potential) are estimated to be around £0.19 higher for 1 kg (i.e. approximately 1 litre) of milk produced in high-input, confinement dairy systems compared with the same amount of milk produced in low-input, pasture-based dairy systems (unpublished study by Compassion in World Farming, cited in Stevenson, 2014).[8] The latter, if well-managed, also affords a much higher standard of animal welfare for dairy cows.

The purported efficiency of intensive systems is often exposed by looking at the whole life-cycle of the product, including what is fed to the animal. Shockingly, more than a third of the world's crop calories are fed to animals, and more than 70% of the calories are then "wasted" in conversion to meat or milk (Compassion in World Farming, 2016). Because feeding crops to animals is so inefficient, more land, water and energy often have to be used to produce a unit of nutrition from industrially reared livestock (with their grain-based diet) than from animals reared on pasture or on mixed (i.e. crop and livestock) farms.

Much of this is avoidable, particularly when it comes to ruminants (i.e. mammals, such as cows and sheep, that have typically four stomach compartments), who consume around 40% of the cereal grain fed to animals. Ruminants graze pastures and can eat hay, silage and high-fibre crop residues that are unsuitable for human consumption. In addition, ruminants (of suitable breeds) can graze in

8 For reference, the UK average farm gate milk price for February 2017 was 27.46p per litre (Defra, 2017).

marginal areas, such as mountainsides or low-lying wet grasslands. This helps to reserve agricultural fields for growing human food.

Reduction in the use of human-edible crops as animal feed is vital. In a world in which resource efficiency is imperative, it's incredibly inefficient to feed so many of our crops to animals. We need to increase the proportion of animals farmed on grasslands or in integrated crop-livestock systems where they can be fed on crop residues. This is also an inherently more resilient set-up which could provide producers, businesses and their customers with a buffer against increasingly volatile commodity prices. Pasture-based systems afford a higher potential level of animal welfare, too.

This is just one way in which environmental sustainability issues and animal welfare intersect. Animal welfare improvements can also often support progress in other pillars of corporate sustainability, and vice versa. Health is one example. Free-range animals who consume fresh forage and have higher activity levels often provide meat of higher nutritional quality than animals reared industrially. For example, meat from slower growing, free-range chickens contains substantially less saturated fat and generally a higher proportion of beneficial omega-3 fatty acids than meat from fast growing chickens reared industrially (Pickett, 2012).

There are, however, times of course when trade-offs are necessary. Goals in different areas of sustainability will not always be aligned. At times, the most efficient system in terms of carbon intensity (for example) is not the best in terms of welfare, biodiversity or livelihoods. To keep within our planetary and moral limits on *all* aspects of sustainability, any attempt to reconfigure our farming systems must necessarily address the volume of the demand as well as how we supply it. Avoiding conventional food waste (as well as grain-based waste) is a theoretical "no-brainer" here, albeit sometimes challenging in practice. It cannot be right that we currently waste the equivalent of 86 *million* broiler chickens in the UK each year (*Household Food and Drink Waste in the United Kingdom 2012*, cited in WRAP, 2013).

Helping companies (and consumers) see the advantages of producing, buying and eating "less and better" meat will certainly be a critical part of our role in future years.

From one to many

Our work will undoubtedly evolve in other ways, too. As farm animal welfare becomes a more important issue for an increasing number of companies, many recognize that they cannot go it alone. Sometimes, individual corporate "will" is not enough, and it is our job as an NGO to help facilitate "the way". Convening multiple companies to address a specific issue is a growing part of the role we need to play. This might be to share evidence-based information and provide practical insights on a particularly complex topic—the aforementioned tail biting in pigs, for instance. It may also be to help forge supply chain connections. To facilitate this type of sourcing conversation requires a high level of trust, and careful attention to be paid to competition laws, but the potential for impact is high. Even the largest companies may source relatively small quantities of a particular type of meat—and, as such, their influence on production standards may be limited. But bring together a number of companies looking to source higher welfare chicken, for example—all of whom need to buy different parts of the bird, and all of whom are willing to invest in a long-term relationship with a particular producer—and suddenly change is possible.

In conclusion

When walking the tightrope of collaboration and challenge, it is easy to wobble. Maintaining a strict stance on ethical issues just as your appreciation of the challenges of a for-profit environment continually deepens requires constant attention. I'm exceptionally proud of the work that Compassion in World Farming and other animal welfare NGOs do to influence corporate practice. There's no magic formula for impact, but on a personal level there are three principles I remind myself of frequently:

1. Be wary of companies who want to "engage" but have no intention of making any meaningful change. We are not there to greenwash (or "hogwash", for want of a more appropriate animal welfare equivalent).
2. Remember no company is perfect. Sometimes it feels wrong to celebrate progress. An example could be a company that is moving to sourcing only free-range eggs, but whose pigs are still suffering in barren conditions. But if you wait for perfection, you'll be waiting a very long time—and missing out on the crucial opportunity to build the animal welfare movement.
3. It doesn't matter why change happens, so long as it's here to stay. Influencing change for animals within a business often means that conversations reference the bottom line, brand equity and supply chain management far more than they reference the lives of the animals who end up on our plates. So long as the outcome for animals is positive and permanent, they won't care why it happened.

References

Barry, M., & Seabright, J. (2014, July 16). It's time for action: The Consumer Goods Forum calls for binding global climate change deal. Forum for the Future. Retrieved from https://www.forumforthefuture.org/blog/it%E2%80%99s-time-action

Bent, D. (2008, May 2). Business case: Getting beyond "virtue". Forum for the Future. Retrieved from https://www.forumforthefuture.org/blog/business-case-getting-beyond-virtue

Compassion in World Farming (2016a, January). Cheap food costs dear. Retrieved from: http://www.ciwf.org.uk/research/policy-economics/cheap-food-costs-dear/

Department for Environment, Food and Rural Affairs (Defra) (2016, August 4). United Kingdom Egg Statistics—Quarter 2, 2016. Retrieved from: https://www.gov.uk/government/collections/egg-production-and-prices

Defra (2017). United Kingdom price, volume and composition of milk: February 2017. Retrieved from: https://www.gov.uk/government/uploads/system/uploads/attachment_data/file/604323/milkprices-statsnotice-30mar17.pdf

Pickett, H. (2012). Nutritional benefits of higher welfare animal products. Compassion in World Farming. Retrieved from: http://www.ciwf.org.uk/research/food-and-human-health/nutrition/

Stevenson, P. (2014). *The European Commission's Forthcoming Communication on Sustainable Food: Impact Assessment by Compassion in World Farming*. Compassion in World Farming. Retrieved from: https://www.ciwf.org.uk/includes/documents/cm_docs/2014/i/impact_assessment_of_failing_to_move_to_sustainable_livestock_production_and_consumption.pdf

WRAP (2013, November 7). Use your loaf and save billions. Retrieved from http://www.wrap.org.uk/content/use-your-loaf-and-save-billions

7 Farm animal welfare as an investment issue

Rory Sullivan

UNIVERSITY OF LEEDS AND BUSINESS BENCHMARK ON FARM ANIMAL WELFARE, UK

Kate Elliot

RATHBONE GREENBANK INVESTMENTS, UK

Abigail Herron

AVIVA INVESTORS, UK

Helena Viñes Fiestas

BNP PARIBAS INVESTMENT PARTNERS, FRANCE

Nicky Amos

NICKY AMOS CSR SERVICES AND BUSINESS BENCHMARK ON FARM ANIMAL WELFARE, UK

Introduction

Investors are an important influence on the manner in which companies manage the social and environmental impacts of their operations. Over the past decade in particular, investors have contributed to significant improvements in corporate governance, in the quality of corporate reporting on environmental, social and governance (ESG) issues (see, for example, the data in KPMG, 2015, p. 30), and in the manner in which companies manage social and environmental impacts. The fact that over 1,500 investment organizations—including over 300 asset owners, over 1,000 asset managers and over 200 service providers—have signed up to the UN Principles for Responsible Investment[1] is further evidence that investors are willing to actively encourage companies to more effectively manage their environmental and social impacts.

Since 2012, when the Business Benchmark on Farm Animal Welfare[2] was launched and the horsemeat scandal hit European retailers and food producers, there has been growing interest in the role that investors might play in encouraging improved corporate practice on farm animal welfare. The aim of this chapter is to

1 See http://www.unpri.org/. Signatory data as at 1 August 2016, http://www.unpri.org/signatories/signatories/

2 The Business Benchmark on Farm Animal Welfare is the first global measure of company performance on animal welfare. It produces an annual benchmark on corporate approaches to farm animal welfare and actively engages with the investment community to encourage investors to take farm animal welfare into account in their company engagement and in their investment research and decision-making processes. See further http://www.bbfaw.com/

provide a wider context for this discussion. It begins with a general review of how investors take account of environmental and social issues in their investment practices and processes. It then discusses the specific case of farm animal welfare, focusing on the reasons why investors might be interested in farm animal welfare and providing high level comments on how investors have incorporated farm animal welfare-related considerations in their investment processes.[3] It concludes with some wider reflections on the role that investors can play.

Why are investors important?

Financial metrics such as share prices and the cost of capital provide companies with a broad measure of how they are perceived by financial markets. They also motivate company management, both because company management see investors as an important stakeholder and because management incentives are often linked to performance on these financial metrics. If investment analysis fails to place sufficient weight on the value of good corporate social and environmental performance, or emphasizes short-term over long-term performance, it risks motivating company management to act in ways that may be harmful to society or the environment. There is evidence that companies respond to the signals sent to them by the financial markets; for example, concern about the market reaction to a failure to meet earnings expectations might cause companies to engage in earnings management to meet these market expectations (see Dallas, 2011, p. 269 and the references cited therein; also, Sullivan, 2011, 2014).

Investors also exert influence in other ways. They have formal rights (e.g. shareholders can vote proxies and call meetings, large investors are often entitled to board seats) and informal influence (e.g. through the views they express in meetings with companies, through the views they express in the press, through their ability to work with other investors). These formal and informal powers mean that shareholders have significant ability, in particular if they act collectively, to influence the behaviour of companies.

What is responsible investment?

Investment is a future-oriented activity. The future determines the returns—or expected returns—on investments made today. Investment also influences the future. For example, a road or a power station built today may well have a lifetime of 20, 50 or even more years. At a very high level, responsible investment can be differentiated from conventional approaches to investment in two ways. First, the goal is the creation of sustainable, long-term investment returns, not just short-term returns. Second, explicit attention is paid to the impacts of investment activities on the stability and health of social, economic and environmental systems.

3 In Chapters 8, 9 and 10, Kate Elliot, Abigail Herron and Helena Viñes Fiestas describe how Rathbone Greenbank Investments, Aviva Investors and BNP Paribas Investment Partners, respectively, take account of farm animal welfare in their investment processes.

There are various reasons why investors may want to pay attention to these issues. The heart of the investment argument is that good environmental and social practices have the potential to strengthen business performance through better downside risk management, through identifying cost savings, and through identifying business opportunities. From an investment perspective, explicitly and proactively evaluating how companies manage ESG issues could help identify business risks and opportunities that might not otherwise be identified or might provide insights into the quality of companies' risk management processes. A similar argument applies to company–investor engagement on these issues. That is, encouraging companies to improve their social and environmental performance should strengthen business performance and, in turn, investment returns (see, for example, Dimson *et al.*, 2015).

A typology of strategies

While the prima facie argument that environmental and social issues can be financially significant is now widely accepted, there is no consensus about how these issues actually affect investment returns or on how best to integrate them into investment processes. Table 7.1 presents a typology of the major responsible investment strategies presently in use. These range from "traditional" negative screening approaches (i.e. where companies are excluded because of their ethical characteristics) through to the more mainstream approaches of engagement and enhanced analysis that have emerged over the past ten years (for data on the market share of these different strategies, see Global Sustainable Investment Alliance, 2014).

Table 7.1 Major responsible investment strategies

Strategy	*Description*
Negative screening	Avoiding (i.e. not investing in) companies on the basis of their products, the sectors they are in, the activities they carry out or their specific management practices.
Positive screening	Preferentially investing in companies on the basis of their products, the sectors they are in, the activities they carry out or their specific management practices.
Best in class	Preferentially investing in companies with better governance and management processes and/or with better environmental or social performance than their industry or sector peers.
Positive/thematic investment	Selecting companies on the basis of their exposure to themes such as climate change or demographic change, or their involvement in a positive area e.g. renewable energy.
Engagement/activism	Using the formal rights (e.g. the ability to vote via shareholdings, the ability to call an emergency general meeting) and informal influence available to investors to encourage companies to improve their management systems, their performance or their reporting.
Integrated analysis (or enhanced analysis)	Proactively considering environmental and social factors in "mainstream" investment research and decision-making.

Source: Sullivan (2011).

When we look at farm animal welfare issues, a similar typology of approaches can be applied. That is, investors could decide not to invest in companies based on the nature of their products (e.g. they do not produce organic food), or because their farm animal welfare practices are considered unacceptable (e.g. they house chickens in barren battery cages). Investors could also preferentially invest in companies with better practices, could engage with companies to encourage them to improve their approach to farm animal welfare, or could build farm animal welfare issues into their investment decisions. In practice, these approaches are often used in combination. For example, an investor might exclude the worst offenders, preferentially invest in best practice companies and engage with companies to encourage improvements in practice or performance.

The approach (or approaches) an investor decides to take will depend on a number of factors such as the significance of the exposure (e.g. the percentage of a company's sales derived from the product/activity in question), the size and profile of the company in question (which could determine how likely it is to face media attention), and the geographical exposure of the company. The decision will also depend on the investor's interest in the issue of farm animal welfare, and its ability (capacity, resources) to analyse and assess company performance on the issue.

Are investors interested in farm animal welfare?

Farm animal welfare is increasingly recognized as an important business issue for companies across the food industry, including retailers, wholesalers, restaurants, service companies, manufacturers, processors and producers. Various factors have contributed to this, including:

- Tightening farm animal welfare-related regulation (in particular within the EU)
- Growing consumer awareness of, and concern about, animal welfare issues and the provenance of food in the supply chain
- The costs of product recalls and of the subsequent remedial or corrective action
- The risks to brand and reputation of being "named and shamed" in high profile media campaigns or food scares/scandals over alleged poor farm animal welfare practices
- The potential to improve operational efficiency, margins and profits through reduced wastage
- The potential to access new markets and customers and to grow existing markets as a result of adopting higher welfare standards ahead of competitors (i.e. first mover advantage) (see further Read, 2011; Fernyhough, 2012)

While the prima facie business case for adopting good animal welfare practices would seem reasonably clear, until recently most investors have paid relatively little attention to farm animal welfare matters, other than reacting in situations where a particular company has hit the headlines for particularly poor or controversial practices. One of the early examples of such a reaction was the 2008

Tesco AGM. Against a backdrop of carefully coordinated media attention, celebrity chef Hugh Fearnley-Whittingstall spearheaded a shareholder resolution calling on the retailer to ensure that all of its chicken met RSPCA Freedom Food standards, or to drop its claim to be kind to animals.

Even among those fund managers managing ethical or screened (retail) funds, farm animal welfare has received relatively little attention, and certainly much less attention than other animal welfare-related issues such as whether the company provides animal testing services, whether the company tests its products on animals, or whether the company is involved in the production or marketing of controversial animal derivatives such as ivory or fur. Where farm animal issues are explicitly considered, they tend to be expressed in terms of whether the company derives sales from intensive farming (i.e. the screen relates to intensive farming in the round rather than specific practices), whether the company is involved in animal slaughter (again, without reference to the specific practices in the company's facilities) or whether the company sells significant amounts of meat (without any consideration of the provenance of these products).[4]

One of the reasons why farm animal welfare issues have tended to receive less investor attention than other social and environmental issues has been the common perception among investors that farm animal welfare is a niche ethical issue rather than a business issue, and that higher welfare animal farming practices inevitably result in higher financial costs for companies. This is compounded by the perceived inevitable need for industrial-scale farming practices to feed ever-growing global populations, with many investors assuming that some compromise of animal welfare standards is probably unavoidable to address this need. There is also a general lack of familiarity in the investment industry of farm animal welfare issues, exacerbated by the fact that there are multiple species and multiple geographies involved. There are signs of change, with investors beginning to recognize that farm animal welfare can be a core business issue, further encouraged by greater awareness of the costs and benefits of good and poor performance, and as clients and NGOs start to ask questions about how farm animal welfare issues are being taken into account in investment decisions (see, for example, the data presented in Sullivan and Amos, 2013, 2014, 2015, 2016).

A specific challenge for investors has been the lack of publicly available information on how companies manage farm animal welfare issues and the lack of comparability between the data that are available. This has made it difficult for investors to differentiate between those companies that do a good job and those that do not. Tools such as the annual Business Benchmark on Farm Animal Welfare (see Chapter 13) have helped to address this problem, both by encouraging improved reporting by companies and by providing a robust framework for assessing companies' approaches to farm animal welfare.

4 There are a number of databases that provide information on the animal welfare (and other) criteria used in ethical funds; see http://www.ethicalinvestors.co.uk/fund_directory.php and http://www.yourethicalmoney.org/investments/ (for UK funds), and http://www.socialfunds.com/funds/chart.cgi?sfChartId=Social+Issues (for US funds).

What actions have investors taken?

The actions that have been taken by investors can be divided into three broad categories: signalling, engagement and investment analysis.

Investors have started to send signals to companies and to the wider investment market about the importance they assign to farm animal welfare. Some have covered farm animal welfare in their communications with clients or with other stakeholders. For example, investors have identified farm animal welfare as a new/emerging issue, have used the results of the Business Benchmark on Farm Animal Welfare to describe the overall characteristics of their portfolios, and have highlighted examples of their engagement with companies on farm animal welfare-related issues (see, further, Sullivan and Amos, 2013, 2014, 2015, 2016).

Another form of signalling has been the move by more than 20 large institutional investors,[5] representing more than £1.5 trillion in assets under management, to sign the Global Investor Statement on Farm Animal Welfare (BBFAW, 2017). This Statement, convened by the Business Benchmark on Farm Animal Welfare, is the first investor statement on farm animal welfare. The signatories to the statement—including Aviva Investors, BNP Paribas Investment Partners and Rathbone Greenbank Investments—state that they believe that farm animal welfare is potentially material to long-term investment value creation in the food sector. They commit to taking account of farm animal welfare when analysing food companies and to encouraging high standards across the food industry.

In relation to engagement, investors have encouraged companies to strengthen their reporting and performance on farm animal welfare (Sullivan *et al.*, 2015a). Individual investors have engaged with companies identified as laggards, often using data from the annual assessments of the Business Benchmark on Farm Animal Welfare (see, for example, Amos and Sullivan, 2015, 2016) to encourage them to improve their management of farm animal welfare-related issues. They have also engaged with leading companies to understand what has enabled these companies to become leaders. This engagement on farm animal welfare is usually integral to these investors' wider company research and engagement processes. Investors typically ask questions about companies' capital expenditure plans, about companies' longer-term strategies for managing and improving performance on farm animal welfare, and about the relationship between farm animal welfare and wider sustainability issues. These engagement discussions often result in investors making suggestions about the actions that could be taken by these companies. Typical suggestions include:

- Adopting formal policies on farm animal welfare or on specific farm animal welfare-related issues (e.g. on close confinement)

5 The founding signatories were: ACTIAM, ASR Netherlands, Australian Ethical Investment, Aviva Investors, BNP Paribas Investment Partners, Central Finance Board of the Methodist Church, Coller Capital, EdenTree Investment Management, Epworth Investment Management, LWCO Trust, NEI Investments, Rathbone Greenbank Investments, Robeco, Schroders, Standard Life, Trillium Asset Management, Triodos Investment Management and Walden Asset Management (Boston Trust). The subsequent signatories (at 1 August 2016) were Hermes, USS and Sonen Capital.

- Assigning senior management responsibility and accountability for farm animal welfare
- Setting farm animal welfare-related objectives and targets
- Strengthening management systems and processes, e.g. auditing, supply chain monitoring, corrective action
- Having product lines assured to higher farm animal welfare standards
- Improving the quality of reporting on farm animal welfare
- Engaging with key stakeholders to better understand current practice and industry expectations

In 2015, the Business Benchmark on Farm Animal Welfare established a structured collaborative engagement programme to supplement the engagement activities of individual investors. The collaborative engagement programme currently has 18 participating investors, including Aviva Investors, BNP Paribas Investment Partners and Rathbone Greenbank Investments. In 2015 it targeted 40 of the companies covered by the Business Benchmark on Farm Animal Welfare, extending this to 67 companies in 2016 (see Box 7.1). This is the first time that investors have collaborated in such a coordinated, structured manner on the farm animal welfare practices of global food companies, and signals a step change in the manner in which investors engage with the issue.

Box 7.1 Investor collaboration on farm animal welfare, 2015–2016

In mid-2015, the Business Benchmark on Farm Animal Welfare initiated an international collaborative initiative aimed at encouraging major global food companies to strengthen their management systems and processes on farm animal welfare. The initiative, which acknowledges leading practice in this area while encouraging major global food companies to strengthen their farm animal welfare approaches, is—at August 2016—supported by 18 institutional investors from the UK, the Netherlands, France, Canada, the USA and Australia. The participating investors are ACTIAM, Australian Ethical Investment, Aviva Investors, BMO Asset Management, BNP Paribas Investment Partners, the Central Finance Board of the Methodist Church, Coller Capital, EdenTree Investment Management, Epworth Investment Management, Loring, Wolcott & Coolidge Trust, NEI Investments, Nelson Capital Management, Rathbone Greenbank Investments, Robeco, Schroders, Trillium Asset Management, Triodos Bank and Walden Asset Management.

The 2015 collaboration focused on both the high (i.e. the ten companies that were ranked in Tiers 1 and 2 of the 2014 Benchmark) and low (i.e. the 40 companies that were ranked in Tiers 5 and 6 of the 2014 Benchmark) performing companies in the Benchmark. The participating investors wrote to the leading companies to commend them for their performance in the Benchmark, and to encourage them to maintain their high level of performance.

The letters to the low performing companies explained that investors see farm animal welfare as a business risk that needs to be managed effectively and as a potential future source of business opportunity and growth. The letters expressed concern about these companies' performance in the Benchmark, and asked them to explain whether they will be taking action to improve their performance and to respond to the recommendations on potential areas for improvement made by the BBFAW Secretariat. These letters also stated that the participating investors would use the annual Benchmark report to monitor their progress.

In 2016, as well as writing to company leaders (i.e. the 11 companies that were ranked in Tiers 1 and 2 of the 2015 Benchmark) and the laggards (i.e. the 36 companies that were ranked in Tiers 5 and 6 of the 2015 Benchmark), the participating investors also wrote to the ten companies that had substantially improved their ranking in the 2015 Benchmark as well as the ten companies that had shown no evident sign of improvement since the 2012 Benchmark. They saw this lack of progress as suggesting that these companies were not paying attention to the issues and concerns being raised by investors.

The early signs are that this engagement is having an effect on company practice. Ten of the low performing (i.e. Tiers 5 and 6) companies in 2015 had substantially improved their performance in 2016. In addition, a number of companies have responded to the participating investors indicating that they intend to take substantive actions ahead of the 2017 benchmarking process.

Furthermore, a number of the participants in the 2016 collaboration have indicated that they are interested in following up the letters with meetings and/or raising farm animal welfare as part of their routine company meetings. Others have expressed an interest in leading a coordinated engagement with companies on behalf of fellow investor signatories.

In relation to investment decision-making, investors have assessed the business risks and opportunities of farm animal welfare for companies, analysed how companies are identifying and managing risks in their supply chains, and used companies' farm animal welfare practices and strategies as a lens into companies' overall management of sustainability-related issues. One of the most interesting findings from interviews with investors on the subject of farm animal welfare is that many see farm animal welfare (or companies' scores in the Business Benchmark on Farm Animal Welfare) as providing them with insights into the quality of companies' risk identification processes, into the calibre of their management, into their stakeholder engagement processes, into their internal governance and management processes, and into their supply chain management processes (Sullivan and Amos, 2013, 2014, 2015, 2016). Investors have analysed these in both absolute terms (i.e. the level of risk to a specific company) and in relative terms (i.e. comparing Company X with Company Y).

Does this mean that all investors are now active on farm animal welfare?

While farm animal welfare is gaining profile and traction as an investment issue, much more needs to be done if investors are to play a fuller and more effective role in encouraging improvements in practice and performance on farm animal welfare. There are important obstacles to progress.

First, for many investors, farm animal welfare continues to be seen as an ethical rather than a mainstream investment issue. Therefore, further work is needed both to set out a compelling business case for action, and to convince mainstream investors that farm animal welfare is an important issue for them to focus on.

Second, there is relatively little demand (from clients, from beneficiaries) for investment organizations to explicitly consider farm animal welfare in their investment processes. Investors have commented that they would look at farm animal welfare in their investment research and their engagement if they saw demand from their clients to do so. However, the common absence of demand means there is limited reason for them to focus on farm animal welfare (Sullivan and Amos, 2014, 2015). An ongoing issue, in particular in North America, is that many investors continue to hold the view that a focus on environmental and social issues (not just confined to farm animal welfare) may be a breach of the fiduciary duties they owe to their clients (for a challenge to this view, see Sullivan *et al.*, 2015b).

Third, corporate disclosures remain limited and it is difficult to make meaningful comparisons between companies. This is starting to change. For example, the 2015 Benchmark revealed that the proportion of companies with a published farm animal welfare policy had increased from 46% in 2012 to 69% in 2015, and the proportion with published objectives and targets for farm animal welfare had increased from 26% in 2012 to 54% in 2015 (Amos and Sullivan, 2016).

Fourth, investment practice remains a barrier. Investors tend to focus most attention on those issues that are seen as financially important over the short term, which is typically over the next one to two years. Issues that may impact on the business beyond that time tend to receive much less attention. Expressed another way, investors are likely to be very interested in an environmental or social issue that has an impact of 10% on a key financial indicator over the next one to two years but may have less interest if the issue may have a 50% impact on the same financial indicator over the next five to ten years (Sullivan, 2011). This also means that investors tend to exclude high-consequence but low-probability events, concluding that the likelihood of these occurring over the timeframe of interest to the investor is relatively low). From a stakeholder perspective, the most important point to take from this discussion is that the investor definition of materiality differs significantly from the definitions adopted by stakeholders (see, for example, Faux, 2002). Mainstream investors' focus on financial materiality means that wider ethical values (other than to the extent that these manifest themselves as impacts on the business through, for example, regulation, damage to brand or reputation, increased costs) tend to be excluded from the assessments made. Even investors with a particular interest in social or environmental matters tend to confine their interest to a relatively narrow set of topics (e.g. the specific screens in a negatively screened fund) rather than the spectrum of social and environmental issues that may be of concern.

Fifth, investor engagement is likely to be less effective in situations where behaving irresponsibly is the profit-maximizing strategy (e.g. when there is a weak or no business case for adopting higher farm animal welfare practices and processes). In such situations, investment analysis and decision-making will tend to reward companies that exploit market failures with a higher share price or a lower cost of capital.

Concluding comments

There has been a step change in the level of attention being paid by investors to farm animal welfare. There are tangible signs that mainstream investor interest in farm animal welfare is increasing. More than 20 major institutional investors have signed the Global Investor Statement on Farm Animal Welfare and 20 are actively participating in a collaborative engagement involving co-signing letters to the CEOs of companies based on their companies' performance in the Business Benchmark on Farm Animal Welfare, conducting direct engagement with companies, and leading coordinated engagements on behalf of fellow investors in the collaboration. It is likely that this interest will grow as awareness of the business case for action is raised, as the breadth and depth of corporate reporting improves and as investors start to talk more publicly about their efforts in this area.

There is also evidence that investor action is encouraging improvements in corporate practice, with 26 (29%) of the 90 companies in the 2016 Benchmark moving up at least one tier since 2015, and 60% (37 of 61) of companies moving up one tier since the 2012 Benchmark.

It is important to be realistic about the extent to which this newfound enthusiasm for responsible investment can or will drive change within companies. The vast majority of investors—including those that could be classed as "responsible investors" and those offering ethical or environmental investment products—are evaluated over relatively short timeframes. Even those that fully accept their responsibilities as long-term investors will face significant pressure to concentrate on shorter-term performance. While these conditions are likely to prevail and may act to dampen progress, it is also important to acknowledge that the progress that has been made by investors on farm animal welfare over the past 5 years has been exponentially greater than in the previous 50.

References

Amos, N. & Sullivan, R. (2015). *The Business Benchmark on Farm Animal Welfare: 2014 Report*. London: Business Benchmark on Farm Animal Welfare.

Amos, N. & Sullivan, R. (2016). *The Business Benchmark on Farm Animal Welfare: 2015 Report*. London: Business Benchmark on Farm Animal Welfare.

Business Benchmark on Farm Animal Welfare (BBFAW) (2017, January 12). *Investor Statement on Farm Animal Welfare.* Retrieved from https://bbfaw.com/investors/get-involved/

Dallas, L. (2011). Short-termism, the financial crisis, and corporate governance. *The Journal of Corporation Law*, 37(2), 264-363.

Dimson, E., Karakaş, O. & Li, X. (2015). Active ownership. *Review of Financial Studies*, 28(12), 3225-3268.

Faux, J. (2002) A stakeholder perspective of material disclosure thresholds for environmental events. *Asian Review of Accounting*, 10(2), 3-16.

Fernyhough, M. (2012). *Farm Animal Welfare and the Consumer. Investor Briefing No. 7 (October 2012)*. London: Business Benchmark on Farm Animal Welfare.

Global Sustainable Investment Alliance (GSIA) (2014). *Global Sustainable Investment Review 2014.* Retrieved from http://www.gsi-alliance.org/wp-content/uploads/2015/02/GSIA_Review_download.pdfKPMG (2015). *Currents of Change: The KPMG Survey of Corporate Responsibility Reporting 2015.* London: KPMG.

Read, K. (2011). *Farm Animal Welfare: The Business Case for Action. Business Benchmark on Farm Animal Welfare. Investor Briefing No. 2 (October 2011)*. London: Business Benchmark on Farm Animal Welfare.

Sullivan, R. (2011). *Valuing Corporate Responsibility: How Do Investors Really Use Corporate Responsibility Information?* Sheffield, UK: Greenleaf Publishing.

Sullivan, R. (2014). *Coping, Shifting, Changing: Strategies for Managing the Impacts of Investor Short-termism on Corporate Sustainability.* New York: Global Compact LEAD; London: Principles for Responsible Investment.

Sullivan, R. & Amos, N. (2013). *How Are Investors Using the 2012 Business Benchmark on Farm Animal Welfare? Business Benchmark on Farm Animal Welfare Investor Briefing No. 10 (June 2013)*. London: Business Benchmark on Farm Animal Welfare.

Sullivan, R. & Amos, N. (2014). *How Are Investors Using the Business Benchmark on Farm Animal Welfare? Investor Briefing No. 15.* London: Business Benchmark on Farm Animal Welfare.

Sullivan, R. & Amos, N. (2015). *How Are Investors Using the Business Benchmark on Farm Animal Welfare? Investor Briefing No. 20.* London: Business Benchmark on Farm Animal Welfare.

Sullivan, R. & Amos, N. (2016). *How Are Investors Using the Business Benchmark on Farm Animal Welfare? 2016 Analysis.* London: Business Benchmark on Farm Animal Welfare.

Sullivan, R., Amos, N. & Herron, A. (2015a). *Engagement on Farm Animal Welfare: A User's Guide. Investor Briefing No. 19.* London: Business Benchmark on Farm Animal Welfare.

Sullivan, R., Martindale, W., Feller, E. & Bordon, A. (2015b). *Fiduciary Duty in the 21st Century.* London: UN Global Compact, UNEPFI, Principles for Responsible Investment and UNEP Inquiry into the Design of a Sustainable Financial System.

8 Investor case study

Rathbone Greenbank Investments

Kate Elliot

RATHBONE GREENBANK INVESTMENTS, UK

About Rathbone Greenbank Investments

Rathbone Greenbank Investments is the dedicated ethical and sustainable investment team of Rathbones, a UK-based provider of investment and wealth management services for private investors, charities, trusts and professional advisers. Rathbones' focus is on the provision of segregated, discretionary investment portfolios: approximately 90% of its £34.2 billion in funds under management[1] is managed on this basis, with the remainder managed by Rathbone Unit Trust Management via its range of unit trusts and open-ended investment companies. Investment managers at Rathbone Greenbank have been involved in ethical and responsible investment since 1992; within Rathbones' total assets under management, we now manage approximately £860 million in ethically screened funds on behalf of over 1,400 clients.[2]

Our investment approach is based on the view that companies with high ethical standards and sustainable business practices make good long-term investments. Rathbones has been a signatory to the UN-backed Principles for Responsible Investment since 2009 and is committed to seeking high standards of corporate governance at the companies in which it invests.

Rathbone Greenbank's in-house ethical research team combines an assessment of companies' overall environmental, social and governance (or ESG) performance—and the financial risks and opportunities this presents—with an understanding of the ethical, social and environmental issues that are of concern or interest to individual clients. We recognize that ESG factors can be financially material, in some cases significantly so, and therefore actively consider these alongside financial metrics as part of our investment process. In addition to this integrated analysis, our clients are able to select specific positive and negative social, environmental and ethical screening criteria to be applied to the management of their portfolios.

The other important element of our approach to responsible investment is shareholder engagement (or active ownership). Rathbone Greenbank takes an

1 As at 31 December 2016.
2 As at 31 December 2016.

active approach in this area. We engage with companies and with policy-makers on behalf of our clients to bring about positive change, in relation to environmental and social impacts and in relation to corporate governance. We seek to be supportive but stretching in our dialogue with companies, in order to address specific areas of concern (e.g. risks that are not being effectively managed) or to encourage improved ESG performance. If companies do not respond appropriately, we may consider voting against management at annual general meetings (AGMs), reducing our holdings in the company or even divesting completely.

Our approach to animal welfare: driving forces

There are two reasons why we focus on farm animal welfare in our investment practices and processes.

The first is that farm animal welfare is an investment issue. A failure to properly manage farm animal welfare can lead to costly product recalls and reputational damage. Furthermore, as investors, we see a company's management of farm animal welfare as a proxy for how well it is managing overall risk across often complex, global supply chains. In addition to these company-specific issues, farm animal welfare is also about the wider risks to the food sector and to society. For example, companies may face tighter regulation and higher costs should voluntary codes and self-regulation fail. Intensive farming may lead to lower short-term prices, but the long-term impacts on human health—for example through increased use of antibiotics and growth hormones in livestock, or higher incidence of food-borne pathogens—and associated costs to society and the economy may well outweigh any short-term benefits. But this is not just about downside risk; companies with higher standards and practices on farm animal welfare may well find that they can access new markets and new business opportunities.

The second is that farm animal welfare is an issue that is of real importance to society and to our clients. For example, 87% of our clients who have expressed a view on this issue have indicated they would wish to avoid investing in companies with poor animal welfare standards, and a similar proportion are interested in supporting companies which demonstrate good practice. This means that there are certain companies that we may exclude from our investment portfolios. Consumer and societal concerns have also led to companies adapting their business models to incorporate higher animal welfare standards, resulting in a wider investible universe for concerned investors.

Addressing farm animal welfare in practice

While there are compelling investment and client reasons for us to take account of farm animal welfare in our investment processes, our ability to do so has been limited by the weaknesses in corporate disclosures on farm animal welfare. Despite the increasing number of food companies that provide a statement or high level policy on farm animal welfare, many fail to back these up with specific details of their objectives and targets or of the performance outcomes that they will track.

This makes it difficult for investors to properly assess the risks and opportunities associated with individual companies' farm animal welfare practices. It also makes it difficult for investors to have a meaningful conversation with companies about these issues.

Since its launch in 2012, the Business Benchmark on Farm Animal Welfare (BBFAW)[3] has played an important role in addressing the lack of corporate disclosure. It provides a standard framework against which all companies can report on their farm animal welfare practices, processes and performance. Its annual ranking of major food companies provides us with information we can use to support both our analysis of companies and our engagement activities. We incorporate BBFAW's rankings into our assessment of a company's performance with regard to animal welfare, both from a positive and a negative screening perspective, and to inform our overall evaluation of that company's management of supply chain risk.

From an engagement perspective, we make food companies aware that we use the BBFAW ranking in our assessment of their practices and we refer them to the BBFAW Benchmark report when they ask for suggestions on how they might improve their practices and reporting.

As a relatively small institution, it can be difficult for us to instigate change in large companies. We have therefore found that working with others on an agenda where there is a clear set of expectations (or a normative framework) can in many cases be much more effective than if we worked on our own. In 2015 and 2016, we worked with some 20 other investors on a collaborative engagement project utilizing the results of the Benchmark. The programme, convened by the BBFAW Secretariat, involved these investors writing to leading companies in the Benchmark to commend them for their performance, and to poor performers to encourage them to improve. While it is too early to offer a definitive assessment, approximately ten companies have responded to this engagement indicating that they plan to increase the level of attention they pay to farm animal welfare.

Case study: Tesco

While most shareholder engagement may take the form of informal dialogue and meetings, more formal methods can be used. For example, in 2008 we utilized new provisions under the UK Companies Act 2006[4] to enable us (on behalf of a number of Rathbone Greenbank clients) to co-file a resolution at Tesco's AGM calling for the retailer to adopt higher poultry welfare standards. There are specific requirements[5] that must be met in order for a shareholder resolution to appear on

3 See, further, Chapter 13 and http://www.bbfaw.com/

4 s153 of the Act deals with the exercise of rights where shares are held on behalf of others, i.e. by Rathbone Nominee Ltd on behalf of our underlying clients; this provision was used in conjunction with s338 which covers the power of members (shareholders) to require the circulation of resolutions for AGMs.

5 Under UK law, shareholder resolutions can be filed at company AGMs if they have the support of either: 100 shareholders who, between them, hold shares with at least £10,000 in nominal value; or, shareholder(s) that represent at least 5% of the voting rights in a company.

the agenda of a company's AGM and, in the UK, this method of engagement is still relatively rare. However, as we knew that many of our clients had a strong interest in farm animal welfare, we lent our support to the initiative (led by the TV chef Hugh Fearnley-Whittingstall and the charity Compassion in World Farming) and ensured the resolution received sufficient support to be tabled for discussion.

On the day, the resolution received 9% of votes in support with a further 10% withheld—well below the 75% necessary for it to pass. However, in an environment where it was common to see almost 100% of votes cast in line with board recommendations, a 20% level of dissent sent a strong message to the company and served to highlight the importance that investors place on animal welfare issues.

While Tesco did not publicly make changes to its farm animal welfare standards in the wake of its 2008 AGM, the group did enter into talks at an industry level on the issue of chicken welfare. The associated "Chicken Out" media campaign also raised public awareness of animal welfare concerns in the poultry supply chain, leading to an increase in sales of higher welfare chickens and thereby providing further incentive for Tesco to improve.

Wider reflections: farm animal welfare as an investment issue

There are three wider points to be made about investors and farm animal welfare.

The first is, unfortunately, that farm animal welfare is still at the earlier stages of being recognized as a material factor in the financial performance of companies. This is partly due to a prevailing perception that it remains primarily an ethical issue, partly because many food companies do not acknowledge farm animal welfare as an important business issue (which reinforces investors' views that it is mainly an ethical consideration) and partly because of the difficulty in obtaining reliable, consistent and relevant information on company practices. This is starting to change. The Business Benchmark on Farm Animal Welfare has played a key role in encouraging better disclosures and in providing a forum for investors to work together on the issue of farm animal welfare. One tangible demonstration of the change is the Global Investor Statement on Farm Animal Welfare (BBFAW, 2017), which has now been signed by 23 investors, including Rathbone Greenbank, from Australia, Canada, France, the Netherlands, the UK and the US. These investors, representing almost £2 trillion in assets under management, have stated that they believe that farm animal welfare is potentially material to long-term investment value creation in the food sector. They have also committed to take account of farm animal welfare when analysing food companies and to encourage high standards across the food industry via their engagement activities.

The second is that change takes time and patience. Returning to the example of Tesco, we have been encouraged by the fact that Tesco's scores in the BBFAW Benchmark have increased year-on-year, although there remains room for improvement in both the group's policy and its performance. Both the Tesco example and the BBFAW investor collaboration also demonstrate how investors can work effectively alongside other stakeholders to achieve real change in companies' approach to farm animal welfare. While it is often difficult to quantify the impact or effectiveness of engagement activity—not least because projects can span years—the dangers of unengaged shareholders failing to hold companies to account for poor management of issues such as farm animal welfare should not be discounted. We act as stewards of our clients' investments. As such, we have a duty to ensure that value is not being destroyed, nor opportunities overlooked, because companies are failing to respond appropriately to material ESG issues.

The third is that companies and investors are becoming increasingly aware of the links between environmental, social and governance factors and financial risks and opportunities. At the same time, we are seeing greater public scrutiny of the role companies and investors play in the economy and society as a whole. But, beneath this underlying trend, there is significant variation in the maturity of debate on individual issues; while climate change and human rights are recognized as material issues by many investors, farm animal welfare still has a long way to go. Data and experiences drawn from pioneering companies—such as those ranking in the top tiers of the BBFAW—will play a key role in strengthening the business case for higher standards of farm animal welfare. And investor engagement will play a crucial role in ensuring companies respond to this issue and begin reporting more detailed information on their policies and performance. Over time, we expect the combined effect will be to put farm animal welfare squarely on the investor agenda. It should ensure that investors have the tools that they need to assess farm animal welfare-related investment risks and opportunities, to identify good and poor performers, and to engage constructively with companies. That, in turn, should help farm animal welfare move from the margins to the mainstream of investor thinking.

Reference

Business Benchmark on Farm Animal Welfare (BBFAW) (2017, January 12). *Investor Statement on Farm Animal Welfare.* Retrieved from https://www.bbfaw.com/media/1446/bbfaw-investor-statement-update-12jan17.pdf

9 Investor case study

Aviva Investors

Abigail Herron

AVIVA INVESTORS, UK

Introduction: Aviva Investor's approach to responsible investment

Aviva Investors is a global asset manager with £400 billion of assets under management.[1] We invest primarily in equities, fixed income, real estate and multi assets. Our core objective is to deliver the investment outcomes—protecting their capital, generating returns, enabling them to plan for their futures and their retirements—that matter most to our clients. Our commitments to responsible investment and stewardship are fundamental to delivering this goal.

At its simplest, stewardship means taking responsibility for something entrusted into our care. In this case, it involves the effort and activities undertaken by and on behalf of asset managers to monitor, engage and, where appropriate, intervene on matters that may affect the long-term value of investee companies and the capital invested in them. This can encompass issues such as strategy, performance, corporate governance, and environmental and social challenges that may materially affect the future sustainability of companies and shareholder value.

We have a bespoke ESG integration approach (policy and process) and aim to have at least one nominated Responsible Investment Officer (RIO) for the relevant asset class or region. Our RIO network currently comprises over 30 fund managers, analysts and support functions with specified responsibility to work with our Global Responsible Investment (GRI) team of seven dedicated governance and responsible investment specialists, who seek to embed ESG data and analysis fully into each team's investment process.

In practice, our approach to responsible investment comprises three core elements: investment integration, active stewardship and market advocacy. Investment integration involves ensuring that ESG issues are fully integrated into our investment decisions, thereby providing us with better insights into investment risks and opportunities, and enabling us to make better informed investment decisions. This involves working closely with our fund managers and analysts, providing them with data and information in a form that is most useful to them, developing research tools and helping them analyse the implications of ESG issues for individual companies and for their investment portfolios as a whole.

1 As at 31 December 2016.

As long-term investors, we see factors such as corporate culture, good governance and strategic responses to changing climate, hard and soft regulatory landscapes, resource availability, and employee and marketplace attitudes as core to the success of our investments.

Our ESG heat map is our key integration tool. It includes a range of material ESG data and analysis, including our governance analysis, which is based on our historic voting records for the individual stocks in which we invest. This is available to all investment teams through the financial data provider Bloomberg. The ESG heat map is supplemented by additional fund manager and analyst briefings that are provided before company meetings, votes or investment decisions. These briefings draw on our heat map and more detailed independent ESG data and research. We use this research, the expertise of the team, bespoke research commissioned from brokers and research organizations, and additional information from less conventional sources such as NGOs and civil society to build up a rich picture of how the ESG issues impact the businesses and other asset classes in which we invest.

Our approach to active ownership and stewardship involves engagement (or dialogue) with companies and the use of the rights (e.g. voting rights for our investments in listed equities) we are granted as investors in companies. We consider engagement to be an important part of our investment process across a range of asset classes. The aim of our engagement is to identify and reduce ESG risks in our portfolios.

For example, by improving our understanding of the quality of the board of directors of a company and its strategy in responding to issues, such as climate change or the living wage, we can gauge how well prepared companies are to deal with current or emerging ESG issues. Where we consider the company's response or performance falls short of the required standards, and that this shortfall will have an impact on our investment decision, we will engage with the board to improve performance. Engagement outcomes are reflected in our voting and thereby feed back into our ESG heat map. For active holdings, engagement is undertaken in close cooperation with the fund manager(s) and the company's response contributes to the investment decision-making process. We use our influence both to understand how companies manage ESG issues and to promote good practice among those companies in which we invest. We focus on generating outcomes that benefit our clients (through enhancing our understanding of risk, through ensuring that companies are well managed and so reducing investment risk on ESG issues) and in many cases society, the environment and the broader economy as well.

Our corporate governance and corporate responsibility voting policy takes into account companies' disclosure of ESG factors including farm animal welfare where relevant. Where companies do not publish this information or where we see poor corporate responsibility performance or management practices, we may vote against or abstain from the resolution to adopt the Report and Accounts to signal our concern. In addition, where we consider this is warranted, we may also withhold support from individual directors with responsibility (such as chair of a board sustainability committee or equivalent). This is applied to constituents of the MSCI World Index and FTSE 350. There were seven cases in 2015 where support was withheld over animal welfare concerns.

We recognize that practically all sustainability and governance issues represent collective problems and generally need collective solutions. Collaborative engagement is the process by which investors, and occasionally other stakeholders, band together (generally in loose coalitions) to pool communications resources and research to encourage companies to improve specific aspects of their environmental or social performance. The process has been institutionalized in a variety of ways, the most all-encompassing being via the PRI Collaboration Platform,[2] formerly known as the Engagement Clearinghouse, which provides a forum for signatories to discuss areas of collaboration and to organize collective activity. We engage via the PRI on topics such as shale gas, water scarcity, palm oil and human rights, as well as vote confirmation. We also engage through other organizations. For example, much of our work on climate change is conducted through the Institutional Investors Group on Climate Change (IIGCC) Corporate Programme,[3] which we chair.

Finally, we look to shape markets for sustainability. We advocate policy measures that support longer term, more sustainable capital markets. We aim to correct market failures such as a lack of corporate disclosure on ESG risks and climate change—at a national, EU, OECD and UN level—to improve long-term policy outcomes.

We also get involved as stakeholders in setting standards in a wide range of industry standards, for instance the Roundtable for Sustainable Palm Oil (RSPO) and the Extractive Industries Transparency Initiative (EITI). An area of current focus for us is the major farm animal welfare assurance labels, such as Red Tractor and RSPCA Assured. We believe they should extend their definition of stakeholders to include the investment community as many of their equivalent standards covering other topics already do.

Aviva Investor's approach to farm animal welfare

Why is farm animal welfare pertinent to Aviva Investors?

Farm animal welfare is an emergent ESG topic. It doesn't occupy as high a profile as more established topics, for example, executive pay or human rights. This may be due to a historical perception of it not being a material issue or simply because of the prevailing culture of shying away from some of the more industrial processes livestock goes through to get on our plates. Nonetheless, scrutiny of corporate performance on farm animal welfare provides useful insights into the culture and robustness of investee companies in several ways:

2 https://www.unpri.org/about/pri-teams/esg-engagements/collaboration-platform
3 http://www.iigcc.org/corporate

- **Governance insights.** How a company approaches the topic of farm animal welfare is an excellent proxy for the overall quality of corporate management and governance. Where farm animals form a significant part of the company's operations we expect management to have detailed knowledge of the various facets of farm animal welfare including the presence, adherence to and sanction flowing from breaches of the policy, antibiotic use and close confinement infrastructure.
- **Reputational risk.** The mismanagement of animal welfare standards in their own operations and in their supply chains exposes companies to reputational risk. In the UK, the horsemeat scandal shone the spotlight on the previously murky supply chains of food retailers and prompted Tesco to take out full-page adverts in a number of national newspapers to apologize. In the US, evidence of animal cruelty triggered the largest beef recall in US history, resulting in the bankruptcy of California-based Hallmark/Westland Meat Packing Company.
- **Regulatory risks and supply chain disruption.** There is potential for laggards to fall foul of legislation, as demonstrated by the EU legislation banning caged eggs. Despite a 12 year lead-in time many companies failed to prepare for the change. We saw poorly managed companies lose ground to those companies that had the foresight to move to free-range eggs throughout their supply chains in advance of this legislation.
- **Future proofing.** As long-term investors we expect oil and gas companies to adjust their strategy to mitigate catastrophic climate change. In a similar vein, food producers and retailers need to demonstrate, by their reporting and strategy, how they will address issues such as the greenhouse gas impact of agriculture, client demands for higher welfare products and protein diversity, and the World Health Authority's recent stance on both the carcinogenic impact of processed meat and the implications of factory farming for antibiotic resistance. The manner in which animals are treated and the welfare of these animals provide many important insights into companies' ability to identify, assess and respond to the present and future challenges facing the food industry.

The catalysts for change

The 2008 Tesco AGM Shareholder Resolution on chicken welfare planted the seed of animal welfare consideration at Aviva Investors. This seed germinated in 2012 with the launch of the Business Benchmark on Farm Animal Welfare (BBFAW),[4] which enabled us to put animal welfare issues firmly onto the spectrum of ESG issues that we consider in our investment process. The Benchmark moved farm animal welfare from being a relatively ad hoc consideration in our investment processes to one that we now consider as a standard part of our assessment of the ESG performance of global food companies. The Benchmark provides us with a

4 See Amos and Sullivan (2016), Chapter 13 by Nicky Amos and Rory Sullivan, and http://www.bbfaw.com/

credible, independent assessment of company performance, it identifies companies' strengths and weaknesses and—as it has started to be used by more and more investors—it is widely seen as the standard framework for the assessment of good and best practice in the food industry.

Integration of farm animal welfare into our investment research and decision-making

When our analysts and fund managers think about ESG issues, they want to understand the company's exposure to the issue, and the company's performance—in both relative and absolute terms—on the issue in question. That is, their assessment of risk relies on understanding both exposure and management quality.

The Benchmark enables us to analyse management quality in a systematic and consistent manner; all of the companies covered by the Benchmark are assessed using the same objective criteria in a credible, robust manner. The results are presented in the form of a ranking which enables us to identify those who manage the issue effectively and those who do not. It also enables us to compare individual companies.

Finally, the fact that the Benchmark is repeated on an annual basis is critical. Investment decision-making is as much about understanding trends and changes in performance as it is about assessing exposure and risk at a defined point in time. The annual Benchmark results allow us to understand whether companies are improving, stagnating or getting worse and to understand whether companies are responding to our engagement. From an internal perspective, it means that our analysts and fund managers have become more familiar with the Benchmark over time, and that they increasingly see the Benchmark as an important input to their decision-making.

Engagement on farm animal welfare

Our decision to engage with food companies on farm animal welfare has several potential triggers:

- The company's performance on the BBFAW ranking.
- A shareholder resolution on farm animal welfare at the companies' AGM. To date, most of these have been filed at US listed companies although the 2008 Tesco shareholder resolution was an important tipping point in UK debates around farm animal welfare.
- Our NGO campaign monitoring system identifies concerns at a particular company or group of companies.
- A routine engagement meeting with management (either where the company raises the issue or where we choose to raise the issue as part of a wider discussion around the management of ESG issues).
- Media stories exposing particular corporate practices or highlighting a new initiative. Tyson Foods is an example of where engagement was arranged

following both positive news flow on its decision to shift away from using human antibiotics, and concerns about the potential regulatory and media scrutiny that might result from undercover footage at a suppliers' farm.

Asking questions of senior management is a powerful way to effect change. During financial year 2015/2016 we engaged with 23 companies specifically on farm animal welfare. These included Whitbread, Tesco, Costco, Tiger Brands, Glanbia, Compass Group, Henan Shuanghui, Grupo Danone and Unilever. Alongside this farm animal welfare was raised as part of a broader meeting agenda with many more companies. Engagement is not always to raise concerns. Where a company has made significant progress we also engage to show our appreciation and explain how it impacts upon our view of the company. For example, we met with Greggs in 2015 to discuss their rise up the BBFAW rankings.

Farm animal welfare, as with most other sustainability and governance issues, is a collective problem and needs collective solutions. Since it was first proposed by its founding organizations Compassion in World Farming and the World Society for the Protection of Animals (now World Animal Protection), we have recognized the potential for BBFAW to be the game-changing intervention that is needed to put farm animal welfare on the agenda of mainstream investors. We have played an active role in the development of the Benchmark and in increasing investor awareness of the Benchmark. Among other activities, we have:

- Promoted the BBFAW investor statement via the PRI Collaboration Platform
- Helped inform the development of the evaluation methodology, by suggesting questions (or criteria) and commenting on the universe of companies proposed for inclusion in the Benchmark
- Hosted two roundtable events to encourage discussion and debate among investors
- Spoken at the 2014 report launch
- Reviewed and commented on a number of BBFAW publications
- Encouraged other investors to use the Benchmark
- Participated in the BBFAW-convened collaborative engagement programme, directed at encouraging high performing companies to maintain their efforts and encouraging poor performing companies to strengthen their management of farm animal welfare

Case study: Hormel

Hormel, a multinational manufacturer of consumer-branded food and meat products including Spam, is considered by us to face significant risks because of the perception of its poor assurance of product quality, sourcing practices, poor labour practices and its reliance on gestation crates for sows (which presents both reputational and operational risks, given the number of US states and countries, including the EU, legislating against their use).

At the 2015 AGM, a shareholder proposal was put forward requesting that the board report the risks associated with its position of indefinitely allowing gestation crates throughout its supply chain. Both of the major proxy voting research providers, ISS and Glass Lewis, issued AGM voting reports supporting the proposal on its economic merits. ISS and Glass Lewis looked at all the data surrounding the issue—including Hormel's statement in opposition—and both concluded that the ongoing use of gestation crates presented significant business risks, that Hormel had not adequately addressed those risks, and that the company should make additional disclosures about the issue. As ISS summarized, a vote in favour "...is warranted, as the company does not provide information about how it is evaluating and managing potential risks related to evolving regulatory and industry trends to shift away from the use of gestation crates".

We supported the shareholder resolution. We also discussed the matter with Hormel's management in person, highlighting the step changes in industry's and regulators' views on gestation cages, and asking when Hormel would take these market level changes into account. As a shareholder in Hormel, we emphasized that we were keen for Hormel to make a supply chain level commitment to phase out the use of gestation crates thus reducing the risk of Hormel being the poster child for outdated and outmoded infrastructure. This is an ongoing engagement.

Case study: antibiotic resistance

One key area of focus for Aviva Investors is antibiotic resistance. The World Health Organization recently warned that the world is fast approaching a "post antibiotic era", where routine operations will be life threatening and common infections would kill once again (WHO, 2014). A major cause of this threat is the misuse of antibiotics in livestock supply chains. Currently, an estimated 80% of antibiotics in the US are currently used for livestock; the corresponding figure for Europe is 50% (Jeremy Coller Foundation, 2016). This is contrary to the stereotypical perception of generous prescription of antibiotics by doctors as the main driver of resistance.

Aviva Investors has significant exposure to the pharmaceutical sector. Furthermore, our parent company, Aviva plc, offers health insurance, meaning that the issue is a very live concern for the Aviva business as a whole.

We have sought to take action on both the supply and demand sides of the antibiotics issue. On the supply side we are engaging with the biotechnology and pharmaceutical industry to stimulate research and development into new antibiotics. We are also focusing on the public policy arena to effect global change. We were pleased to see that antibiotic resistance took centre stage at the 2016 United Nations General Assembly and supported several related side events. At a UK level we have cultivated a good relationship with the Review on Antimicrobial Resistance team (AMR). As part of our Superbugs and SuperRisks initiative we hosted the Chair of the AMR, Lord Jim O'Neill, as keynote speaker at our inaugural investor event on antibiotic resistance: Superbugs and Super Risks—What impact will antibiotic resistance have on the capital markets?

In collaboration with Farm Animal Investor Risk and Return (FAIRR) and the Alliance to Save our Antibiotics we produced a briefing for investors: *Superbugs and Super Risks: The Investment Case for Action* (Wardle *et al.*, 2016). This was launched in London and New York and is a "how to guide" for engagement on this topic including a detailed list of questions for investors to ask of companies.

We have also collaborated with FAIRR on the demand side. In 2015 Aviva Investors became a founder signatory to the FAIRR initiative, which provides investors with publications and other materials to help them understand and manage farm animal welfare risks and opportunities. We were founder members of a $2 trillion coalition of 64 institutional investors, under the FAIRR umbrella, on the topic of antibiotic resistance. The coalition is calling upon ten of the biggest US and UK restaurant chains for an end to non-therapeutic use of antibiotics important to human health in their global meat and poultry supply chains. The investor coalition is concerned that a failure to confront irresponsible antibiotic use poses significant risks to our investment portfolio. This includes the substantial risk of regulation as antibiotic overuse has increasingly become a target for stricter regulation in both the EU and US and further regulation is highly likely. There is also the reputational risk of contributing to a global threat to human health which currently kills an estimated 700,000 people per year.

Wider reflections

Investors—individually and collectively—have a critical role to play in encouraging higher standards of corporate governance and corporate responsibility (or sustainability) in the companies in which they invest. As such, they are a key stakeholder in efforts to encourage companies to better manage ESG issues in the round and to encourage companies to improve their management of specific issues.

BBFAW has changed the conversation between us and our investee companies and has succeeded in adding farm welfare to the spectrum of ESG issues that are considered by investors. So why has it succeeded? Or, more precisely, how has it succeeded where previous efforts to engage investors on farm animal welfare have had relatively little success? In my view there are five factors that have been of particular importance.

First, BBFAW has always sought to be a tool for investors. It has consistently engaged with investors to understand the information that investors are interested in, and to ensure that its outputs are relevant to investors. For example, the Benchmark structure and questions were developed with the investment community and are reviewed annually in conjunction with the investment community. The BBFAW assessment framework—policies, governance, objectives and targets, management systems, performance—aligns with the way in which investors analyse and assess companies' practices and performance on any ESG issue. In response to feedback from investors, the BBFAW provides investors with web-based access to individual company summary reports highlighting trends in performance as well as comparative data based on the average sector scores.

Similarly, the universe of companies has been designed with investors' needs in mind. BBFAW has not just focused on the largest food companies but has made sure to include those companies that are relevant to investors. For example, the Benchmark covers Waitrose which, while not one of the largest retailers, is a key comparator (or reference) for investors interested in the UK retail sector.

Beyond the Benchmark, BBFAW has also produced a series of briefing notes for investors on relevant issues. Examples include briefing notes on animal welfare issues such as overuse of antibiotics (Bond and Jewell, 2014) and farmed fish (Cooke, 2016). They also include practical guidance notes for companies on issues such as disclosure (Sullivan and Amos, 2015), and for investors on farm animal welfare-related legislation (Stevenson, 2014), company engagement on farm animal welfare (Sullivan *et al.*, 2015) and the investment case for farm animal welfare (Sullivan *et al.*, 2012).

Second, BBFAW's core deliverable is a highly credible and robust Benchmark. The assessment methodology is transparent, the Benchmark is conducted by highly experienced and trained business and animal welfare specialists, and the Benchmark has comprehensive review processes including a company review stage. Importantly, despite being funded by Compassion in World Farming and World Animal Protection, the Benchmark is independent of both.

Third, the Benchmark addresses the core obstacle to investors taking account of farm animal welfare in their investment processes by enabling investors to quickly and easily compare companies with others in their sector. BBFAW allows greater comparison by the creation of a robust and authoritative benchmark of corporate farm animal welfare performance, with results publicly available. By democratizing this data BBFAW also helps give the public access to knowledge about businesses' performance both as individual investors and more generally as stakeholders. Of critical importance has been the fact that the Benchmark is repeated annually, thereby enabling the progress of companies over time to be assessed.

Fourth, BBFAW has actively engaged with the sell-side and with responsible investment research organizations to raise their awareness of farm animal welfare and to encourage them to pay attention to the issue in their research processes and in the advice they offer to their clients. This is important because fund managers (or investment managers) place considerable credence in the opinions of brokers or sell-side analysts. Therefore, brokers' views on farm animal welfare issues are influential. Brokers have attended BBFAW report launches and events, and a number have issued notes on the issue of farm animal welfare. While there is a long way to go, this interest suggests that farm animal welfare is starting to be taken seriously as an investment issue. Specialist responsible investment research providers are also important influences. Their views on the scope of ESG issues (specifically, whether farm animal welfare is an important ESG issue) and the research they conduct on farm animal welfare have an important influence on the weight assigned by investment managers in their company analysis.

Fifth, BBFAW has provided an important signal to companies and to the wider investment market. For example, when companies question why we are asking them whether farm animal welfare is on the board agenda and embedded into corporate strategy, we point them to the BBFAW Global Investor Statement on Farm Animal Welfare which currently has over 20 investor signatories representing over £1.5 trillion in assets under management. Aviva Investors was proud to be a founding signatory to this, the world's first investor statement on farm animal welfare, and we consider it a useful way of signalling not only our interest and intent to the capital markets, but also that this is an issue that many other investors are also concerned about and rapidly becoming a mainstream investor concern.

Ultimately, BBFAW has catalysed change within the investment community by presenting farm animal welfare in terms that are relevant to investors, aligning with investors' interests and, critically, removing the excuses (lack of practical tools, lack of consensus, lack of disclosure) that investors have hid behind. There is, of course, much to be done. However, the Business Benchmark on Farm Animal Welfare and strong and consistent support provided by its founders, Compassion in World Farming and World Animal Protection, show how the influence and enthusiasm of a key stakeholder group—in this case, the investment community—can be harnessed in support of the goal of raising company practices and performance on farm animal welfare.

References

Amos, N. & Sullivan, R. (2016). *The Business Benchmark on Farm Animal Welfare: 2015 Report*. London: BBFAW.

Bond, V. & Jewell, J. (2014). *The Impact of Antibiotic Use in Animals on Human Health and Animal Welfare*. BBFAW Investor Briefing No.17. London: BBFAW.

Cooke, M. (2016). *Animal Welfare in Farmed Fish*. BBFAW Investor Briefing No. 23. London: BBFAW.

Jeremy Coller Foundation (2016). Human Consequences of Animal Factory Farming. Retrieved from http://www.jeremycollerfoundation.org/wp-content/uploads/2016/12/Animal_Factory_Farming_-_pitchbook_2016_online.pdf

Stevenson, P. (2014). *Farm Animal Welfare: The Regulatory and Policy Landscape*. BBFAW Investor Briefing No.13. London: BBFAW.

Sullivan, R. & Amos, N. (2015). *Farm Animal Welfare Disclosure Framework*. BBFAW Investor Briefing No. 18. London: BBFAW.

Sullivan, R., Ngo, M. & Amos, N. (2012). *Farm Animal Welfare as an Investment Issue*. BBFAW Investor Briefing No.4. London: BBFAW.

Sullivan, R., Amos, N. & Herron, A. (2015). *Engagement on Farm Animal Welfare: A User's Guide*. BBFAW Investor Briefing No. 19. London: BBFAW.

Wardle, R., Rose, E. & Herron, A. (2016). *Superbugs and Super Risks: The Investment Case for Action*. FAIRR, Aviva Investors & Alliance to Save Our Antibiotics. Retrieved from http://www.fairr.org/wp-content/uploads/Superbugs-and-Super-Risks-The-Investment-Case-for-Action-Briefing-November-2016.pdf

World Health Organization (WHO) (2014). *Antimicrobial Resistance: Global Report on Surveillance*. Retrieved from http://www.who.int/drugresistance/documents/surveillance report/en/

10 Investor case study

BNP Paribas Investment Partners

Helena Viñes Fiestas

BNP PARIBAS INVESTMENT PARTNERS, FRANCE

Introduction: responsible investment at BNP Paribas Investment Partners

BNP Paribas Investment Partners is the dedicated, autonomous asset management business of the BNP Paribas Group. It has US$590 billion of assets in assets under management (as of 30 June 2016). It offers institutional (e.g. pension funds, sovereign wealth funds) and retail (or individual) clients around the world a wide scope of asset management services across the full range of asset classes.

As a long-term global asset manager, BNP Paribas Investment Partners is committed to being a responsible investor in all aspects of its business. We believe in responsible practices for ourselves, and for the companies in which we invest. We are a signatory to the UN-backed Principles for Responsible Investment (PRI) and we ensure that our activities align with the BNP Paribas Group's commitment to corporate responsibility and sustainable development.

Consistent with our duty to act in the best long-term interests of our clients, our responsible investment policy commits us to incorporating environmental, social and governance (ESG) factors into our investment decision-making and ownership practices.

Helping our clients achieve their investment objectives and protecting their interests

We are aware that ESG issues may impact the value and reputation of companies in which we invest. We are committed to incorporating ESG standards in our investment criteria to protect the value of their investment in line with our fiduciary duty to help our clients achieve their investment objectives and protect their interests.

For corporate issuers, these ESG standards are based on the ten principles of the United Nations Global Compact. This shared framework is recognized around the world and applies to all industry sectors, based on the international conventions in the areas of human rights, labour standards, environmental stewardship and anti-corruption. We expect companies to comply with these principles, and companies that violate one or more principles may be excluded, while those at risk of breaching them are closely monitored.

We supplement the United Nations Global Compact principles with our own investment criteria for potentially controversial sectors and products, including palm oil, wood pulp, nuclear power stations, coal-fired power stations, controversial weapons, asbestos, mining, oil sands and agriculture. The criteria for these sectors and products are based on international conventions and regulations, BNP Paribas Group CSR Policies and voluntary industry standards. In each sector, we highlight mandatory requirements which have to be met for BNP Paribas Investment Partners to invest and evaluate criteria which provide a framework for further analysis and dialogue with companies.

Our commitment as shareholders

Voting at general shareholder meetings is an integral part of our investment responsibilities and a key component of the dialogue with companies in which we invest on behalf of our clients. By exercising our voting rights, we aim to enhance the long-term value of our shareholdings and foster corporate governance best practices, social responsibility and environmental stewardship.

Promoting and developing environmental, social and governance practices

We work closely with a range of organizations dedicated to responsible investment with the aim of jointly promoting sustainability and improving our shared practices. These include the United Nations-supported Principles for Responsible Investment (PRI), the Institutional Investors Group on Climate Change (IIGCC), French Asset Management Association (AFG), the European Fund and Asset Management Association (EFAMA), the Forum pour l'Investissement Responsable (FIR, a French organization that promotes sustainable and responsible investment), the United Nations Environment Programme Finance Initiative (UNEP FI) and the International Corporate Governance Network (ICGN).

Our implementation

We created a dedicated Sustainability Research Team more than 15 years ago. Since then, the team has expanded, and is in charge of the development and implementation of our responsible investment policy, including in-depth research. The team carries out systematic research on the issuers held in our investment portfolios; it follows and monitors companies throughout the year, and at least once a year reviews companies' ESG performance scores against relevant sector and sub-sector benchmarks.

The results of this research are disseminated to all of our investment centres. ESG correspondents have been appointed in these teams, in order to raise awareness and to facilitate the integration of this research into our wider investment research and decision-making processes.

The Sustainability Research Team is also in charge of the Stewardship Strategy. We fully adhere to the idea that stewardship is more than just voting. This is why we have developed an engagement strategy and appointed a Proxy Voting Committee (PVC). It has developed a proactive strategy to maximize its impact as a good steward of assets, involving a clear communication and disclosure policy. Our engagement strategy sets our current and medium-term priorities for our dialogues with our investee companies.

Analysts from the Sustainability Research Team run engagement actions directly with investee companies in order to encourage better ESG practices and risk management. We engage with companies to address a wide range of issues, but with a particular emphasis on human rights, climate change and corporate governance. Engagement activities are carried out individually but also in conjunction with other investors or as part of our active membership of different associations. For example, we signed and became an active founding member of the Institutional Investor Group on Climate Change (IIGCC) in 2003 and of the United Nations-supported Principles for Responsible Investment (PRI) in 2006.

Lastly, we aim to help improve public policy frameworks for sustainability and responsible investment. To this end, we work alongside our peers to foster sustainable and responsible investment in a series of initiatives and working groups such as the policy working group at IIGCC.[1]

The investment case for farm animal welfare

There are various reasons why we as an investor are concerned about farm animal welfare. The first is that there are clear linkages between food production processes and key product parameters such as quality, taste and safety. The intensification of food production has brought many benefits, not least in terms of the volume of food that is produced each year. However, it has also become clear that intensification raises a whole series of issues, for the welfare of the animals kept in these systems, for product quality and for human health. We are interested in farm animal welfare both because of its direct impact on these product parameters—we discuss these below—and because of what company performance on farm animal welfare might tell us about companies' management of these wider issues.

When assessing investment risk and opportunity, we do not confine our attention simply to impacts on product quality, taste and safety. We recognize that these impacts have knock-on effects across the companies in which we are invested. First, they affect corporate brand and reputation; we have seen many companies suffer reputational damage as a result of being "named and shamed" in high profile media campaigns resulting from food scares/scandals or from poor farm animal welfare practices. This is also a collective reputation issue. High profile scandals undermine not only the brands of the firms involved but they also affect trust in the food industry as a whole. Second, they can create pressure for regulatory action. The progressive tightening of European Union, in particular, and US legislation on farm animal welfare has increased costs for food producers

1 http://www.iigcc.org/programmes/programme/policy

both in terms of increased capital expenditures and in terms of monitoring and oversight processes. Third, consumer demand for higher welfare products has grown, often catalysed by media stories and NGO campaigns. This creates opportunities for companies to access new markets and customers, and to grow existing markets as a result of adopting higher welfare standards. It has also meant that companies have faced pressure to help their clients respond to these consumer demands; an example is the pressure on food producers to meet the corporate responsibility standards of the retailers that they supply.

Of taste, quality and human health: animal welfare and business risk

We believe that safety, health and nutrition are, alongside responsible and sustainable sourcing, undoubtedly the number one responsibility and the most relevant ESG risk for the food industry. It was these issues that first catalysed our interest in farm animal welfare. We found, and continue to find, a whole series of relationships between farm animal welfare and the food industry's ability to deliver on its core objectives; sometimes these are causal, sometimes these are indirect, sometimes they are indicative of other aspects of corporate practice.

When we look at safety, health and nutrition risks in the food industry, we find that the conditions under which animals are reared, how they are fed, treated, transported and finally slaughtered have a direct impact on the quality and safety of the meat, dairy and eggs that we eat. For example:

- About 75% of all new infectious diseases affecting humans over the past 10 years were caused by bacteria, viruses and other pathogens that started in animals and animal products.[2] While not all of these resulted from poor animal welfare, there is evidence that intensive farm production plays a role (D'Silva, 2006; Sims, 2007; EFSA, 2009).
- Since 2009 the number of food, beverage and private label food retail alerts of the top 47 companies within Europe and North America has almost tripled, with food-borne pathogens accounting for 33% of all recall cases (Societe Generale Cross Asset Research, 2013).[3]
- Significant human health issues result from intensive farming. Of particular concern are the risks associated with common food-borne infections such as salmonella, campylobacter and *E. coli*, and the risks associated with the manner in which animals are fed: for example the use of hormone growth promoters. The US Centers for Disease Control and Prevention estimates that, each year, roughly one in six Americans become ill, 128,000 are hospitalized and 3,000 die from food-borne diseases.[4]

2 WHO. 10 Facts on food safety. Retrieved from http://www.who.int/features/factfiles/food_safety/facts/en/index3.html

3 The SG SRI Cross Asset Research provides us with an annual update of the product recalls and safety incidents of food companies.

4 US Centers for Disease Control and Prevention. Retrieved from https://www.cdc.gov/foodborneburden/

- Poor animal welfare can reduce the taste, tenderness, colour and quality of meat. Scientific evidence shows that, for example, when an animal is stressed before and during slaughter, or subjected to fighting in the pens, the quality and taste of the meat are reduced (FAO, 2001). For example, stress, pre-slaughter and post-slaughter handling of animals can cause pale soft exudative (PSE) and dark firm dry (DFD) meats; PSE and DFD are two of the major quality defects facing the meat industry and its profitability (Adzitey and Nurul, 2011).
- High-density animal production processes have contributed to the emergence of new, often antibiotic-resistant diseases. To help prevent disease (and sometimes to promote weight-gain) associated with intensive farming, animals are given sub-therapeutic doses of antibiotics. Concerned by increasing animal antibiotic resistance—which allegedly causes around 23,000 deaths each year in the US alone[5]—in May 2016 the US Food and Drug Administration (FDA) issued a new requirement for pharmaceutical companies to report the amounts of antibiotics sold to the food-producing livestock industry as a first step towards monitoring consumption (US FDA, 2016). In the European Union the use of substances having a hormonal action for growth promotion in farm animals is prohibited, but that is not the case elsewhere. In the US and Canada, while permitted (except for bovine growth hormones—rBGH), organic meats and poultry have experienced the fastest growth within the agricultural sector.

The Business Benchmark on Farm Animal Welfare

While farm animal welfare has been an important focus in our investment research into the food industry for a number of years, our ability to integrate the issue systematically into our research has been constrained by both weaknesses in corporate disclosures on farm animal welfare and by the lack of a standardized framework or assessment tool that we can use to make meaningful comparisons between companies' practices or performance. This has changed with the introduction of the Business Benchmark on Farm Animal Welfare.[6] Since its launch in 2012, the Benchmark has provided us, investors, with a standard framework against which they can assess global food companies on their farm animal welfare practices, processes and performance. Its annual report (e.g. Amos and Sullivan, 2016) analyses the practices and performance of almost 100 global companies, ranking them from those where farm animal welfare is fully integrated into their business practices and processes, through to those that provide little or no information on their approach to farm animal welfare. Investors can also access company-specific assessments that provide an evaluation of each company's strengths and weaknesses, that analyse trends in company

5 US Centers for Disease Control and Prevention. Retrieved from https://www.cdc.gov/drugresistance/

6 See, further, Amos and Sullivan (2016). See, also, Chapter 13 and http://www.bbfaw.com/

performance, and that discuss the company's engagement with stakeholders on the issue of farm animal welfare.

We have actively supported and promoted the Business Benchmark on Farm Animal Welfare since its inception in 2012. We have actively encouraged investors to support the Benchmark, we have posted details of the Benchmark to the PRI Clearinghouse, and we have spoken about it at different conferences and roundtables. In 2016, we were delighted to become founding signatories to the Global Investor Statement on Farm Animal Welfare, the first ever investor-backed global statement on farm animal welfare (BBFAW, 2016).

We use the Business Benchmark on Farm Animal Welfare in two ways. First, it is now a standard input to our investment research process. Our Sustainability Research Team analyses all BNPP IP investee companies annually in terms of their ESG performance, giving each a score of between 0 and 100. Companies are benchmarked against a set of ESG indicators developed internally, and each benchmark will group companies according to their activities, business model, size and where they are listed. Our ESG food sector analysis—with some differences depending on whether it is a retailer, a restaurant, a food producer or a food ingredient company—focuses on two areas (a) safety, health and nutrition; and (b) responsible and sustainable sourcing. Animal welfare is a consideration in both of these areas. For example, in supply chain management, our product safety management score for food producers includes three areas: policies and leadership, implementation in production and implementation at suppliers. We use the BBFAW data to inform our assessments of company performance on these issues. Similarly, on safety and product quality, we assess whether or not the company has a clear position on the reduction or avoidance of antibiotics for prophylactic use or whether or not they avoid growth-promoting substances.

The second way we use the Benchmark is in our engagement. We engage with food companies annually as part of our annual review on ESG practices. Since 2012, we have raised farm animal welfare with those companies that have been ranked in the lowest tiers of the Benchmark, and we have encouraged them to improve their practices, performance and disclosures on farm animal welfare. In May 2015, alongside six other investors and with the support of the BBFAW Secretariat, we committed to work collectively on encouraging global food companies to strengthen their management systems and processes on farm animal welfare. The programme involved writing to leading companies in the Benchmark to commend them for their performance, and to poor performers to encourage them to improve. This engagement programme continued in 2016 (having increased to 19 participating investors), supplementing these letters with face to face meetings with companies. By joining the collaborative engagement we aim to join forces with our peers and to formalize our engagement in this area.

Closing comments

Farm animal welfare can no longer be seen as a niche ethical issue, or as simply a matter for ethical investment funds. It is an issue that is relevant right across the food industry, and is one that investors need to pay attention to in their investment research and in their engagement with companies. However, the fact that it is important does not mean that, from an investment perspective, it should be treated as a stand-alone issue. Of course, the issue is important in and of itself. However, it is also important because it is often an indicator of other, deeper issues (for example, the use of antibiotics to prop up intensive production systems) and as an indicator of the wider quality of management within food companies.

The key contribution of the Business Benchmark on Farm Animal Welfare has been that it has enabled us to translate animal welfare into terms and into a tool that is relevant to the way in which investors look at companies; its focus on policies, governance, objectives and targets, management systems and performance aligns with the way in which investors analyse and assess companies' practices and performance on any ESG issue. By enabling investors to quickly and easily compare companies with others in their sector, and by providing annual updates, BBFAW aligns directly with the way in which we look to analyse and assess companies.

The work of the Business Benchmark, and the support provided by the wider investment community, is starting to drive real change. To provide just one example, a growing number of the food companies we invest in have identified farm animal welfare as presenting significant downside business risks. These include risks to brand and reputation as a result of being "named and shamed" in high profile media campaigns and the risks of food scares and scandals over alleged poor farm animal welfare practices. Others have started to talk about the business opportunities, including the ability to access new markets and customers, the ability to grow existing markets, and the need to respond to supplier expectations and demands.

References

Adzitey, F. & Nurul, H. (2011). Pale soft exudative (PSE) and dark firm dry (DFD) meats. *International Food Research Journal*, 18, 11-20.

Amos, N. & Sullivan, R. (2016). *The Business Benchmark on Farm Animal Welfare: 2015 Report*. London: BBFAW.

Business Benchmark on Farm Animal Welfare (BBFAW) (2016, May 23). *Investor Statement on Farm Animal Welfare.* Retrieved from https://www.bbfaw.com/media/1435/investor-statement-on-farm-animal-welfare.pdf

D'Silva, J. (2006). Adverse impact of industrial animal agriculture on the health and welfare of farmed animals. *Integrative Zoology*, 1(1), 53-58. doi: 10.1111/j.1749-4877.2006.00013.x

EFSA (European Food Safety Authority) (2009). *Scientific Report of EFSA. Effects of Farming Systems on Dairy Cow Welfare and Disease: Report of the Panel on Animal Health and Welfare.* Retrieved from http://www.fao.org/fileadmin/user_upload/animalwelfare/EFSA%20Report%20on%20dairy%20cow%20welfare%20final.pdf

Food and Agriculture Organization (FAO) (2001). *Guidelines for Humane Handling, Transport and Slaughter of Livestock*. Bangkok, Thailand: FAO.

Sims, L.D. (2007). *Risks Associated with Poultry Production Systems*. Palm Cove, Australia: Asia Pacific Veterinary Information Services. Retrieved from http://www.fao.org/Ag/againfo/home/events/bangkok2007/docs/part2/2_1.pdf

Societe Generale Cross Asset Research (2013). *Food Safety: Sorting the Wheat from the Chaff*. Paris: Societe Generale Cross Asset Research.

U.S. Food & Drugs Administration (2016, May 10). FDA issues rule for data collection of antimicrobial sales and distribution by animal species. Press release. Retrieved from https://www.fda.gov/NewsEvents/Newsroom/PressAnnouncements/ucm500149.htm

11 Bringing farm animal welfare to the consumer's plate

Transparency, labelling and consumer education

Minna Autio

UNIVERSITY OF HELSINKI, FINLAND

Jaakko Autio

UNIVERSITY OF HELSINKI, FINLAND

Ari Kuismin

AALTO UNIVERSITY SCHOOL OF BUSINESS, FINLAND

Brigit Ramsingh

UNIVERSITY OF CENTRAL LANCASHIRE, UK

Eliisa Kylkilahti

UNIVERSITY OF HELSINKI, FINLAND

Anna Valros

UNIVERSITY OF HELSINKI, FINLAND

Introduction

The welfare of farm animals (which includes cattle, pigs, sheep, goats and poultry) has become a high profile issue in Western societies. Food crises such as mad cow disease (BSE) in the early 1990s, bird flu A(H7N9) in the 2000s and, most recently, the 2013 horsemeat scandal (Jaskari *et al.* 2015) have raised the awareness of global health risks and ethical issues related to food production and consumption. Media coverage of animals' living conditions and of animal slaughter practices has further raised the profile of animal welfare (Evans and Miele, 2012; Jokinen *et al.*, 2012).

These high profile cases—as well as wider debates around the ethics of farm animal welfare, the environmental impacts of meat production and the health effects of meat consumption—have catalysed at times intense discussions about how individual consumers and society as a whole should act. The manner in which different stakeholders think about solutions to the "problem of farm animal welfare" is critically dependent on their views on the ethical, environmental and nutritional issues at stake (see, for example, the diverse views and arguments advanced in de Bakker and Dagevos, 2012; Diamond, 1978; Graça *et al.*, 2015;

Miele *et al.*, 2013; Cembalo *et al.*, 2016; Sandøe *et al.*, 2003; Springmann *et al.*, 2016), on the way in which they define the "problem" and on the views they hold about the roles, responsibilities and influence of different actors. As a result of these divergent views, a whole series of solutions have been advanced, including (among many others): completely eliminating meat and animal-derived products from diets; significantly reducing the volume of meat consumed; raising the welfare standards of animals farmed for food; encouraging sales of higher welfare products; better product labelling; and transitioning away from animal-based proteins to meat produced in laboratories (see, for example, de Bakker and Dagevos, 2012; Dilworth and McGregor, 2015; Jallinoja *et al.*, 2016; Vainio *et al.*, 2016).

These and other solutions may face practical challenges. For example, they may have economic and social impacts on the livelihoods of farmers and food businesses, they may also have negative environmental impacts, or they may have adverse or unknown effects on public health. Even if these challenges could be addressed, the proponents of these solutions then need to consider how they can change consumer preferences. This can be described in very simple terms: could consumers be persuaded to give up tasty beef and delicious tandoori chicken meals, or could they be persuaded to replace meat with new plant protein food made of oats and beans? Put another way, if the aim is to change consumers' eating habits, we must first start by understanding their views and their motivations, and locating these in the context of individual and collective views on issues such as animal welfare and the use of animals for food, the relationship between farming and farm animal welfare, the economic and societal importance of farming and of farmed animals, and ideas of place, location and landscape.

In this chapter, we explore the potential for food labelling to change or influence Finnish consumers' views on animal welfare and their food choices. Our central argument is that labelling can play an important role in changing patterns of food consumption (in this case, encouraging the consumption of meat farmed to higher welfare standards) but only where such labelling aligns with the issues that are of concern to consumers (e.g. produced in Finland) and where labelling is implemented as part of wider processes of consumer education and awareness raising.

Consumers' views on farm animal welfare: between meat and hot pot

As Miele *et al.* (2013, p. 22) have pointed out, the scientific study of animal welfare is a relatively young but well-established scientific discipline. The authors argue that it is generally accepted that animal welfare is about *the animal itself*, and the increasing integration of biological sciences is contributing towards a greater understanding of the link between the animal's biology (e.g. species-typical behaviour and nutrition), its wellbeing and objective assessments of welfare. However, while animal welfare is increasingly focused on the individual animal, research in the social sciences suggests that consumers do not share this perspective. Instead, consumers tend to position welfare issues among broader ethical and value-laden conceptions of the human–animal relationship, such as pets and their wellbeing (Kylkilahti *et al.*, 2016; Miele *et al.*, 2011).

The increased media and public attention focused on animal welfare has stimulated discussions on animal rights and suffering. These have covered issues such as beating animals, raising chickens in cages, abnormal animal behaviours and inhumane treatment in slaughtering, all of which are well-known issues in large-scale food production (e.g. Kupsala *et al.*, 2015). While these debates have led to increases in sales of organic and higher animal welfare products such as free-range eggs, the reality is that most meat continues to be produced intensively, where legislation and regulations define the welfare standards that are expected to be achieved.

Although the issues of farm animal welfare are increasingly recognized in Western consumer cultures, studies have also shown that consumers do not necessarily show any affinity towards animal wellbeing (e.g. Davidson *et al.* 2003; Schröder and McEachern 2004). For example, Evans and Miele (2012) have noted that eating meat and the use of animals for food are often taken for granted in certain affluent Western societies. They also argue that the main reason why consumers do not take animal welfare "seriously" is that consumers do not recognize or acknowledge the connection between food (meat) and its origins (animal). Expressed another way, people "de-animalize" the meat (Buller and Cesar, 2007). For example, a living pig (animal) is transformed first to carcass (dead meat) and then to pork ribs and bacon (food ingredients). The journey of buying and eating meat for consumers usually begins in supermarkets where they choose, for example, between steak (beef) and chops (lamb). Furthermore, animal flesh is often sold in products using culturally familiar names (e.g. Lancashire hotpot, Karelian stew) which blur the distinction between living animal and "dead" meat.

Another issue is that the majority of Western consumers' knowledge of farm animals' living conditions is no longer based on personal experience. Most people now live in urban environments and their understanding of animal welfare is based on information from the television, the internet, newspapers and social media, rather than on knowledge gained from visiting farms and seeing living animals (Evans and Miele, 2012; Vanhonacker and Verbeke, 2014). In addition, intensive farming techniques generally involve raising animals out of sight, for example inside cowsheds and piggeries. The consequence is that more people interact with animals through zoos and through the lives of their pets, rather than through farming and the lives of farm animals.

Despite these barriers to greater public understanding, empathetic attitudes towards animal rights have strengthened in the Western world (Franklin, 1999). Recent academic studies suggest that consumers are willing to pay more for higher welfare in animal-based products (e.g. Napolitano *et al.*, 2010), that consumers with pro-environmental attitudes are also concerned about the wellbeing of farm animals (e.g. Vanhonacker and Verbeke, 2014), and that some consumers are transitioning from meat consumption to plant-based diets as part of wider moves towards more sustainable consumption (Vinnari and Vinnari, 2014; Jallinoja *et al.*, 2016; Vainio *et al.*, 2016).

Despite this, many people, if they can afford it, continue to eat meat on a daily basis. As Harrington (1991) indicated 25 years ago, the majority of consumers have little interest in production systems' effect on animal wellbeing. There are many countries where there is limited consumer demand for higher welfare meat products (Lusk, 2011), higher welfare products remain a niche market in most countries, and also those few consumers who buy meat directly from farmers' markets or from farms are engaged in a niche activity. Therefore, the route whereby meat products go from the farm to the dinner table is rather difficult to perceive and trace for many consumers; consumers do not see the processes of farming, slaughtering, cutting or packing, but they tend to assume that transportation and other practices are done following the rules and regulations imposed by animal welfare legislation.

Food labelling: communication and animal welfare

Consumers' understanding of the path from farm-to-fork is not particularly helped by the complicated EU legislative frameworks which govern animals on farm, animals as food and the information allowed on food labels. The relevant EU legislation which exists to address animal products (albeit from more of a human-health and food safety perspective) includes the so-called "Hygiene Package" (consisting of EU Regulations EC 852/2004, EC 853/2004 and EC 854/2004) and the General Food Law Regulation (EC 178/2002), which enshrines the "farm-to-fork" concept into law and places responsibility on the food business for things like traceability of the food product (Heyder *et al.*, 2010).

Country-of-Origin Labelling, or "COOL labelling", dictates how production and processing must be clearly presented to consumers to avoid any uncertainty. For example, bacon that contains pork from Denmark but has undergone significant processing in another country such as the UK, must indicate this on the label, for example, phrased as "Produced in Britain using Danish Pork". Earlier regulation of COOL labelling was replaced by the recently introduced Food Information to Consumers (or the FIC) EU Regulation 1169/2011. The FIC is a broad piece of legislation which also covers allergen information and nutritional labelling. It is expected that the COOL regulations will either remain the same or possibly become more stringent to avoid any issues of food fraud particularly involving blended meat products.

More directly related to animal welfare, however, the EU signed in 1998 its Council Directive 98/58/EC Concerning the Protection of Animals kept for Farming Purposes, which came into effect in 2009. This provides a baseline for animal welfare standards across the EU, although EU Member States can set stricter standards within their own country. This ability to set stricter standards has opened up many opportunities for the meat industry to appeal to broader markets of concerned consumers, but it has also resulted in a wide array of logos and labelling marks indicating varying levels of animal welfare, along with standards and logos on a variety of other food issues that often get bundled together with animal welfare such as organic, fair trade and sustainability (Grunert *et al.*, 2014; Heerwagen *et al.*, 2015).

Beyond the legislative requirements, there are independent body or industry-driven standards circulating in the European market which are able to go beyond the minimum standards required by the EU. These are identifiable to consumers often in the form of logos appearing on the label and packaging. The existing animal welfare labels in Europe include, for example, the Danish label (Dyrenes Beskyttelse), Beter Leven in the Netherlands, Label Rouge in France, Krav in Sweden, and the Freedom Food label developed by the UK Royal Society for the Prevention of Cruelty to Animals (RSPCA) (Heerwagen *et al.*, 2015). There are also industry standards and labels which cover animal welfare as part of wider requirements such as food safety. For example, the UK Red Tractor scheme covers all farm products including vegetable and dairy, food quality and safety, animal disease contingency plans and quality management systems. It also includes some farm welfare conditions, for example hatchery conditions for chicks and untethered exercise for cows and lambs (Krieger and Schiefer, 2004). In Finland, the only national quality system concerning animal welfare is the industry-driven Laatuvastuu (quality responsibility) that focuses on responsible pork production. This certification was created by the Association for Animal Health ETT, and was approved as a national quality system by the Finnish Food Safety Authority (EVIRA) in 2013 (Kaljonen, 2016).

To complicate matters further, the scope of organic logos and labelling sometimes overlaps with animal welfare standards. Organic is often presumed by consumers to mean that foods are minimally processed without the addition of chemicals, fertilizers in the soil or hormones in meat, and that there is a certain degree of attention to animal welfare, alongside a commitment to sustainable production along the food chain (Makatouni, 2002). Not all logos appearing on food labels are created equally, however, and the level of organic purity or degree of animal welfare may be different. In 2010, the European Union (EU) introduced a mandatory logo for organic foods in order to make the identification of organic products easier for consumers (Janssen and Hamm, 2012). The EU logo became mandatory for all pre-packaged organic produce within the EU; such products must now have at least 95% organic ingredients and the ingredients not grown organically must be listed on the label (European Commission, 2007). The "Euro-leaf" logo is meant to symbolize the marriage of "Europe" (the stars derived from the European flag) and "Nature" indicated by a stylized leaf and the pale green colour, and also meant to represent high standards of animal welfare (European Commission, 2016). The animal welfare specifications indicate that farm animals must be "freely grazing in open-air" and treated "according to enhanced animal welfare conditions" and (perhaps somewhat vaguely) ensuring 100% organic feed, although in some cases the use of "minimal additives and processing aids" is permitted (European Commission, 2007). The United Kingdom's Soil Association has produced organic standards for food destined for human consumption and meets (or in some cases exceeds) the minimum standards of the EU's legislation.

The wide array of available logos and underlying standards in the EU means that it is difficult for consumers to differentiate between logos (even those directly focused on animal welfare), let alone to understand the animal welfare standards or performance that underpin terms such as "organic" and "sustainable" (Ramsingh, 2017). Research suggests that consumers tend to conflate these terms and assume that higher animal welfare, higher quality and safer food are all related, and that products that perform well on one dimension will also perform well on the others (Harper and Makatoumi, 2002; Grunert *et al.*, 2014).

European Union, Welfare Quality® assessment and consumers

Changing consumer attitudes towards farm animals and meat production have highlighted the need to strengthen the dialogue between producers, legislation, trade and consumers. Labelling has been identified as one tool that can be used to structure this dialogue although, reflecting the discussion above about the problems with multiple labels creating confusion for customers, the EU concluded that it needed to develop a common strategy and standards on the European level. Starting in 2004, the European Commission funded a Welfare Quality® research programme (which ran from 2004 to 2009) to develop European standards for on-farm welfare assessment and product information systems, as well as practical strategies for improving animal welfare (Evans and Miele, 2007; Miele and Kjærnes, 2009).

The Welfare Quality® research programme was designed to enable an open dialogue between animal welfare scientists, consumers, producers and other stakeholders (Miele *et al.*, 2011). When the research programme was launched in 2004, consumers' viewpoints on farm animal welfare were studied by conducting focus group discussions in European countries such as the UK, the Netherlands, Norway, Sweden, Hungary, France and Italy (Evans and Miele, 2012). The use of focus groups to produce information on consumers' thinking was based on the idea that researchers wanted to explore the opinions of "ordinary" consumers rather than of individuals who were already highly motivated on animal welfare issues (Evans and Miele, 2008, p. 13).

The central aim of the Welfare Quality® research programme was to develop an effective welfare assessment framework that would both reflect the understanding of animal welfare scientists, and also be accepted by the public and other interest groups. As described by Blokhuis *et al.* (2010), the Welfare Quality® research programme attempted to deliver reliable, science-based and understandable production information on the wellbeing of poultry, pigs and cattle. As a result of dialogue between different stakeholders, the research programme proposed a farm animal welfare assessment framework comprising four high-level principles and 12 supporting criteria (see Table 11.1; see also Veissier *et al.*, 2011). While some companies already use (elements of) the Welfare Quality® framework, the framework is still in the process of being developed and updated (Blokhuis, 2015).

Table 11.1 Principles and criteria of the Welfare Quality® assessment

Principle	*Description of the assessment criteria*
Good feeding	1. Animals should not suffer prolonged hunger and they should have sufficient and appropriate diet.
	2. Animals should not suffer prolonged thirst and they should have sufficient and accessible water supply.
Good housing	3. Animals should have comfort around resting.
	4. Animals should have thermal comfort, i.e. not too hot or too cold.
	5. Animals should have enough space to be able to move around freely.
Good health	6. Animals should be free of physical injuries.
	7. Animals should be free of disease, i.e. farmers and handlers should maintain high standards of hygiene and care.
	8. Animals should not suffer pain induced by inappropriate management, handling, slaughter, or surgical procedures.
Appropriate behaviour	9. Animals should be able to express normal, non-harmful, social behaviours, e.g. grooming.
	10. Animals should be able to express the behaviours characteristic of their species, e.g. foraging.
	11. Animals should be handled well in all situations, i.e. handlers should promote good human–animal relationships.
	12. Negative emotions such as fear, distress, frustration or apathy should be avoided whereas positive emotions such as security or contentment should be promoted.

Finnish context of studying animal welfare

While the Welfare Quality® assessment framework offered the potential to address at least some of the issues around product labelling, it was also important to understand whether and how it would work in practice. Of particular importance was understanding the relevance of the assessment framework to (the majority of) consumers who have limited knowledge of the natural behaviours of farm animals, or of the implications of current farming practices for farmed animals.

To explore these questions, we now look at consumer research conducted in Finland. Kupsala *et al.* (2011, p. 29) have shown that around 25% of Finnish consumers consider animal welfare issues while they are shopping for groceries. In their study, a majority of the respondents felt that it was difficult to establish what an individual consumer could do in order to improve the living conditions of farm animals. Interestingly, almost half of consumers in the study questioned the reliability of information directed to consumers on choices promoting animal welfare. Furthermore, further research by Kupsala *et al.* (2015) indicated that female gender, young age, urban residency and a non-farming background as well as social-equality attitudes were all linked to greater concern for farm animals.

As a part of a national Welfare Quality® research project, Finnish consumers' perceptions of farm animal welfare were explored in the autumn of 2013. As in earlier studies conducted in other countries, the focus group was chosen as the method to gain information (Munsterhjelm *et al.*, 2014). Five workshops were conducted and the participants were recruited from different backgrounds: (i) university students, (ii) social sector workers, (iii) hunters, (iv) home economics teachers, and (v) vegans and semi-vegetarians. A total of 23 people participated in workshops, of whom 15 were women and 8 men. The participants' ages ranged from 22 to 61 years. The workshops were planned and coordinated by the third author of this chapter (Kuismin, 2014).

Using the specific example of pigs' welfare, farm animal welfare was discussed in the workshops under four themes: daily shopping and consumers' relationship with meat and meat products; the origin of animal products and farming practices; participants' views on the defining features of farm animal welfare; and the proposed principles and criteria of the Welfare Quality® assessment. The participants were also asked to think of possible ways of presenting the assessment results to consumers, and to consider how the welfare assessment might affect their willingness to pay for meat products.

Two distinct, albeit overlapping, themes emerged from the research. The first was that, for consumers, farm animal welfare is of secondary importance compared with the role of meat as food, price and indigenous production (also Evans and Miele, 2012). The second was that, when talking about animal welfare, consumers emphasized the importance of living a natural or nature-like existence; that is, farm animals' dignity and their individual welfare were central elements of consumers' interpretation of farm animal welfare. We discuss each of these below.

Eating meat: the distinction between animals and meat

We found that most consumers' understanding of farm animals is limited to meat as a product. For example, a pig is seen as pork or bacon to be consumed. When consumers are making food choices, the animal is often absent and the link to animal welfare is weak. This highlights how the connection between animal and food is dismissed (Evans and Miele, 2012), although consumers did favour indigenous meat production (also Niva *et al.*, 2004; Autio *et al.*, 2013) and food packaging as important factors in their consumption decisions. It seems that the route of meat products from a farm to a dinner table is rather difficult to perceive for consumers; as Evans and Miele (2012, p. 312) have argued, the act of eating an animal is an astonishingly smooth and unremarkable practice in everyday life.

In fact, the workshops suggested that not only do consumers not think about the origins of the meat that they consume but they are alienated and distant from these animals. Participants in the workshops argued that the recognition of the connection between animal and meat is associated with negative meanings. They commented that, when they were cooking meat, they did not think about the origins of the meat or differentiate between meat and meal. In fact, the terms that consumers used when talking about meat (e.g. "home-made", "Karelian stew") could well be interpreted as an attempt to avoid thinking about the origin of the meat. The following quotations show how ordinary consumers can consciously alienate themselves from the origin of meat products:

> Package says: "Karelian stew meat". I put these in the oven, and it becomes Karelian stew. I do not have a clue what I have had. Karelian stew anyway. That's easy.
>
> (Female, 39 years, home economics teacher)

> I admit I've fallen for that myself, like when I started getting grossed out by eating animals, it made it easier for me, you know if … it didn't remind you the food [of an animal]. I didn't want to think where it came from … the more processed it is or more manufactured, somehow it distances you from the idea or the guilt or whatever sensation of it having ever been an animal and what it has gone through in all its life before it got here to our table.
>
> (Female, 29-years, vegans and semi-vegetarian group)

That is, Finnish consumers appear to conceptualize animal eating in similar ways to the consumers in the UK, the Netherlands, Norway and Sweden, where they emphasize meat as a significant attribute rather than the animal itself. It is interesting to note that research has suggested that consumers in France, Italy and Hungary are able to link animal welfare in a broader sense to meat quality (Evans and Miele, 2012, p. 308).

Packaging and appearances can further alienate consumers from the origin of the meat product. Our data suggested that if a package includes a picture of a "happy" chicken or has a picture of cows happily walking in green meadows, consumers felt more informed about the product and where the food comes from. Yet, in fact, this kind of information can be highly misleading as a description of animals' actual living conditions.

Meat packaging usually provides information not only on the content, but also on the country of origin, on the producer (or company) and, on occasion, the farmer. From a business perspective, packaged meat has an obvious advantage in comparison with meat counters, because the packaging allows the use of persuasive and positive descriptions of the product such as "examined and supervised domestic production". In our study, the focus group participants agreed that domestic production was the primary factor they considered when buying meat products. This implies trust in the ethicality of domestic products (Pettersson and Bergman, 2007 reached a similar conclusion in Sweden), but also in the superiority of domestic over overseas products in relation to animal welfare practices. In general, Finnish consumers see domestic production to be safer, more reliable and purer compared with imported food (Niva *et al.*, 2004). This is reinforced by, as in other Nordic countries, Finnish consumers having high levels of trust in regulatory authorities (e.g. Kupsala *et al.*, 2011; Skarstad *et al.*, 2007). In fact, workshop participants were almost dogmatic in the level of trust they had in domestic meat:

> It is for me at least with all the food I buy it is important for it to be Finnish. That's why all the package labelling is really important for me, so that there'd be a clear indication, it being Finnish.
>
> (Female, 31-years, social sector worker)

> I can't say that I would buy that [Welfare Quality®] ... Especially if there would be a price difference I don't think I would do. I reckon you'd still get the domestic stuff ... in a way if you had ... produced overseas or cheap, and domestic and then you had this kind of ethical meat, then I'd still buy the domestic... if it was the same price then I might buy the ethically produced stuff.
>
> (Female, 25-years, university student)

Other studies have confirmed that, for Finnish consumers, one of the main motivating principles behind their food choices is that it is domestically produced (Niva *et al.*, 2004, p. 23; Autio *et al.*, 2013), even if this makes it more expensive than imported products. In fact, Pettersson and Bergman (2007) found that, among Swedish consumers, low-priced imported meat invoked suspicion and opposition. Similarly, Vanhonacker *et al.* (2016) concluded that Belgian consumers considered domestic broiler production and its meat to be significantly superior to imported products.

The other important consideration is cost. The workshops suggested that, when consumers have the option of purchasing ethically and organically produced but more expensive foreign meat, the price of ethically produced overseas meat needs to be close to the price of favoured domestic meat for customers to switch to the more ethical product. More generally, the workshops pointed to the importance of indigenous production, the information received from food packaging (in particular, country of origin and details of the producer and the farmer) and lower prices as the most important criteria when making purchasing decisions. Animal welfare was seen as a much less important consideration.

Naturalness and animals' good life: animal welfare on a plate

When talking about animal welfare, the consumer workshops suggested that consumers see this as comprising three elements. First, farm animal welfare is defined in relation to the animal's living conditions, in particular where these can be described as natural or species-typical (also Spooner *et al.*, 2014). Second, the animal itself has a value and dignity. Third, when consumers talk about the transparency of meat production while pursuing animal friendly products, they value indigenous production. From an animal welfare perspective, the ideal situation was described as one that combined both a "natural" life and a "good" life for animals.

Yet, even those, mainly carnivorous, workshop participants who stressed the importance of natural behaviour and of species-typical nutrition justified meat production, and thus "exploiting" the animal for human purposes, when it was done with dignity and respect. They did not identify eating meat as a problem as such but stressed the importance of offering animals purposeful nutrition (non-genetically modified (GM) feed) and of treating these animals well. They perceived that keeping animals tied up had the effect of distancing the animal from its natural living conditions (also Spooner *et al.*, 2014), and were critical of Finnish meat production practices, seeing them as leading to farmers being alienated from understanding what is best for farm animals:

> It is just unbelievable how … these farmers, how alienated they are from living their life with the animals. There was a TV programme that showed … pigs and they said we are fine for space here. The pigs could not even turn or pass each other. How can they say in front of the TV that that is fine? Yeah so, that is right in line with EU regulation.
>
> (Female, 61-years, social sector worker)

When workshop participants identified attributes other than low price as important, they indicated that they might be willing to pay a premium price for domestically produced meat and for higher welfare meat, such as meat certified to Welfare Quality® standards. This finding is in line with consumer willingness to pay more for organic products.

> I am prepared to pay little extra for domestic meat, because I want to believe that the quality of Finnish production is controlled. For example, Polish imported meat is cheaper compared to Finnish one.
>
> (Female, 39-years, home economics teacher)

> I would pay [extra]. I mean if you could make sure that … the animal has lived, been able to carry out species-typical behaviours and have a species-specific diet, then absolutely. It is an investment in one's own health. I also think the label [Welfare Quality®] is practical for consumers. But I think there has to be also transparency that you can check from the Internet page information on that specific meat package.
>
> (Male, 29-years, hunter)

This young man connects an animal's wellbeing to his own health and welfare. As Autio *et al.* (2013) have noted, Finnish consumers are increasingly unhappy with industrial global food production systems, which they see as harmful both personally in terms of health and globally in terms of social and environmental justice. When consumers talk about natural living conditions and species-typical nutrition, they appear to view animals as having meaning or uses beyond being a component of a meal or a source of energy (protein). In that context, the quality of an animal's life is seen as more important than satisfying individual needs of consumers. That is, consumers see that the animal's welfare is important, and that the animal should be treated with respect throughout its life. In the following quotation, the consumer is picturing mass produced broiler meat as plastic and artificial:

> In a way you should respect the life of the animal too. Even though it's raised and born into dying in a way… I for example feel precisely that something like broilers, it's as if they're plastic, the way they go around like that.
>
> (Female, 25-years, home economics teacher)

The quotation suggests that animal dignity has been compromised as a result of mass production and intensive farming. Thus, the food industry could be said to be breaking the link between humans and animals, and creating distance between the two. Among our interviewees, the group that had the closest link to animals being used as food, namely the hunting group of young males, had a strong ethical orientation towards animal welfare and naturalness (in the sense of species-typical, organic and GM-free feed). They appreciated domestic, even local, production and often had a personal or recognized direct relationship to food production.

When considering an animal itself, workshop participants commented that the Welfare Quality® criteria were obvious; in fact, some expected that farmers could and should be expected to do even more. They also believed that small farm size delivered better animal welfare more than mass production farms (a conclusion which mirrors research by Spooner *et al.*, 2014 into the views of Canadian consumers). According to Autio *et al.* (2013) Finnish consumers value small producers' artisanship and small-scale organic farming.

A final issue raised in the workshops related to the wider question of the scale of meat production and consumption. As noted by one participant:

> Nevertheless, I mean somehow, I do not want it to be factory farmed meat because ... we do not, in my opinion, really need to produce meat as efficiently as we do now. We would get by with less meat production, and meat consumption specifically. That is where the change should be made. Nobody needs to consume as much meat as we currently do.
>
> (Female, 26-years, university student)

The extract illustrates that at least some consumers view intensive farming and eating meat as being unsustainable (also de Bakker and Dagevos, 2012). These consumers are most likely to transform their eating habits—as least partially—towards a more plant-based diet, which responds to two challenges: sustainable consumption (Vinnari and Vinnari, 2014) and farm animal welfare. Yet such a decision requires information, reflection and a willingness to give up "tasty beef and delicious tandoori chicken meals" at least to some extent.

Consumers: labels, education and transparency

Our study has given insight into consumers' views on farm animal welfare and its meanings in everyday life. It seems that Finnish consumers do consider farm animal welfare when making grocery purchasing decisions (also Kupsala *et al.*, 2011), or at least they know that animal welfare requirements are higher (for example) in organic production than in traditional meat production. Because there is no animal welfare labelling of Finnish meat, it seems that consumers' views on animal welfare are based on the presumption that authorities (e.g. through legislation, policy and guidelines) take care of major ethical problems in food production.

It is challenging for consumers to see a connection between animal, meat products and welfare (Buller and Cesar, 2007; Evans and Miele, 2012). Many consumers are distanced from farm animals and they often see low prices and domestic production as being of more importance than welfare issues. However, the interviewees were almost unanimously of the opinion that the only ways to drive higher levels of farm animal welfare—apart from supporting organic production—were to have either a transparent, impartial and supervised communication system (e.g. labeling) indicating the level of animal welfare (also Heerwagen *et al.*, 2015), or to tighten the legislation to create more stringent animal welfare requirements.

The workshops, and other literature on consumers and farm animal welfare, also pointed to a number of other factors that are important to raise awareness and facilitate changes in consumers' behaviour. First, the provision of reliable information about the entire meat chain (through packaging, labelling and internet sources) is essential to engage consumers with animal welfare issues. Food labels and easy to recognize logos could help in this process.

Second, the development of markets for medium and premium certified levels of animal welfare plays an important role in raising consumer awareness and, over time, attracting new consumer segments (Heerwagen *et al.*, 2015, p. 81). For example, the workshop findings suggested that the creation of a Finnish animal welfare labelling system (e.g. EU Welfare Quality®, national certified system or a voluntary certification standard) would affect food choices especially for those consumers who already recognize the connection between meat products, animals and farming practices.

Third, consumer education about the general state of living conditions of farm animals is needed. Bringing animal production closer to consumers (e.g. visibility, direct exposure to farms) would educate consumers that meat comes from animals, and thus reduce their alienation from the animal itself (Spooner *et al.*, 2014, pp. 155, 157). This could be achieved through, for example, engaging schools to participate in farm-based education, attracting consumers to agri-tourism or encouraging consumers to buy meat directly from farmers. Some retailers in the UK, for instance, have launched education programmes aimed at primary school children. An example is Tesco's Farm to Fork programme which teaches children about where food comes from (Tesco, 2014). In addition, adults could benefit from similar information while planning, purchasing and preparing the household meals; however, educating adult consumers remains a challenge for the food business.

Concluding comments

Through better labelling and more effective communications, higher animal welfare could be turned into an asset, not only for animals, but also for food companies and the wider food industry. However, there are challenges. In the case of Finland, these include the fact that higher welfare meat is still a niche market, that consumers do not see the link between animal welfare and meat, and that customers prioritize domestic (or indigenous) production and affordability over higher animal welfare. Therefore, for labelling to play a meaningful role in changing consumers' attitudes and practices, there is also a need for consumer education on animals and animal welfare, for the wider availability of higher welfare products, and for the gap between consumers and animals to be narrowed.

References

Autio, M., Collins, R., Wahlen, S. & Anttila, M. (2013). Consuming nostalgia? The appreciation of authenticity in local food production. *International Journal of Consumer Studies*, 37(5), 564-568.

de Bakker, E. & Dagevos, H. (2012). Reducing meat consumption in today's consumer society: questioning the citizen-consumer gap. *Journal of Agricultural and Environmental Ethics*, 25(6), 877-894.

Blokhuis, H.J. (2015). From the WQN coordinator. Welfare Quality Network, Newsletter 4, 1-2. Retrieved from http://www.welfarequalitynetwork.net/downloadattachment/53877/25781/WQN%20Newsletter%204%20June%202015.pdf [accessed 1 June 2016].

Blokhuis, H.J., Veissier, I., Miele, M. & Jones, B. (2010). The Welfare Quality® project and beyond: Safeguarding farm animal well-being. *Acta Agriculturae Scandinavica, Section A –Animal Science*, 60(3), 129-140.

Buller, H., & Cesar, C. (2007). Eating well, eating fare: farm animal welfare in France. *International Journal of Sociology of Food and Agriculture*, 15(3), 45-58.

Cembalo, L., Caracciolo, F., Lombardi, A., Del Giudice, T., Grunert, K.G. & Cicia, G. (2016). Determinants of individual attitudes toward animal welfare-friendly food products. *Journal of Agricultural and Environmental Ethics*, 29(2), 237-254.

Davidson, A., Schröder, M.J. & Bower, J.A. (2003). The importance of origin as a quality attribute for beef: results from a Scottish consumer survey. *International Journal of Consumer Studies*, 27(2), 91-98.

Diamond, C. (1978). Eating meat and eating people. *Philosophy*, 53, 465-479.

Dilworth, T., & McGregor, A. (2015). Moral steaks? Ethical discourses of in vitro meat in academia and Australia. *Journal of Agricultural and Environmental Ethics*, 28(1), 85-107.

European Commission (2007). Council Regulation (EC) No. 834/2007 of 28 June 2007 on organic production and labelling of organic products. *Official Journal of the European Union*, L189/1-L189/23.

European Commission (2016). Organic Farming Questions & Answers. Retrieved from https://ec.europa.eu/agriculture/organic/sites/orgfarming/files/docs/body/organic_logo-faq_en.pdf [accessed 28 March 2016].

Evans, A., & Miele, M. (2007). *Consumers' Views about Farm Animal Welfare: Part I National Reports Based on Focus Group Research*. Welfare Quality® Reports No. 4. Cardiff: Cardiff School of City and Regional Planning.

Evans, A., & Miele, M. (2008). *Consumers' Views about Farm Animal Welfare: Part II European Comparative Report Based on Focus Group Research*. Welfare Quality® Reports No. 5. Cardiff: Cardiff School of City and Regional Planning.

Evans, A.B. & Miele, M. (2012). Between food and flesh: how animals are made to matter (and not matter) within food consumption practices. *Environment and Planning D, Society and Space*, 30(2), 298-314.

Franklin, A. (1999). *Animals and Modern Cultures: A Sociology of Human-Animal Relations in Modernity*. London: Sage.

Graça, J., Oliveira, A. & Calheiros, M.M. (2015). Meat, beyond the plate: Data-driven hypotheses for understanding consumer willingness to adopt a more plant-based diet. *Appetite*, 90, 80-90.

Grunert, K.G., Hieke, S. & Wills, J. (2014). Sustainability labels on food products: consumer motivation, understanding and use. *Food Policy*, 44, 177-189.

Harper, G.C. & Makatouni, A. (2002). Consumer perception of organic food production and farm animal welfare. *British Food Journal*, 104(3/4/5), 287-299.

Harrington, G. (1991). Consumer perception of meat. *Development in Animal of Meat and Meat Production*, 25, 159-178.

Heerwagen, L.R., Mørkbak, M.R., Denver, S., Sandøe, P. & Christensen, T. (2015). The role of quality labels in market-driven animal welfare. *Journal of Agricultural and Environmental Ethics*, 28(1), 67-84.

Heyder, M., Hollmann-Hespos, T. & Theuvsen, L. (2010). Agribusiness firm reactions to regulations: the case of investments in traceability systems. *International Journal on Food System Dynamics*, 1(2), 133-142.

Jallinoja, P., Niva, M. & Latvala, T. (2016). Future of sustainable eating? Examining the potential for expanding bean eating in a meat-eating culture. *Futures*, 83(October 2016), 4-14.

Janssen, M., & Hamm, U. (2012). Product labelling in the market for organic food: Consumer preferences and willingness-to-pay for different organic certification logos. *Food Quality and Preference*, 25(1), 9-22.

Jaskari, M., Leipämaa-Leskinen, H. & Syrjälä, H. (2015). Revealing the paradoxes of horsemeat: The challenges of marketing horsemeat in Finland. *NJB*, 64(2), 86-102.

Jokinen, P., Kupsala, S. & Vinnari, M. (2012). Consumer trust in animal farming practices: exploring the high trust of Finnish consumers. *International Journal of Consumer Studies*, 36(1), 106-116.

Kaljonen, M. (2016). Welfare certificates contested. *TRACE.: Finnish Journal for Human-Animal Studies*, 2(1), 82-87.

Krieger, S. & Schiefer, G. (2004). Quality management schemes in Europe and beyond. In *Joint Congress on IT in Agriculture. Proceedings of the AFITA/WCCA 2004* (pp. 258-263).

Kuismin, A. (2014). Kuluttajien näkemyksiä eläinten hyvinvoinnista ja sen mittaamisesta. In C. Munsterhjelm, A. Valros & A. Kuismin (Eds.). *Sikojen hyvinvointi kilpailuvaltiksi—Welfare Quality® -järjestelmän pilotointi Suomessa.* Final report of Welfare Quality® -project in Finland (in Finnish) (pp. 45-61). Helsinki: University of Helsinki.

Kupsala, S., Jokinen, P., Vinnari, M. & Pohjolainen, P. (2011). Suomalaiset näkemykset tuotantoeläinten hyvinvoinnista. *Maaseudun uusi aika—Maaseutututkimuksen ja -politiikan aikakauslehti* 19(3), 20-35 (in Finnish).

Kupsala, S., Vinnari, M., Jokinen, P. & Räsänen, P. (2015). Citizen attitudes to farm animals in Finland: a population-based study. *Journal of Agricultural and Environmental Ethics*, 28(4), 601-620.

Kylkilahti, E., Syrjälä, H., Autio, J., Kuismin, A. & Autio, M. (2016). Understanding co-consumption between consumers and their pets. *International Journal of Consumer Studies*, 40(1), 125-131.

Lusk, J.L. (2011). The market for animal welfare. *Agriculture and Human Values*, 28(4), 561-575.

Makatouni, A. (2002). What motivates consumers to buy organic food in the UK? *British Food Journal*, 104(3/4/5), 345-352.

Miele, M. (2011). The taste of happiness: Free-range chicken. *Environment and Planning A*, 43(9), 2076-2090.

Miele, M., & Kjærnes, U. (2009). Investigating societal values on farm animal welfare: the example of Welfare Quality®. In L. Keeling (Ed.). *An Overview of the Development of the Welfare Quality Project Assessment Systems* (pp. 43-55). Cardiff: Cardiff University, School of City and Regional Planning.

Miele, M., Veissier, I., Evans, A. & Botreau, R. (2011). Animal welfare: establishing a dialogue between science and society. *Animal Welfare*, 20(1), 103-117.

Miele, M., Blokhuis, H., Bennett, R. & Bock, B. (2013). Changes in farming and in stakeholder concern for animal welfare. In H. Blokhuis, M. Miele, I. Veissier & B. Jones (Eds.). *Improving Farm Animal Welfare: Science and Society Working Together—the Welfare Quality Approach* (pp. 19-47). Wageningen: Wageningen Academic Publishers.

Munsterhjelm, C., Valros, A. & Kuismin, A. (2014). *Sikojen hyvinvointi kilpailuvaltiksi—Welfare Quality® -järjestelmän pilotointi Suomessa.* Final report of Welfare Quality® -project in Finland (in Finnish). Helsinki: University of Helsinki.

Napolitano, F., Girolami, A. & Braghieri, A. (2010). Consumer liking and willingness to pay for high welfare animal-based products. *Trends in Food Science & Technology*, 21(11), 537-543.

Niva, M., Mäkelä, J. & Kujala, J. (2004). *Trust Weakens When the Distance Grows.* Finnish Results of the OMIaRD Consumer Focus Group Study on Organic Foods. Helsinki: National Consumer Research Center.

Pettersson, L., & Bergman, H. (2007). Swedish consumers' views on animal welfare. In A. Evans & M. Miele (Eds.). *Consumers' Views about Farm Animal Welfare: Part I National Reports Based on Focus Group Research* (pp. 205-252). Welfare Quality® Reports No. 4. Cardiff: Cardiff School of City and Regional Planning.

Ramsingh, B. (2017). "What it says on the tin": the food label as an evolving form of communication. *Proceedings of the Oxford Symposium on Food and Cookery* (forthcoming).

Sandøe, P., Christiansen, S.B. & Appleby, M.C. (2003). Farm animal welfare: the interaction of ethical questions and animal welfare science. *Animal Welfare*, 12(4), 469-478.

Schröder, M.J., & McEachern, M.G. (2004). Consumer value conflicts surrounding ethical food purchase decisions: a focus on animal welfare. *International Journal of Consumer Studies*, 28(2), 168-177.

Skarstad, G.Å., Terragni, L. & Torjusen, H. (2007). Animal welfare according to Norwegian consumers and producers: definitions and implications. *International Journal of Sociology of Food and Agriculture*, 15(3), 74-90.

Spooner, J.M., Schuppli, C.A. & Fraser, D. (2014). Attitudes of Canadian citizens toward farm animal welfare: A qualitative study. *Livestock Science*, 163, 150-158.

Springmann, M., Mason-D'Croz, D., Robinson, S., Garnett, T., Godfray, H.C.J., Gollin, D., Rayner, M., Ballon, P. & Scarborough, P. (2016). Global and regional health effects of future food production under climate change: a modelling study. *The Lancet*. doi: 10.1016/S0140-6736(15)01156-3

Tesco (2014). One million children to learn where food comes from. Press release. Retrieved from http://www.tescoplc.com/index.asp?pageid=17&newsid=926 [accessed 28 March 2016].

Vainio A., Niva, M., Jallinoja, P. & Latvala, T. (2016). From beef to beans: Eating motives and the replacement of animal proteins with plant proteins among Finnish consumers. *Appetite*, 106(November 2016), 92-100.

Vanhonacker, F., & Verbeke, W. (2014). Public and consumer policies for higher welfare food products: challenges and opportunities. *Journal of Agricultural and Environmental Ethics*, 27(1), 153-171.

Vanhonacker, F., Tuyttens, F.A.M. & Verbeke, W. (2016). Belgian citizens' and broiler producers' perceptions of broiler chicken welfare in Belgium versus Brazil. *Poultry Science*, 95(7), 1555-1563.

Veissier, I., Jensen, K.K. & Sandøe, P. (2011). Highlighting ethical decisions underlying the scoring of animal welfare in the Welfare Quality® scheme. *Animal Welfare*, 20(1), 89-101.

Vinnari, M., & Vinnari, E. (2014). A framework for sustainability transition: the case of plant-based diets. *Journal of Agricultural and Environmental Ethics*, 27(3), 369-396.

12 The human–animal bond

A risk and asset for animal-based agriculture

Emily Patterson-Kane and Cia Johnson

AMERICAN VETERINARY MEDICAL ASSOCIATION, USA

Introduction

The welfare of agricultural animals is determined not just by their immediate environment, but also by the structures, institutions and economics of agriculture that the farm operates within. That is, animals are subject to layers of control exerted by a complex web of human relationships, attachments and attitudes. And this relational environment operates largely outside the realm of empirical data and overt rationality. It is instead governed by the processes of human social subjectivity. Social subjectivity encompasses the way in which our attachments to individuals and groups are governed by processes such as intuition, unconditioned and conditioned emotion, and implicit learning, which underlies assessments of authenticity and trust.

The agricultural professionals of the future will increasingly face a choice that they may not be explicitly aware of. One option is to undertake a comprehensive trust-building approach to participating in agriculture. To do this agricultural professionals will need to distinguish between practices that are humane and those that pass as acceptable simply because they are commonplace and deeply entrenched; between practices justifiable in the present to create a lesser evil, and those that are welfare affirming and acceptable in the long term. These distinctions emerge clearly only when relationships between animal caregivers, managers and the public support free communication leading to the development of a more-or-less shared understanding of how animals should, and therefore *must*, be treated.

Alternatively stakeholders in agriculture that have control of animals may decide to take an approach more along the lines of a quotation attributed to dramatist Jean Giraudoux: "The secret of success is sincerity. Once you can fake that you've got it made." When emphasis is placed on achieving a goal, such as securing public trust in a product, rather than internalizing the need to actually deserve this trust throughout the whole supply chain we see this play out. Within agriculture, if stakeholders seek to provide for animals in a way that matches the broadest possible informed consensus when it comes to welfare, rather than meeting the requirements only of narrowly proscribed and relationally isolated subsets of human stakeholders (be they poorly informed consumers, efficiency-focused producers, those who derive profit from the activity or even academically trained animal welfare scientists), deserved trust will be afforded. However the latter choice (i.e. focusing on achieving trust rather than delivering better animal welfare outcomes) leaves agricultural activities constantly at risk of a catastrophic failure of public trust when real or perceived animal welfare abuses are exposed anywhere in their industry.

In this chapter we will show how the scientific study of animal welfare is necessary, but not in itself sufficient, for the development of humane agricultural practices. The knowledge gained about animals' objective and subjective wellbeing must be combined with an understanding of human social subjectivity, especially the manner in which people develop positive emotional responses and feelings of trust in relation to people who carry out agricultural activities. Knowledge of animal welfare can be of enormous benefit, but often does very little in itself to create clarity and change in massive and complex activities such as animal-based agriculture. It is through understanding relational psychology that we may continue to move agriculture towards providing conditions that honour the nature of the animal while allowing for its responsible use for human purposes such as the production of fibre, meat, milk and eggs.

In this chapter we outline the benefits of relational thinking in animal-based agriculture, the advantages for the animals, for human caregivers, for farmers and agricultural brands. We also discuss the obstacles to relational approaches, and offer suggestions for moving large-scale supply chains towards relationship-based sustainability.

Moving from categorical to relational thinking

The disciplinary basis for studying networks of human and animal relationships is often described as the human–animal bond (HAB) or human–animal interactions (HAI). However work in this area tends to focus on companion and service animals, predominantly dogs. This means that the qualities of normal or good human–animal relationships are often seen predominantly in this context, leaving the role of agricultural animals to be neglected or even vilified (see Croney, 2014). In this context it is common for entire species to be deemed "pet" species rather than assessing the actual roles of individual animals. This categorical rather than relational approach often leads to societal disagreement.

For example, in 2014 the House Rabbit Society and other pet rabbit advocates protested the supermarket chain Whole Food's decision to start stocking rabbit meat. Whole Food's response was that their rabbit meat suppliers met "WFM's high animal welfare standards" (Whole Foods, 2014). This welfare science-based communications strategy failed to engage with the basis of the protestors' objections, which was that the only valid relationship to have with a domesticated rabbit was that of owner and pet. Meanwhile demand for rabbit meat continues to grow, in part due to its use in raw dog food diets favoured by owners who consider kibbles and other commercial pet food diets unwholesome. Who is a pet, and who is food? So long as each species is permitted only one role this will remain a hotly contested matter. Other examples include the contested nature of dogs, horses and cetaceans as sources of "food" (for people) or "feed" (for animals).

There also seems to be a somewhat open question around whether an animal "being food" (or other tangible products) is fundamentally inconsistent with being treated well, and being cared for by an ethical and compassionate person (and/or company). Although research on this subject is predominantly recent, dating from the mid-1990s, there is, in fact, ample basis for characterizing conscientious owner and livestock relationships as mutually beneficial and positive (within a mainstream, largely utilitarian framework, and accepting that a contrary animal rights/vegan argument can be made). That is, when all other things are equal, a positive human–animal relationship benefits humans, animals and productivity.

Farmers report feeling a close connection between their wellbeing and the welfare of their animals (Kauppinen *et al.*, 2010), and farmers commonly have an intrinsic motivation to advance animals' welfare and conservation (Ryan *et al.*, 2003). Research has demonstrated that agricultural animals display variable personality types (Ruis *et al.*, 2000) and respond to people as individuals. Similarly, farm workers also vary greatly in personality and attitudes (Matthis, 2005), and in ways that affect how they treat animals (Hemsworth *et al.*, 2000; Hemsworth, 2004; Bertenshaw and Rowlinson, 2009). These effects are most obviously beneficial in settings where people and animals interact over long periods (such as dairy farming), or when the interaction involves animals that are highly vulnerable (such as raising juvenile animals, during surgical modifications, or slaughter). And it should not be forgotten that most farm animals are themselves social and that animal–animal interactions are key drivers of good or compromised welfare (see Galindo and Broom, 2000).

Including animals as voluntary participants in agriculture

Broadly speaking, animal husbandry systems tend to rely on handling animals either based on the animals responding fearfully (driving or dragging), or based on them responding mainly through positively motivated and cooperative behaviour patterns (approaching or accepting guidance calmly). The preference to move towards positive handling within agriculture, notably championed by Temple Grandin (2016), echoes that of the positive training movement relating to dogs and other companion animals (AVSAB, 2016), and the positive psychology movement in the realm of human psychology (Gable and Haidt, 2005).

In large and small ways agricultural systems need to move towards soliciting animals' cooperation rather than forcing their compliance. For example, a study in 1997 found that cows were more likely to approach an automated milking system on days when music was played (Uetake *et al.*, 1997). Further, in 2001 psychologists at the University of Leicester in the UK played music of different tempos to herds of Friesian cattle and found that milk production increased with slow tempo music (Briggs, 2001). These findings were followed by the British Columbia Dairy Association contest, "Music Makes More Milk" where the public was invited to create and submit songs that cows would "vote" on based on milk production (O'Brien, 2014). Additionally music replay in weanling piglets facilitated play behaviour (de Jonge *et al.*, 2008) and reduced stress (Dudinka *et al.*, 2006).

Classical style music has a calming effect on both the animals and caretakers (North and Hargreaves, 2009) and improves the human–animal relationship. A recent example of a positive relationship between a farmer and his beef herd is shown in the viral video clips of Derek Klingenberg serenading his cows with his trombone (Mazza, 2014).

In a parallel move some experts have long pushed for the science of animal welfare to move its focus away from mitigating the negative and towards embracing the role of positive experiences (e.g. Mellor, 2015) which can benefit animals even if they are living in very challenging conditions. However it may take a paradigm shift towards anthrozoology or other interaction-based disciplines for this recommendation to be fully implemented. And when this occurs, opportunities for positive experiences are a natural building block for caregivers to reconnect with animals in environments where their duties are currently neutral or aversive and where these duties lead to avoidance and disengagement from animals.

Far from being theoretical ideas, the fact is that in modern systems we often have the option of making the animals perform (rather than inviting their cooperation) in order to meet most if not all production goals. Previously described primarily as "low stress handling", new programmes now emphasize replacing aversive interactions with neutral or positive ones. For example Merck's beef cattle handling programme entitled "Creating Connections™: working together for cattle well-being" explicitly recognizes and values the inter-generationally understood art of stockmanship.[1] This recapturing of an ethologically informed handling skill base becomes ever more vital as animals are made more prone to stress by larger herd sizes, lean genetics, metabolic conditions (e.g. porcine stress syndrome, fatigued cattle syndrome) and potentially some pharmaceutical products (AVMA, 2014).

However further work is needed to support routinely positive interactions in farming facilities where the association of humans with unconditioned rewards like feeding, cooling or exercising is lost through automation of these systems. This severing of meaningful connections can have far-reaching consequences due to the loss of routine positive human–animal interactions.

Humans as beneficiaries of good human–animal interactions

When they do occur, interactions between people and animals can create a powerful feedback loop that is positive or negative and has wide implications. For example, even when carrying out the difficult task of euthanasia, it was found that workers were not excessively stressed when they deemed the animal was suffering, and they were able to use a technique they felt caused little pain (Matthis, 2005). Conversely when healthy animals are being killed (Whiting and Marion, 2011) and are not able to be used for their intended purpose (Hall *et al.*, 2004), or questionable techniques are used, the people involved can suffer serious and lasting psychological consequences.

1 http://www.creatingconnections.info/en-us/Home/Index

Essentially a properly understood and supported HAB will tend to support the use of practices that are better for both animal welfare and worker psychological wellbeing. For example, in a study comparing a cognitive-behavioural intervention on stockpersons to modify behaviour towards pigs with a control group it was found that the behaviour modification treatment resulted in increases in the total score given by the stockperson to those attitude questions relating to petting and talking to pigs. This attitude change corresponded to a significant reduction in the percentage of negative physical interactions displayed by the stockperson. These changes led to an increase in both the time that pigs spent close to the stockperson as well as the number of interactions with the stockperson relative to pigs at the control farms (Hemsworth *et al.*, 1994). Programmes such as the We Care^{SM} initiative in the US (a joint effort of the Pork Checkoff, through the National Pork Board, and the National Pork Producers Council) have the potential to assist with improving stockperson behaviour through resources such as the Employee Care Toolkit. These behaviour changes can lead to improved employee–animal relationships and ultimately lead to improvements in overall animal welfare.

However, when the HAB turns sour, a cascade of negative consequences can drive a situation towards ever poorer performance. For example, employees in jobs that involve the euthanasia of animals often meet with disapproval from their immediate family members, which can leave them socially isolated and more vulnerable to suffering stress. This contributes to increased burnout and turnover in positions where both compassion and a high level of skill are required to ensure humane treatment of vulnerable animals (Rogelberg *et al.*, 2007). In these cases managers that are fair and communicate empathically with their workers represent a crucial safety net for people and the animals under their care and control (Reeve *et al.*, 2005).

Obstacles to caregivers adopting relational approaches

The choices available to agricultural workers are often greatly limited and constrained. The average farm herd/flock has increased dramatically in size (e.g. Barkema *et al.*, 2015) and has become more vertically integrated in order to maintain profitability. In addition supply chains, from raw ingredient to end consumer, are often global in scale. As such, the connection between management, labour, animals and consumers is increasingly indirect. As an example it is not unusual in the United States for management and workers to speak different languages, with some or all of the animal-handling employees speaking Spanish (Matthis, 2005). As such the animal and worker dyad are often less autonomous, and so are more vulnerable to abusive exploitation as the intended or unintended result of choices made by physically and sociologically distant decision-makers.

Work previously done by local community members may be outsourced to cheaper migrant worker gangs or even slave labour. For example, the use of slave labour in all levels of the farmed shrimp production industry, predominantly in South Asia, has been widely reported by international media for at least eight years. When it is suppressed in one area it quickly springs up in another and has proved impossible to exclude from the sprawling supply chain that ultimately puts shrimp on the affluent Western consumer's table (Kara, 2014). The routine use of child and slave labour in this industry has failed to resonate with consumers who have not demanded, and thus have not received, assurances of fair labour practices in relation to the shrimp they consume, despite this being a product most could avoid without suffering serious inconvenience.

In turn, workers handling animals may feel less connected to non-local consumer populations, and thus may be more willing to compromise or even actively adulterate their product. For example, in 2007 melamine was deliberately added to pet food ingredients to create high protein readings when products were diluted or made from poorer grade ingredients. Many pets sickened or died as a result. At that time the deadly potential of high doses of melamine was not well understood, but this was not the case the following year when melamine adulteration not only occurred again, but this time the contaminated product was milk formula and six infants in China died as a result. Rather than being an isolated event, the Chinese Government determined that 22 different dairy companies had been employing melamine on a large scale. It was a practice that had become routine and eventually escalated to the levels where the products became acutely toxic.

In terms of animal welfare, larger farms do not consistently provide better or worse welfare for animals than smaller farms (Patterson-Kane, 2011). But large-scale and highly integrated industries make certain welfare problems difficult to address as their cause may be deeply embedded in the overall structure of the industry and difficult for any single stakeholder to change (and as a result professions such as veterinary medicine may have their ethical stances questioned; Rollin, 2009). Examples from the dairy cattle industry include calves not receiving colostrum (Beam *et al.*, 2009), poor uptake of polled genetics (which would remove the need for invasive dehorning), and lameness in cows (von Keyserlingk *et al.*, 2009). Animal welfare mistakes can rapidly infiltrate a large agricultural sector, but then take decades or longer to reverse (for example tail docking of dairy cattle which was ultimately determined to have no animal health or productivity benefits but remains common in some regions). Empirically impressive-seeming goals may be pursued in the absence of true gains, for example increasing the number of piglets born per litter rather than the number successfully weaned (Levis, 2016).

These trends have also affected the perception of agriculture by consumers in many developed nations, who are now predominantly urban or suburban and lack direct experience of agricultural practices; most will not even have set foot on a farm in years (McKendree *et al.*, 2013). Most community members must now rely heavily on a producer or brand's reputation or assurances that are provided about their standards. This audience is regularly presented with evidence of animal abuse occurring on farms, during transport, or at slaughter. Initially each release would have a discernible impact in the media cycle and provoke both industry and regulatory responses, for example the Hallmark meat packing case (2008) in the US which resulted in restriction on dragging prone cows (Perry and Brandt, 2008). Brands might feel some complacency that, with repetition, such revelations seem to be having an increasingly temporary effect. Even a widespread outcry in

Australia against live export of sheep and cattle by sea caused only a temporary moratorium on the practice which resumed in 2016. However when culturally salient, welfare revelations can still lead to permanent changes such as those relating to the use of the *puntilla* technique (using a blade to severe the spinal cord in the neck) to slaughter horses in Mexico (Sandberg, 2007).

Implications for farmers and brands

When welfare exposés occur frequently, this naturally leads to questions about the apparent disparity between the animal welfare assurances being provided, and video footage that whistle-blowers and activists continue to be able to acquire. Even simple factual statements on product labels can be revealed as untrue; an example was the 2014 disclosure by a dairy farmer (Dairy Carrie, 2014) that her non-organic milk was being used in a Lifeway kefir beverage labelled as organic, despite her proactively notifying them several times that they were sourcing their milk from a non-organic farmer co-operative. The evidence suggests that the inaccurate labelling was allowed to continue until the farmer chose to go public with the issue. Faced with scenarios of this type it is not surprising that consumers are treating simple written assurances with increasing scepticism.

And, as if that was not complicated enough, animal welfare (as most people understand it) is not a scientifically defined concept—not even a clearly distinct category. While there is a science of animal welfare, it is a subset of the overall meaning of what "animal welfare" is to people, and science is not in the driving seat when it comes to controlling the term's scope and meaning. Surveys repeatedly show that the idea of animal welfare is innately intermingled with other concepts like "organic" and "free-range" (Harper and Makatouni *et al.*, 2002). The public may not, on the other hand, directly equate welfare with cleanliness, and may be willing to compromise in some aspects of animal health and safety to provide naturalistic habitats. The public also tends to overestimate its knowledge of agricultural practices (Dietrich, 2016). In this context the public, farmers and anointed animal welfare experts may be speaking of very different things when welfare is being discussed (Vanhonacker *et al.*, 2008). The existence of these conflicting dialects supports our assertion that the respective communities do not communicate openly or frequently enough to have created a functional shared language.

There is a melting pot of animal welfare (and welfare-adjacent) issues where much of the relevant knowledge base rests in the so-called "hard" sciences, but the full meaning is at best within the social sciences and more likely broader even than other subjects (e.g. food safety, pollution, social justice). And while this fuzziness is often deemed a problem and source of inaccuracy, it is still often treated as if it can be solved by coming up with that perfect definition or perfectly phrased survey question.

This approach is fundamentally flawed. It is likely that there will never be a universal definition of animal welfare or an agreed upon way to objectively measure it. Instead it is the duty of the agriculture professionals and para-professionals to work within the culture of their community and attempt to engage in dialogue in order to capture and respond to public expectations. Within this dialogue the complexities of animal husbandry and economics are distilled down to their essentials and communicated honestly; because choices will be made on both sides of the equation.

To the extent that there is middle ground for this debate, it may be formed by recognizing that farming of animals can occur within the context of carer–animal bonds. Much is made these days of an assumed inconsistency in caring for an animal that will be killed. It is referred to variously as the caring/killing paradox, the sentient commodity problem and seen as occurring within agriculture, research and other settings where animals are placed in peril or killed. However in our experience committed farmers and other animal caretakers often do not experience dissonance between love of an animal and killing it. This is often due to the significant moral and/or ethical worth placed upon the animal's "purpose", as wholesome food or other important and useful product, and the heritage value of the breed. As such, an appropriate death has intrinsic value within agriculture similar to its value within a natural ecosystem; that is, "...deaths, always to the disadvantage of individuals, are a necessity for the species" (Rolston, 1994).

It is in this context that we sometimes observe a cultural difference between caretaking and research staff. Moving a specific animal between research and production herds can create different levels of satisfaction or discomfort depending on which outcome the individual is primarily involved in and therefore considers morally significant. Caretakers may differ in how they value the outcomes of a pig producing the intangible product of scientific data (with an endpoint of euthanasia and disposal as "waste"), and the use of the carcass as food.

However, it is entirely possible that the proportion of farmers motivated by the intrinsic value of their role, versus those purely motivated by economic outcomes (see Kauppinen *et al.*, 2010) may be changing over time. The formalization for training in agriculture has undoubtedly had great benefits for animals in areas such as nutrition, disease prevention and hygiene—but research is lacking into whether there may have been some losses due to the interruption of inter-generational and apprenticeship pathways into agricultural careers that fostered transmission of deeper philosophies of duty, meaning and worth. Having said that, it should be recognized that, at the present time, "family farms" with direct inheritance remain the norm in farming both in the United States and worldwide (Lowder *et al.*, 2014).

The path forward

The dominant approach to an instance of animal abuse or other "moral" failings being discovered in an agricultural facility is to distance management from responsibility, reinforce the theoretical ideals of the company, maintain the overall system and wait out bad press. Prior to online animal welfare exposés, a landmark example was that of the US company Jack in the Box and its response to *E. coli* (O157:H7) in its product which caused widespread illness and was linked to two infant deaths. While internally deemed a success as the brand survived and remains an economically viable franchise to this day, its communications at the time focused on deflecting blame up the supply chain while emphasizing its compliance with (selected) legal standards. To many this is also a prime example of lack of commitment to the relationship with the consumer, relative to the goals of avoiding blame and reducing legal liability (Ulmer and Sellnow, 2000). As such the company's strategy to ensure survival may have been at the cost of a less obvious long-term loss of market position due to an erosion of public trust. It is not possible to know how the outcome might have differed if the company had taken a more candid approach to acknowledging the role of its delayed response to State-level requirements to cook meat products at high temperatures. In any case, the media and social media environment has changed a great deal even from this event in the early 1990s. A strategy that embraces qualified and arguably obfuscatory messaging is increasingly risky as exposés and reactions become more rapid; although brands can gamble that if they weather the storm the crisis may also pass from the public mind more rapidly than used to be the norm.

One tacit "solution" some players are attempting is to avoid crisis by directly controlling the information consumers have to work with. For example there are multiple bills proposed that would prevent states from legislating farm animal standards (Andre, 2016), limit the ability to film animals on farms (Shea, 2014) or expose whistle-blowers to disproportionate liability even when they film under otherwise legal conditions (also known as "agricultural disparagement laws"; Semple, 1995). There has also been a tendency to manage, rather than overtly oppose, ambiguous or misleading product packaging. For example, producers may support moves to ban misleading labelling of products such as "hormone-free" milk, but also oppose accurate labelling for categories such as GMO (genetically modified organism) ingredients and national origin. Producers often seem to want to decide on the consumer's behalf which product variables are "valid" considerations using value criteria from other groups such as scientists or other anointed experts. An interesting contrast has been the Campbell Soup Company which recently began voluntarily labelling its products that contain GMO ingredients and supporting mandatory GMO labelling (Patnaik and Cavale, 2016).

As an aside, it should be noted that an unwillingness to embrace transparency is often very rationally motivated. For example, during the period when workers in animal laboratories were being targeted by destructive or violent animal rights activists, anonymity was a reasonable response for many who feared the potential consequences for their security and their family. However, the professional and brand messaging began to change as this danger diminished and most animal rights groups moved to pursuing educational, advocacy or legal approaches to opposing the use of animals in research. This shift to using the law to pursue animal rights or muscular animal welfare agendas has ratchetted up the potential consequences of accepting any liability—especially in the system in the United States where damages are more likely to correlate to the magnitude of the harm done, rather than the severity of the error or oversight that led to this harm occurring.

Even in contexts where errors are dealt with routinely in a system that arguably favours the actor over the victim, fear of consequences drives non-disclosure or ambiguous reporting of errors; an analogous example relates to errors by doctors

(Hyman and Silver, 2004; Gallagher *et al.*, 2003). In large-scale production facilities, where even minor oversights have the potential to affect very large populations of animals and humans, these psychological factors will be present and will require explicit targeting to ensure that problems, including practices that compromise animal welfare, are discovered and addressed at the earliest opportunity. This detection requires relational systems that are positively motivated, where workers are actively rewarded for problem identification and problem solving over apparent flawless performance. In this realm having explicit standards to conform to is a great asset. It should also be noted that these fears of costly liability may well be disproportionate and overly precautionary—as the actual costs to companies of lawsuits over errors such as handling practices leading to food-borne illness have been so small as to be arguably negligible (Buzby *et al.*, 2001).

However in a market where creating, maintaining and conforming to standards beyond the legal minimum can be costly, some production groups' strategy is to suggest that those who choose not to do so should not be punished. They argue that, when retailers require certain welfare standards, the retailers are robbing the consumers of "choice" (e.g. Andre, 2016). However the retailers have learned that when they choose to offer products that many find unconscionable, their reputation suffers. There is clearly an expectation that valid consumer choice can only operate within an envelope of ethically acceptable variation. This envelope is somewhat contested: for example in relation to access to cheap food for low income families; the leeway that should be given for religious slaughter; or to supply animals to distant markets such as Canada to Hawaii where the cultural preference is to receive the animal alive rather than via the cold chain.

In terms of animal welfare, most producers and providers currently rely primarily on assurances resting upon on science-based standards for animal care. These standards have improved welfare for innumerable animals and are to some extent known and respected by the public (McKendree *et al.*, 2013). This approach has a great deal of merit. However, it is directly undermined by consumer scepticism in the face of animal abuse exposés and other perceived evidence of the brands/producers/retailers as unreliable narrators for their industry. One example from the authors' personal experience involved listening to a speaker representing Monsanto who began a talk by referring to data about how the public trusts farmers, and asserting "Monsanto *is* farmers". Following that assertion, the speaker referred to the farmers as "originators" for the rest of the presentation. This is a clear sign that speaking in the warm language that the public trusts simply does not come naturally to many large players in the sphere of vertically integrated agriculture.

When it comes to bolstering the public's faith in assurance schemes, some programmes have retained traction through radical simplification of their messages. For example, the "no animals were harmed" assurance in relation to television and motion picture activities extends animal welfare protection even to ants and other "lower order" animals that most people would squash without a second thought. They do this less because of an assessment of potential sentience in these animals, and more in order to avoid any appearance of equivocating or carrying out any activity that could be seen as counter to their assurance. Most agricultural welfare messaging relates to complex husbandry and management systems and so is unlikely to be able to achieve this level of clarity. Furthermore, attempts to house these schemes under umbrella terms the public may find easier to understand have already become the subject of litigation challenging their accuracy (e.g. "humane"; see *Hemy v. Perdue Farms Inc.* in Justia US Law, 2013).

In contrast, when sincere, advertising campaigns based on relationships of different types can be both simple and compelling. For example, in Australia, the MasterFoods "Let's Make Dinner Time Happen" campaign showed that when adults were asked who they would like to have dinner with they suggested celebrities, but their children choose parents or family (MasterFoods, 2016). This reinforces the view that food is not just nutrition but also a type of emotional connection with people close to you. Research demonstrates that feelings of this type are relevant to how people form attachments and loyalty to products and brands. And that a perception of shared ethical/moral standards is measurably more important in these decisions than establishing science-based animal welfare standards (Center for Food Integrity, 2015).

Efforts to achieve similar feelings of attachment between consumers and producers have met with limited success. For example Monsanto's "America's Farmers" campaign, while not overtly rejected by mainstream commentators, seems to have had limited impact on the public consciousness (Monsanto, 2010; Morris, 2011). Perhaps it is because the use of images of the farming family are not explicitly linked with "factory farming" and so do not challenge their beliefs in relation to the identity of the underlying brand (Simon, 2013). By comparison take the recent attempts by companies such as Hill's Pet Nutrition in the US to let the public know that they carry out pet food nutrition research. Despite advertisements running in prime time showing these research centres, most viewers probably did not consciously realize that the dogs shown were research (aka "laboratory") animals, and thus their concept of the necessity for using research animals or ideas about how laboratory animals are treated was probably not challenged or changed. Part of the reason for this is that the positive portrayal material very rarely shows the animals within the context in which they are routinely housed (the cage or pen) but focuses instead on wide open pastoral vistas in which the animal-housing facility is a minor feature.

The path to relationship-based sustainability

How can vertically integrated, long supply chain agriculture make relationship-based assurances? A non-relational approach would deal with lack of trust by outsourcing trust to third-party assurance schemes (often while trying to retain some degree of control over these entities). By contrast, relationship-based approaches focus on attempting to retain trust—and both can be used in parallel. Trust retention depends on competence and projects this competence via honesty, transparency and long-term thinking.

Honesty at a basic level means not making strategic use of lies, obfuscation or misdirection. For example, it does not directly affect the potential visitor of a

SeaWorld facility, that SeaWorld has historically had their employees "go undercover" and join animal activist groups in order to monitor their activities. But they are wise to have ended that activity (BBC, 2016) as it undermines the honesty of the staff making animal welfare assurances to the public. In a relational setting integrity is seen as a core trait that a person/entity displays across all settings. So patterns of communication that obfuscate or minimize, even if not outright dishonest, toe the line in a way that builds distrust and invites ridicule (e.g. referring to beak trimming in poultry as "beak conditioning"). And this distrust is generalized to a variable extent to the category the listener applies to the speaker, be it that brand, that industry or that type of agriculture (i.e. "factory farming").

Transparency in its most obvious form can be seen in those farms that are open to the public such as Fair Oaks and Kreider Farms. It is also seen in communications that have a similar tone regardless of whether they are internal to the company or directed to the public or other stakeholders. While some groups may be more important than others economically they should be seen as morally/relationally equivalent, and even economic factors should be seen through a long-term lens. Consider for example the small circulation magazine *Farm News* that by dropping a long-term cartoonist at the behest of an advertiser was seen as cravenly privileging advertisers over subscribers and stifling criticism of large brands such as Monsanto (albeit not at Monsanto's request)—thus suffering a widely reported blow to its reputation and forcing it to reverse the decision (Munson, 2016).

Because public distaste for most forms of conventional agriculture is not as widespread, visceral or entrenched as for slaughterhouses or animal laboratories, the idea of a fun day out at the farm still resonates and provides opportunities for extensive and relatively nuanced edutainment experiences akin to what might be experienced at a zoo (although this ship has probably sailed in sectors such as fur farming, foie gras or veal production). Even more extensive experiences can be garnered through extended stays in the form of agri-tourism.

And, to return to the assumed quality of competence, farms, feedlots, auction houses, transporters, slaughterhouses, and every facility where a live animal is touched, must employ expert animal handlers who constantly strive to relate to each animal as an individual. In settings where doing so is difficult or impossible, changes will need to be made. Managers should spend time with the people and animals they manage and receive explicit training in how to communicate with both stakeholder groups and the wider public. This animal-centred ethic should generalize to more distant participants. For example the genetics expert should be committed to setting animals up to have normal or even unusually bold or calm (as opposed to fearful) temperaments through their genetic breeding goals, alongside, or above, production goals (Boissy, 2005). Not only will a bold or calm animal suffer less under the same stresses, they will be more cooperative with relational/positive handling techniques than a timid animal.

The broader network of support workers, providers and service suppliers, and neighbours should be made familiar with what every facility does, who works and lives there, and their commitment to each other. In those areas where workers find they are met with a lack of support or pushback from their family and community, active steps should be taken to address the situation with outreach and a genuine openness to the concerns being expressed. Even where minds cannot be changed, opposition expressed within a relationship is more respectful and less stressful and can include a mutual recognition of good intent. Workers without home support may be offered formal or informal alternative sources of support in the workplace.

Where people are not working directly with agricultural animals on a regular basis, a finding that may be relevant is this: across all settings the more people know about the animals (on the level of their natural history) the more they tend to like them, and the more they like them the more they are naturally concerned about their welfare. In a setting of extreme specialization some workers may lose sight of the fact that they are directly affecting the experiences of animals of a certain species. As such, there should be a reasonable expectation that every worker in a livestock or other animal-based activity has an interest in the species they work with, and be involved in ongoing education relating to its way of life, needs, welfare and nature. Voluntary contact with animals of other species, such as pets, is also associated with more concern for farm animal welfare (McKendree *et al.*, 2013). It could be suggested, therefore, that a demonstrated and ongoing interest in animals should be used in decisions relating to hiring, placement and promotion. (And, interestingly, learning about traits like sentience that animals share with humans affects attitudes not only about animals, but also towards commonly "dehumanized" people such as refugees; Costello and Hodson, 2009.)

At every level a core competence must be relational, and all relationships must be given equivalent moral value. When a company has a beautiful lobby and offices but outdated and disgusting animal handling facilities, it is saying that some kinds of relationships, such as between visitor and office worker, are valued, and others, such as between handler and animal, are not. Investment is visible in time and money no matter what verbal protestations might be made. This is not to say that pigs entering a slaughterhouse should have a sofa and a magazine. But they should be provided with a non-slippery surface and a race that encourages them to move smoothly. This, in turn, gives the handler animals that are easy to move and does not produce frustration or motivation to use harsh driving techniques to meet throughput goals (whether or not the use of these techniques is permitted "on paper").

Economic entities tend to understand the financial benefits that come from people forming attachments to their product or brand. This is why people pay a premium for luxury brands and every retailer tries to win consumers with incentivized "loyalty" schemes. However there is a need to understand that this principle often has a limited time horizon. Knowing people like to see animals in pastures leads many brands to use advertising and packaging showing animals on pasture. In the long run, however, this exposes them to being seen as dishonest when these images are placed side-by-side with accurate images of their actual animal-housing facilities. The veracity of simplified welfare claims are now being dragged through the courts around the world. Examples include Baiada Poultry in Australia for its "free to roam" campaign (Bowling, 2013) and the California Milk

Advisory Board in the United States for its "Happy Cows" campaign (Winn, 2012). "Animal welfare" itself has taken on a negative connotation in some farming circles as it is raised overwhelmingly in a context of criticism rather than praise, and they become conditioned to avoid engaging with it.

There is a fine line between presenting a product well, and the animal welfare version of "greenwashing", and indeed, there is probably no bright line between the two. But there is a long-term benefit to making the public more familiar with what farming, transport and perhaps even slaughter (see, for example, the American Meat Institute's "Glass Walls Projects", 2012) actually look like. This will allow a distinction to be made between what practices are modern but widely acceptable to a fully informed community and those that simply go too far in compromising animal welfare for reasons of efficiency and will have to change.

Even with a focus on attachment and sustainability, there may be a natural limit to the relational wisdom that can be shown by entities whose only core value remains efficiency. Ultimately ethical and moral standards need to be built such that the value of authentic (trustworthy) relationships is an integral part of the value model. Experience suggests that over time industry sectors are more likely to begin with these cultures and lose them, than to gain them over time as new participants come on board for purely economic reasons (e.g. organic agriculture). The role of participating professionals (e.g. veterinarians, expert stockpersons) may be key in continually bringing the welfare of animals to the forefront.

Conclusions

Sentient animals, even as products, occupy a unique space. It is not realistic to move all animals into a category like "pet", but it is equally impossible to try to insist that they be treated as mere objects obscured from public view and consideration. As sentient property, animals have special qualities which come with special obligations.

For this reason we have proposed that those involved in the food industry:

- Select and support people who care about animals as part of their professional calling at every level of all agricultural activities
- Maximize positive interactions between animals and people at all levels and in all settings
- Require that integrity and transparency trump goals of efficiency, "image" and compliance
- Treat all interactions with sincere stakeholders as bi-directional, morally significant and not competing

A final addition to this list is that agricultural stakeholders must have an awareness and concern for the *full lifespan of the animal*, whether or not this occurs within individual or company ownership. Once a person or brand has "touched" an animal their integrity inevitably remains "attached" to that animal, throughout its life until its eventual death and consumption of all related products. This principle of attachment reaches backwards as well as forwards in time (Maloni and Brown, 2006). This reality is on display with retailers such as supermarkets and chain restaurants worldwide reaching back through their supply chain to make assurances in relation to how those animals that contributed to their products were raised. And this avenue is especially important in the United States where "top down" federal regulation of agriculture is rare and likely to remain so. In practical terms this reality suggests future options such as attended "handovers" of animals, with caretakers accompanying their stock to auction and slaughter rather than having them transported and resold without committed caretakers present to protect their interests during these transitions.

Active resistance to this relational ideal is most apparent in the United States where attempts to uniquely identify animals (such as by ear tags) were opposed and defeated. Accountability was seen, at least partially, as a threat because each player does not trust the other participants in their overall supply chain or the federal government itself. As long as this is the case how can the consumer and animal welfare advocate have faith in these industries? Even as more and more stakeholders understand that standards and policies do not create attachment and trust, there is a desire to subvert what the public wants rather than bend to it. Like "animal welfare", trust and integrity are themselves becoming buzzwords that some in agriculture, a sector that still largely operates and self-regulates under an assumption of ethical accountability, are trying to co-opt rather than conform to. There is a gratifyingly widespread recognition of the need for relational thinking; however the mainstream adoption of the necessary transparency and long-term thinking will be very difficult for the established structures of large-scale, conventional agri-business to embrace.

References

American Meat Institute (2012). The Glass Walls Project. Retrieved from http://animalhandling.org/ht/d/sp/i/80622/pid/80622

American Veterinary Medical Association (AVMA) (2014). Welfare Implications of the Use of β-Adrenoreceptor Agonists. Retrieved from https://www.avma.org/KB/Resources/LiteratureReviews/Pages/Use-of-Beta-Agonists.aspx

American Veterinary Society of Animal Behavior (AVSAB) (2016). The use of punishment for behavior modification in animals. Retrieved from http://www.vetmed.ucdavis.edu/vmth/local_resources/pdfs/behavior_pdfs/AVSAB_Punishment_Statements.pdf

Andre, S. (2016, May 10). Oklahoma Farm Bureau official touts 'Right to Farm' proposal. Retrieved from http://www.tulsaworld.com/news/state/oklahoma-farm-bureau-official-touts-right-to-farm-proposal/article_b93e0a73-c7e0-52ef-af71-39316970794d.html

Barkema, H.W., von Keyserlingk, M.A.G., Kastelic, J.P., Lam, T.J.G.M., Luby, C., Roy, J.P., LeBlanc, S.J., Keefe, G.P., & Kelton, D.F. (2015). Invited review: Changes in the dairy industry affecting dairy cattle health and welfare. *Journal of Dairy Science*, 98(11), 7426-7445.

BBC (2016, February 25). SeaWorld admits its employees spied on animal rights groups. Retrieved from http://www.bbc.com/news/world-us-canada-35662207

Beam, A.L., Lombard, J.E., Kopral, C.A., Garber, L.P., Winter, A.L., Hicks, J.A., & Schlater, J.L. (2009). Prevalence of failure of passive transfer of immunity in newborn heifer calves and associated management practices on US dairy operations. *Journal of Dairy Science*, 92(8), 3973-3980.

Bertenshaw, C., & Rowlinson, P. (2009). Exploring stock managers' perceptions of the human–animal relationship on dairy farms and an association with milk production. *Anthrozoös*, 22(1), 59-69.

Boissy, A., Fisher, A.D., Bouix, J., Hinch, G.N., & Le Neindre, P. (2005). Genetics of fear in ruminant livestock. *Livestock Production Science*, 93(1), 23-32.

Bowling, D. (2013, July 9). Baiada busted for misleading "free to roam" claims. Retrieved from http://www.foodmag.com.au/news/baiada-busted-for-misleading-free-to-roam-claims

Briggs, H. (2001, June 26). Sweet music for milking. Retrieved from http://news.bbc.co.uk/2/hi/science/nature/1408434.stm

Buzby, J.C., Frenzen, P.D., & Rasco, B. (2001). *Product Liability and Microbial Foodborne Illness*. Washington, DC: US Department of Agriculture, Economic Research Service.

Center for Food Integrity (2015). A clear view of transparency and how it builds trust. Retrieved from http://www.foodintegrity.org/research/consumer-trust-research/current-research/

Costello, K., & Hodson, G. (2009). Exploring the roots of dehumanization: The role of animal-human similarity in promoting immigrant humanization. *Group Processes & Intergroup Relations*, 13(1), 3-22.

Croney, C.C. (2014). Bonding with commodities: Social constructions and implications of human–animal relationships in contemporary livestock production. *Animal Frontiers*, 4(3), 59-64.

Dairy Carrie (2014, October 6). Lifeway is lying about our farm. Retrieved from http://dairycarrie.com/2014/10/06/lifewaykefir/

de Jonge, F.H., Boleij, H., Baars, A.M., Dudink, S., & Spruijt, B.M. (2008). Music during play-time: Using context conditioning as a tool to improve welfare in piglets. *Applied Animal Behaviour Science*, 115(3), 138-148.

Dietrich, C.N. (2016). *How Did We Get Here? Understanding Consumers' Attitudes Toward Modern Agriculture Practices*. Doctoral dissertation, The Ohio State University.

Grandin, T. (2016). Livestock behaviour, design of facilities and humane slaughter. Retrieved from http://www.grandin.com/

Dudinka, S., Simonse, H., Marks, I., de Jongea, F.H., & Spruijta, B.M. (2006). Announcing the arrival of enrichment increases play behaviour and reduces weaning-stress-induced behaviours of piglets directly after weaning. *Applied Animal Behaviour Science*, 101(1-2), 86-101.

Gable, S.L., & Haidt, J. (2005). What (and why) is positive psychology?. *Review of General Psychology*, 9(2), 103.

Galindo, F., & Broom, D.M. (2000). The relationships between social behaviour of dairy cows and the occurrence of lameness in three herds. *Research in Veterinary Science*, 69(1), 75-79.

Gallagher, T.H., Waterman, A.D., Ebers, A.G., Fraser, V.J., & Levinson, W. (2003). Patients' and physicians' attitudes regarding the disclosure of medical errors. *Jama*, 289(8), 1001-1007.

Hall, M.J., Ng, A., Ursano, R.J., Holloway, H., Fullerton, C., & Casper, J. (2004). Psychological impact of the animal-human bond in disaster preparedness and response. *Journal of Psychiatric Practice®*, 10(6), 368-374.

Harper, G.C., & Makatouni, A. (2002). Consumer perception of organic food production and farm animal welfare. *British Food Journal*, 104(3/4/5), 287-299.

Hemsworth, P.H. (2004). Human-livestock interaction. In G.J. Benson & B.E. Rollin (Eds.). *The Well-Being of Farm Animals: Challenges and Solutions* (pp. 21-38). Ames, IA: Blackwell Publishing.

Hemsworth, P.H., Coleman, G.J., & Barnett, J.L. (1994). Improving the attitude and behaviour of stockpersons towards pigs and the consequences on the behaviour and reproductive performance of commercial pigs. *Applied Animal Behaviour Science*, 39(3-4), 349-362.

Hemsworth, P.H., Coleman, G.J., Barnett, J.L., & Borg, S. (2000). Relationships between human-animal interactions and productivity of commercial dairy cows. *Journal of Animal Science*, 78(11), 2821-2831.

Hyman, D.A., & Silver, C. (2004). Poor state of health care quality in the US: Is malpractice liability part of the problem or part of the solution. *The Cornell Law Review*, 90, 893.

Justia US Law (2013). HEMY v. PERDUE FARMS, INC. *et al*, No. 3:2011cv00888 - Document 60 (D.N.J. 2013). Retrieved from http://law.justia.com/cases/federal/district-courts/new-jersey/njdce/3:2011cv00888/253801/60/

Kara, S. (2014). *Bonded Labor: Tackling the System of Slavery in South Asia*. New York: Columbia University Press.

Kauppinen, T., Vainio, A., Valros, A., Rita, H., & Vesala, K.M. (2010). Improving animal welfare: qualitative and quantitative methodology in the study of farmers' attitudes. *Animal Welfare*, 19(4), 523.

Levis, D.G. (2016). The modern sow: top production issues. In *Proceedings of the London Swine Conference: A Platform For Success, 5–6 April 2016, London, Ontario* (pp. 19-34).

Lowder, S.K., Skoet, J., & Singh, S. (2014). What do we really know about the number and distribution of farms and family farms worldwide? Background paper for *The State of Food and Agriculture 2014*. ESA Working Paper No. 14-02. Rome: FAO.

McKendree, M.G.S., Olynk, N.J., & Ortega, D.L. (2013). *Consumer Perceptions of Livestock Products and Animal Welfare*. Center for Food and Agricultural Business. Retrieved from http://www.agribusiness.purdue.edu/files/resources/r-7-2013-mckendree-olynk-widmar.pdf

Maloni, M.J., & Brown, M.E. (2006). Corporate social responsibility in the supply chain: an application in the food industry. *Journal of Business Ethics*, 68(1), 35-52.

MasterFoods (2016, February 19). MasterFoods make dinner time happen. Retrieved from http://theinspirationroom.com/daily/2016/masterfoods-make-dinner-time-matter/

Matthis, J.S. (2005). Selected employee attributes and perceptions regarding methods and animal welfare concerns associated with swine euthanasia. NCSU Libraries. Retrieved from http://repository.lib.ncsu.edu/ir/bitstream/1840.16/4993/1/etd.pdf

Mazza, E. (2014, August 4). Cows come running to hear farmer play Lorde's "Royals" on trombone. *Huffington Post*. Retrieved from http://www.huffingtonpost.com/2014/08/04/cows-royal-trombone_n_5646726.html

Mellor, D.J. (2015). Positive animal welfare states and reference standards for welfare assessment. *New Zealand Veterinary Journal*, 63(1), 17-23.

Monsanto. (2010). America's Farmers. Retrieved from http://www.americasfarmers.com/

Morris, F. (2011, March 7). Big ads for big ag. Harvest Public Media. Retrieved from http://harvestpublicmedia.org/article/467/big-ads-big-ag/5

Munson, K. (2016, May 13). How Iowa's farmer cartoonist became a national free-speech martyr. *Des Moines Register*. Retrieved from http://www.desmoinesregister.com/story/

news/local/kyle-munson/2016/05/13/iowa-cartoonist-farm-news-rick-friday-free-speech-profit/84243968/

North, A.C., & Hargreaves, D.J. (2009). The power of music. *The Psychologist*, 22, 1012-1013.

O'Brien, A. (2014, February 10). Milking to music. Modern Farmer. Retrieved from http://modernfarmer.com/2014/02/milking-music/

Patnaik, S., & Cavale, S. (2016, January 8). Campbell Soup becomes first major company to start GMO labeling. Yahoo News. Retrieved from http://news.yahoo.com/campbell-soup-says-supports-mandatory-gmo-labeling-055100694--sector.html

Patterson-Kane, E.G. (2011). Reply to: The well-being of farm animals on larger operations is disregarded in the pursuit of higher profits. Best Food Facts. Retrieved from http://www.bestfoodfacts.org/farm-size-animal-welfare/

Perry, N., & Brandt, P. (2008). A case study on cruelty to farm animals: Lessons learned from the Hallmark Meat Packing case. *Michigan Law Review First Impressions*, 106(1), 117-122.

Reeve, C.L., Rogelberg, S.G., Spitzmüller, C., & DiGiacomo, N. (2005). The caring-killing paradox: euthanasia-related strain among animal-shelter workers. *Journal of Applied Social Psychology*, 35(1), 119-143.

Rogelberg, S.G., Reeve, C.L., Spitzmüller, C., DiGiacomo, N., Clark, O.L., Teeter, L., Walker, A.G., Starling, P.G., & Carter, N.T. (2007). Impact of euthanasia rates, euthanasia practices, and human resource practices on employee turnover in animal shelters. *Journal of the American Veterinary Medical Association*, 230(5), 713-719.

Rollin, B.E. (2009). Veterinary medical ethics. An ethicist's commentary on veterinarians and production diseases. *The Canadian Veterinary Journal. La revue veterinaire canadienne*, 50(11), 1128-1132.

Rolston, H. (1994). Value in nature and the nature of value. *Royal Institute of Philosophy Supplement*, 36, 13-30.

Ruis, M.A., te Brake, J.H., van de Burgwal, J.A., de Jong, I.C., Blokhuis, H.J., & Koolhaas, J.M. (2000). Personalities in female domesticated pigs: behavioural and physiological indications. *Applied Animal Behaviour Science*, 66(1), 31-47.

Ryan, R.L., Erickson, D.L., & De Young, R. (2003). Farmers' motivations for adopting conservation practices along riparian zones in a mid-western agricultural watershed. *Journal of Environmental Planning and Management*, 46(1), 19-37.

Sandberg, L. (2007, September 30). Horse slaughter ban has gruesome results. *Houston Chronicle*. Retrieved from http://www.chron.com/news/houston-texas/article/Horse-slaughter-ban-has-gruesome-results-1817383.php

Semple, M.W. (1995). Veggie libel meets free speech: a constitutional analysis of agricultural disparagement laws. *Virginia Environmental Law Journal*, 15, 403.

Shea, M. (2014). Punishing animal rights activists for animal abuse: rapid reporting and the new wave of ag-gag laws. *Columbia Journal of Law and Social Problems*, 48, 337.

Simon, M. (2013). *Best Public Relations that Money Can Buy: A Guide to Food Industry Front Groups*. Washington, DC: Center for Food Safety. Retrieved from http://www.centerforfoodsafety.org/files/front_groups_final_84531.pdf

Uetake, K., Hurnik, J.F., & Johnson, L. (1997). Effect of music on voluntary approach of dairy cows to an automatic milking system. *Applied Animal Behaviour Science*, 53, 175-182.

Ulmer, R.R., & Sellnow, T.L. (2000). Consistent questions of ambiguity in organizational crisis communication: Jack in the Box as a case study. *Journal of Business Ethics*, 25(2), 143-155.

Vanhonacker, F., Verbeke, W., Van Poucke, E., & Tuyttens, F.A. (2008). Do citizens and farmers interpret the concept of farm animal welfare differently? *Livestock Science*, 116(1), 126-136.

Von Keyserlingk, M.A.G., Rushen, J., de Passillé, A.M., & Weary, D.M. (2009). Invited review: The welfare of dairy cattle—Key concepts and the role of science. *Journal of Dairy Science*, 92(9), 4101-4111.

Whiting, T.L., & Marion, C.R. (2011). Perpetration-induced traumatic stress: A risk for veterinarians involved in the destruction of healthy animals. *The Canadian Veterinary Journal*, 52(7), 794.

Whole Foods (2014). Company News: Whole Foods market rabbit standards development process. Retrieved from http://media.wholefoodsmarket.com/news/rabbits

Winn, P. (2012, September 6). Calif. judge tosses out PETA lawsuit against California "Happy Cows" ads. CNSNews.com. Retrieved from http://www.cnsnews.com/news/article/calif-judge-tosses-out-peta-lawsuit-against-california-happy-cows-ads

Part III

Corporate practice

13 Global food companies and farm animal welfare

The state of play

Nicky Amos

NICKY AMOS CSR SERVICES AND BUSINESS BENCHMARK ON FARM ANIMAL WELFARE, UK

Rory Sullivan

UNIVERSITY OF LEEDS AND BUSINESS BENCHMARK ON FARM ANIMAL WELFARE, UK

Introduction

Farm animal welfare is now recognized as an important business issue for companies in the food industry. As has been discussed by the various authors in this volume, a variety of factors have driven this change, including the 2013 European horsemeat scandal, food scares, tightening regulatory requirements on animal welfare and on food safety and quality, investor concerns about how food companies are managing animal welfare and other risks in their supply chains, consumer interest in issues such as food quality and safety, provenance and traceability, and public concerns about the welfare of animals in food supply chains.

In response to these pressures, an increasing number of global food companies have started to pay more attention to the issue of farm animal welfare. They have adopted policies, established governance and management systems, improved their reporting and taken action to improve farm animal welfare performance.

In this chapter, we present the results of the 2015 Business Benchmark on Farm Animal Welfare (BBFAW), which assessed how 90 of the world's largest food companies are managing farm animal welfare. We discuss these companies' governance and management systems, processes and performance, we analyse how these have changed over time, and we offer some high level reflections on the drivers for change.

The Business Benchmark on Farm Animal Welfare

The Business Benchmark on Farm Animal Welfare (BBFAW)[1]—an initiative supported by leading farm animal welfare organizations, Compassion in World Farming and World Animal Protection, and by Coller Capital—is designed to raise farm animal welfare standards and performance in the world's leading food businesses.

BBFAW's key tool for the delivery of these objectives is an annual Benchmark of global food companies' performance on farm animal welfare. The Benchmark provides investors, governments, academics, NGOs, consumers and other

1 http://www.bbfaw.com/

stakeholders with an independent, impartial and reliable assessment of individual company efforts to adopt higher farm animal welfare standards and practices. To date, Benchmarks have been published for 2012, 2013, 2014 and 2015 (Amos and Sullivan 2013a, 2013b, 2015a, 2016a). The Benchmark describes how global food companies are managing and reporting on farm animal welfare, and assesses the progress that has been made in terms of these companies' management practices and farm animal welfare performance.

BBFAW also produces guidance and other materials for companies and investors on issues such as the business case for farm animal welfare, best practices in corporate management and reporting, and new and forthcoming farm animal welfare-related regulations and policies.[2] In addition, BBFAW engages with investors and with companies to encourage investors to pay more attention to farm animal welfare in their investment processes and in their company dialogue, and to encourage companies to improve their practices, performance and reporting on farm animal welfare.

The 2015 Benchmark

The 2015 Benchmark covered 90 global food companies. The companies were broadly spread across the three food industry subsectors, i.e. food retailers and wholesalers, restaurants and bars, and food producers (see Table 13.1). They were geographically dispersed (see Table 13.2), and included both listed and unlisted companies (private companies, partnership companies, cooperatives). Companies were primarily selected on the basis of their size (i.e. turnover) and the scale of their farm animal footprint (see, further, Amos and Sullivan, 2013a, 2016b).

The Benchmark assessed company practice and performance in four core areas—management commitment, governance and management, leadership and innovation, and performance reporting—as indicated in Table 13.3. Within each of these areas, companies were evaluated against a number of criteria, with scores awarded according to how close they were to best practice (Amos and Sullivan, 2016a, b). The categories were weighted as indicated in Table 13.3.

The framework was designed to be relevant to all food companies, irrespective of their sector or business model. Furthermore, it was designed to align with the manner in which companies manage and report on other social and environmental issues (see, further, Amos and Sullivan, 2013c; Sullivan, 2011).

Table 13.1 Companies by sub-sector

Sub-sector	*Number of companies*
Food retailers and wholesalers	31
Restaurants and bars	25
Food producers	34
Total	90

2 See, further, www.bbfaw.com

Table 13.2 Companies by country of listing or incorporation

Country of listing or incorporation	*Number of companies*
USA	23
UK	19
France	8
Germany	8
Italy	6
Netherlands	4
Switzerland	4
Brazil	3
Australia	2
Denmark	2
Norway	2
Sweden	2
Spain	2
Canada	2
Belgium	1
New Zealand	1
People's Republic of China	1

Each company was assessed on the basis of its own non-confidential published literature, including its annual reports, corporate social responsibility (CSR) reports and website content. This information had to be publicly available at the time of the company assessment; for the 2015 Benchmark, company assessments were conducted in August and September 2015.

The reasons for relying on published information were twofold. The first was that encouraging companies to provide a better account of their approach to farm animal welfare was, and remains, a core objective of the Business Benchmark on Farm Animal Welfare. The second was that we wanted to ensure that companies were assessed consistently, and to avoid any suggestion that companies that worked with Compassion in World Farming and/or World Animal Protection were in any way favoured by the assessment methodology.

Draft results were emailed to companies in October 2015. In the period October–November 2015, 32 companies responded with written comments or requested further dialogue on the assessment approach and scoring. Company scores were revised only in situations where there had been errors in the assessment process, either because of incorrect scores being awarded or because information that was in the public domain at the time of the assessment (i.e. August/September 2015) had been overlooked or misinterpreted (Amos and Sullivan, 2016b).

Table 13.3 Benchmark elements

Pillar	*Key elements*	*No. of points*	*Weighting (% of total score)*
Management commitment	General account of why farm animal welfare is important to the business, including discussion of the risks and business opportunities. Overarching farm animal welfare policy that sets out core principles and beliefs on farm animal welfare and that explains how these are addressed and implemented throughout the business. Specific policy positions on key welfare concerns such as the close confinement of livestock, animals subjected to genetic engineering or cloning, routine mutilations, antibiotic usage, slaughter without stunning, and long-distance live transportation.	70	34%
Governance and management	Defined responsibilities for the day-to-day management of animal welfare-related issues as well as strategic oversight of how the company's policy is being implemented. Objectives and targets including process and performance measures, with an explanation of how these objectives and targets are to be delivered and how progress is to be monitored. Reporting of performance against objectives, targets and company policy, including discussion of the factors that have affected performance. Internal controls such as employee training on farm animal welfare and responses in the event of non-compliance with the farm animal welfare policy. Policy implementation through supply chains, including the incorporation of farm animal welfare in supplier contracts, supply chain monitoring and auditing processes, and supporting suppliers in meeting the company's standards on farm animal welfare.	85	41%
Leadership and innovation	Company involvement in research and development programmes to advance farm animal welfare. Company involvement in industry or other initiatives directed at improving farm animal welfare. Independent third-party acknowledgement of farm animal welfare performance from notable award or accreditation schemes. Company initiatives to promote higher farm animal welfare among customers or consumers.	30	15%
Performance reporting	Company reporting on specific performance measures, namely the proportion of animals in supply chains that are free from confinement, the proportion of animals that are subject to pre-slaughter stunning, and the average, typical or maximum permitted live transport times for animals. Company reporting on other farm animal welfare outcome measures.	20	10%

Results[3]

Overall findings

We graded the surveyed companies into one of six tiers, as indicated in Table 13.4. Table 13.5 shows how the number of companies in each tier changed over the period 2012 to 2015. The 2015 Benchmark suggested that corporate practice and reporting on farm animal welfare remained relatively underdeveloped, certainly in comparison with other corporate responsibility topics, such a climate change mitigation and human rights. Forty per cent (40%), or 36 out of the 90 companies, were placed in Tiers 5 and 6; that is, they provided little or no information on their approach to farm animal welfare, or that farm animal welfare was even recognized as a business issue.

While the data in Table 13.5 suggest that there is much work to be done to even get farm animal welfare on the business agenda of many large global food companies, the proportion of companies in Tiers 5 and 6 has been declining consistently, from 60% in the 2012 Benchmark, to 53% in 2013, 50% in 2014 and 40% in 2015. In fact, 12 of the 40 companies that were in Tiers 5 and 6 in the 2014 Benchmark had improved their performance enough to move up at least one tier in the 2015 Benchmark. Furthermore, between 2014 and 2015, five companies (2 Sisters Food Group, Compass Group, Greggs, Metro, and Mitchells & Butlers) moved up two tiers and one company, Whitbread, moved up three tiers.

Table 13.4 BBFAW tiers

Tier	*Percentage score*
1: Leadership	>80%
2: Integral to business strategy	62–80%
3: Established but work to be done	44–61%
4: Making progress on implementation	27–43%
5: On the business agenda but limited evidence of implementation	11–26%
6: No evidence that on the business agenda	<11%

Table 13.5 Number of companies by tier

Tier	*Number of companies*			
	2012	*2013*	*2014*	*2015*
1: Leadership	0	2	3	4
2: Integral to business strategy	3	5	7	7
3: Established but work to be done	6	10	14	16
4: Making progress on implementation	18	16	16	27
5: On the business agenda but limited evidence of implementation	18	14	19	17
6: No evidence that on the business agenda	23	23	21	19
Total	68	70	80	90

3 This section is based on Amos and Sullivan (2016a) unless otherwise indicated.

There was also a group of clear leaders. These 11 companies—Coop Group (Switzerland), Cranswick, J Sainsbury, Marfrig, McDonald's, Migros, Marks & Spencer, Noble Foods, The Co-operative Food (UK), Unilever and Waitrose—had made strong commitments to farm animal welfare, had well-developed management systems and processes, and had a clear focus on farm animal welfare performance measures. They represented all three of the food industry sub-sectors (i.e. food retailers and wholesalers, restaurants and bars, and food producers), they were distributed across the countries (of listing or incorporation) covered by the Benchmark, and they encompassed a range of ownership structures (public, private and co-operatives). This is encouraging as it suggests that it is realistic for food companies, irrespective of their sub-sector, geography or ownership, to aspire to and achieve high standards of farm animal welfare.

The other notable point about the 2015 Benchmark was that the restaurants and bars sector continued to be a noticeably poorer performer than the other two sectors. This appeared, at least in part, to reflect companies' proximity to consumers or the public. The average score for those companies with a strong high street presence and trading under the corporate brand name (e.g. Domino's Pizza, Greggs, JD Wetherspoon, McDonald's, Quick, Starbucks, Subway and Wendy's) was broadly similar to that for the other sectors. In contrast, business-to-business companies that had less proximity to the public (or are relatively unknown) or that trade under multiple service brands scored significantly lower. For example, the average score for Compass Group, Cremonini, Elior, Gategroup Holding, Olav Thon Gruppen, SSP Group Limited and Umoe Gruppen (a group that is representative of business-to-business companies) was approximately half that of the other sectors covered by the Benchmark.

Is farm animal welfare recognized as a business issue?

Acknowledging farm animal welfare as a business issue is a necessary first step in developing and implementing an effective approach to the management of farm animal welfare. Of the 90 global food companies covered by the 2015 Benchmark, 84% recognized farm animal welfare as a business issue, a noticeable improvement on the 71% in the 2012 and 2013 Benchmarks.

In their published materials, companies presented different reasons for focusing on farm animal welfare. For some, ethical arguments were identified as the most important. For others, more conventional business arguments such as the need to comply with legislation and relevant voluntary and industry standards, the need to meet stakeholder, customer and consumer expectations, and market opportunities (for example, for higher welfare products) dominated their thinking. What was striking was that relatively few commented on the overall significance of farm animal welfare to their business, e.g. the costs likely to be incurred to comply with legislation, the potential sales of higher welfare products. This makes it difficult for investors or other stakeholders to assess whether farm animal welfare is a financially material risk or opportunity for these companies.

Do companies publish overarching policies on farm animal welfare?

In large companies, the adoption of a formal policy on a specific corporate responsibility issue is generally seen as the essential starting point for the effective management of the issue. If management systems and processes are not well developed or if management sees animal welfare primarily as an operational issue, such factors can attenuate or dampen the influence of external pressures. Conversely, companies with well-developed and responsive management systems and processes, coupled with management recognition of farm animal welfare as a strategic value driver, are more likely to respond effectively and quickly to external governance pressures.

While the specific content of policies will inevitably vary, high quality farm animal welfare policies should include:

- A clear statement of the reasons why farm animal welfare is relevant to the business
- A commitment to compliance with relevant legislation and to other relevant standards
- A commitment to continuous improvement in farm animal welfare performance
- A description of the processes in place to ensure the policy is effectively implemented
- Clear accountabilities for the implementation of the policy
- A commitment to public reporting on performance

Of the 90 companies covered by the 2015 Benchmark, 49 (54%) had published comprehensive farm animal welfare policies. Another 13 (14%) had published basic policy statements that provided limited information on how the policy statements would be implemented. While these numbers were broadly the same as the 2014 Benchmark, they did represent a step change improvement from the 2012 Benchmark when just 34% of companies had comprehensive policies and 12% had basic policy statements.

Many of these policies, however, were limited in their scope. Of the 62 companies with published farm animal welfare policies, 46 applied their policies to all geographies, 33 applied their policies to all relevant animal species and 30 applied their policies to all products produced, manufactured or sold. In discussions with BBFAW, a number of companies pointed to the difficulties they faced in imposing their policies on suppliers, in particular in situations where suppliers—or other purchasing companies—are more powerful than the food company and/or where the food company accounts for only a small part of a supplier's turnover. Another interesting point raised by food companies was that they wanted to prioritize action on their key ingredients, which were typically those representing the largest volume or the largest business spend. This has resulted in companies prioritizing the development and implementation of policies for these key ingredients rather than for all of the animals in their supply chains.

Do companies have specific policies on farm animal welfare?

In practice, overarching farm animal welfare policies set the broad direction but do not prescribe the specific actions that need to be taken. The Benchmark therefore assessed whether companies had adopted policies on seven priority farm animal welfare-related issues identified by Compassion in World Farming and by World Animal Protection (see, further, Sullivan and Amos, 2015). These were: close confinement, the use of genetically modified or cloned animals, the use of growth promoting substances, the use of antibiotics for prophylactic purposes, routine mutilations, pre-slaughter stunning, and long-distance live transportation.

In Figure 13.1, we indicate the proportion of companies that had made at least partial commitments on these issues and—with the exception of the question on the prophylactic use of antibiotics which was first asked in 2014—how these compared with the 2012, 2013 and 2014 Benchmarks.

The data presented in Figure 13.1 suggest that companies—albeit from a low base in many cases—are slowly starting to establish formal policies on specific farm animal welfare issues. This reflects the normal evolution of practice on corporate responsibility issues, where companies tend to start with high level policies and then, over time, supplement these with more detailed policies on specific issues.

Our interviews with companies covered by the Benchmark suggested that the high proportion of companies with policies on close confinement reflected changes in animal welfare legislation, in particular the banning of barren battery cages and sow stalls (gestation crates) in the EU, the threat of similar legislation in other jurisdictions, and the impact of NGO campaigns and public concerns about eggs from caged hens and the use of sow stalls. In many cases these commitments were limited to those markets where NGO pressures, public concerns and legislation pressure were the greatest.

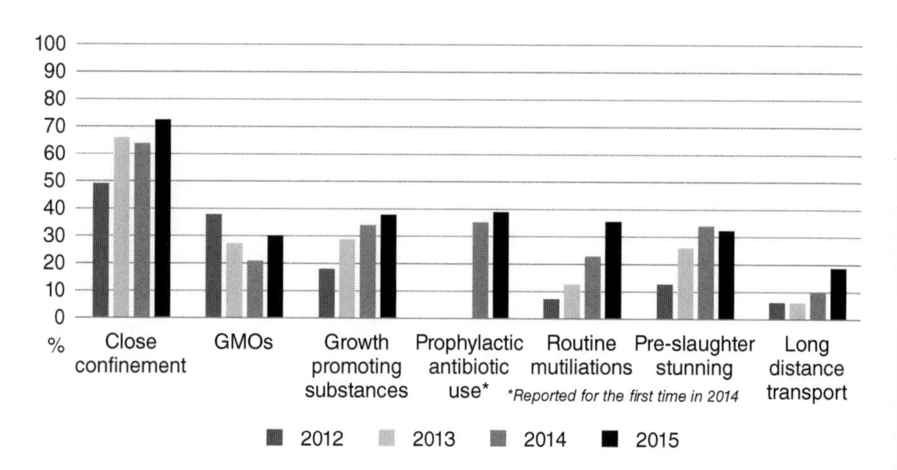

Figure 13.1 Percentage of companies with specific animal welfare policies
Source: data from Amos and Sullivan (2016a).

A wider point is that many of these issues are a direct consequence of the systems and conditions in which animals are reared. For example, the routine use of antibiotics on-farm is frequently prophylactic (used to prevent disease rather than treat it). That is, they are used to "prop up" environments where the welfare potential of animals is very low. Confined, cramped conditions, where animals are bred to operate at their physiological limits and are weaned at a young age, can be stressful, and can compromise animals' immune systems, making sickness more likely. Intensive farming, therefore, often relies on the prophylactic use of antibiotics to compensate for an inherently low-welfare environment.

Similarly, many farm animals are subjected to procedures that alter their bodies, often with no anaesthesia, causing immediate and often long-term pain and distress. Examples include: beak trimming (where part of the bird's beak is removed using a hot blade, secateurs or an infra-red beam), surgical castration of beef cattle, branding of animals with hot irons, disbudding of dairy calves with hot irons or caustic paste, dehorning adult cattle with wire or saws, the castration and tail docking of pigs, and fin clipping, which is used to mark the origin of hatcheries in farmed fish. The root cause of many of these issues is that these practices are frequently integral to the operation of highly intensive production systems, such as large-scale beef feedlots, battery cages for laying hens, broiler chickens reared indoors in high stocking densities, veal crates for calves, tether systems for cows, calves and sows, and sow stalls and farrowing crates for pregnant and lactating sows, respectively. The majority of these mutilations can be avoided if animals are kept in well-managed conditions, are provided with plenty of space to move freely and are given a varied environment in which to express the range of natural behaviours that are important to them (for example, foraging, scratching and pecking for broiler (meat) chickens).

Do companies define management responsibilities for farm animal welfare?

In most large companies, there is generally a clear delineation between those staff members who are responsible for the oversight of a policy and those staff members who are responsible for day-to-day implementation of the policy. Policy oversight is usually the responsibility of senior management or the board, and encompasses tasks such as defining the overall policy goals, monitoring the implementation of the policy, acting in the event of the policy not being complied with and ensuring that the policy remains relevant to the organization. In contrast, day-to-day implementation is commonly the responsibility of specific individual(s) or team(s), and encompasses tasks such as developing and implementing management systems and processes, setting objectives and targets, measuring and monitoring performance, and reporting.

Understanding how companies structure their governance and management is particularly important in the case of farm animal welfare given that farm animal welfare continues to be a relatively new area of management attention for many companies. Companies need to have the technical and operational staff to enable them to be confident that the issues associated with farm animal welfare are being effectively managed. Companies also need to ensure that their senior management and boards are aware of the business implications of farm animal welfare and are prepared to intervene when needed, both to ensure that their farm animal welfare policy is effectively implemented (e.g. in situations where there are tensions between the company's farm animal welfare policies and other business objectives) and when evidence emerges of failures in the company's management systems and controls.

The results of the 2015 Benchmark suggested that many companies had yet to formalize their management of farm animal welfare issues. In fact, 44 (49%) of the companies reviewed did not publish details of who is responsible, at either a senior management or operational level, for farm animal welfare. While this is an improvement on the 59% in the 2014 Benchmark, it was frequently difficult to tell how much, if any, senior management attention was actually being focused explicitly on farm animal welfare. In the majority of cases, farm animal welfare was presented as just one of a range of corporate responsibility-related issues that needed to be managed by these companies.

Have companies set objectives for farm animal welfare?

Objectives and targets are the point where policy commitments are translated into substantive action, and where resources and responsibilities are allocated for the delivery of these policy commitments. Of the 90 companies covered by the 2015 Benchmark, 49 (54%) had set farm animal welfare-related objectives and targets, a markedly higher proportion than the 26% who had set objectives and targets in 2012. Many of these companies—35 out of the 49 that had published objectives and targets—provided a reasonable amount of information on how the target was to be achieved (for example, who was responsible, what resources were allocated, what the key steps or actions towards the target were).

Many of the targets focused on management processes (e.g. to formalize farm animal welfare management systems, to introduce audits) and/or on a single farm animal welfare-related issue (e.g. to eliminate sow stalls, to move towards cage-free eggs). This is not unsurprising. The relative novelty of farm animal welfare as a management issue means that many companies are at the early stages of developing and implementing their management systems, processes and reporting. Where they do focus on performance, the objectives tend to be framed in relatively narrow species-specific terms.

The other point to note is that many companies are not "closing the loop" on their reporting. While, 62 of the 90 companies covered by the Benchmark had established formal policy commitments on farm animal welfare, only 33 reported on how they had performed against these policies. Similarly, of the 49 companies that had set formal farm animal welfare-related objectives and targets, just 33 reported on their performance against these or against previous objectives and targets that they had set for themselves.

Do companies describe their control systems for farm animal welfare?

Thirty-six (or 40%) of the 90 companies covered by the 2015 Benchmark reported that they included farm animal welfare in supplier conditions, compared with 34% in the 2014 and 2013 Benchmarks and 15% in the 2012 Benchmark. Of these, 25 stated that they included farm animal welfare in all relevant contracts and 11 that they included farm animal welfare in some but not necessarily all contracts.

From our discussions with companies, the emphasis on supplier contracts seemed to be a result of companies focusing on supply chain management more generally, rather than animal welfare in particular. The 2013 European horsemeat scandal heightened the level of company attention being paid to supply chains, and led to companies shortening their supply chains for particular products, increasing the quantities channelled through existing producers and emphasizing food provenance and local sourcing.

Auditing and traceability processes are essential building blocks for improving the management and oversight of farm animal welfare. Fifty-eight per cent (58%) of the companies covered by the Benchmark described how they audit the farm animal welfare performance of their suppliers (compared with 45% in 2014, 43% in 2013 and 35% in 2012) and 47% described their supplier education and capacity-building initiatives (compared with 36% in 2014, 34% in 2013 and 31% in 2012). While these numbers are relatively low, companies have started to collaborate with their suppliers on developing innovative online tools, sharing knowledge and best practices, and improving management understanding of performance through enhanced monitoring and reporting practices.

The Benchmark also asked about whether companies provided training on farm animal welfare to their internal staff and whether they had corrective action processes in place to take action in the event of non-compliances with their farm animal welfare policies. This is an area of weakness, with just 29% of companies reporting that they provided farm animal welfare-related training to their staff and a similar number describing their internal controls for farm animal welfare.

Are companies reporting against farm assurance schemes?

There is a general absence of global standards for higher animal welfare. In the absence of such standards, formal farm animal welfare assurance schemes have a critical role to play in driving higher standards, in providing robust auditing and assurance processes, and in providing reassurance to consumers and stakeholders about the performance outcomes being achieved. Examples of schemes which offer many welfare advantages relative to standard industry practice include the Soil Association, RSPCA Assured, Animal Welfare Approved, Beter Leven, KRAV, Label Rouge, Best Aquaculture Practices (Global Aquaculture Alliance), Global GAP Aquaculture Standard and the Global Animal Partnership (GAP) 5-Step® Program.

Most assurance schemes tend to have limited geographic scope—there are many national schemes—and they tend to have species-specific criteria. That is, companies may find that they need to sign up to multiple assurance schemes in order to ensure all their farmed animals are covered by the relevant assurance standard using criteria that match companies' own internal standards on farm animal welfare. Furthermore, it is often difficult to compare schemes because of differences in the requirements of participating schemes (e.g. in relation to the space requirements specified, the training requirements for those companies involved in animal handling, monitoring and corrective action processes, the welfare outcomes that are required) and because of differences in schemes' auditing and assurance processes (e.g. the frequency of auditing, the qualifications of the auditors).

Moreover, many of the widely cited assurance standards (for example, ISO 9001 and British Lion) are actually primarily concerned with quality and safety-related issues, and have relatively little or nothing to say about farm animal welfare other than, perhaps, that producers or suppliers should comply with relevant legal requirements. While these assurance standards are not farm assurance scheme standards *per se* (and should not be presented as such), they do provide many of the core process elements (e.g. on auditing, on traceability) that companies need if they are to implement effective farm animal welfare management processes in their supply chains. That is, companies should be able to build their animal welfare implementation processes on the back of the systems and processes that they have established to meet the requirements of these quality and safety assurance standards.

The 2015 Benchmark found that 73% of the 90 companies made reference to at least one farm assurance scheme standard in their reporting. However, as with other issues covered by the Benchmark, this reporting tended to be confined to specific species and specific geographies.

Performance reporting

The central finding from the 2015 Benchmark was that reporting on farm animal welfare performance remained in its infancy, although there were early signs that companies were starting to respond to increased interest in their performance against key policy commitments. For example, 30 of the 90 companies (33%) provided some information on the proportion of animals that are free from close confinement, 10 reported on the proportion of animals that are stunned prior to slaughter and 8 provided quantitative information on transport times. In the majority of cases, the scope of this reporting of performance was limited.

Our discussions with companies pointed to a number of reasons why the performance reporting scores were relatively low: many companies are still focusing on strengthening their internal management systems and processes; reporting on performance is largely seen as being for internal rather than external audiences; companies generally have multiple animal species; companies frequently manage animal species to different standards; and there is an absence of universal global performance standards for animal welfare. A number of companies commented that, over time, they expect to face greater customer and NGO pressure to report on their performance impact (that is, the welfare outcomes for animals managed in farm production systems). Some also cautioned that such reporting will only become standard when there is a consensus on the performance data that needs to be reported and a critical mass of companies are already reporting this information.

Concluding comments

There are three headline findings from the 2015 Benchmark. The first is that practice and reporting on farm animal welfare remain relatively underdeveloped across all four of the strategic pillars considered in the Benchmark (management commitment and policy, governance and management, innovation, and performance reporting).

The second and more encouraging finding is that we appear to be reaching a tipping point on farm animal welfare. Increasing numbers of food companies publicly acknowledge that they have responsibility for managing farm animal welfare-related issues and have started to establish the systems and processes they need to manage farm animal welfare effectively. There are various reasons for this change. Our interviews with companies suggest that consumer and client demand are the most important influences on their approach to farm animal welfare (Amos and Sullivan, 2015b). Other drivers include: regulatory pressure, the annual Business Benchmark on Farm Animal Welfare, media pressure and NGO pressure (Amos and Sullivan, 2015b). Interestingly, these pressures do not appear to be limited to Europe, with some companies citing animal welfare in the top five issues for global customers, and others noting customer interest in the responsible sourcing of meat as part of a wider societal concern around food quality, safety, provenance and authenticity.

The third finding is that we are starting to see early signs of companies demonstrating their leadership on farm animal welfare. These companies (which appeared in Tiers 1 and 2 of the Benchmark) include Coop Group (Switzerland), Cranswick, J Sainsbury, Marfrig, McDonald's, Migros, Marks & Spencer, Noble Foods, Co-op (UK), Unilever and Waitrose. These companies have all made strong commitments to farm animal welfare, have well developed management systems and processes, and have a clear focus on farm animal welfare performance measures. Interestingly, the 11 leadership companies cover all three of the food industry sub-sectors (i.e. food retailers and wholesalers, restaurants and bars, and food producers), they are well distributed across the countries (of listing or incorporation) covered by the Benchmark and they encompass a range of ownership structures (public, private and co-operatives). This is encouraging as it suggests that it is realistic for food companies, irrespective of their sub-sector, geography or ownership, to aspire to and achieve higher scoring in this Benchmark.

Reflecting on these findings, our overall impression is that the current state of play, with most companies at the early stages of developing and implementing farm animal welfare management systems, is probably best seen as the early stages of what is likely to be a long journey towards systematically raising standards of animal welfare across the food industry. Achieving higher welfare standards in food supply chains will take time, given that systemic change will be contingent on the industry being prepared to invest in higher welfare methods, the development of financial instruments to support and reward producers, and the continuous improvement in farm animal welfare performance through the implementation and integration of policies and standards into business strategy.

Given that progress on farm animal welfare standards in the food industry is at a relatively early stage, some food companies may regard the current focus on animal welfare as a transient issue that may not be as deserving of management attention as some other social or environmental concerns. Others may regard it as an inherent risk to be managed in the supply chain and focus their attention on ensuring compliance with minimum regulatory and industry standards. However, more forward-thinking businesses are starting to realize the competitive advantage in having clearly defined standards on farm animal welfare and a commitment to advancing farm animal welfare, along with a willingness to account for their performance in a transparent way. These companies will likely find that they are less prone to challenges from external stakeholders and can in fact benefit from increased engagement with their customers, suppliers and investors on their efforts to improve farm animal welfare.

References

Amos, N. & Sullivan, R. (2013a). *The Business Benchmark on Farm Animal Welfare: 2012 Report*. London: Business Benchmark on Farm Animal Welfare.

Amos, N. & Sullivan, R. (2013b). *The Business Benchmark on Farm Animal Welfare: 2013 Report*. London: Business Benchmark on Farm Animal Welfare.

Amos, N. & Sullivan, R. (2015a). *The Business Benchmark on Farm Animal Welfare: 2014 Report*. London: Business Benchmark on Farm Animal Welfare.

Amos, N. & Sullivan, R. (2015b). *How Are Companies Using the Business Benchmark on Farm Animal Welfare? Investor Briefing No. 21*. London: Business Benchmark on Farm Animal Welfare.

Amos, N. & Sullivan, R. (2016a). *The Business Benchmark on Farm Animal Welfare: 2015 Report*. London: Business Benchmark on Farm Animal Welfare.

Amos, N. & Sullivan, R. (2016b). *The Business Benchmark on Farm Animal Welfare: 2015 Methodology Report*. London: Business Benchmark on Farm Animal Welfare.

Sullivan, R. (2011). *Valuing Corporate Responsibility: How Do Investors Really Use Corporate Responsibility Information?* Sheffield, UK: Greenleaf Publishing.

Sullivan, R. & Amos, N. (2015). *Farm Animal Welfare Disclosure Framework. Investor Briefing No. 18*. London: Business Benchmark on Farm Animal Welfare.

14 Case study

Barilla – Good for You, Good for the Planet

Leonardo Mirone

BARILLA GROUP, ITALY

Background

Founded in 1877, Barilla started out as a shop producing pasta and bread. Today the Barilla Group has become a world leader in the market for pasta and ready-made pasta sauces in continental Europe, for bakery products in Italy and for crispbreads in Scandinavia. Barilla's international headquarters are in Parma, Italy, and it has 26 offices and 30 production sites around the world. The company produces more than 1 million tonnes of pasta every year and has annual revenues of over €3.2 billion.

Barilla cooperates with more than 1,200 suppliers across the world in the sourcing of 800 raw materials. Durum wheat, common wheat, rye, tomatoes, eggs and sugar, the main ingredients in pasta, bakery products and sauces, are defined as "strategic" raw materials.

Responsible sourcing integral to business strategy

Barilla first formally acknowledged the importance of sustainability in 2009 when the Group established the Barilla Center for Food & Nutrition (BCFN), a think-tank aimed at studying and analysing major global issues linked to food and nutrition. Since then, Barilla has increasingly recognized the importance of food sustainability at the corporate level.

In recent years, the Barilla Group has been following through on its aim to increase revenues while reducing the Group's environmental footprint and promoting healthy lifestyles through balanced diets. Its sustainability programme, "Good for You, Good for the Planet", outlines Barilla's plan to purchase all its strategic raw materials responsibly by 2020. In this context, the quality, food safety and nutritional value of products are a priority, and higher farm animal welfare is integral to these values.

Animal welfare has been a key focus for Barilla since 2011 when the company made its first commitment to sourcing cage-free eggs. By the end of 2015, Barilla had made Good for You, Good for the Planet core to the company's purpose. The purchasing team works closely with suppliers to encourage their participation in initiatives aimed at improving sourcing standards. For animal welfare, this means that Barilla expects its suppliers to comply with its new animal welfare standards in all regions where they are farming, sourcing, processing and marketing animal products.

Farm animal welfare: policy and implementation

With the development of the Good for You, Good for the Planet programme, animal welfare forms one of the key elements of Barilla's corporate policy. In 2010, Barilla engaged with the animal welfare organization, Compassion in World Farming ("Compassion"), to support its aim to improve animal welfare in its supply chain. Barilla began by identifying farm animal welfare issues along its supply chain, from birth to slaughter, and has since been working on specific animal welfare issues, addressing issues such as housing, feed and water supply, health and antibiotics management, transport, slaughter and traceability. Through this engagement, Barilla developed a formal position paper on animal welfare, launched in 2015, which sets out a clear and detailed farm animal welfare policy.

The Barilla Guidelines on Animal Welfare require suppliers to manage their farm animals with full respect to the five fundamental freedoms of animal welfare: freedom from hunger or thirst, pain, fear and distress and freedom to have a suitable physical environment. The principles also specify the standards on key welfare issues that suppliers are required to meet. For example, suppliers must define the maximum stocking densities for animals in production systems, ensure that the use of cloned animals and growth hormones is prohibited, and limit live animal transport to eight hours or less. Barilla only purchases ingredients from suppliers that adhere to these guidelines. The guidelines and standards are included in the contracts signed by egg and meat suppliers, and they are regularly checked through specific audits. In situations where a supplier is found to be non-compliant with the standards, a recovery plan is set depending on the gravity of the non-conformity.

The process of developing these Guidelines also led to Barilla's landmark decision to phase out caged eggs across all brands by 2020, a decision that will improve the lives of more than 2 million laying hens. With around 24,500 tonnes of shell and liquid eggs purchased annually, eggs represent one of the most important supply ingredients for the Group. Of the eggs purchased, 75% are used in Italy and the rest are used in the manufacture of Barilla's products in France, the United States, Russia and Brazil. At the end of 2011, Barilla took its first major step in introducing higher welfare standards across its business by committing to source only cage-free eggs for its bakery brands Mulino Bianco and Pavesi. The following year, Barilla's cage-free policy was extended to the pasta brands, Le Emiliane and La Collezione.

In 2014, to extend its higher welfare commitment beyond eggs, Barilla began an important project to engage existing meat suppliers to ensure that the meat used to prepare sauces and filled pasta comes from higher welfare systems. This led to the development of animal welfare guidelines for Barilla's pork and beef suppliers. Since 2015, Barilla's Italian meat suppliers have signed up to these higher welfare standards and have begun to implement them.

Progress towards higher welfare eggs and meat products

Barilla is making good progress towards its 2020 goal of sourcing eggs only from cage-free hens. In Italy, 100% of category "A" eggs are from cage-free hens, meaning that all eggs used in Barilla, La Collezione, Le Emiliane, Mulino Bianco and Pavesi brand products are cage-free. From 2017, 100% of the eggs used in Harrys brands in France will come from cage-free hens. In the United States and Brazil, Barilla is conducting ongoing analysis to identify suppliers of eggs from cage-free hens. In total, 80% of the eggs (by volume) used in Barilla's products are from cage-free hens.

In addition, all beef and pork meat sourced in Italy for use in sauces and filled pasta is sourced exclusively from certified sources, ensuring that the meat is traceable to the individual animal supply chains. Since 2016, 2,100 tonnes of product, representing 80% of all meat purchased annually by Barilla, is sourced from selected farms that are in accordance with the Barilla Guidelines on Animal Welfare.

Notwithstanding this progress, the economic implications of introducing higher standards of animal welfare are complex and are affected by factors such as the cost of land, feed and labour, as well as building infrastructure and equipment. Unlike crops, where farmers can change their crop choice in response to market trends, livestock farming involves capital investment in infrastructure. As investment is a major determinant of a producer's ability to integrate higher welfare considerations into existing systems, timing is critical. Not only does this require long-term finance and resource planning, but it also means that producers must speculate on how the market will develop when making decisions to invest in higher or lower welfare systems. Investing in a higher welfare system can provide market advantages, but only if buyers (i.e. manufacturers, retailers, wholesalers) and, ultimately, consumers are prepared to pay a premium for higher welfare products. By the same token, failure to invest in a higher welfare system can disadvantage producers if they are unable to respond to market demands for higher welfare products.

When the EU Directive on the Welfare of Laying Hens was introduced in 1999, egg producers were given almost 13 years to transition into enriched or alternative systems for laying hens. During this period, egg producers had to decide on whether to focus their investments on lower welfare (e.g. enriched cage) systems or on higher welfare (e.g. barn) systems. Those producers who invested in enriched cages may today find themselves needing to transition out of cages altogether and to supply only cage-free eggs, whereas producers who invested in barn eggs are likely to be better equipped to meet changing market demands. This was the case for one of Barilla's egg suppliers in Italy, which made the decision ahead of 2012 to transition out of caged eggs altogether, anticipating that the market would gradually shift towards cage-free eggs. This supplier has had to manage higher production costs in a market where consumers in Italy have, at least in the short term, been unwilling to pay a premium for cage-free eggs. In this instance, Barilla supported the supplier by guaranteeing to purchase volumes of cage-free eggs, even when the market for higher welfare eggs had not yet been fully developed.

Transitioning Barilla's egg supply chains to higher welfare systems has required careful management and collaboration with suppliers. The company appreciated that requiring egg producers to transition away from caged production was a major commitment, and not one that suppliers could meet entirely on their own. In preliminary conversations with each supplier Barilla established whether the supplier was entering egg production for the first time, constructing a new building as part of its business development, or looking to convert an existing building and/or replace equipment. At the end of the design phase it was clear that, for most suppliers investing in newly installed buildings or equipment, the cost differential between providing a lower versus a higher welfare system was marginal. However, retrofitting an existing production facility was generally more burdensome economically and could increase production costs by 15% or more. It therefore made sense for most suppliers to delay any transition until their existing system was due to be upgraded. Table 14.1 provides illustrative production costs associated with different systems in Barilla's egg supply chain.

As can be seen from Table 14.1, producing eggs in a new multi-tier barn rather than in barren battery cages adds on average €225 per tonne to egg production costs. Table 14.1 further shows that free-range eggs cost at least €500 per tonne more than eggs from enriched cages, and organic eggs cost at least €1,300 per tonne more to produce than eggs from enriched cages.

It is important to point out that feed price has a marked impact on cost differentials, with the conversion rate from feed to eggs in different systems varying significantly. Hens in enriched cages have little chance to move about and burn calories, so they eat less feed; approximately 2.2 kg of feed is needed to produce 1 kg of shell eggs during the fertility period of hens when they are raised in enriched cages. In higher welfare (e.g. non-cage) systems, more feed is needed for every kilogram of eggs produced. It therefore follows that when the price of feed is low, the extra feed needed for higher animal welfare systems has a lower impact on the cost, and when the price of feed is high, the additional feed required has a higher impact on the cost differential. This variation is included in the costs in Table 14.1.

What these figures underline is that the cost differential between the different systems is important to farmers. They simply cannot invest in high animal welfare systems if there is no certainty of market benefit. If a farmer decides to build a more costly system and is then obliged to compete with a farmer using a cheaper system, the business may not be sustainable.

Table 14.1 Differential costs (capital and operational) of egg production systems in Barilla's supply chain (2016)

System of production	*Differential costs (€/tonne of de-shelled pasteurized eggs)*
Multi-tier cage (enriched)	–
Existing barn (single-tier)	250–300
New multi-tier barn	200–250
Free-range	500–600
Organic	1,300–1,500

Note: Differential costs are based on medium-size farming systems (100,000–200,000 hens)

Rewarding suppliers with strategies based on volumes and transparent pricing mechanisms

Given the considerations outlined above, Barilla takes active steps to support producers transitioning to higher welfare systems. In general, eggs are supplied at regular (e.g. monthly, quarterly) prices, and contracts typically run at least for the duration of the egg-laying period (i.e. 14 months minimum). Prices are calculated according to feed prices; once the price of feed is fixed between the supplier of eggs and the sub-supplier of the feed, the total cost of eggs for the period is calculated and used as the basis of the final price in the contract.

Given that there is no predictor of how much consumers are prepared to pay for higher welfare eggs, Barilla has chosen to pay producers a price based on the cost of production, which takes into account the fixed production costs (e.g. the cost of investment, plus variable costs, for feed, energy, etc.). This way, suppliers are able to plan their activities, and they do not have to negotiate prices based on the auction price of feed or compete on price against other suppliers.

Suppliers understand that the issue of caged hens is an emotive one for some consumers and is one of the more high-profile welfare issues cited by the media, animal welfare organizations and, increasingly, investors. However, there are some suppliers who are yet to be convinced that cage-free is the way forward for the egg market. At an intellectual level, farmers and producers accept that market success of animal welfare schemes can improve conditions for animals on the farm. Consumers play a big role in determining the extent to which conditions improve; the more animal welfare-friendly products consumers buy, the better the conditions will be for farmed animals. Barilla understands that not all producers are prepared to take the chance or sustain higher production costs if the market does not change quickly enough. It should also be appreciated that, while suppliers of whole eggs can seek market opportunity from marketing their eggs as higher welfare products (e.g. through Label Rouge certification), suppliers of eggs as ingredients do not always have the same opportunity to command a higher price premium for their products. For all suppliers, they accept that higher production costs do not necessarily translate into higher prices being paid for their products, and that much of this depends on market dynamics. Furthermore, some markets can leverage price increases while others might struggle to do so. In Switzerland, for example, Barilla has benefited from increased market demand for higher welfare products because it predicted the market trend for higher animal welfare. Here, Barilla was ahead of the curve in being cage-free, whereas in Italy the market is taking longer to shift towards higher welfare products, and Barilla must therefore continue to support suppliers that are having to manage the burden of higher production costs associated with cage-free systems.

Barilla has adopted the same principle of rewarding suppliers who invest in higher welfare pork and beef production systems. It is understandable that increases in production costs associated with higher welfare products are only viable if farmers receive a price premium to cover the additional investment costs, although Barilla acknowledges that there is a learning curve and that the unit costs of new systems often decline over time. Higher costs are associated with land and physical infrastructure, feed and labour, as well as the cost of auditing farm animals to prescribed assurance standards. This is made more complex by the plethora of species-specific and geographically nuanced assurance standards and certificates (e.g. agroVet, Label Rouge, CAT) that producers are obliged to meet by their buyers. Complying with multiple and often conflicting assurance standards can be time and resource intensive. It can also require producers to invest in the training of personnel so that they are familiar with and able to understand the audit and certification processes of the varying assurance standards.

Engaging consumers on higher animal welfare

In the absence of a universal farm assurance scheme, Barilla welcomes the emergence of award schemes, such as Compassion in World Farming's Good Animal Welfare Awards, which provide a proxy for the management of welfare schemes across multiple supply chains. Following the first Good Egg Award received by Barilla in 2011, a TV advert was produced to promote the move to cage-free eggs for the leading biscuit and bakery brand, Mulino Bianco. The advert gained a lot of public attention and helped to raise the importance of higher welfare and cage-free systems in Italy. It also publicly promoted Barilla's welfare commitment as a leading Italian manufacturer.

To further promote its welfare credentials to Italian consumers, Barilla communicates to consumers on the packaging for egg pasta and bakery products, and has also dedicated sections of its websites to communicate the higher welfare achievements and high quality brands.[1]

Business benefits of higher welfare

Many global brands now report on animal welfare as part of their corporate social responsibility and sustainability programmes because of the greater consumer concern about how animals produced for food are reared. Farm animal welfare is also an emerging issue for the investor community and one that is set to become as important as carbon, water and waste in the future.

By introducing its cage-free policy and by engaging with meat suppliers to improve welfare standards in the supply chain, Barilla is demonstrating its leadership position in the market. As part of its sustainability plan, Barilla has aligned welfare with quality as part of its brand and has communicated this to customers through a variety of marketing channels, reaching a widespread audience.

External recognition of the animal welfare approach is strategically important to the Group. Since its first iteration in 2012, Barilla has been one of the companies benchmarked in the annual Business Benchmark on Farm Animal Welfare (BBFAW), the leading global measure of company policy, practices and

1 See, for example, http://www.goodforyougoodfortheplanet.org/ and http://www.barillagroup.com/our-position

performance on farm animal welfare.[2] Thanks to its successful engagement with the suppliers and the journey to continuously improve welfare standards across the business, Barilla has been moving up the benchmark tiers year on year. In the 2015 Benchmark, Barilla asserted its position as the highest ranking Italian company, moving up to Tier 3, alongside other world leading food companies, such as Compass Group, Sodexo, and Subway (Amos and Sullivan, 2016).

Barilla has also received multiple awards from Compassion in World Farming for its commitment to sourcing cage-free eggs. In fact, between 2011 and 2016, Barilla has received four Good Egg Awards for using 100% cage-free eggs in Mulino Bianco, Le Emiliane, La Collezione, Pavesi and Harrys brand products.[3]

Although moving to higher welfare standards requires a long-term perspective and careful planning, Barilla sees animal welfare as an integral part of its business strategy, and as vital to meeting stakeholders' expectations of improved sustainability. By working closely with suppliers and engaging consumers in this area, Barilla is showing leadership by not only meeting its customers' expectations but also improving traceability and risk management throughout its supply chain.

Key reflections and learning

Barilla has always put a huge effort into supplying ingredients from the most reliable supply chains. A willingness to collaborate with reliable stakeholders (NGOs, suppliers and institutions) is critical to setting the strategy and building a roadmap. Transitioning global supply chains to higher welfare standards is a significant commitment, requiring engagement with suppliers to manage the risks and opportunities associated with changing farming production systems. The timeliness of any transition is also critical to ensuring that suppliers are not compromised in their efforts to move to higher welfare systems. Risks associated with these transitions—which can range from higher production costs and lower volumes to competing standards set by buyers—must be mitigated through close cooperation with suppliers. The company is proud of the progress made and confident that there are processes and networking in place to work hand-in-hand with suppliers to achieve the best welfare outcomes for animals in the egg, pork and beef supply chains in ways that are commercially viable and sustainable for suppliers.

Reference

Amos, N. & Sullivan, R. (2016). *The Business Benchmark on Farm Animal Welfare: 2015 Report.* London: Business Benchmark on Farm Animal Welfare.

2 https://www.bbfaw.com/

3 https://www.ciwf.org.uk/our-impact/food-business-programme/good-farm-animal-welfare-awards/good-egg-award/

15 Case study

Animal welfare as a part of the DNA of BRF

Géraldine Kutas

BRF, BRAZIL

Introduction

It took 30 years for sustainability to be fully integrated in the business strategy of companies. Sustainability-related issues were historically seen as matters of corporate philanthropy, with the costs invariably accounted for on a public relations line under marketing. While the scope of sustainability-related activities was limited and often with little to do with core business, these activities were inevitably promoted with considerable fanfare. This thinking has changed. Today, an increasing number of top executives believe that the benefits of efforts to achieve sustainability far outweigh the costs, and that sustainability should be a core (or integral) part of business practice.

The question we in business now face is, how long will it take for animal welfare to reach a similar level? As we survey the business landscape, it appears likely that animal welfare will be seen as a core business issue within the next ten years. Why? NGO pressure, consumer concerns and the economic benefit of providing greater wellbeing for animals are all incentivizing companies to include welfare in their business strategies and to have effective management systems and processes in place to effectively manage farm animal welfare on a day-to-day basis.

In this chapter, I discuss the case of BRF, as it shines a light on the drivers for corporate action and on some of the practical challenges faced by companies aiming to strengthen their approach to farm animal welfare. BRF, a global leader in poultry and pig production and export, has, for many years, taken action to improve animal wellbeing. Whereas, previously, the corporate approach was not formally organized and there was no formal communication on the subject, since 2011 the company has a published policy, and structured management processes in place, with performance being monitored and progress communicated in a transparent way. This has not occurred overnight. BRF has faced many challenges and has learned, and is continuing to learn, from, its own experiences. A steadfast commitment to continuous improvement, where the company reflects on its experiences, is helping BRF on the journey towards sustainable and responsible meat production.

BRF: a world giant in animal protein

BRF is a multinational food company, headquartered in Brazil. The company is the world leader for poultry meat exports and is the world's third largest poultry producer. BRF is a fully integrated business, controlling the industrialization of ingredients, from the production of animal feed right up to retail distribution. In addition to chicken and turkey meats, it is also involved in the production and export of swine meat as well as products such as margarine, pasta and ready-to-eat meals.

Born from the merger of Sadia and Perdigão in 2009, the company is one of the world's animal protein giants. BRF is a publicly listed company that produces approximately 4,000 references (meaning unique product codes known as stock keeping units or SKUs) that are distributed in more than 150 countries. It employs approximately 110,000 people around the world and controls 35 meat processing plants in Brazil and 18 production units located in four continents, serving 47 distribution centres. In total, the company produces more than 4 million tonnes of food every year. In 2015, BRF's net operating revenue increased by 11% reaching US$8.8 billion, with a net profit of US$833 million.

BRF's growth model involves innovation (with over 300 innovations and new product lines launched per year), acquisitions and partnerships. Its objective is to have an efficient end-to-end business model, in line with the needs of consumers, and to have a global supply and delivery capacity.

Why invest in improving animal welfare?

The way BRF does business is organized around five core values: a company inspired by consumers, products for a healthy life, a team environment, eager for performance and immediate service.

These core values naturally led BRF to engage in the improvement of animal welfare. Perdigão and Sadia were internationally recognized for respecting the wellbeing of animals under their control. In addition, specific conditions in Brazil, such as the weather, facilitate the adoption of good animal welfare practices. For example, birds have access to natural light and fresh air because they can be grown in open-houses given the favourable climatic conditions. In 2011, two years after its creation, BRF built on the foundations provided by Perdigão and Sadia by developing and publishing a formal animal welfare policy and committing to implementing the policy as part of its overall sustainability practices.[1]

BRF took the decision to prioritize animal welfare for a number of reasons. First, animal welfare is important because consumers increasingly care about how animals are treated. In Brazil the legislation for the protection of farm animals is not as advanced as in the European Union (EU). But there are plenty of governmental and private initiatives moving in that direction and an increasing number of Brazilian consumers are asking for improved animal welfare policies. The international exposure of the company is also a key element. Being active in

1 https://www.brf-global.com/brasil/en/corporate-responsibility/animal-welfare-0

Europe, with two processing plants and various offices, has naturally increased BRF's level of awareness and the sensibility to animal welfare.

Second, products for a healthy life (one of BRF's five core values) means, among other things, having access to safe and high quality food. This is not possible if animals are poorly treated. Poultry and pork reared in facilities with a lower density, with access to natural light and sufficient food and water, as well as adequate veterinary treatment when necessary, are animals with the right conditions to be healthier. There is also a financial case as safe animals generally mean higher economic returns.

Third, BRF's own employees are convinced that animal welfare is a must-have. There is a great collaboration between several departments such as agricultural production, quality insurance and sustainability to deliver yearly measures that will concretely improve animal wellbeing. Although some measures might need time to be implemented throughout this large industry, the sentiment that actions cannot be delayed runs from BRF's top management through to day-to-day operations.

Nonetheless, it is not always easy to find one's way in the world of animal welfare. On the one hand, animal welfare should be based on relatively standard welfare key performance indicators (KPIs), which acknowledge or take account of specific local conditions; an example is the prevalence of dark houses in some parts of Brazil because of the high outside temperature. While the use of welfare KPIs aligns with how companies generally manage social and environmental issues, there is of course an emotional dimension when dealing with farm animals as sentient beings. Although this is understandable, we should not forget that we are talking about animals that are produced for the purpose of being sold as food. Far from the romantic notion of collecting eggs at the farm gate that many people have from their childhoods, the reality is that industrial production is about scale and cost competitiveness for mainstream markets. The challenge for companies is how to choose the right indicators, based on sound science, that allow them to respond to these emotional claims, while also aligning with business needs and objectives.

In that sense, the absence of international certification on animal welfare presents a major difficulty. The World Organisation for Animal Health's (OIE's) terrestrial code and technical chapters (transport, slaughter, broilers) is currently the only existing global animal welfare standard (OIE, 2016). The ISO Technical Standard approved by 41 countries, including Brazil, on 9 May 2016, will provide a management tool to facilitate its implementation. However, countries still have different legislation, with different industry bodies adopting different guidelines and standards, often going beyond the OIE standard. Non-governmental organizations (NGOs) have also developed certification schemes; again, these tend to exist, for the most part, at the national level and there is limited consistency between different jurisdictions.

To help address these problems of inconsistent standards and inconsistent frameworks, BRF has chosen to work in partnership with World Animal Protection. This NGO is one of the few with a truly international presence—with offices in the locations where BRF actually raises animals—and it has made the choice to cooperate with the industry to work on mainstream production, not just on animals produced for niche markets such as organic farming. BRF and World Animal Protection signed a memorandum of understanding at the end of 2014 and, since then, the partnership has been fundamental in developing projects that focus on animal welfare in all stages of production—from breeding to humane slaughter—and in raising awareness among company employees through specific training initiatives. Schedules were also created to include activities to develop and implement procedures that will improve the efficiency of BRF's supply chain production activities. For instance, as part of the partnership actions, in 2015 the company, in collaboration with World Animal Protection, trained 250 employees on animal welfare and held five awareness events for company leaders and key operators.

From policy to day-to-day implementation

BRF believes not only that animal welfare is an integral component of the ethical principles which inform its approach to animal production, but also that higher standards of animal welfare allow for improvements in the working environment, in human–animal relationships and, consequently, in productivity. For these reasons, BRF works on the basis of continuous improvement in production practices, using animal welfare indicators based on the "five freedoms" of animals:

- **Physiological freedom**. Animals free from hunger, thirst and malnutrition
- **Environmental freedom**. Animals free from discomfort
- **Sanitary freedom**. Animals free from pain, injury and disease
- **Behavioural freedom**. Animals free to express their normal behaviour
- **Psychological freedom**. Animals free from fear and distress

Taking these into account, BRF has defined criteria for animal welfare (such as avoiding cloned animals, growth-promoting substances and the routine use of antibiotics) based on the results of scientific research, prevailing legislation and client requirements. In addition to its stated welfare positions, BRF has set a target to transition to the collective gestation system for 100% of its pig breeding stock by 2026. Since there are no Brazilian rules on this matter, the company followed the laws of the European Union. As such, sows will remain in individual accommodation for the minimum required period and will later be released into collective crates, following animal welfare precepts. To implement its commitments, the company appointed professionals responsible for animal welfare on its farms and in its processing plants. One of their key roles is to educate employees and suppliers about farm animal welfare and about BRF's expectations.

All indicators of animal welfare are monitored and audited, and BRF establishes responsibilities for the implementation of corrective actions whenever necessary. This policy does not only apply to BRF itself, but it extends also to third parties. In fact, the company audits and encourages its suppliers and partners to develop good practices of animal welfare in line with international animal welfare procedures. In case of non-conformity with the animal welfare guidelines, the stakeholders involved are notified to ensure that corrective measures are taken. Finally, BRF regularly discloses its commitments and the progress made in its annual report available on its website.

The inclusion of BRF in the Business Benchmark on Farm Animal Welfare (BBFAW) in 2014[2] is an additional motivation for the company to increase communication efforts around its animal welfare practices. Simply put, prior to participating in the BBFAW, many people in the company had no sense that it was important to communicate on industry practices, such as the ban on hormones for instance, plans for improvement and the progress being made by the company against them. With the publication of the 2014 BBFAW Report (Amos and Sullivan, 2015) and the comments received from the authors, the company realized that the initiatives in this area should not only be highlighted but also organized and reported in a more systematic way. In addition, BRF's inclusion in the BBFAW allowed the company to compare its animal welfare performance with that of other companies operating in the same segment, enabling BRF to identify areas of strength and potential areas for improvement. One of the most encouraging findings from BRF's perspective was that country of origin is not a guarantee of higher standards, with many of the companies from emerging markets performing as well as if not better than their European and American peers. This is important as it encourages emerging market companies to continue investing in animal welfare. More generally, the Benchmark is significantly contributing to raising global awareness on animal wellbeing, and is one of the key references for companies looking to develop and implement animal welfare management systems, processes and reporting.

Elimination of sow gestation crates

BRF has engaged in a series of modifications to its production processes with a view to improving the welfare of chicken, turkeys and pigs.

One of the most important commitments the company has taken is the gradual elimination of sow gestation crates. A gestation crate, also known as sow stall, is a metal enclosure used in intensive pig farming, in which a female breeding sow may be kept during pregnancy and for most of her adult life. This practice may sound inappropriate, but we need to understand first why the industry uses sow stalls.

Their use is a consequence of indoor housing. Keeping animals inside is not necessarily bad. In fact, it protects both animals and farmers from weather, predators and parasites, and it improves animal performance, as well as making the production more predictable. The problem is that traditional group housing for pregnant sows does not work well indoors and producers must turn to individual housing as a practical solution (even though such housing increases capital costs). Why do pregnant sows not get along well? They will fight, wound and even kill one another when they think their access to feed is at risk. As a result, weaker sows will be injured or starved of their allotted feed portion. At the same time, the stronger sows will eat too much, making them overweight, which could eventually

2 See Chapter 13 by Amos and Sullivan.

harm their ability to give birth to and feed a healthy set of piglets. By using gestation crates, producers ensure that each individual sow has the correct amount of feed and the ability to eat it in peace and safety.

Furthermore, individually confined animals can improve the producer's ability to manage them, by making it easier and quicker to give them medications, check their condition and feed them.

Despite the economic implications, in 2014, BRF decided that it was time to turn the page and to engage in a process of gradual elimination of sow gestation crates. Many factors helped determine this decision such as a change in legislation in key regions (EU, Canada and some US states) which banned their use, BRF's dialogue with NGOs (especially World Animal Protection), and the availability of other production techniques which, even if imperfect, allowed the elimination of stalls.

BRF has committed to eliminating the use of gestation crates by 2026 and, to date, has succeeded in transitioning some 15% of its sows (300,000 in total) to collective housing systems. The period of transition could be criticized for being too long, but one must take into account the model used by BRF and the impact on small producers. BRF partners involved in pig rearing invariably do not have the financial resources to immediately change production systems. The company therefore provides technical and financial assistance. It works with financial entities to agree preferential interest rates and ensures that the transition period for any major changes is structured so that major impacts on small producers are avoided. Furthermore, the relatively long transition time allows BRF time to search for and test alternative collective rearing techniques.

Individual management of sows in a group housing system is now under control, but the problems linked to behaviour, such as aggressiveness, remain a challenge. Once again, the support of World Animal Protection has been critical to helping BRF to successfully manage this transition to collective housing. World Animal Protection has helped BRF to define the measures and investments that are necessary for each type of third-party partner. The investment required is significant, but the company expects a financial return as many multinationals from the food service area, including retailers, are asking their suppliers to eliminate this practice.

BRF's announcement in November 2014 to eliminate sow gestation crates had a positive domino effect (BRF, 2014). In fact, a year after BRF's statement, its main competitors, JBS and Aurora, also announced their commitment to eliminate sow gestation crates by 2025 and 2026, respectively. Together, these three companies account for 50% of Brazilian swine meat production. At the same time, the Brazilian Ministry of Agriculture, Livestock and Food Supply signed agreements with the Brazilian Association of Pig Farmers and the European Union (EU) to encourage the country's pig producers to end the use of this practice. Under the agreements, Brazilian pig producers will be provided with research and training to facilitate their successful transition to collective gestation systems.

This shows how the decision of a company to be a first-mover can rapidly change the practices of a whole sector, before any legislation is passed. BRF wants to continue to lead this industry transformation that will put animal welfare at the centre of the sustainability strategy of any company. Group housing system is a first move, but the company is working on other measures to continually improve its animal welfare practices.

Meat for thought

Animal welfare is comparable to sustainability. It is a journey; a long process of continuous improvements. BRF continues to face challenges and is learning from its own experiences. However, animal welfare is in the DNA of the company; an essential pillar of its strategy. BRF does not want to simply comply with existing rules. Rather, it intends to be a leader and is permanently working on how it could advance animal wellbeing. With time, the topic is becoming more structured and organized.

The absence of an international set of criteria accepted in a large majority of countries still constitutes a challenge. The common baseline is the OIE standard (OIE, 2016, pp. 277-401), although this is relatively basic. Of course, higher welfare standards can be implemented in order to meet customer requests or national regulations; BRF now exports to 150 countries and has to comply with multiple regulations and client requirements that are not necessarily compatible. For this reason, the company has certified parts of its production to different standards including GlobalGap, STS and ALO Free Switzerland.

The company is also committed to facing the different conditions of production in the countries where it has recently made acquisitions. The main production base remains Brazil, but BRF is also producing in Argentina and Thailand. Studies must be made in each of the sites and conformity plans scheduled for them. This often takes longer than originally expected and can generate some frustration.

In order to invest in animal welfare best practices, a company needs to make money and see an economic return. Some investments reduce costs, increase productivity and therefore are easily implemented. These are the "low-hanging" fruit. However, sometimes this is not the case, as the money spent is simply an additional cost. The meat sector is an extremely competitive market and consumers are not necessarily willing to pay more for something they nevertheless care about. On the contrary, they expect food prices to decline and the majority of them buy entry-level products. So under these circumstances, how can a company invest heavily in improving animal welfare, above the baseline standards that are a pre-competitive requirement? If there is no premium for a company that offers what others do not, it is hard to maintain a high level of investment. This is difficult, but not impossible. BRF has been able to make progress through its specialization in innovative, value-added products, such as ready-to-eat meals, through establishing preferential supplying agreements with major food business customers, and by leading the way and encouraging others to follow. BRF intends to combine all these alternatives, but sometimes it is not enough to allow all the investments the company would like to make to improve the lives of animals to materialize quickly. Animal welfare is a continuous improvement process and has to be framed over the long term. Some steps take longer, but what really matters is to see progress.

Finally, BRF has realized that the best way to respond to pressures—from NGOs, from consumers, from customers—while seeking to gain business is to have an established policy, to adopt commitments and to report on progress in a transparent way. It may not yet have all the answers, but animal welfare is an issue that is here to stay and BRF is embracing the challenge, continuously learning from its experiences, and is committed to demonstrating its leadership on this issue and contributing to the advancement of higher welfare within the industry.

References

Amos, N. & Sullivan, R. (2015). *The Business Benchmark on Farm Animal Welfare: 2014 Report.* London: Business Benchmark on Farm Animal Welfare.

BRF (2014, November 25). BRF and World Animal Protection announce global partnership. Press release. Retrieved from https://imprensa.brf-global.com/release-detalhe.cfm?codigo=534&idioma=PT

OIE (World Organization for Animal Health) (2016). *Terrestrial Animal Health Code* (25th edn). Paris, France: OIE.

16 Case study

COOK and animal welfare

Richard Pike

COOK, UK

COOK: our history

COOK is an independent ready meals producer. The company was set up in 1997 by Edward Perry and Dale Penfold with the slightly mad idea of trying to cook and sell frozen ready meals that would "look and taste like a good cook would make at home". This founding principle holds true to this day.

The early years were pretty traumatic as the fledgling business worked out how to master the techniques for bulk producing "by hand" frozen products that would be indistinguishable from anything you had at last night's dinner party. During this process, there were three main things that were sacrosanct: first, quality; second, our founding statement—that is, to cook using ingredients and techniques that a good cook would use at home so that it looks and tastes homemade; third, to maintain the independence of the business. All three precepts were extremely challenging for a growing business that didn't have any money and wasn't making any either!

In 2006, we begged and borrowed enough cash to be able to build our new kitchen in Sittingbourne, Kent and to allow the aggressive shop opening plan that was needed to start to realize some real growth. This was a huge gamble and one that looked like paying off—until the financial crash in 2008. The next three years were traumatic, but the core values held firm despite the obvious temptation to sell up, compromise quality or put in "machines"!

Today COOK continues to grow and we employ around 700 staff, operate 85 stores across the country and serve around 400 independent retailers who operate COOK-branded freezers in a concession format. We produce some 145 different products, the majority of which are made in our main kitchen in Sittingbourne, Kent and our pudding kitchen in Ilton, Somerset.

Our customers are predominantly discerning food lovers who have an expectation that we are doing things right, and who value quality and honesty. They are also not backwards in coming forwards to tell us when we have got something right or wrong.

The COOK business as a force for good

Our business by its nature is entrepreneurial and creative. While it has always had purpose at its heart, it wasn't clear to either the founders or the rest of the team until fairly recently exactly what this meant. What was clear, however, was that it was important to try to use business as a force for good in society and to ensure that it enriched the lives of all those it touched, either through our employment practices, our community activities or our work with suppliers.

In 2013, in an attempt to try to frame some of these ambitions, we became one of the first UK certified B Corporations, or "B Corps". B Corps are certified by the non-profit organization, B Lab, to meet rigorous standards of social and environmental performance, accountability and transparency.[1]

As part of this process we began, really for the first time, to both identify and measure what matters to us in relation to our business, to our community and to our planet. Becoming a B Corp required us to really challenge what we were doing across the three core pillars of the framework—community, environment and people—and to complete a rigorous assessment in an effort to gain the minimum 80 points that was required for certification. Helpfully, the structure of the assessment allows businesses that want to be a force for good in society to be rewarded in areas that they are performing well in and highlights those areas where focus may be needed to improve, but the certification doesn't require a level of excellence across all areas.

Our approach to sourcing and welfare

Our primary purpose has always been to make a product that was the best that money could buy. Within this, it was taken as given that quality meant "good", and that animal welfare considerations, therefore, should be built into what we do. We routinely visited all of our suppliers and checked the conditions at their farms and facilities. These visits covered basic compliance checks around quality, traceability and provenance, as well as environmental performance, animal welfare and working conditions for both permanent and seasonal staff.

However, all of this work was done within the confines of what was seen as "accepted" in the industry, with commercial viability and quality as primary considerations. During these visits, farm animal welfare was considered and discussed. We met some very passionate farmers who were clearly concerned about the welfare of their animals. However, the system was clearly geared towards profit and not sustainability.

Given the other much more direct imperatives that existed in the business during this time, this status quo was considered to be acceptable and defendable to our consumers, although, in reality, we knew that we were not doing enough and needed to find a way to change within a commercial framework. However, while it was clear that our customers expected a certain level of welfare consideration to be in place,

1 http://bcorporation.uk/

they were also highly cost sensitive and so it was going to be difficult to make direct changes in our sourcing provenance and pass the costs on.

Churchill said that "A cat looks down upon a man, a dog looks up to a man but a pig will look a man in the eye and see his equal".[2] We use this saying as a tool to encourage openness and honesty with our people, our customers and our suppliers. We soon realized that we were not being true to the core value of "Churchill's Pig" and were allowing purely commercial considerations to cloud our judgement. Our founder, Ed, made it very clear that he wanted to be able to answer any question from the readers of a certain tabloid newspaper, and feel confident that he was happy with our position. We dubbed this our *Daily Mail* test; that is, could we demonstrate that our practices and processes were aligned with our values?

What happened next?

In 2011, we began the process of seriously looking at our supply chain, our commitments and our ambitions. We met with Compassion in World Farming (Compassion) for the first time for advice and to help us frame the discussion. In particular, we looked at the business and ethical justification for a "business as usual" approach and we realized that we were falling behind our competitors in our approach while failing to live up to our own and our customers' expectations. Using our *Daily Mail* test, we were unable to justify to ourselves, let alone anyone else, the continued lack of direct focus on our ingredient provenance.

Our initial meeting with Compassion was a result of a chance conversation with their food business manager, Caroline Saunders, who invited us to their offices to offer us some support in defining where our priorities may lie. As a result of this discussion, we identified egg sourcing—at the time, the use of "standard" egg was in the news—as one of our welfare priorities and one of the areas where we could most easily make changes to our supply chain and engage the rest of the business in those changes. There was a plentiful supply of free-range product available, so we began the process of making a significant investment in our raw egg ingredients by switching all of our supply into UK and EU free-range eggs for both in-house and external products.

A tangible benefit of this transition came in the same year, 2011, when we applied for and received a Good Egg Award from Compassion in World Farming, recognizing our commitment to sourcing only free-range egg products. From this point on, we were able to use this acknowledgement in our marketing activities and, by the following year, all of our branded and unbranded products contained only certified free-range eggs. Of course cost was a concern, especially as free-range eggs are more expensive. We managed to offset this by increasing our sales volumes and through more direct sourcing. Together, these meant that there was a zero net increase in the unit purchase price of our eggs.

On the back of this early success, we began to look at the rest of our ingredient portfolio and we realized the enormity of the task ahead of us. With around 750

2 http://www.notable-quotes.com/c/churchill_sir_winston.html

ingredients and packaging lines from around the world, we rapidly found that our sourcing ambition was not simply about ensuring the quality, value, welfare, provenance or ethics of the individual products; what we needed to do was to develop a much more holistic approach to sustainable sourcing which encompassed all of these elements as well as wider sustainability concerns.

Our challenge was, and remains, whether we could be a pioneering business in some areas, but potentially fall below expectations in others, and how we could reconcile these tensions with our stated aspirations to be a force for good in society. In 2014, in an effort to give the whole project some real focus, we created our sourcing panel comprising senior members of the team from across all business activities, to devise our strategy, develop our aspirations and steer our procurement strategy. As a part of this exercise, we identified chicken, pork and duck as those areas most needing urgent attention.

Sustainable sourcing: three successes and a work in progress

When we began to discuss our options in these areas of supply in detail, we initially believed that the solution was a simple one, in that we just needed to work out how to afford "higher welfare" labelled product. However, very quickly, it became apparent that this approach was unlikely to answer all of our questions and that what we needed to work out was actually how to source materials "sustainably", by taking into account all of the elements that were important to us (such as provenance, ethics, biodiversity, supplier relationships and animal welfare). One of our key findings was that this would require us to think beyond labels such as "free-range", "local" or even "higher welfare".

Duck

We use a confit of duck leg in one of our bestselling dishes as well as in certain other smaller lines.

Originally all of our duck was from a single supplier in France. It was a good product that met all of our quality aspirations. However, it did not meet our desire to source closer to home and its welfare standards were unclear. When reviewing our options, we spoke to many potential suppliers and consistently came across the same issue—we required a size specification for our duck leg that was not widely available, and this led to either a significantly increased cost or lower available volumes.

Having established our sourcing panel and having a decent forum in place to debate these issues, we were able to review our requirements in the light of possible solutions rather than being constrained by current convention. We realized that we could redevelop the dish to allow the use of a slightly smaller duck leg with a wider specification. This meant that we could make much better use of the supplier's raw material with the added benefit that it also helped us to reduce costs. The result is that we now use a wonderful, higher welfare product, from a single farm in Ireland that meets all of our needs. We have also been able to develop a proper collaborative partnership, which allows us to respond much better to each other's needs and means that we are better placed to resolve unexpected challenges as they arise. For example, we have been able to manage issues relating to security of supply in instances where the volume of duck legs is at risk from the supplier through unforeseen circumstances. In these instances, we are able to adapt and change our production requirements and schedules to accommodate such a short-term issue, by reducing the availability of certain lines. This, in turn, removes some of the pressure from the supplier.

Pork

Our sourcing requirement for pork had been for it all to be certified to the UK Red Tractor standard.[3] Our initial thinking was that we would aspire to a particular higher welfare standard. However, when we looked into the detail of the Red Tractor standard, there were elements that we were not comfortable with, in particular those that permitted routine mutilations (such as tail docking and teeth clipping). These activities were permitted because the minimum space requirements around outdoor finishing paddocks meant that the potential for boredom or aggression to manifest itself existed and, in such instances, to protect the welfare of the herd, certain actions were acceptable. We believed that a better method of control would be for the pigs to have enough space and stimulation to prevent such issues arising in the first place.

When looking for new suppliers we use networking and recommendations from like-minded businesses to find potential partners and invite them to come and see if we are a business that they would like to be involved with. As a result, we are extremely lucky to now be working with two excellent farmers who are supplying us with 100% free-range pork that meets the Compassion in World Farming criteria for the supply and use of higher welfare pork meat (CIWF, 2013, 2016). In the wider sustainability context, both farms are also heavily into biodiversity and they are extremely efficient and effective, thus making the best use of their available resources.

The commercial impact has been that we have seen an increase of around 18% in the cost of pork. However, this has been outweighed by the marketing benefit of being able to promote the fact that we use free-range ingredients from two UK farms, and being able to showcase the farms involved in our marketing material and on our products. This, in turn, helps to promote the farms and their methods and raise awareness among consumers.

The harder challenge for us has been to move all of the other pork products that we use (such as bacon, sausages, gammon and chorizo) to higher welfare standards, given that the volumes involved are much lower and less available. Once again though, the developing relationships with our two existing pork meat suppliers have opened up other opportunities, offering ideas for using other cuts, manufacturing different products and introducing us to other potential partners.

3 http://assurance.redtractor.org.uk/

By the end of 2016 we had moved all of our pork products to a level that we are comfortable with and as part of this process we have now developed a UK chorizo product in partnership with one of our suppliers to replace our current traditional Spanish version. While this could be considered less authentic, it will ensure a consistency in our approach to farm animal welfare and will add further value to our customer message.

We are still aspiring to complete the final step in this process and move our bacon across to a higher welfare source which will be complete by the end of 2017.

Salmon

Fish is one of the product groups that presents the most challenges when determining what a suitable standard for supply looks like. Some salmon is farmed, but welfare standards do not cover all finfish species, and supply chains are generally more fragmented than for other animal products.

We use a large volume of salmon on a weekly basis. This is mainly diced and is farmed to RSPCA Assured standards.[4] We must admit to not actually being fully aware of the fact that the product was farm assured; we actually only found this out when we began to look deeper into the supply of salmon and discovered that these standards were in place, even though they were not being widely advertised.

This finding raises interesting questions around the reasons for businesses to adopt a higher welfare approach. Is it simply because of their interest in responding to demand for a higher welfare product, or is it more to do with the commercial imperative of operating a single system of supply rather than operating multiple systems of varying standards? Or, is it because fish farming is a relatively emotive subject (albeit that the media focus has been largely centred on fish conservation and human rights issues), so farming to a higher standard has become a form of business protection? Irrespective of the answer, it meant for COOK that we had a degree of assurance that our fish were being farmed to high standards and that there was and will continue to be sufficient supply to meet our needs in the future.

Chicken

One of the most emotive and difficult to solve welfare questions relates to chicken. Interestingly, this is one area where there is a wide public assumption that higher welfare birds are routinely used. According to Compassion and Defra, around 899 million broilers are slaughtered each year in the UK (Defra, 2015) and, of these, only around 23% are from higher welfare systems, including free-range and organic systems. Thus, the supply of higher welfare birds is limited and expensive, especially when you compare this with the fact that some 53% of eggs are free-range or organic (CIWF, 2010).

We use around 11 tonnes of chicken a week, made up of, predominantly, whole and diced breast together with some legs and thighs.

4 https://science.rspca.org.uk/sciencegroup/farmanimals/standards/salmon

In the past, we used "standard" chicken from Holland and the UK. Over time, however, we have progressively moved to UK-based supply, sourcing predominantly from one farm and requiring all chicken to be Red Tractor certified.

We did explore the potential to move to an entirely free-range supply of chicken, but we calculated that this would increase our chicken purchase price by 34%, which is not currently commercially viable and is arguably not the most sustainable approach.

Of course, by not using free-range chicken, we need to be able to respond to the *Daily Mail* question, and we need to be satisfied that indoor bred birds are managed to higher welfare standards and are acceptable to our ethos. This challenge has led to us creating our own standards that encapsulate our view of welfare issues in the context of a wider sustainability approach and our belief that the two go hand in hand. So, while it is currently uneconomical for us to move to free-range supply, there is much that we can do, and have done, to ensure higher welfare standards for our chicken supply. For example, we have begun by working with all our stakeholders to create our own standards and plan to move to a maximum stocking density of 31 kg/m^2 (compared with 33 kg/m^2 under EU legislation) by the end of March 2018. Furthermore, by redesigning dishes to use different parts of the bird, educating customers to understand the value and quality of brown meat over breast, passing part of the cost on to the consumer and working in a truly collaborative partnership with farmers to fully understand and reduce unnecessary cost, it becomes viable to move to a truly higher welfare proposition in a fully sustainable manner.

Some wider reflections

Our world is facing many challenges; we are currently using three planets' worth of resources; one in three calories of global food production is wasted; and by 2025 two-thirds of the world's population may be facing water shortages.[5] We also see repeated media exposés of poor animal welfare practice and increasing customer awareness. The question for us is less and less about whether businesses can be commercially viable by moving to higher welfare sourcing but whether they can be commercially viable if they do not.

Here at COOK we recognize that we are still in the discovery phase of our welfare and sourcing aspirations. We are excited about what we have achieved so far and the possibilities that have been unlocked, and we are looking forward to the challenges that still lie ahead. So what have we learned so far?

The first lesson is that partnerships are key. For a medium-sized business like COOK—which is too big to absorb a higher cost base but too small to interest high volume suppliers—it is only by working with like-minded, progressive farmers and processors who truly want to come along for the ride that the story can be one of success; these people are out there just waiting for the opportunity to realize

5 See WWF web pages on Food waste, https://www.worldwildlife.org/initiatives/food-waste; and Water scarcity, https://www.worldwildlife.org/threats/water-scarcity

their own ambitions. The tricky bit is finding them, but networking through industry organizations, transparency in our communications and showcasing our success stories on our website and through our products can help individual businesses to grow, tell their story and to increase consumer demand for higher welfare products.

Partnerships and collaboration are also the way we deliver change across the food industry. Working collaboratively, sharing experiences, finding joint solutions and demonstrating success are all essential to delivering wider change. It is often the innovations that have been pioneered by smaller companies that become the sustainability strategies of the larger companies and drive a step change in purchasing attitudes as it becomes socially unacceptable over time not to care.

The second lesson is that there is no one-size-fits-all standard that suits every business's sourcing aspirations. Standards and certifications are useful, and many have made important contributions to improving animal welfare and the wider sustainability of the food industry. However, the reality is that none enables a company such as COOK to develop its own truly sustainable supply chain standard, covering all of the issues that are important to it (including cost!), while also ensuring that the business is resilient to the inevitable disruptions and challenges faced by every business.

The third lesson is that internal change processes are critical. While high animal welfare standards should be a given, if standards are not where you would wish them to be from the outset, implementing a mind-set change throughout the business can be extremely difficult. Finance directors, in particular, are notoriously difficult to influence! However, our experience is that robust arguments, coupled with passion and conviction can deliver real, meaningful change. When we began the process of reviewing our supply chain and our aspirations for it, we were guilty of a fairly dogmatic approach and believing that we knew from the outset what the outcome was going to be. The reality is that rushing to a conclusion is a bigger waste of that time than not rushing your decisions and coming to an appropriate conclusion that fits the individual business model.

The fourth lesson is that once a plan is in place it is critical to maintain momentum and to implement the plan without delay to avoid losing those hard-won hearts and minds. Central to this is a willingness to reflect on experience. Each decision provides lessons for the next time, and any decision can be revised at a later date to improve the process as long as it is done in collaboration with all the interested parties. We have chosen to take an approach that gives an honest, warts-and-all answer to any question and this is powerful. We firmly believe that if we are not prepared to stand up and justify a decision we have taken, then we should not have taken that decision—which is quite a leveller in a senior meeting. Nevertheless, it is important to be flexible because what works today may not be what works best in a few years' time when we suddenly find ourselves out on a limb because we thought that all our welfare issues were "fixed".

The fifth lesson is that customers appreciate honesty. While there is a risk that some will walk away, most will engage and appreciate it regardless of whether or not they completely agree with the company's approach.

In conclusion, developing an animal welfare or sourcing strategy is daunting and complicated, and it should not be done in isolation. When developed in collaboration with staff, customers and suppliers, as well as independent NGOs with welfare expertise, and when it pays due consideration to other business demands and to the needs and interests of stakeholders, the strategy can deliver real business benefits.

References

Compassion in World Farming (CIWF) (2010, April 8). UK consumers vote for higher welfare chicken and eggs. Press release. Retrieved from https://www.ciwf.org.uk/includes/documents/cm_docs/2010/n/nr1009.pdf

CIWF (2013, May 17). Pig welfare sheet. Retrieved from https://www.ciwf.org.uk/media/5235121/Welfare-sheet-Pigs.pdf

CIWF (2016). Good Pig Award criteria. Retrieved from https://www.compassioninfoodbusiness.com/awards/good-pig-award/

Defra (2015). Poultry and poultry meat statistics notice. Retrieved from https://data.gov.uk/dataset/poultry_and_poultry_meat_statistics_notice/resource/3323909c-a829-4091-932f-46256004b5b0

17 Case study

The business of farm animal welfare at Greggs

Malcolm Copland

GREGGS PLC, UK

About Greggs

With over 1,800 shops, and 20,000 employees serving millions of customers each week, Greggs is the UK's leading bakery food-on-the-go retailer. We have recently diversified our growth strategy to transform Greggs from a traditional bakery business into a modern, attractive food-on-the-go retailer. This in turn is bringing about significant changes to the quality and relevance of our product offer, as well as the positioning and refurbishment of our shops. Our offer is differentiated by the fact that we freshly prepare food and drinks in our shops each day. Greggs owns and operates a vertically integrated supply chain, from production through to distribution to point of sale. This means that we can make great tasting, high-quality bakery food at great prices, offering value for our customers.

Our strategic plan, launched in 2013, focuses on growing like-for-like sales by improving the quality of our existing estate and making our operation simpler and more efficient. The plan has four key pillars, which are supported by our commitment to having a positive impact on people's lives:

- Great tasting, freshly prepared food
- Best customer experience
- Competitive supply chain
- First class support teams

We believe it is our responsibility to do business in a way that brings benefits to the people who shop with us, work for us, supply us or live near us. In addition, we recognize our broader responsibility to respect the environment. As such, we have identified five focus areas in our social responsibility programme. These are:

- **Customer health.** We encourage healthy food-on-the-go choices
- **Responsible sourcing.** We care about where our ingredients come from
- **Community.** We share our success with the people around us
- **Environment.** We aim to use energy efficiently and minimize waste
- **People.** We are a great place to work

Each area has a defined commitment, which is delivered through a variety of projects, and we track our progress using time-bound, measurable targets.

A focus on responsible sourcing

For Greggs, responsible sourcing is about making sure that our purchasing decisions are made as sustainably, ethically and responsibly as possible within our commercial framework. It is also about ensuring that our supply needs are produced and delivered in a way that avoids abuse or exploitation of workers, animals and the environment. We consider the wider implications of our business decisions when making sourcing choices.

We acknowledge that we are not large enough as a business to drive significant change on our own in our UK or our worldwide supplier bases. We always seek, however, to continuously drive improvements, and we positively support the actions of others through the adoption of industry accepted standards. We have a commitment to our customers, people and shareholders to maintain our reputation for great value products. Inevitably there will be occasions where commercial considerations will conflict with ethical sourcing concerns—we recognize this and we seek to achieve a balanced outcome in our decision-making. Notwithstanding this, the area on which we will never compromise is the use of quality ingredients; we want our customers to be confident that our food contains high-quality ingredients that have been sourced and produced in line with good practice.

The Greggs farm animal welfare strategy

Farm animal welfare remains a priority for Greggs; it is consistent with our values of doing the right thing when it comes to responsible sourcing and avoiding the abuse or exploitation of animals. Since 2013, Greggs has been assessed by the annual Business Benchmark on Farm Animal Welfare (BBFAW) (see Chapter 13 by Amos and Sullivan). The BBFAW provides a practical and respected framework against which our business can assess our progress and highlight areas for improvement. It was also an important catalyst for Greggs to develop its animal welfare policy and strategy in 2014.

The scope of our animal welfare strategy and policy includes all animal and fish species that are reared or caught for supply to Greggs. Recognizing the need to be pragmatic in our approach, we initially focused on our high-volume, primary sourced raw pork, beef and mutton, cooked chicken and whole/shell eggs. In 2016, we added milk, cream, liquid egg and wild caught skipjack tuna to the scope. Other animal-derived ingredients are scheduled for inclusion in the policy as part of our strategic plan. As a minimum, we require our raw materials to be from livestock, poultry and seafood reared or caught according to the requirements of EU and source-country farm animal welfare legislation. Where possible we will exceed these requirements. Our wild-caught skipjack tuna is now caught without fish aggregating devices (FADs) or by pole and line fishing.

The Greggs farm animal welfare strategy is based on existing legislation and on farm animal welfare certifications and standards, such as the Farm Animal Welfare Council's (FAWC) "Five Freedoms" and the British "Red Tractor" assurance scheme. The FAWC Five Freedoms on which we anchor standards for livestock reared to provide our ingredients are:

- Freedom from Hunger and Thirst—by ready access to fresh water and a diet to maintain full health and vigour
- Freedom from Discomfort—by providing an appropriate environment including shelter and a comfortable resting area
- Freedom from Pain, Injury or Disease—by prevention or rapid diagnosis and treatment
- Freedom to Express Normal Behaviour—by providing sufficient space, proper facilities and company of the animal's own kind
- Freedom from Fear and Distress—by ensuring conditions and treatment which avoid mental suffering

In addition to basing our farm animal welfare strategy on recognized standards, we also developed it in consultation with our suppliers and through engagement with NGOs, including Compassion in World Farming (CIWF).

Our focus on farm animal welfare has provided us with a range of benefits, including:

- Demonstrating that we strive to do the right thing when it comes to farm animal welfare and ethical sourcing
- Confirming the importance we assign to farm animal welfare and enabling us to demonstrate this commitment to our consumers, our investors and our external stakeholders
- Helping to build consumer trust and improving the profile of our brand
- Encouraging our suppliers to comply with our farm animal welfare policies
- Reducing business risk by assuring traceability and reducing the likelihood of product recalls
- Reducing the level of business risk for, and the attractiveness of Greggs to, institutional investors
- Providing opportunities for recognition and consumer communication through awards such as CIWF's Good Egg Award

The Greggs farm animal welfare strategy is governed by our operating board and is championed by the commercial director, who is supported by a cross-functional customer health and responsible sourcing team. Implementation of the strategy through our supply chain is achieved through ongoing supplier engagement using questionnaires backed up by audits and site visits. Our farm animal welfare questionnaires, which are based on the Five Freedoms, go far beyond simply assessing performance against legal requirements. The questionnaires also specify the welfare outcome measures (WOMs) that are to be used to monitor the welfare of the livestock and poultry. These measures are used both to track our performance and to help us identify areas where we need to improve performance or raise our farm animal welfare requirements. Open questions are used to confirm compliance and to seek further information on farm animal welfare and to identify areas for improvement.

Beyond monitoring supplier performance, we actively engage with suppliers and the industry on the issue. In 2015, we attended a joint conference of the Responsible Use of Medicines in Agriculture Alliance (RUMA) and the Veterinary Medicines Directorate (VMD), and a forum organized by the International Seafood Sustainability Foundation (ISSF) on tuna sustainability.

Recognizing that improving farm animal welfare is a continuous process of monitoring and improvement, we employ benchmarking against recognized schemes adopted by our industry. Greggs also invests in educating our people in farm animal welfare, as demonstrated by our supplier technologists who completed Animal Welfare Officer training at Bristol University during 2015. In the same year our Retail Management Conference included a workshop on farm animal welfare.

The Business Benchmark on Farm Animal Welfare continues to provide a practical and respected third-party framework against which we can assess our progress. The BBFAW's annual evaluations and feedback provide a helpful analysis of our strengths and our weaknesses, and enable us to focus on improvement areas for the materials that we purchase.

In depth: Greggs' farm animal welfare policies

Following a review of existing standards, supplier questionnaires and the current leading farm animal welfare issues, Greggs has established seven policies on key farm animal welfare issues. These are used to manage the main aspects of farm animal welfare that are relevant to Greggs' business and are subject to regular review. These policies are:

- **Greggs' Close Confinement and Intensive Farming Policy** states that livestock and poultry should be protected from experiencing unnecessary discomfort and from unnecessary fear and distress by providing a suitable environment.
- **Greggs' Avoidance of Growth-Promoting Substances Policy** states that livestock and poultry must not be provided with growth-promoting substances irrespective of whether these are antibiotics.
- **Greggs' Antibiotics Policy** states that Greggs recognizes the potential risk to human health from the development of antimicrobial resistance as a result of the overuse of antibiotics in the rearing of livestock. Greggs supports the responsible use of antibiotics, which it defines broadly as using as little as possible but as often as necessary to avoid further suffering. It does not allow the prophylactic use of antibiotics or the use of antibiotics as growth promoters in the livestock and poultry supplied to Greggs. Finally, Greggs maintains an active oversight of the scientific and policy debates around the use of the

highest priority critically important antibiotics (CIAs) in human health in the rearing of the livestock.[1]

- **Greggs' Routine Surgical Interventions Policy** states that livestock and poultry should be protected from avoidable pain, injury and disease through timely diagnosis and treatment. Surgical interventions such as tail docking and the reduction of corner teeth or tusk reduction for pigs reared for supply to us should only be practised to prevent further suffering or when alternative solutions have been unsuccessful. The policy also states that, where routine and non-routine surgical interventions are performed, the use of pain relief and anaesthetic must be provided where appropriate.
- **Greggs' Pre-Slaughter Stunning Policy** states that the livestock and poultry supplied to Greggs should be protected from experiencing unnecessary fear and distress during lairage and slaughter. We require that all meat supplied to us is from livestock which has been stunned before slaughter. Greggs also requires that there is a contingency in place when there is a failure of the stunning equipment or failure to deliver an effective stun. It accepts the use of gas as a stunning technique, as the livestock and poultry are unconscious and insensible to pain at the time of death. Greggs does not exclude meat from livestock or poultry produced using religious slaughter such as halal, but it does require that an effective pre-slaughter stun has been delivered to these animals.
- **Greggs' Live Transport Policy** states that livestock and poultry should be protected from unnecessary discomfort, fear and distress during transport, and that they must not be subjected to long live journey times (exceeding eight hours) from the time of loading to unloading.
- **Greggs' Genetically Modified and Cloned Livestock and Poultry Policy** states that no livestock or poultry that have been genetically modified and no cloned livestock or poultry or their progeny can be supplied to Greggs.

Measuring farm animal welfare performance

Establishing effective farm animal welfare policies for key welfare issues provides a foundation from which to improve welfare standards. Improving welfare should be viewed as a journey, where progress is made in steps. Progress can be measured through the improvement in the welfare of animals providing the ingredients. It can also be measured through the range of ingredients produced to accredited animal welfare standards.

We seek continuous improvement in farm animal welfare standards from our suppliers through defined targets and objectives. These are implemented through our supply chain using a collaborative approach whereby we explain our requirements, encourage transparency and work with suppliers to drive progress.

1 The highest priority CIA antibiotics are listed as the 3rd and 4th generation cephalosporins, macrolides, fluoroquinolones and glycopeptides by the World Health Organization (WHO) in 2011 (see WHO, 2012).

We have selected five key performance indicators (KPIs) for monitoring farm animal welfare performance in the most critical welfare areas:

- The proportion of animals that are stunned before slaughter
- The proportion of live animals transported over eight hours
- The proportion of animals that are reared without close confinement
- The proportion of animals that are reared without using growth promoters
- The proportion of animals which are genetically modified or cloned

It is appropriate that performance reporting and impact reporting feature in the Business Benchmark on Farm Animal Welfare, which is placing increased emphasis on the weighting of performance scores. We include both KPIs and WOMs in our supplier questionnaires, and we work with and engage key suppliers in providing these in a collaborative, open spirit.

What we have learned

We recognize that improving farm animal welfare is an incremental process. Our five-year animal welfare strategy covers all relevant animal-derived products and ingredients, and we review our plan annually to make sure that it remains aligned with our business and industry practices, and with stakeholder expectations. We continue to engage with suppliers and NGOs such as CIWF to build knowledge and develop our farm animal welfare processes and approach. Through our farm animal welfare questionnaires, we have begun to see the value in asking open questions of our suppliers, thus enabling us to better understand their current situation and capacity to drive welfare standards in the short and the longer term.

As with other environmental and social issues, we have found that progress in farm animal welfare standards is best achieved through a concerted approach to continuous improvement within and across the food industry. This is principally facilitated by purchasers of food ingredients—mainly retailers and food processors—specifying higher farm animal welfare requirements for the products that they source. Demand for higher welfare animal products is mainly driven by consumer pressure and, allied to this, the competitive advantages of offering products that differentiate companies and brands in the marketplace. However, food companies need to be prepared to work in partnership with their suppliers to respond to demands for higher welfare products. Change of the scale required by the food industry will take time, especially given the costs associated with training and educating employees in animal welfare, auditing and certifying products to recognized standards, and the investment required to modify or upgrade production systems.

The transition from risk to opportunity

Given that progress in farm animal welfare standards in the food industry is at a relatively early stage, some food companies may regard animal welfare as a transient issue that may not be as deserving of management attention as some other social or environmental concerns. Others may regard it as an inherent risk to be managed in the supply chain and focus their attention on ensuring compliance with minimum regulatory and industry standards. However, more forward-thinking businesses are starting to realize the competitive advantage in having clearly defined standards on farm animal welfare and a commitment to advancing farm animal welfare, along with a willingness to account for their performance in a transparent way. These companies will likely find that they are less prone to challenges from external stakeholders and can in fact benefit from increased engagement with their customers, suppliers and investors on their efforts to improve farm animal welfare.

At Greggs, we have experienced more interest from institutional investors in recent years, as they seek to understand how we are managing risks as well as opportunities linked to farm animal welfare. Undoubtedly, these investors have been spurred on by the Business Benchmark on Farm Animal Welfare to assess the quality of companies' policies, practices and performance on farm animal welfare and to play their role in demanding better standards and reporting across the food sector.

Today, we regard farm animal welfare as a business opportunity more than simply a risk to be managed. We have made progress in the standards of farm animal welfare of the materials that we purchase by working closely with CIWF and our suppliers. In 2013 we produced our first farm animal welfare supplier questionnaires and standards. Our progress has been recognized; while we only achieved a Tier 5 rating in the 2013 and 2014 BBFAW reports, we were delighted to have progressed to a Tier 3 rating in the 2015 BBFAW report and then go on to achieve a Tier 2 rating in 2016. I was also a panel member at the 2015 BBFAW report launch (see Amos and Sullivan, 2013, 2015, 2016).

From our humble beginnings as a small family business in the north-east of England, to the UK's leading bakery food-on-the-go retailer, responsible sourcing has been, and will continue to be, at the heart of our strategy.

References

Amos, N. & Sullivan, R. (2013). *The Business Benchmark on Farm Animal Welfare: 2013 Report*. London: Business Benchmark on Farm Animal Welfare.

Amos, N. & Sullivan, R. (2015). *The Business Benchmark on Farm Animal Welfare: 2014 Report*. London: Business Benchmark on Farm Animal Welfare.

Amos, N. & Sullivan, R. (2016). *The Business Benchmark on Farm Animal Welfare: 2015 Report*. London: Business Benchmark on Farm Animal Welfare.

World Health Organization (2012). *Critically Important Antimicrobials for Human Medicine, 3rd revision 2011*. Geneva: WHO. Retrieved from http://www.who.int/foodsafety/publications/antimicrobials-third/en/

18 Case study

Animal welfare at the epicentre of a perfect storm

Steven McLean

MARKS & SPENCER PLC, UK

Farm animal welfare at M&S

There are many reasons for food businesses to focus on farm animal welfare in their supply chains. But, for lots of organizations, one of the most significant motives will be customer perception—with animal welfare being used either to enhance or differentiate a brand among competitors or to protect an existing brand position.

UK retailer Marks & Spencer (M&S) has built a unique brand position over the last 130 years and much of this is down to customer trust. M&S is an own-label retailer, selling food, clothing and home products through its 1,330 stores and online, both in the UK and internationally. M&S is renowned for providing consumers with unique, innovative products sourced and marketed with an industry-leading approach to provenance, ethics and environmental standards. This position has evolved over decades, and the business is focused on protecting that position by always acting with the integrity its customers have come to know and expect.

In 2015 the business revised its core values, introducing four new values built on the principles that have guided the business since it was founded in 1884. The new values—Inspiration, Innovation, Integrity and In Touch—are at the heart of every decision the business makes. Perhaps not surprisingly then, M&S has a long-held position as a leader in farm animal welfare. It was one of only two retail organizations globally to achieve Tier 1 status in the 2015 Business Benchmark on Farm Animal Welfare (Amos and Sullivan, 2016), and has won a number of awards from Compassion in World Farming and the RSPCA.

How does M&S approach farm animal welfare?

M&S's approach to farm animal welfare has evolved over many years. At its core, M&S has always insisted that high standards of farm animal welfare are met and maintained at all stages of the animal's life—on the farm, during transport and at the place of slaughter. For many years, M&S has had a dedicated team of agriculture and fisheries specialists responsible for delivering and implementing its agriculture policies. All these agriculture managers are externally trained in animal welfare by Bristol University and are certified every three years. In addition, M&S has worked with external advisers, NGOs and other specialist providers to help determine what best practice welfare looks like.

Back in the 1990s, M&S was one of the first retailers to develop its own sourcing standards—M&S Select Farm standards—which included specific welfare requirements alongside food safety and animal health standards. At the same time, it started auditing supplying farms to ensure compliance with these requirements, in order to demonstrate to its customers that it acts ethically and with integrity. Historically, like the rest of the industry, M&S followed an input measure-led approach—setting requirements for how animals were managed and how much space they were provided with, among other things. The criteria for this were regularly updated based on practical observations, evolving industry standards and following discussions with experts in animal welfare. As thinking has evolved, however, M&S has developed its welfare approach to ensure it maintains leading standards. M&S's animal welfare approach now comprises four main elements:

- Best practice baseline standards
- Codes of practice and farm assurance
- Outcome measure collection
- Research and innovation projects

Best practice baseline standards

All M&S producers must adhere to current legislative requirements and abide by the UK Red Tractor standard. Above this, M&S baseline standards include additional criteria that producers must meet in order to be accepted into the supply chains as an M&S Select Farm. For some species, this requirement is in line with current legislation and industry standards. For many species, this means continually going beyond industry norms to ensure M&S food animals are produced to a higher welfare standard (see Box 18.1).

Box 18.1 M&S's best practice baseline standards

Eggs: M&S sells 100% free-range eggs in its fresh shell eggs and ingredient eggs used in its prepared products.

Turkeys, geese and ducks: All M&S fresh whole turkeys and ducks are produced to higher welfare standards. All M&S geese are produced free-range and it does not sell foie gras or its by-products.

Pork: All M&S fresh pork is outdoor bred or free-range. M&S prohibits the use of farrowing crates in its fresh pork supply.

Chicken: All M&S Oakham fresh chicken is reared in barns with increased space (stocked at 30 kg/m^2), natural daylight and provision of environmental enrichment.

Dairy: The herds supplying M&S with fresh milk must follow an enhanced health and welfare programme, which is audited by a specialist veterinary surgeon each year. In addition, all farms are currently undergoing RSPCA Assured accreditation.

Beef: M&S does not permit the rearing of calves for white veal, only rose veal.

Wild fish: All M&S wild fish is caught from the most sustainable sources available (certified, undergoing assessment or involved in a credible improvement programme).

Farmed fish: M&S sources all farmed fish and fish feed from the most sustainable sources available.

The following minimum standards exist across all M&S meat, dairy, egg and fish supply chains:

1. M&S does not allow specific breeds that have inherent welfare issues associated with them, e.g. Barbary duck.
2. M&S does not allow genetic engineering or cloning of livestock.
3. M&S does not sell meat and by-products from exotic species, including bison, crocodile, kangaroo or frogs' legs.
4. M&S does not allow meat, bone meal or any unauthorized feed products in its livestock diets.
5. M&S does not permit the routine mutilation of farm animals in its supply.
6. Humane slaughter methods must be used on all livestock and M&S requires pre-slaughter stun for all animals in its supply chain.
7. M&S insists that all live animal transport is kept to a minimum and that long-distance transport is avoided. To ensure this, it specifies a maximum transport time of 8 hours and has a target of less than 4 hours. The majority of live animal transport in its supply is less than 2 hours.
8. M&S requires that all livestock are maintained in good health and that all sick or injured animals receive prompt treatment. All producers must implement a livestock health plan in conjunction with their veterinary surgeon that is regularly reviewed and updated.
9. M&S insists that producers adhere to its policy on responsible antimicrobial use. It does not permit routine use of antimicrobials and the use of growth promoting antibiotics is prohibited.

Source: Marks & Spencer Farm Animal Health & Welfare website*

* https://corporate.marksandspencer.com/plan-a/our-approach/food-and-household/product-standards/farm-animal-health-and-welfare#ba707bfdd3ce4aa081caea3521c904b3

Codes of practice and farm assurance

All livestock used in M&S supply chains must be produced according to M&S livestock codes of practice, which build on its baseline standards and include specifications on all areas of sustainability including animal welfare, people welfare, environment and efficiency. It continually seeks to improve standards and carries out an annual independent review of its codes of practice alongside its partners. To ensure these standards are being met the retailer uses M&S Select Farm assurance and national farm assurance. Audits are carried out at farm, transport and slaughter by M&S trained supply personnel and independently verified by SAI Global. In addition, M&S's team of animal welfare specialists carries out periodic inspections to verify that its suppliers are providing leading standards of animal care.

Welfare outcome measures

In recent years, M&S has introduced a range of species-specific welfare outcome measures—metrics collected by directly observing the animals—that provide ongoing information about the health and welfare of the animals in its supply. As an example, the number of animals that have fallen ill or that have suffered an injury are typical outcome measures recorded on farm. This is a relatively new approach; at the current time, welfare outcome measures are being collected across M&S's integrated supply chains, and this process is being rolled out to other livestock sectors.

Research and innovation

M&S works closely with industry experts and scientists to constantly review its animal welfare approach. It has a long-term partnership with independent welfare specialists, FAI, which provides animal welfare knowledge and direction and is responsible for managing its independent data collection and supply chain research on outcome measures. In addition, M&S liaises regularly with centres of excellence in animal welfare and engages regularly with responsible NGOs, including RSPCA, Compassion in World Farming and the Humane Slaughter Association to ensure its approaches and policies are current and meaningful, using these NGOs as "critical friends". It also engages with NGO partners on outcome measure findings to drive continued improvement in its supply chains.

One of the key advantages of using an outcome-based approach to welfare monitoring is that it provides robust information about the welfare standards on farm but, importantly, allows farmers to pioneer their own solutions and innovations to make progress. This flexibility and creativity is crucial for tackling some of the long-standing challenges to sustainable food production. It also provides information that can help shape research requirements, with M&S then investing in research to trial new approaches that can deliver meaningful change in welfare outcomes.

Key reflections

One of the key learnings from the way that M&S approaches farm animal welfare is that having leading standards can clearly support a differentiated brand position based on ethics and trust. M&S is recognized for its leading position on farm animal welfare, which reflects its core value of integrity and is in line with its wider ethical programme, Plan A. What is also clear is that this is not a position one can develop overnight; it has taken sustained effort over a long period. Furthermore, it is evident that it takes considerable investment in terms of internal resources, consultation with external advisers and auditors, and liaison with the supply chain.

Put simply, customers expect M&S to do the right thing in terms of animal welfare but they do not always know what the right thing is, so they also trust M&S to establish the best approach. The approach it takes is to be led by science; that way it can justify its standards. M&S, therefore, spends a lot of time consulting with industry and working closely with independent advisers to review the latest scientific research.

Inevitably, there is "noise" in the industry, with competitors perhaps following a slightly different approach from that taken by M&S. There are many grey areas where judgement calls are required. M&S's view is that it is important to not simply "follow the pack" but to have independently verified policy positions that fit with its own supply chain and commercial positioning.

This is a challenge in itself: how does a business like M&S balance the different requirements and views of a number of stakeholders to agree policies that are acceptable to its supply chain and maintain its brand position? Every issue is different. Sometimes it is clear cut—consumers expect certain practices from a business such as M&S and it has to deliver them—and a good example would be free-range eggs. Other issues are less clear or involve significant changes to production methods to achieve the desired end result. In those situations, M&S needs to work with its supply base to move towards its aspired position in a practical timeframe and provide support in terms of information to help farmers evolve welfare practice. Ultimately, M&S is just one of a number of retailers in the supply chain, which means that farmers and processors can choose to supply elsewhere if M&S makes its welfare requirements too onerous or if the cost of meeting these requirements is too high. You can't jump from nothing to leading standards overnight so you need a clear strategy and long-term relationships to succeed.

One definite advantage that good farm animal welfare has over other supply chain issues is that generally it makes commercial sense for farmers, and this is definitely something that M&S factors into supply chain engagement. Of course, big changes that involve significant differences to production methods take time and investment and companies need to create supply chain models that make it worthwhile for farmers to consider making changes on this scale. But incremental improvements in animal welfare generally deliver improved bottom line performance at a farm level—healthier animals have higher production efficiency—and so this is an easy sell to farmers. What M&S does is support this kind of ongoing incremental improvement with veterinary advice so that farmers are given clear guidance on what is required and how to achieve it on their own farm.

It is one thing to engage the supply chain, but another to engage consumers, who often get mixed messages from lobbying groups and the media, while having little practical knowledge of what good animal welfare really means. Customer engagement is a really important part of animal welfare policy. M&S is constantly striving to be more transparent about its sourcing standards and to explain to customers through its website, in-store messaging and marketing about what makes its approach to animal welfare different and about how it arrives at its policy positions. It also tries to explain some of the rationale behind its decisions and its aims and aspirations for the future so that customers that are interested can see where it is on its welfare journey.

The word "journey" is key. What is clear from the way that M&S has approached farm animal welfare over many years is that the situation is constantly evolving—what is seen as good today will change as new information and new technology become available. Businesses must, therefore, be prepared to invest in animal welfare for the long term. Animal welfare is not something that you can address today and then forget, as good practice is constantly changing; achieving today's leading standards will not get you any credit tomorrow. Maintaining leading standards requires investment, resources, expertise, collaboration and ongoing effort. If you are going to lead, then you have to be prepared for others to follow and therefore you have to make it a long-term approach. It is no good going for quick headlines today.

Perhaps inevitably, aiming for leading welfare standards also means addressing difficult issues and finding solutions that are credible and commercially viable. You have to be prepared to deal with the difficult challenges. If you are starting from scratch, then there is plenty of low-hanging fruit to address and you can make fairly rapid progress. But there are some big issues that require a fundamental change in mind-set, production approach or even supply chain structure. Some of these challenges are pre-competitive and it is on these issues—things like antibiotic use—where the whole industry should be collaborating to drive change rather than individual businesses trying to gain competitive advantage. Of course, we operate in a competitive world and every retailer is trying to carve out its own positions in the marketplace, but an industry-led approach to major challenges can often deliver better results faster and that is in everyone's interests.

Current and future opportunities and challenges

With such a longstanding position on farm animal welfare it must seem as if everything is simple for a business like M&S—gradual evolution of policy and incremental improvement of welfare performance are all that are required to maintain a leading position. In some situations, that is probably the case, but things are not always clear cut. The food retail environment is fast-paced and ever-changing and farm animal welfare is one issue among a whole host of issues that M&S needs to consider as part of its sourcing approach.

Probably the two biggest factors for M&S are the wider sustainability challenges we all face and the competitive nature of food retail. Animal welfare is important to M&S because its core brand values see that it acts ethically and with integrity. But this means that it also needs to consider a wide range of other factors when setting sourcing standards and approach. Ethical sourcing is multi-factorial and so M&S has to balance animal welfare against sustainability issues such as a product's carbon footprint, the resources that are used in its production, the impact on human welfare, the environmental impact and the overall efficiency of production. This is an area that is becoming increasingly complex as the wider sustainability agenda gains momentum. The oft-quoted "perfect storm" of growing population and the demand for more food, balanced against energy security, water security, resource availability and climate disruption, mean that food production is under increasing pressure and efficiency is a key driver. The sustainability agenda sees the whole food industry under increasing pressure to produce more food from fewer inputs to ensure that we can continue to feed the growing global population. While this makes good sense from an environmental point of view and from a financial point of view, it can present some interesting ethical dilemmas around animal welfare. By its very description, a "more from less" approach would tend to point towards intensification of agriculture to get higher production from fewer inputs, ensuring better resource utilization and improved food security. This approach is hard to argue with from an environmental viewpoint and matches the wider drive in society to reduce energy use, water use and waste. Yet many welfare input measures focus on indicators such as space provision and freedom of movement—a more extensive production environment—for the welfare of the animals concerned. These pressures are often motivated by a desire to provide animals with the freedom to exhibit more natural behaviour. The ethical debate is also clouded by emotion and the anthropomorphism that inevitably colours our collective view on how animals should be managed and cared for.

Establishing where farm animal welfare fits within the M&S sustainability hierarchy and decision-making is far from simple. Its approach to welfare is to be science-led and that also shapes its wider sustainability thinking. Therefore, M&S tries to consider welfare within the wider context of ethics. But it is not always easy to determine what the most important factor is, and external pressures—whether from NGO or competitor activity or consumer awareness—unavoidably shape the approach. Sometimes preconceived ideas on what good welfare performance looks like also make the right decision harder to accept. M&S has to ensure that at all times it can justify its policy decisions in respect of animal welfare, sustainability and customer opinion and that those decisions stand up to scrutiny.

One of the key ways that M&S is hoping to smooth this decision-making process is through the adoption of welfare outcome measure recording. Welfare outcome measures provide far more meaningful information than has ever been available before. Historically welfare performance has been all about setting input parameters, and these have always been based on a specific set of circumstances. However, welfare outcome measures provide a way of seeing how different production systems and approaches affect welfare, either positively or negatively.

They allow comparison of completely different production systems and show whether these systems can achieve similar welfare performance through different management approaches. Welfare outcome measures also facilitate the consideration of animal welfare in an impartial way within the wider sustainability agenda, as they provide a way of objectively assessing whether sustainable intensification really does have a negative impact on animal welfare.

One area where objective measures aren't so readily available is that of animal behaviour. Many will argue that a key welfare requirement is the ability to exhibit normal behaviour; indeed it is one of the Five Freedoms and, as such, is entrenched within many definitions and interpretations of good welfare practice. Yet some changes to production that can appear to make good sense from a sustainability point of view, and have no detrimental impact on welfare outcome measures, are still seen as unacceptable by many due to their constraints on behaviour. One notable example of this challenge would be housed dairy production, where environmental performance, resource utilization and welfare outcome measures can be better than grazed production systems. However, despite these potential benefits, concerns remain about the impact on cow behaviour. Is this simply anthropomorphism—assuming that cows are happier with the freedom to roam outside because it feels more natural—or is there real justification on welfare grounds? So much depends on the housing conditions and design, space allowances and management practices, but it is issues like this that present obvious challenges to a business like M&S.

M&S's whole approach to animal welfare is based on being science-led but sometimes the science is inconclusive and it has to make a decision based on all the factors surrounding an issue and on the impact that such a decision can have on brand reputation. The debate around housed dairy cows is a great example of this. Although the scientific evidence does not clearly favour one system over another in terms of animal welfare (assuming both systems are run to a high standard), M&S's decision was to have a grazing requirement for the herds that supply it with milk. The reason is that, at the current time, public opinion is firmly in favour of cows grazing and so that is what customers expect M&S to do. This is a great example of the need to be pragmatic when setting welfare policy, using science as a basis for informing decisions but not being blinkered to wider issues.

The other major challenge facing food retailers is the balance between good welfare practice and the commercial reality of the huge pressure on retail food prices. To an extent a business such as M&S is insulated from this, but the pressure remains there as a backdrop to any commercial discussions. The reality is that consumers increasingly expect food prices to be low, but they also expect high welfare standards, which can add to cost of production. This is where transparency and clarity over welfare standards is important, so that consumers can quickly and easily determine the differences between products and make a value judgement accordingly. It is also where product labelling becomes important particularly in those critical few seconds when a customer is looking at products on the shelf and making buying decisions.

Concluding remarks

Marks & Spencer provides an example of a business that clearly differentiates itself based on leading standards of farm animal welfare. This is not by accident; it is the result of sustained focus on animal welfare over a long period of time, supported by a significant investment in time and resources to manage and develop that welfare position. The advantage to M&S is clear: reinforcement of positive brand positioning as an ethical retailer that operates with integrity; and brand protection through proactive action to improve animal welfare and therefore avoid contentious and potentially negative publicity around welfare concerns.

Reference

Amos, N. & Sullivan, R. (2016). *The Business Benchmark on Farm Animal Welfare: 2015 Report.* London: Business Benchmark on Farm Animal Welfare.

19 Case study

The Co-op's agricultural journey

Rosie Barraclough and Ciara Gorst

THE CO-OP, UK

Introduction

Co-op ("The Co-op" and previously known as The Co-operative Food) is part of The Co-operative Group, one of the world's largest consumer cooperatives, owned by more than 8 million members. We are one of the UK's leading convenience retailers, operating across the country with over 2,800 stores located in every postal area across the UK. This commitment to be the UK's leading community food retailer means we serve 14.5 million customers every week.

The purpose of The Co-op business is "To provide our customers with delicious food conveniently" with a vision "To be the best local food retailer in the UK". We are making significant strides in offering more home-grown produce for sale in our stores, with a focus on extending our farming group model and progressing our local sourcing initiative. In 2015, we published our report, *Backing British* (The Co-operative Food, 2015), which detailed our new local sourcing initiative and our commitments to sourcing British food.

Co-op supports British farmers and we know that clarity on the provenance of food is important to our customers and our members. In 2015, we committed to spending £1.5 billion over three years to source own-brand meat, produce and dairy products from the UK; since then we have made significant strides in offering more home-grown produce for sale in our stores. From May 2017, we will have further extended our commitment to back UK farmers by switching all of our fresh bacon and lamb to 100% British. This new sourcing initiative will make Co-op the only major UK food retailer to stock 100% British own brand fresh beef, chicken, pork, lamb, bacon and turkey, having already been the only retailer to use British meat in all its chilled ready meals, pies and sandwiches.

At The Co-op, we have championed the values that matter to our customers and members for many years. We have long known that animal welfare is an important concern and we are, therefore, committed to upholding the principles of our customers and members and to ensuring that animal welfare is an integral part of our business.

The business case for animal welfare

The retail environment is a very competitive one, so it is crucial that Co-op delivers what our customers expect of us. The Co-op is recognized for its ethical credentials by our customers, members and colleagues. We listen to what is important to them and we ensure that this is reflected in our sourcing policies and commitments. Our customer research tells us that British farming, healthy eating and animal welfare—in particular, good standards of practice and good animal husbandry—are the key priorities alongside price, quality and service that our customers expect from us. We carry out regular customer insight into these areas, which allows us to measure our like-for-like performance in these as well as other policy areas. This process ensures that we are focused on customers' key priorities and that we act in a timely manner to respond to their needs. Animal welfare is consistently identified as a priority issue, providing further incentive to ensure that we implement good standards of welfare across our supply chain and that our monitoring schemes are robust.

At The Co-op, our aim is to develop high-quality, fairly priced products that have been produced to good animal welfare standards (see Box 19.1). It is vital that our customers and members know that their principles and values are being incorporated into our actions and we are proud to state that we have made improvements in the way that we govern, manage and report on animal welfare.

Our animal welfare journey

Animal welfare is a key business priority for The Co-op. We understand it is important to our customers, our members and to our employees. For many years, we have endorsed good animal welfare. This started in the 1990s when we labelled the living conditions of hens on egg boxes. This then led to us becoming the first retailer to use only free-range eggs as an ingredient in all our own-brand products.

Box 19.1 In brief: Co-op's animal welfare standards

All Co-op own-brand fresh, frozen and prepared meat and poultry products are produced, as a minimum, to Red Tractor Farm Assurance Scheme (a UK accredited body) standards, or the equivalent whenever products are sourced outside of the UK.

Co-op only sells shell eggs (own-brand and branded) that are, as a minimum, British, free-range and RSPCA Assured. We only use free-range eggs as ingredients in our own brand products. From 2015, we ensured that the ingredients for all of our premium pork, bacon and pork sausage products were produced to RSPCA Assured standards from outdoor-bred pigs, and that our premium-brand fresh Atlantic salmon and smoked salmon were sourced according to RSPCA Assured standards.

We know our customers want transparency so in 2015 Co-op made a commitment to report on farmers' compliance with our input, outcome and quality and consistency measures on our website. We have taken this commitment further and in 2016 we identified our key performance indicators per species and, as a first step towards broadening our performance reporting, we started to report on animals' average journey time to abattoir.

The Co-op Farming Groups

Over the past five years, we've been on a journey that has culminated in the development of close partnerships with our farmers who provide us with meat, milk, eggs and fish for our stores. We established our first Farming Group, The Co-op Dairy Group, in 2011, to support British dairy farmers and to cement relationships with producers, to provide high-quality milk and a transparent supply chain. Following on from the success of The Co-op Dairy Group, we developed a further five groups: The Co-op Hereford and Aberdeen Angus Beef Farming Group, The Co-op Cambrian Lamb Farming Group, The Co-op Chicken Farming Group, The Co-op Egg Farming Group and The Co-op Pork Farming Group.

These Farming Groups allow us to have clear oversight of our supply chain and enable us to work collaboratively with British farmers and suppliers. We now have long-term relationships with almost 400 carefully selected farmers, who are each focused on producing food to the highest standards. In turn, we have been able to invest in British farmers through a number of different agricultural initiatives, such as the Agricultural Research & Development programme, Open Farm Sunday, The Co-op Integrated Calf Scheme and our young farmer programme, The Co-op Farming Pioneers. We have also established a Farming & Food team to ensure that animal welfare standards are upheld, and this team provides a strong link between farmer, supplier and the business.

The Farming Group model is based around five pillars:

- Health, welfare and quality
- The Co-op brand
- Sustainability
- Environmental
- Ethical and training

As part of the health, welfare and quality pillar, our farmers are expected to submit key performance indicator data for each of the months that they have supplied us with meat, poultry or milk. These data, based on input, outcome and quality, and consistency measures, are analysed by our Farming & Food team. A set procedure is in place when an animal welfare issue is identified and we work alongside the farmer, a veterinarian and the supplier to rectify the issue.

How we govern and manage farm animal welfare

In 2013, we established The Co-op Farming & Food team as a central function. This is a team of seven agricultural specialists that have experience of working within the dairy, pork, poultry, fish, beef and lamb industries. The team is dedicated to ensuring that good animal welfare standards are maintained and to promoting best practice on-farm. The team works to deliver core standards covering animal welfare, sustainability and environmental impacts. It also leads on a number of other agriculture-related initiatives and works closely with our Farming Groups. The team is able to carry out thorough animal welfare inspections. In 2015, we visited 233 sites including farms, hatcheries and abattoirs to monitor animal welfare.

Co-op invests in specific animal welfare training for the team, through accredited courses in animal welfare, such as Animal Welfare Officer training at the University of Bristol, as well as specific training on key species. We also actively encourage the further development of the team through attendance at industry events and workshops in animal welfare and other areas, so that our team is up to date with key industry issues.

It is important for us to have our performance analysed by an independent body. In 2015, we worked with Food Animal Initiative (FAI), a team of agricultural specialists, veterinarians and scientists, to ensure that our livestock standards and key performance indicator measures were up to date with the latest science and industry best practice. An independent review of our farm animal welfare standards and performance against these standards was conducted by FAI and their findings were published in a Governance Report, which we published on our website for our customers and members (FAI, 2015).

Alongside animal welfare inspections carried out by the Farming & Food team, we also work with an independent animal welfare audit body, which audits the beef, lamb, pork and chicken farms within our Farming Groups. We only use auditors that are trained to assess our farms to UK animal welfare standards. The farms are audited against our five pillars of achievement (see Figure 19.1), and are rated bronze, silver or gold according to their performance across these pillars. For

Health, welfare and quality	Co-op brand	Sustainability	Environmental	Ethical and training
Agricultural KPIs	Attendance at producer group meetings	Water/electricity usage and conservation	Carbon footprint assessments	Ethical component
Audit performance	Community awareness/ membership	Alternative energy practices on farms	Environmental pollution controls	Formal training and development programmes
Quality and consistency	Engagement with the Co-op	Alternative soya usage/Soya from responsible source	Environmental scheme memberships	Apprenticeships
Research and development	Hosting of producer group farm visits	Local sourcing of materials	Pesticide/Heavy metal usage on farms/diets	Industry scheme memberships

Figure 19.1 The Co-op five pillars of achievement
Source: Co-op Farming Groups website.[1]

1 http://www.co-operativefood.co.uk/food-matters/farming-food/farming-groups/

Table 19.1 Farming Group performance

	2014 (Year 1)	2015 (Year 2)
Farms achieving gold	2%	10%
Farms achieving silver	6%	17%
Farms achieving bronze	36%	31%

Source: data from Co-op Farming Group audits, 2015.

a farm to be rated bronze, the first two pillars ("Health, welfare and quality" and "Co-operative brand") must be met. The other three pillars ("Sustainability", "Environmental impact" and "Ethical and training") determine whether a farm is classified as silver or gold.

The Co-op is committed to progressing and raising the standards of the farms within our Farming Groups. 2015 was the second year that our Farming Groups have been in place and compared with the previous year, 15% more farmers achieved bronze, silver or gold for their increased compliance against the pillars, and 10% achieved the gold standard (compared with just 2% in 2014) (see Table 19.1).

We have regular contact with the farmers within our Farming Groups through regular meetings that occur two to three times per year. The purpose of these meetings is to disseminate best practice, improve animal welfare and highlight key industry issues.

A 2015 survey showed that almost nine out of ten farmers participating in these groups believed that being a member of a farming group benefited them.[2] In the future, we are looking to create Farming Groups for turkeys, standard beef & lamb, and Atlantic salmon. Through our Farming Groups, we want to be able to assure our customers that we are working closely with the farmers that produce the meat, milk, eggs and fish for our stores.

Case studies

Transparency in farm animal welfare

Co-op customers and members expect transparency and honesty, and we have a responsibility to be open in the way that we govern, manage and report on animal welfare. We receive monthly key performance indicator data from our Farming Groups. In order to effectively manage these data, we have invested in an online database called Pyramid. Pyramid allows us to monitor trends in our performance and to investigate any animal welfare concerns with particular suppliers and farmers.

We are investing in upgrading our dairy platform further. This investment will enable our Co-operative Dairy Farming Group farmers to benchmark themselves against one other. We are hopeful that this will help drive improvements in animal health, welfare and improve efficiency on farm.

2 Co-op customer and farmer survey.

We have collated, monitored and managed animal welfare data from our Farming Groups since early 2013. In 2015, we made a commitment to report on compliance with our key performance indicators. In 2016, we identified and started to track these performance measures, and also started to report on compliance by species using both welfare input and output measures.

Free-range eggs

Animal welfare has always been an integral part of how we operate; it is The Co-op way of doing business. We are proud that Co-op was at the forefront of helping to develop the RSPCA Freedom Food (now RSPCA Assured) standard in 1994 and then became the first national retailer to sell RSPCA Accredited Freedom Food products, with the launch of "Freedom Food Free Range eggs" in our stores.

In 1995, we recognized the poor welfare status of caged hens and we became the first retailer to label battery eggs as "Intensively Produced", as we felt that it was important to be transparent and honest with our customers about how their eggs were produced.

In 2006, we committed that all own-brand Co-op eggs must be British, free-range and RSPCA Freedom Food approved. In 2008, we extended this policy to apply to all whole eggs we sold (including own-brand and other branded eggs).

By 2006, all eggs in our stores were either RSPCA Freedom Food Free Range or organic. We know how important "free-range" is to our customers and members, so after a number of years' work, in 2010, we were able to move to using only free-range eggs as an ingredient in all our own brand products, such as sandwiches, mayonnaise and desserts.

Farm animal welfare research and development

It is The Co-op's pioneering spirit that has allowed us to improve the way we operate as a business. One of the key benefits to having our collaborative supply base is that it enables us to invest in our farmers. In 2015 we launched our research and development programme with Food Animal Initiative (FAI). Through this work, we are able to address some of the key health and welfare issues that challenge our suppliers.

We are working on a range of projects that may change the way we focus on animal welfare. Currently, we have projects covering our main species (dairy, beef, pork, chicken and lamb), and we plan to expand the research programme to cover more species, such as turkey and laying hens.

One project under way, in conjunction with FAI, our chicken supplier, the University of Bristol and SRUC, is the trialling of a novel method of measuring chicken welfare called qualitative behavioural assessment (QBA). Traditionally animal welfare has been addressed in terms of the inputs provided; however, more recently animal welfare scientists are also making efforts to develop outcome measures, considering how an animal experiences the situation in which it lives. QBA is a method used to assess animals' expressive behaviour ("body language"), and our study aims to explore QBA as a method of formalizing stockpersons' observations of bird expressions as a management as well as a training tool.

Another example of our R&D projects involves working with our dairy farmers on a bovine virus diarrhoea (BVD) eradication programme across The Co-op Dairy Group. Our aim is to achieve BVD-free status, with ongoing monitoring to ensure that this status is maintained.

Lessons learned

At the heart of our decisions are the principles and values of our customers and members. We know that animal welfare is important to our customers and members, and we are committed to upholding animal welfare as an integral business priority.

In the last five years, we have made significant investments in British farming through our Farming Groups, through our Farming & Food team and through other key initiatives. These have enabled us to develop close relationships with our farmers and our suppliers. We believe our collaborative approach to farm animal welfare has been fundamental to the success of our animal welfare policies and management.

In all areas we constantly review our performance. Every month we produce a compliance report which tracks our performance on our farming standards covering health, welfare and quality. The performance of our supplying farms and partner suppliers is analysed and we provide them with feedback on their performance and trends. Our Farming Group structure and meetings provide a collaborative forum for our Food & Farming team and our suppliers and farmers to exchange knowledge and insights into the challenges and issues linked to our farm animal welfare standards and to find solutions.

In line with our strategy of providing our customers with delicious food conveniently, we continually analyse how we can better respond to our customers' needs. Our future vision is an integrated supply chain supported by activities to deliver a sustainable industry. Driving improvements in agriculture within a retail environment, however, is not always simple; it requires a commitment of time and resources, and it requires a commitment to the long haul. Prior to 2011, our relationships tended to be transactional and short term. Following the successful launch of our Dairy Group (the first of our Farming Groups) in 2011, we have now launched five more Farming Groups to help us deliver our vision. We have also invested in a new agricultural team, increased the amount of British meat and poultry we sell, and worked with our farmers and suppliers to shorten our supply chains. These actions have enabled us to build relationships with producers, deliver a continued investment in quality, and provide customers with a more consistent and transparent supply chain. They have also enabled us to maintain our strict animal welfare policies and have encouraged us to invest in training and research linked to finding improvements in farming efficiencies.

An ongoing challenge that we face as a convenience retailer is the amount of space that is available in our stores to display our product ranges; in some stores, we may only have a single one-foot wide bay for displaying fresh meat. Such logistics reduce our customer proposition and hamper our ability to compete with other retailers who are able to offer a wider choice to customers. We therefore need to ensure that we have in place the best choice of products, based on intelligence linked to customer demographic and purchasing needs.

Concluding comments

We will continue to listen to our customers to ensure that they know about The Co-op brand credentials and feel as proud of these as we are. We take great pride in the progress our business has made and our commitment to support British food and farming. We have made every effort to strengthen our ties with the industry, our farmers and suppliers, and we seek to work together to deliver a transparent supply chain that benefits the farming community and meets the needs of our customers. We have worked hard to raise the bar, through launching Co-op Farming Groups involving more than 400 farmers and activities aimed at supporting young people, the environment and animal welfare, as well as our ongoing investment in research into issues identified through our supply chain. Our passion and support for British food and farming continues to grow, and we remain committed to furthering our efforts in this area.

Our view is that successfully delivering on our vision for British food and farming and for higher standards of farm animal welfare will enable us to be successful and sustainable in the long term. The commercial imperatives are clear; in today's society, consumers have a growing interest in the provenance of their food and how this food is produced. We therefore need to respond to these demands, and ensure that we are at the forefront of the food industry on these issues, ensuring that we operate to higher standards and report honestly and openly about our performance.

By doing so, we know that we will not only benefit the animals that enter our food chain, but hope to also encourage other food companies to act, thereby improving the way in which animal welfare is governed, managed and reported on across the food industry. We believe that, together, our industry has in its power the ability to profoundly change the way that animals are reared for food.

References

FAI (2015). Governance report. Retrieved from www.co-operativefood.co.uk/globalassets/policy/pdfs/animal-welfare.ppt

The Co-operative Food (2015). *Backing British: A Better Way of Doing Business for Communities and Farming.* Manchester, UK: The Co-operative Group. Retrieved from http://www.co-operativefood.co.uk/globalassets/policy/british/cop67-brit_pr_report_singles_aw.pdf

20 Case study

Unilever and farm animal welfare

Bronwen Reinhardt

COMPASSION IN WORLD FARMING, UK

Background

Unilever is one of the world's leading suppliers of food, home and personal care products, with sales in over 190 countries and reaching 2 billion consumers a day. It has 169,000 employees and generated sales of €53.3 billion in 2015. Its acquisition of Best Foods in 2000 brought Unilever leadership in the culinary category with market-leading brands such as Knorr and Hellmann's. With its Wall's and Ben & Jerry's brands, Unilever is also the world's leading ice cream producer.

Unilever has created a company culture whereby sustainability is a key element in its processes. It has managed to do this and retain profitability despite introducing major changes within its supply chain.

Understanding where animal welfare features in sustainability

Unilever believes that growth and sustainability go hand in hand. Half of Unilever's raw materials come from either farms or forests and, given the scale of its footprint, sustainable agricultural sourcing is a strategic priority for its business and brands. Sustainable sourcing helps Unilever to manage core business risk by ensuring security of its supply for the long term. Unilever recognizes that many consumers have concerns about animal welfare, and it takes these concerns very seriously. It also recognizes, and has demonstrated, the brand value of communicating higher welfare ingredients as an inherent part of product quality.

Farm animal welfare has been included in Unilever's *Sustainable Agriculture Code* (Unilever, 2015) since 2010 and it has actively encouraged its suppliers to participate in initiatives to improve animal welfare standards in the countries where it sources, processes and markets products from animal origin.

Since 2007, Unilever has introduced a number of welfare policies across its business, brand by brand, demonstrating its commitment to continuous improvement in farm animal welfare. It continues to work closely with its supply chain partners to ensure that they support the high animal welfare standards it wants to achieve for animal-derived ingredients (Box 20.1).

Box 20.1 Unilever's position...

Unilever is not a significant buyer of animal-derived ingredients and, therefore, its approach to farm animal welfare requires successful implementation by its supply chain partners.

In November 2010, Unilever introduced its Sustainable Living Plan,* committing to a journey towards sustainable growth right across its business, setting out key sustainability targets for its direct operations, suppliers and distributors.

One of the three key outcomes of its Sustainable Living Plan is to source 100% of its agricultural raw materials sustainably by 2020. So in order to meet this target, Unilever is working closely with all of its suppliers to encourage good animal welfare practices and improvement programmes, as well as ensuring that its suppliers comply with legal requirements and accepted industry standards with respect to animal welfare.

Unilever's Sustainable Agriculture Code is supplemented by detailed implementation guides, which set out clear standards of care that Unilever expects of its suppliers. Through working with these suppliers, Unilever has established a transparent supply chain in relation to the specific welfare standards used for animal-derived ingredients and it reports openly on a regular basis about its performance against these standards.

* Unilever, Sustainable living web page. Retrieved from https://www.unilever.com/sustainable-living/

Policy and commitment on farm animal welfare

Since 2007, Unilever has been developing animal welfare criteria as part of its sustainable sourcing programme in partnership with Compassion in World Farming. These criteria address issues such as housing, hygiene, feeding and feed, health management and the management of antibiotics, water supply, mutilations, transport, slaughtering practices and traceability. Unilever's working method for monitoring and improving animal welfare is based on the "Five Freedoms" (Farm Animal Welfare Council, 2009).

Based on the volumes purchased, its initial focus was on sourcing cage-free eggs and on its dairy supply chain, where it has made significant progress in partnership with its suppliers. Specifically, Unilever has made a policy commitment to source only cage-free eggs for all of its mayonnaises and dressings in Europe, including its market leading brands, Hellmann's, Amora and Calvé. Continuing its roll-out of cage-free products, in 2010 Hellmann's in North America launched a Light mayonnaise using cage-free eggs. Unilever's Ben & Jerry's ice cream brand has been using only free-range eggs in Europe since 2004 and by the end of 2011, 99% of all eggs used in its ice cream mix worldwide were cage-free (Compassion in World Farming, 2013).

As well as addressing the welfare of laying hens, Unilever has committed to putting the welfare of dairy cows at the centre of its sourcing strategy through its Ben & Jerry's Caring Dairy programme. It is also actively campaigning for better welfare rules, including good housing, good feeding, good health, and the ability to express appropriate behaviours, for all dairy cows across Europe.

Knorr has been working with Compassion in World Farming to develop global criteria for good animal welfare and a framework to start transforming its supply chain. The comprehensive set of criteria behind Knorr's plan caters to the specific welfare needs of chickens, cows and pigs. Knorr has worked with independent external experts to assess current practices and is engaging supplier partners on the improvements needed to bring consistent and positive change across its supply chain. Building knowledge and capacity of its suppliers and providing meaningful information to its consumers are key elements of Knorr's commitment to animal welfare.

Through its Unox brand, Unilever has started to introduce higher welfare into its chicken supply chain, addressing welfare issues such as the growth rate, stocking density and enrichment for broiler chickens.

These efforts have had a measureable effect on the business as a whole. In 2015, 45% of Unilever's global egg supply was cage-free and 59% of its dairy ingredients were from sustainable sources. More recently, Unilever has extended its focus to meat, where it is working together with animal welfare organizations and its suppliers; in 2015, 38% of the pork meat used in Europe for Unilever brands was sourced against higher animal welfare standards.[1]

Research and implementation

Cage-free eggs in mayonnaise

Unilever was one of the first global companies to work with egg suppliers to start providing cage-free eggs for its leading brands, Hellmann's, Amora and Calvé; together, these make up the largest dressings business in the world and Hellmann's is the world's number one mayonnaise brand. These brands have been trading on "realness" for many years and have recognized the benefits of being able to further substantiate this claim by improving the attributes of their ingredients.

For its mayonnaises, the most logical place to focus its attention was on a primary ingredient, so Unilever set out to explore consumer associations with cage-free eggs and how to improve the perceptions of the product and brand. It did this by conducting research across six different countries. Based on the findings from this research, in 2009, Hellmann's, Amora and Calvé committed to using only cage-free eggs in their products. With its marketing and promotional activity centred on "Good Eggs" as a key ingredient, Unilever saw a subsequent growth in its sales and market share across Europe.

1 Unilever, Farm animal welfare web page. Retrieved from https://www.unilever.com/sustainable-living/what-matters-to-you/farm-animal-welfare.html

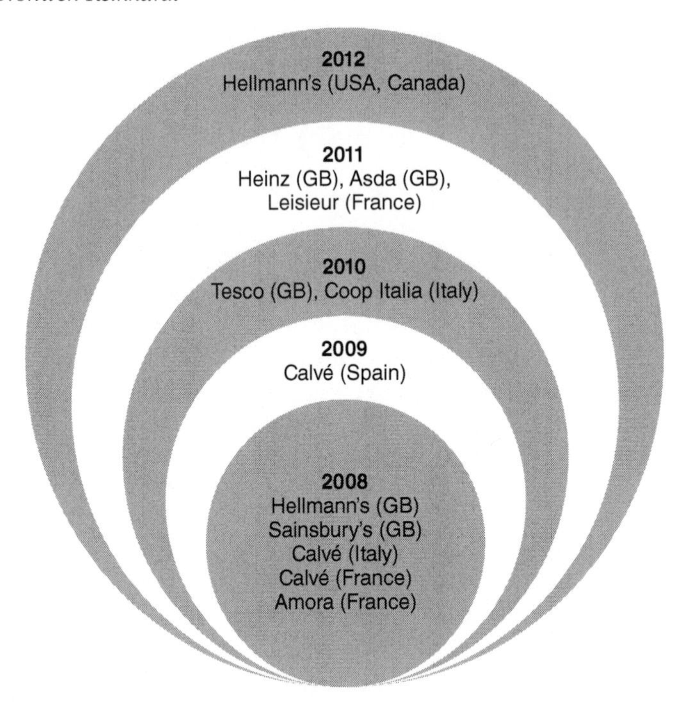

Figure 20.1 The "ripple effect" of companies adopting cage-free eggs in mayonnaise
Source: adapted from Compassion in World Farming material.[2]

Unilever's cage-free commitment for its mayonnaise and dressings has been rolled out across its entire European operation. This has caused a ripple effect across the industry as other supermarkets and brands, recognizing the advantage of moving to cage-free eggs, have followed suit; this is illustrated in Figure 20.1 which is adapted from materials prepared by Compassion in World Farming to encourage other organizations to adopt higher standards of farm animal welfare. By making this important commitment to the welfare of laying hens in its supply chain, Unilever has enabled a market shift towards higher welfare mayonnaise across the industry.

Sourcing of cage-free eggs

Unilever is aware of the concerns raised about global egg industry standards by which breeders of egg-laying hens eliminate male chicks, even though these methods are included in EU Directives and in American Veterinary Medical Association guidelines. The process involves chick sexing to identify, separate and cull male chicks because they are not relevant to egg production. While this is a standard practice in egg production, and although Unilever uses only a small percentage of eggs produced in the market, Unilever takes these concerns seriously.

2 https://www.compassioninfoodbusiness.com/media/7427146/ciwf_ripple_effect_diagram_final.pdf

Unilever is engaged with the egg production industry, the animal welfare community and R&D companies to develop alternative options to current practice. Unilever is committed to providing support to the market introduction of *in-ovo* gender identification (sexing) of eggs, a new technology that has the potential to eliminate the hatching and culling of male chicks in the poultry-breeding industry.

Ben & Jerry's Caring Dairy programme

Unilever has made progressive welfare commitments in the dairy sector through its Ben & Jerry's Caring Dairy programme that sources milk for its ice cream. The Caring Dairy programme is a partnership between Ben & Jerry's and CONO,[3] the makers of Beemster cheese in The Netherlands, involving about 200 farmers. The programme offers farmers a way to measure and improve 11 sustainability indicators on their farms, and helps each farmer to develop a unique action plan to improve practices. In exchange for participating, Caring Dairy farmers receive a financial incentive for their produce.

Ben & Jerry's believes that caring for a cow's health and wellbeing is not only good for the cow but it can also improve the overall performance of the farm. Ben & Jerry's works closely with dairy farmers to ensure that their cows are provided with the best conditions. In the EU programme, the focus is on grazing and longevity. This means that all farms in the EU programme need to apply grazing for the dairy cows and need to participate in the Cow Compass to monitor animal health and welfare. In the US a similar Caring Dairy programme is implemented with the local supplier in Vermont.

Supporting Better Dairy

Since its Food Business programme began in 2007, Unilever has had a longstanding and productive relationship with Compassion in World Farming. As a result, its Ben & Jerry's brand joined forces with Compassion in World Farming and the World Society for the Protection of Animals (now World Animal Protection) in 2012 to launch the Supporting Better Dairy[4] campaign, with the aim of securing an EU Dairy Cow Welfare Directive.

With standards of dairy cow welfare varying greatly across Europe, the campaign aims to seek a guarantee of minimum welfare standards to protect the welfare of the 23 million dairy cows in Europe, by proposing new rules for good housing, good feeding, good health and appropriate behaviour.[5]

To help raise awareness of the campaign, Ben & Jerry's launched its Cow Power ice cream in October 2012. The coalition also set up a dedicated website[6] to

3 http://www.cono.nl/
4 http://www.benjerry.co.uk/values/issues-we-care-about/supporting-better-dairy
5 *Ibid.*
6 http://www.benjerry.com/caringdairy

encourage consumers across Europe to sign up to the campaign in support of the new EU Directive. The campaign has reached more than 115,000 consumer sign-ups.

Antibiotics usage

In its Sustainable Agriculture Code, Unilever states that antibiotics should only be used prudently with the aim of optimizing therapeutic efficiency and minimizing the development of antibiotic resistance. In 2015, its Breyers® brand in the USA committed to only sourcing milk and cream from cows not treated with artificial growth hormones.

Global recognition

Unilever's efforts in relation to animal welfare have been recognized with a number of successes at the European Good Farm Animal Welfare Awards, organized by Compassion in World Farming. In 2008, Unilever received a Good Egg Award for its welfare commitment to source only cage-free eggs for all of its dressings sold in Western Europe. It has made a further commitment to move to 100% cage-free eggs in all of its products, including Ben & Jerry's ice cream and Hellmann's, Amora and Calvé mayonnaises globally by 2020, and this commitment is already taking shape.

Ben & Jerry's (Europe) received a Good Egg Award in 2011 from Compassion in World Farming, as well as one of Compassion in World Farming's first Good Dairy Awards for its commitment to using higher welfare dairy systems for cows and calves in its supply chain. Ben & Jerry's also received a Good Egg Award in 2012 for using cage-free eggs across its entire US business. Unilever won an additional Good Egg Award in 2012 for extending its cage-free commitment to its Hellmann's brand in the USA.

In 2015, the Knorr brand was recognized for its commitment to animal welfare and presented with Compassion in World Farming's first Special Recognition Award. This recognizes the brand's ambition to advance animal welfare practices in its own global supply chain and how it is contributing to raising standards across the industry.

In some European countries, farm animal welfare is not high on the agenda for consumers, so it is vital that large, global companies such as Unilever are demonstrating and communicating their leadership and commitment to improving farm animal welfare across their businesses. In 2012, Compassion in World Farming awarded one of its first ever European Leader Awards to Unilever, for making farm animal welfare integral to its brand values, thus celebrating the positive impact it is having on farm animal welfare both at a brand level and across different regions, and for the good example they are setting to the food industry as a whole. The European Leader Award reflects an organization's commitment to improving welfare across more than one species; to demonstrating continuous improvement in farm animal welfare as part of its corporate social responsibility strategy; and to continually promoting the importance of higher welfare to consumers as part of its marketing and communications activities.

Unilever: communicating higher welfare

Through its market-leading brands, Unilever has made considerable investments in communicating and promoting its higher welfare products to consumers, focusing its campaigns on positive messages around good, honest, real ingredients. For example, Hellmann's ran an advertising campaign costing more than £2 million (including TV, outdoor posters, direct mail and press) to promote its cage-free Hellmann's mayonnaise and Good Egg Award in 2008, reaching millions of consumers in the UK (see Figures 20.2 and 20.3).

Figure 20.2 Outdoor advertising, Hellmann's

Figure 20.3 Direct mail advertising, Hellmann's

Lessons learned

While Unilever has made significant progress and is now beginning to realize the significant commercial benefits for its approach to higher farm animal welfare practice, it has not all been plain sailing. Unilever has learned many important lessons along the way. Those of wider relevance to discussions around business and farm animal welfare are set out below.

The first point to make is that it takes time to change a business, and it can take even longer for the business benefits to appear; Unilever started its animal welfare journey in 2005 and, even after a decade, recognizes there is still more to do.

In order to make the changes achieved to date, Unilever has taken a variety of actions including launching its internal "champions for change", building a secure business case from its research and experience, finding solutions that were workable at the scale relevant to its business growth and encouraging and supporting suppliers to meet its needs. This leads to the second point which is that Unilever relies on its suppliers to deliver many of its animal welfare-related commitments and objectives. It is often assumed that companies of the size of Unilever have the power to impose whatever conditions they choose on suppliers. However, the reality is very different. Because of the nature of the business and the volumes required, Unilever is rarely the largest customer of any individual supplier; in fact, Unilever is actually a relatively small player in the agricultural commodities market. In addition, like every other food company, it and its suppliers are under constant price pressure and face tight constraints on investments, in particular when there is not a clear commercial case for investment.

These factors mean that Unilever needs to work with others—not just suppliers but also governments and other actors—to deliver the changes needed in its markets. Whether this is increasing supply, setting minimum standards or reducing costs, Unilever has an influence, but maximizing its overall impact means that it must focus on what it can do and think creatively about how it uses its influence for positive change.

The third point is that the business case for action on farm animal welfare goes far beyond the direct costs and benefits. For example, Unilever has seen benefits in terms of its brand and product positioning, in terms of press coverage and in terms of sales of products with higher welfare claims. Unilever also sees the benefits in terms of mitigating risk to its business; as a consumer brand, Unilever simply cannot afford to be found to have treated the animals in its care or in its supply chains badly.

The fourth point is that, while there is a clear case for action for Unilever, this case may not be as clear-cut for others in the food industry. For example, companies that are not consumer facing may be less concerned about their brand. Even among Unilever suppliers, the question of whether or not to invest in higher animal welfare is frequently very narrowly drawn, and focused on the direct costs (e.g. capital, disruption to production) and benefits. Because many of the benefits are uncertain (e.g. will customers really pay a premium for higher quality products) and because the costs of existing production systems are already sunk, Unilever finds that suppliers are often reluctant to invest unless the financial case for action is overwhelmingly positive (e.g. they may look for payback periods of 12 to 18 months).

Leaders for change

Unilever's commitment to farm animal welfare and its holistic approach to integrating key welfare issues into its business culture is a model of best practice for the global food industry. By assessing and prioritizing its biggest welfare impacts, tackling them systematically and making both its policies and progress publicly available, Unilever has built trust among its key stakeholder groups, notably its consumers and investors. Brands such as Hellmann's, Calvé, Amora and Ben & Jerry's remain market leaders in their categories and are synonymous with quality and real ingredients.

Through its sustainable sourcing and animal welfare initiatives, Unilever has received a positive response from consumers who recognize its core brand values. By promoting its Good Farm Animal Welfare Awards and higher welfare ingredients, Unilever has seen an increase in sales and market share across Europe. Its dedication to continuously address welfare in its supply chain is having a positive effect on an increasing number of farm animals across the globe.

Furthermore, Unilever was recently ranked among the top food companies by the Business Benchmark on Farm Animal Welfare (BBFAW),[7] a key tool for investors to understand the relative performance of global food companies on their farm animal welfare management and reporting practices. Unilever's position in Tier 2 of the Benchmark reflects the fact that farm animal welfare is integral to its business strategy through commitments made in the Unilever Sustainable Living Plan, and that these are implemented via the Unilever Sustainable Agriculture Code. This further demonstrates the company's leadership in managing its risks and its commitment to continuous improvement in this sphere. Farm animal welfare is an emerging issue for the investor community and one that is set to become as important as other sustainability issues, such as carbon, water and waste. Unilever is very much ahead of the game globally in being able to demonstrate that its ethics and approach to sustainable sourcing are integral to the sustainability of its business.

References

Compassion in World Farming (2012, June 20). New campaign "Supporting Better Dairy". Retrieved from http://www.ciwf.org.uk/news/2012/06/new-campaign-supporting-better-dairy

Compassion in World Farming (2013, June). Case Study: Working in Partnership: Unilever. Retrieved from https://www.compassioninfoodbusiness.com/media/5818194/unilever-case-study_final_pdf.pdf

Farm Animal Welfare Council (2009). *Farm Animal Welfare in Great Britain: Past, Present and Future*. London: FAWC. Retrieved from https://www.gov.uk/government/uploads/system/uploads/attachment_data/file/319292/Farm_Animal_Welfare_in_Great_Britain_-_Past__Present_and_Future.pdf

Unilever (2015). Sustainable Agriculture Code 2015. London: Unilever Plc. Retrieved from https://www.unilever.com/Images/sac-2015_tcm244-427050_en.pdf

7 http://www.bbfaw.com/; see also Chapter 13 by Amos and Sullivan.

Part IV

Wider reflections

21 Revisiting the business case for action

Nicky Amos

NICKY AMOS CSR SERVICES AND BUSINESS BENCHMARK ON FARM ANIMAL WELFARE, UK

Rory Sullivan

UNIVERSITY OF LEEDS AND BUSINESS BENCHMARK ON FARM ANIMAL WELFARE, UK

Introduction

The central premise of this book is that food companies in the modern food system have a direct influence on the welfare and wellbeing of many of the billions of animals that are farmed for food. These companies decide the species that are bred, how animals are reared and how animals are slaughtered. Their views and attitudes towards animals and towards farming in general shape the systems in which farm animals are kept and how their wellbeing is managed.

While there are a variety of ethical reasons for companies to act on farm animal welfare, the core theme of many of the chapters in this book is that the actions taken by companies depend on what is commonly referred to as the "business case for action". This business case is shaped by the external drivers for action (for example, legislation, consumer concerns, media attention, civil society pressures), the financial costs and benefits of taking action, and companies' views on the importance of farm animal welfare to their business over the short, medium and long term. The "business case" is often cited as the main reason why companies refrain from taking concerted action to improve farm animal welfare standards.

Given its central importance to business decision-making, we have decided to focus the concluding chapter of Part IV on the business case for action on farm animal welfare. We divide our analysis into two parts. In the first, we describe the reasons why companies might act on farm animal welfare; effectively, the drivers for action. We then discuss how companies analyse and interpret these drivers, how they reconcile the costs with the benefits of taking action, and the implications for their strategies and approach to farm animal welfare. We argue that a conventional business case-driven approach to farm animal welfare tends to result in companies focusing on actions that deliver short-term financial returns rather than longer-term business benefits. In the second part, we build on the evidence and experience presented in this book to argue that companies that aspire to be successful and sustainable over the longer term approach decision-making in a different way. While still requiring investments to deliver appropriate financial returns, these companies locate the business case for higher welfare standards in the context of their goals of being successful and sustainable over the medium to long term. In turn, the actions that these companies take—for example, working with suppliers to achieve higher farm animal welfare standards, auditing suppliers and monitoring performance, engaging with customers—change the business case for other food companies.

We conclude this chapter by revisiting the wider case for higher standards of farm animal welfare. We note that the food industry faces a series of structural drivers and pressures that may make higher standards simply a requirement of doing business. We also suggest that farm animal welfare can create significant opportunities for companies that adopt progressive, leadership approaches, and create significant risks for those companies that do not.

Drivers for action

Why do food companies need to pay attention to farm animal welfare? Ethical values have played a notably important role. An increasing number of companies now acknowledge that animals are sentient beings and that this imposes a moral obligation on them as corporate citizens to protect and respect the animals in their care and in their supply chains. This is being reflected in corporate animal welfare policies, where it is more common to see companies both acknowledge animals as sentient beings and commit to the Five Freedoms—freedom from hunger and thirst; freedom from discomfort; freedom from pain, injury or disease; freedom to express normal behaviour; and freedom from fear and distress—as a framework for their approach to managing farm animal welfare.

Aside from the ethical case for action, there are other, more conventional, business reasons for companies to pay attention to farm animal welfare. These include:

- To comply with legislation and relevant voluntary and industry standards (see, further, Chapter 4 by Heleen van de Weerd and Jon Day)
- To meet stakeholder expectations (Chapter 6 by Jemima Jewell)
- To meet client and customer expectations (see the corporate case studies in Chapters 14 to 20)
- To meet general public and consumer expectations (Chapter 5 by Sally Healy)
- To access market opportunities (for example, for higher welfare products)
- To enhance their brand and reputation (e.g. through recognition in Compassion in World Farming's Supermarket Survey and Good Farm Animal Welfare Awards and in the Humane Society of the United States' Henry Spira Corporate Progress Award)

For food retailers, service companies and brand manufacturers, customer perceptions are of key importance; animal welfare is often used either to enhance or differentiate a brand among competitors or to protect an existing brand position. Similarly, for food producers, improved welfare standards can help increase market share and improve profitability (for example from improved health and wellbeing, the reduced need for medicines to prevent or treat disease and injuries, better product quality in terms of reduced bruising, for example, and reduced stress levels and lower mortality, resulting in fewer rejects and a higher grading of produce). More generally, companies that address or enhance animal welfare may be able to win or retain a competitive advantage through, for example, accessing new opportunities for food produced in higher animal welfare systems or becoming a producer of choice for retailers and consumers concerned about animal health and welfare, food safety and quality, human health and the environment. Companies also need to manage the downside risks. These can include food scares (e.g. salmonella in eggs, avian flu in poultry, swine flu, and BSE in beef); food scandals (e.g. milk and infant milk formula adulterated with melamine in China in 2008, the 2013 European horsemeat scandal); and media exposés of poor animal welfare practices (e.g. US-based Hallmark/Westland's recall of beef in 2008, the 2011 scandal in China of pigs fed the steroid clenbuterol). History has shown that such incidents can damage corporate reputations, reduce sales, and increase regulatory and other business costs.

While the general drivers for companies to adopt higher standards of farm animal welfare are widely recognized and accepted by the food industry, they do not necessarily make a compelling case for companies to take action. There are three aspects that we wish to highlight: the relevance of the drivers for action differs between companies, the drivers for action may not be particularly strong, and the drivers for action may lack dependability.

In relation to relevance, we see that the drivers for action differ between geographies, between companies, between food industry sub-sectors (e.g. between retailers and producers), and between species. That is, the business case for action for a specific company must be analysed in the context of that company's products, markets, location in the food industry, countries of operation and so forth. For instance, despite European Union legislation being widely seen as world-leading in terms of the standards required, there are gaps in legislation (e.g. there are groups of animals not covered by current legislation), and there are variations in the enforcement of this legislation between countries. Company size and profile is another factor that may be of relevance; larger, high-profile companies are more likely to receive scrutiny and criticism than smaller, lesser-known companies. Moreover, consumer-facing companies are likely to be more sensitive to the issues that are of concern to consumers whereas business-to-business companies are likely to be more sensitive to the needs and interests of their customers.

Furthermore, many of the drivers for action may not be particularly strong. For example, legislative requirements may be incomplete, the penalties and sanctions for non-compliance may be relatively limited, and the enforcement of legislation may not be a regulatory priority. Similarly, while consumers are widely identified as a key driver of action for consumer-facing companies, such as retailers and restaurants and bars, the reality is that relatively few meat-eating consumers feel sufficiently strongly about animal welfare for it to be the key determinant of their purchasing decisions; in fact, as discussed by Autio *et al.* in Chapter 11, purchasing decisions are typically driven by factors such as cost and convenience. Furthermore, those consumers who do care about animal welfare can often find their ethical concerns addressed through isolated higher welfare product lines (e.g. cage-free eggs or antibiotic-free chicken products) rather than through wholesale, systemic changes within the companies in question. Similarly, media pressure is variable; the media can be fickle, moving from one corporate scandal to the next. This is not just about the intensity of the pressure or driver for action, it is also about the intensity relative to other drivers. For example, a company that is engaged in a price war or in a struggle for market share may simply not have the time or resources to strengthen its approach to farm animal welfare, no matter how much pressure is placed upon it to do so.

Finally, many of the drivers for action lack dependability and longevity. For example, the issues that are of concern to consumers can change over time. So too can corporate commitments, where promises to act on animal welfare or to support suppliers of higher welfare products may not translate into increased sales or longer-term contracts.

The business case for action

Before we discuss the business case in more detail, we need to start by acknowledging that the food industry is highly cost competitive. All companies in the food industry face constant pressure to reduce costs and improve efficiency (as measured in the unit cost of animal protein produced), with minor changes in pricing having potentially large impacts on sales and on profit margins. Over the last century, the food industry has moved inexorably towards more intensive animal production systems. This has boosted production yields but has also led to significant and widespread negative impacts on animal welfare. With intensive agriculture commonly practised across the global food industry, and with many food companies obliged to meet minimum legislative requirements on farm animal production standards, most food producers have invested significant capital in infrastructure systems and processes designed to manage large-scale production of food. This sunk capital is a major barrier to change, as companies are reluctant to adapt or replace existing production systems, especially when the requirement for change does not match their investment cycles, when there is no impending change to existing legislation, when there is limited capital to invest, and when there is no certainty over how the market is likely to respond to higher welfare products.

But the issues around the business case for action are not only related to the question of existing capital investment (or sunk capital). Of perhaps more significance is the manner in which companies frame the business case (in particular, the emphasis on relatively short-term financial costs and benefits), the nature and characteristics of the drivers for action (as we discussed above), and the perceptions that companies have about the economic case for action on farm animal welfare. We discuss each of these points below.

When making investment decisions, companies tend to focus most attention on the financial costs and benefits of these investments, with particular emphasis on the short-term financial returns. Indeed, it appears that many of the actions taken by companies on farm animal welfare (especially those that involve significant capital investment or significant organizational resources) can be explained simply by considering the direct financial costs and the financial benefits of the actions taken. This does not mean that companies do not realize other benefits from these actions (e.g. brand or reputational benefits from presenting business efficiency and supply chain improvements as farm animal welfare improvements); rather, it is that these benefits are ancillary to the core financial case for investment. These findings mirror the findings of recent research into the climate change performance of supermarkets, where virtually all the actions taken by supermarkets could be explained simply in terms of the direct costs and benefits of the actions taken (Gouldson and Sullivan, 2013, 2014; Sullivan and Gouldson, 2013, 2016). Furthermore, the required rates of return are strikingly common; most companies expect their capital investments to pay for themselves within two or three years, although, as the Unilever case study (in Chapter 20 by Reinhardt) suggests, some may have even shorter target rates of return.

In practice, the requirement to ensure that capital investments deliver (or meet) short-term financial targets frequently trumps wider corporate commitments to higher animal welfare standards. The practical consequence is that corporate leaders can adopt ambitious, long-term targets on farm animal welfare knowing that only measures supported by a strong business case will be adopted. Expressed another way, in most cases and irrespective of the corporate commitments that have been made, there is limited evidence that companies will invest capital in situations where the financial costs outweigh the financial benefits of such investments.

The characteristics of the drivers for action mean that companies tend to be reluctant to invest in situations where the returns will take several years to materialize or where there are questions about consumer or customer willingness to pay for higher welfare products. Despite the strong moral arguments for higher animal welfare, because many of the drivers for action are relatively weak and many of the potential benefits lack dependability or certainty, the majority of companies will only invest in higher welfare systems if such investments deliver clear financial returns (e.g. improved efficiency) or if buyers (i.e. manufacturers, retailers, wholesalers) and, ultimately, consumers are prepared to pay a premium for higher welfare products.

The third point is that the business case for higher standards of farm animal welfare remains relatively unproven and, consequently, companies tend to be sceptical about the arguments for adopting higher standards. In preparing this book, we reviewed the academic and other published literature on the business case for action on farm animal welfare. We observed that the literature is thin; there have been relatively few robust studies on the relationship between higher animal welfare and production outcomes. We also observed that while there is some evidence that higher standards of farm animal welfare can deliver better production outcomes (see Box 21.1), relatively little effort has been made to discuss the financial implications of investments in farm animal welfare.

Box 21.1 Evidence that higher standards of animal welfare improve production efficiency

The general argument for investing in farm animal welfare is that animals tend to be healthier in better welfare systems. This can lead to savings from, for example, lower expenditures on antibiotics and other veterinary medicines, better quality products (and, therefore, fewer rejects or lower-grade products) and lower mortality rates. Healthier animals also can have better feed conversion ratios, higher growth rates, fewer injuries, better immune responses and a greater ability to resist disease.

Studies on the relationship between animal welfare and production efficiency include the following:

- Beattie *et al.* (2000) compared the rearing of fattening pigs in barren and enriched environments, where the latter incorporated extra space and an area with peat and straw in a rack. They found that, during the finishing period (15–21 weeks), mean daily food intakes were higher and food conversion ratios were better for pigs in enriched environments compared with those in barren environments. Growth rates were also higher for the pigs in enriched environments during this period resulting in heavier carcass weights. The authors also reported that environmental enrichment had a small but significant effect on meat quality; pork from pigs reared in barren environments was less tender and had greater cooking losses than pork from pigs reared in enriched environments.
- A World Animal Protection (Lemme *et al.*, 2014) case study on sow housing in Brazil found that the group housing of sows is viable and advantageous to productivity, promotes better animal welfare and allows sows to express natural behaviour. World Animal Protection compared data from two farms—ECO-BEA (using group housing of sows) and Miunça (using individual sow stalls)—and found that, although the investment per sow resulting from the electronic sow feeding (ECO-BEA) was 38% higher than in individual sow stalls (Miunça), this investment was compensated by a 30% decrease in the cost of direct labour per sow and a 16% increase in revenue per sow. The study further concluded that allowing the expression of natural behaviour, good handling and good animal–human relationships are important in achieving good productivity in pig production.
- Norgaard and Olsen (1995) analysed housing systems for slaughter pigs in Denmark and found that the straw-flow system (which provides separate areas for lying and excretion) provided higher profitability than traditional systems with fully or partially slatted flooring. The study reported that the straw-flow system required higher labour input and straw consumption costs but that these costs were offset by a 20% reduction in capital costs.

- RSPCA (2006) compared the benefits of rearing broiler chickens to basic and higher animal welfare standards, and concluded that the RSPCA higher welfare (now known as RSPCA Assured) standard for rearing chickens indoors provided significantly better animal welfare compared with the industry standard. The study found lower proportions of hock burns and food pad burns, lower mortality rates and a lower percentage of rejects at the slaughterhouse in chickens reared to higher welfare standards. The study indicated that if 25,000 birds were reared to the RSPCA's higher welfare standards and the same number of birds were reared to basic industry standards, more than 900 additional birds under the RSPCA standard would reach the slaughter age (primarily owing to lower mortality) and 4,755 more birds would be produced to a higher quality grade.
- A World Animal Protection (2014a) case study on silvopastoral beef and dairy production (the practice of combining forestry and grazing of domesticated animals in a mutually beneficial way) in Colombia concluded that intensive silvopastoral systems are more productive, more manageable and more profitable than cattle ranching systems. The study—a partnership project involving the Colombian Cattle Ranching Association (FEDEGAN-FNG), the Centre for Research on Sustainable Agricultural Production Systems (CIPAV), the global assessment network agri benchmark of the Thünen Institute of Farm Economics, and World Animal Protection—assessed three farms with intensive silvopastoral systems and one control (cattle ranch) farm. The assessment found intensive silvopastoral systems produce higher feed quantity and better quality (digestibility, nutrient contents), higher milk yields in cows; higher daily weight gains in finishing cattle, allowing the reduction of finishing periods and increasing the cattle numbers; and higher stocking rates and land productivity. It also found that in the three silvopastoral farms, the animals were healthier and had better body condition (scoring 3.5 on a 5-point scale compared with 2.5 on the cattle ranch).
- A World Animal Protection (2014b) case study on large-scale broiler and egg production in Brazil described the actions taken by Korin, a Brazilian company based in Ipeúna, São Paulo State, to improve the health and welfare of the animals at the centre of its activities while still achieving strong productivity. The actions taken by Korin included keeping birds at stocking densities that were approximately 30% lower than those in conventional farms, using relatively slower growing bird strains, providing perching and nesting facilities for laying hens, ensuring that contract farms were no further than a 90-minute drive from the slaughterhouse (thereby reducing the stress experienced by animals during transport) and producing meat and eggs without the use of antibiotic growth promoters or other chemical treatments in the feed. Korin found that while its birds were still fast growing, this production system resulted in fewer incidences of lameness, less competition for food and more space for the birds to behave naturally.

We note that Lusk and Norwood (2011), in their review of the economics of farm animal welfare, drew a similar conclusion, arguing that additional research on the costs of animal welfare is needed to improve cost-benefit analysis, as well as to understand the extent to which rising prices resulting from the higher costs of new animal housing systems will curb consumer purchases of higher welfare animal products. While there have been several studies on consumer willingness to pay for higher welfare (see, for example, Bennett *et al.*, 2012 and the references cited by Sally Healy in Chapter 5), it is not clear how this willingness translates into actual purchasing decisions.

There has been some analysis of the cost impacts of legislation. For example, papers on the economic impact of animal welfare legislation in the State of California (Mullally and Lusk, 2015; Malone and Lusk, 2016) suggested that legislation introduced in 2015 had led to a price increase of between $0.50 and $1.00 per dozen eggs.[1] The first study (Mullally and Lusk, 2015) estimated that while the value of sales had increased by about 12%, the quantity of eggs sold had decreased by around 8%. They also noted that the positive impacts on producers may have been short-lived and were likely to be concentrated among producers located in California. Malone and Lusk (2016) subsequently concluded that while the first study showed marginal changes in the quantities of eggs sold, the price change was a result of increased cost (or reduced supply) rather than because of increased consumer demand for eggs from hens in improved living conditions.

A report commissioned by the European Commission to assess farmers' costs of compliance with EU legislation in the fields of environment, animal welfare and food safety (Menghi *et al.*, 2014) found that on animal farms, food safety and animal health legislation creates the highest compliance costs for all types of legislation investigated, primarily affecting capital costs linked to changes of production systems. The report concluded that pig and broiler farms are most affected by legislation in all three (environment, animal welfare and food safety) policy fields, with costs ranging between 5 and 10% of production compared with a range of 2 to 3% for dairy, beef and sheep meat. However, the authors cautioned against drawing generalized conclusions on the impact of costs of compliance on competitiveness of EU Member States relative to non-EU Member State countries, noting that a wide range of calculated costs of compliance had been observed and noting that the impact of compliance costs on competitiveness can vary significantly across sectors, products and countries.

One of the important features (and limitations) of the literature on the costs and benefits of investing in farm animal welfare is that little has been written about the manner in which the costs and benefits are distributed (and, specifically, whether the individual or organization making the investment will realize the benefits) or about the likelihood that consumers or customers will pay a premium

1 The legislation, effective from 1 January 2015, includes both Proposition 2 (2008), which bans the confinement of farm animals (including laying hens, veal calves and gestating sows) in systems that prohibit freedom of movement and natural behaviours, and the California state legislature (AB 1437 (2010)), which bans the sale of eggs in California produced under conditions that do not comply with Proposition 2.

for higher welfare products (and whether some or all of that premium will revert to the organization making the investment). This latter point also highlights the dependency of organizations on others; for farmers or producers to benefit financially from higher standards of farm animal welfare, they often require their clients to share financial benefits with them (e.g. through higher prices or other incentives). Put another way, if there is no financial benefit to the organization making the investment, then there is no rational economic choice to be made. This is a blind spot in much of the literature. For example, McInerney (2016) argues that the husbandry changes required for higher welfare methods (e.g. stocking density, housing provision, feeding regimes, health management, transportation standards, etc.), might emerge as perhaps a 10% increase in overall production cost and as a 2.5% increase in the retail cost of a high-welfare food product. He also observes that individual items on the supermarket shelf typically vary by this much on a regular basis depending on season, local conditions and wider market prices, among others, and so should represent no serious basis for concern. He concludes that most animal welfare improvements would cost consumers merely a few extra pennies per week but would collectively contribute substantial additional economic value to society. While this is a compelling argument it takes no account of who bears the costs of improvements and whether such costs can be absorbed. For example, a report by the Farm Animal Welfare Committee (FAWC, 2011) on the economics of farm animal welfare concludes that the low profitability of livestock farming is a key challenge and that animal welfare cannot be left to market forces alone.

Reframing the business case for action

While the discussion above may provide limited comfort for those concerned about farm animal welfare, a more interesting and encouraging picture emerges from the case studies presented in Chapters 14 to 20. What these, and other leading companies (such as those ranked in Tiers 1 and 2 of the Business Benchmark on Farm Animal Welfare; see Chapter 13) have in common is that they aspire to be successful and sustainable over the short and long term, and that their approaches to risk assessment, risk management, strategy and capital allocation reflect this imperative. While the specific reasons for adopting higher standards of farm animal welfare differ between these companies, most identify one or several of the following as reasons for action:

Achieving corporate responsibility objectives or sustainability goals. For these companies, farm animal welfare is recognized as an important corporate responsibility issue. As such, they acknowledge that they are expected to commit to appropriate animal welfare standards, to manage their performance against these standards and to report on the progress they are making on a regular basis.

Complying with current and prospective farm animal welfare legislation. Legislation is the most commonly used policy instrument for achieving minimum welfare standards for animals on farm, during transportation and at slaughter. Leading companies see compliance with legislation as a minimum expectation across their business. Given the absence of universal standards on farm animal welfare, companies looking to position themselves as global-scale producers of meat and other animal-derived products (an example is BRF as described in Chapter 15) use the legislation and standards developed by the European Union (generally seen as the most stringent in the world) to define their minimum corporate standards.

Complying with voluntary standards and codes or developing company welfare standards. A range of voluntary standards exist in individual markets such as Australia, the UK, Germany, Scandinavia and the United States. Farm assurance schemes, designed primarily to address standards of food quality, increasingly reflect criteria on animal welfare, along with criteria on food safety and environmental protection, in response to growing consumer demand for assurance about how animal-derived food products are produced, transported and supplied. Higher welfare standards, such as the RSPCA Assured standard in the UK and the Animal Welfare Approved standard in the United States, provide food companies with a structured mechanism to identify and manage farm animal welfare risks within their supply chains, and provide an independent mark of quality, which is particularly attractive to businesses operating nationally. The Global Animal Partnership's 5-Step® programme provides the closest example of a universal standard and has been developed in response to growing demand from consumers and multinational companies for a global benchmark against which food supply chains can be measured. While some food companies maintain a commitment to independently certified products, others (see for example the case studies of COOK and The Co-op in Chapters 16 and 19) have developed their own standards for the auditing and management of animal welfare in their supply chains.

Controlling costs and enhancing business longevity. Leading firms explicitly recognize farm animal welfare issues in their business planning and capital investment processes, and aim to invest in ways that enable them and their suppliers to "future-proof" their capital investments against regulatory and market demands. They recognize that a failure to take animal welfare issues into account could lead to them investing significant amounts of capital in costly retrofits, being unable to utilize their facilities as they were intended or, in the worst case, having facilities that effectively become obsolete.

Ensuring security of supply. Leading companies recognize that regular and structured engagement with the companies in their supply chains on farm animal welfare, as on other sustainability issues, enables them to strengthen the resilience of their supply chains. They can do this both through signalling their commitments and strategic direction of travel on farm animal welfare and through providing appropriate incentives (e.g. preferential or extended contracts which guarantee supply volumes) to suppliers that are able to meet their demand for higher welfare products.

Managing risk and reputation. Irrespective of whether animal welfare is considered a financially material issue, leading food companies recognize that the identification, assessment and monitoring of farm animal welfare impacts through the supply chain is important to ensuring that they can identify any potential legal, financial, reputational or physical risks associated with their production systems, thereby enabling these risks to be mitigated before they impact negatively on the company. It is interesting that all three of the investor case studies (see Chapters 8 to 10) point to the manner in which investors are using information on how companies manage farm animal welfare to draw wider inferences about these companies' quality of management and risk management processes.

Creating and taking advantage of market opportunities. Leading companies see that their risk management processes should enable them to identify and benefit from upside opportunities as well as minimizing downside risks. These risk assessment and management processes can also help companies to identify their business strengths and the related PR opportunities linked to these.

Demonstrating leadership and innovation. With growing consumer concerns around the quality and provenance of food, many companies now draw attention to animal welfare issues in their product marketing and brand communications. This is leading to the creation of large markets for higher animal welfare products, such as cage-free eggs, higher welfare indoor chicken and antibiotic-free meat. For example, a company achieving accreditation to the RSPCA Assured standard will be able to demonstrate the quality of its management approach on farm animal welfare, which, in turn, can be used to engage customers and enhance brand loyalty. As highlighted by Unilever (see Chapter 20), progressive food companies are adopting leadership positions on farm animal welfare and are investing in research and development projects and industry-based initiatives to share knowledge, trial new technologies and inform and promote the development of higher farm animal welfare practices across the industry.

How companies can change the business case for farm animal welfare

One of the most interesting features of the company case studies (see Chapters 14 to 20) is that leading companies are adopting innovative techniques and adaptive strategies aimed at encouraging and incentivizing their suppliers to introduce higher standards of farm animal welfare. They are doing this in a variety of ways. One strategy is to align investments in farm animal welfare with suppliers' capital investment cycles. For example, through working with its suppliers, Italian pasta manufacturer Barilla (Chapter 14) found that capital investment in new buildings and infrastructure delivers only marginal differences in the cost of producing eggs to basic welfare or higher welfare standards, whereas retrofitting an existing production facility becomes more burdensome economically, increasing production costs by at least 15%. Given that such a cost differential is unlikely to be met by the market, Barilla understands the need to work with suppliers to consider the lifespan of existing systems when planning any transition to higher welfare production systems.

Another strategy is to make improvements that do not require significant capital investments. For example, Brazilian-based meat producer BRF (Chapter 15) stresses that improving animal welfare standards in a cost-effective way does not necessarily require capital investment. BRF argues that addressing welfare issues (such as overcrowding, poor hygiene and compromised behaviour due to the absence of manipulable substrates) can improve health and welfare, reduce the financial losses associated with negative productivity issues, and enable higher yields, reduced downgrades and higher profit margins.

Companies are also looking to integrate farm animal welfare into their wider business activities and strategies. For example, global food manufacturer Unilever (Chapter 20) was one of the first global companies to work with egg suppliers to start providing cage-free eggs for its leading brands, Hellmann's, Amora and Calvé. In 2008, Unilever invested more than £2 million (including TV, outdoor posters, direct mail and press) in promoting its free-range Hellmann's mayonnaise and its Good Egg Award from Compassion in World Farming, reaching millions of consumers in the UK. This example illustrates that the business case for action on farm animal welfare extends beyond direct costs and benefits to include brand enhancement, product positioning, press coverage and sales of higher welfare products. Unilever also sees the benefits of proactively managing its business risks associated with animal welfare, explaining that as a consumer brand, it cannot be found to be poorly treating the animals in its care or in its supply chains.

Food companies can also adapt their business models to enhance animal welfare. The case of UK-based food company COOK (Chapter 16) provides a good illustration of this. COOK reformulated one of its recipes to allow the use of a slightly smaller duck leg with a higher animal welfare specification without increasing the retail price. It also transitioned to 100% free-range pork supplied by two local suppliers. While this transition led to an 18% increase in the cost of pork, this additional cost was justified through the marketing benefit COOK obtained from using free-range ingredients from local farms and showcasing the farms in its marketing material and on its product packs. The COOK case study also highlights the practical challenges faced by companies when aiming to improve welfare standards. For example, COOK found that transitioning to an entirely free-range supply of chicken would increase its chicken purchase price by 34%, rendering the proposition commercially unviable. Instead, COOK is creating its own standards that exceed the Red Tractor standard for broiler chickens which will see it reduce its maximum stocking density from 33 kg/m^2 (the current EU regulatory standard) to 31 kg/m^2. It has also begun to redesign dishes to use different parts of the bird, educating customers to understand the value and quality of brown meat over breast, passing part of the cost onto the consumer and working in collaboration with farmers to understand and eliminate unnecessary costs.

Companies can also make animal welfare a central part of their business proposition. For The Co-op (Chapter 19), the commercial imperatives of farm animal welfare are clear. The Co-op has a long-standing commitment to sourcing higher range animal products, reporting an almost 300% increase in sales of higher welfare meat between 2009 and 2012, demonstrating that consumers are increasingly demanding food that has been produced to higher welfare standards, and they are willing to pay for it. In 2015, Co-op committed to spending £1.5 billion over three years to source own-brand meat, produce and dairy products from the UK. In September 2016, it further extended its commitment to back UK farmers by switching all its fresh bacon and lamb to 100% British. This new sourcing initiative made The Co-op the only major UK food retailer to stock 100% own-brand fresh British beef, chicken, pork, lamb, bacon and turkey, having previously been the only retailer to use British meat in all its chilled ready meals, pies and sandwiches.

Finally, companies can do much to alter the business case analysis and in turn the decisions of their suppliers. They can alter the economics (i.e. the balance of costs and benefits) and they can encourage suppliers to take a more holistic and longer-term approach to investment decision-making. This can lead to the adoption of improved welfare practices, both through the upgrading of existing facilities—when and where feasible—to ensure that these facilities take proper account of the changing regulatory and industry standards and by changing expectations around animal welfare. The specific strategies differ between companies and between suppliers but the sorts of practical steps that companies can take to ease the financial burden of implementing higher welfare production systems and processes include:

- Ensuring that the transition period for any significant changes is structured so that major impacts on producers are avoided by allowing existing infrastructure to be upgraded or replaced as part of existing financial cycles
- Working with financial entities to agree preferential interest rates
- Securing preferential lending rates for capital investments in infrastructure that is designed for higher welfare production
- Maintaining a dialogue with producers to help them to understand market dynamics (e.g. the potential for premium priced products, market expansion, brand and reputational benefits) associated with higher welfare products
- Conducting trials with producers to evaluate the risks and benefits of improved welfare processes
- Providing extended contracts that guarantee levels of supply, allowing for any time lag between higher production costs and higher prices paid by the market
- Providing preferential contracts with guaranteed higher volumes of supply
- Paying a premium price for higher welfare products
- Providing pro bono professional advice on issues such as animal handling, certification schemes and performance measurement
- Reformulating product recipes to use fewer but higher welfare ingredients
- Introducing labelling and/or brand marketing to promote higher welfare products to consumers

An agenda for change

The material presented in this chapter and in the book as a whole points to three strategic imperatives for food companies. First, farm animal welfare should be a core issue for the sustainability and business agenda of all food companies. Second, by reframing the business case for action, companies could make very significant progress in improving their approach to farm animal welfare and that of their suppliers. Third, the structural challenges faced by the food industry mean that the industry needs to work together to address some of the key barriers to progress on farm animal welfare. We discuss each of these themes briefly here.

Make farm animal welfare a strategic priority

It is clear that farm animal welfare is, and should be recognized as, a core business issue for all food companies. Through this book we have identified a series of drivers (or pressures) for companies to act on farm animal welfare. While many of these drivers remain weak, it is noteworthy that the drivers are relatively aligned and, as such, reinforce and amplify each other. For example, while legislation has had important direct impacts on animal welfare, the more significant impacts have often been through the setting of precedents, and through showing what can be achieved. This is particularly the case with the EU, given that it is such an important market for many food producers. To take just one example, the EU ban on sow stalls is being replicated by several global food companies, including BRF, Smithfield Foods and Cargill, which have committed to ban pork from gestation crates. Expressed another way, legislation in combination with other drivers for change—companies' responsible sourcing or sustainable agriculture programmes, consumer and societal pressure, voluntary animal welfare initiatives, company and supply chain innovations—can, albeit sometimes relatively slowly, be a real driver for improving the welfare of farmed animals around the globe. Furthermore, there is a general acceptance in the food industry that there will continue to be progressive tightening of legislation on farm animal welfare, growing consumer interest in the issue, and increased customer and investor pressure for companies to improve their practices, performance and transparency on farm animal welfare.

Build the business case for action

In relation to the business case for action, narrowly focused, financially oriented, and short-term risk assessment and cost-benefit assessment processes can lead to companies making decisions that do not take account of the full range of business risks associated with farm animal welfare. Companies that take a more holistic and longer-term approach are likely to reap a range of benefits from building their internal capacity and being able to access new market opportunities, to building their brand and reputation as leaders. Taking a proactive approach also allows companies to influence the markets in which they operate, to shape market norms, to demonstrate that higher animal welfare practices are technically feasible and economically viable, to influence consumer awareness and to shape public policy.

Even for those companies that continue to frame the business case in a relatively financially oriented, short-term way, the balance point is clearly moving towards higher standards of farm animal welfare. For companies that are starting from scratch, the evidence and cases presented in this book suggest that there is likely to be a range of cost-effective actions they can take to improve their business simply by applying a farm animal welfare lens to their practices and processes. For example, they may be able to deliver significant improvements through relatively low cost measures, such as improved training of staff involved in animal handling and in purchasing, through supplier engagement and through improvements in processes and systems. Companies may also find that the business case for investment is much more attractive in situations where they align their investments in higher animal welfare systems with their overall capital expenditure planning (e.g. making welfare standards an integral part of new builds rather than retrofitting or upgrading existing facilities) and with their wider marketing efforts (e.g. encouraging clients to support investments in higher animal welfare as part of wider contract negotiations). Perhaps the more significant development is the greater number of companies and customers that are taking a more proactive approach to farm animal welfare. This interest will be cascaded through their purchasing decisions and through supply chains creating increased demand for higher welfare products and increasing the pressure on companies to ensure consistent and appropriate standards of farm animal welfare. These companies may also change the economics of investment, by providing financial and other incentives for investment to their suppliers.

Despite the growing strength of the business case for action on farm animal welfare, we acknowledge that many in the food industry are yet to be convinced that there is a business case for adopting higher standards of farm animal welfare. Unless or until the literature and the evidence base on the economic, financial and non-financial case for farm animal welfare is strengthened, many business leaders will continue to be sceptical about the business case for investing in farm animal welfare and, as a consequence, will be less willing to make such investments. It is, therefore, recommended that future studies on the business case for farm animal welfare consider both the financial costs and the financial benefits, and the wider potential for business value creation through, for example, improvements in brand profile and recognition, enhanced reputation, consumer awareness and willingness to purchase higher welfare products, and customer and employee trust and loyalty.

Work together to address the structural challenges

The realities of the food industry are well understood. It is a highly competitive sector, companies want to differentiate themselves across a whole range of dimensions, downward pressures on costs are an ever-present challenge, and companies have a multitude of commercial and sustainability challenges that they need to address. Companies must also balance animal welfare against other sustainability issues such as the carbon footprint of a product, the resources that are used in its production, the impact on human welfare, the environmental and ecological impact and the overall efficiency of production.

These challenges need to be understood in the context of the need to feed the world's burgeoning population (which is expected to reach 9.6 billion people by 2050) and changing dietary preferences (e.g. the ongoing growth in the world's per capita meat and milk consumption, especially in China and India). Against this backdrop, animal welfare is not only an important issue for individual food companies but a systemic challenge for the industry as a whole. The pressure to boost production yields in recent decades has resulted in the use of cheap and often subsidized feed grain, cheap fuel, cheap labour, limited breed selection and rapid technological change particularly in poultry, pork and dairy production systems, often to the detriment of both the animals and the people involved in livestock production. Furthermore, as over 70% of all emerging infectious diseases in humans are derived from the animal kingdom (Blancou *et al.*, 2005), animal-related public health risks are being viewed with increasing urgency and importance. This is an issue that extends beyond the needs and interests of individual companies. In fact, the negative consequences of animals being reared in conditions that deny them a "life worth living" are starting to have a detrimental effect on the business case for intensive production and, in turn, on the structure of the global food industry as a whole. At the same time, as we have discussed above, the business case for action is not clear cut; it is not clear how consumers or markets will respond to products produced from animals in more sustainable and higher welfare production systems, nor, in turn, is it clear whether such investments in higher welfare systems and processes will be economically viable.

Having noted these challenges, it is probably fair to say that the manner in which the food industry—individually and collectively—responds to these pressures will be key to its future success. Of course, change of the scale required to advance animal welfare standards will take time, especially given the costs associated with training and educating employees in animal welfare, auditing and certifying products to recognized standards, and the capital investment required to modify or upgrade production systems. Thus, driving improvements requires all stakeholders to take a long-term view of effecting change. Historically, the nature of company–supplier relationships has been transactional and short term, yet systemic change requires companies to work with their suppliers to deliver mutual and sustainable benefits. It requires companies to leverage their influence for change, it requires companies to create a robust commercial case for their suppliers to invest in farm animal welfare, and it requires companies to work in collaboration with their suppliers, governments and other actors.

This is clearly an ambitious agenda and one that may appear a long way from where we are today. Yet the central message of this book is that, through the actions of leading companies, we can expect to see changes in the way that the industry as a whole manages farm animal welfare. Many of the companies that we now consider leaders began with a focus on risk management and cost reduction (which is where many companies are now). Over time, this can lead companies to explore and develop new strategies to create business value; many leading companies have moved beyond simply reducing costs and increasing value to adopting strategies focused on product quality, brand and product differentiation and innovation. We are beginning to see the next evolutionary stage in farm animal welfare, as companies move away from outperforming their competitors on regulatory compliance, production cost management and risk management to strategies aimed at outperforming the market through re-engineered product formulations, processes and whole systems that optimize higher animal welfare standards. That is, we are moving towards a point where innovation in animal welfare is becoming a major source of new revenue and growth, as companies shift towards offering products with provenance, traceability, quality, safety and animal welfare attributes. Looking to the future, we expect more companies to regard animal welfare not simply as a risk to be managed but as a source of market differentiation and long-term value creation.

References

Beattie, V.E., O'Connell, N.E., & Moss, B.W. (2000). Influence of environmental enrichment on the behaviour, performance and meat quality of domestic pigs. *Livestock Production Science*, 65, 71-79.

Bennett, R., Kehlbacher, A., & Balcombe, K. (2012). A method for the economic valuation of animal welfare benefits using a single welfare score. *Animal Welfare,* 21(S1), 125-130.

Blancou, J., Chomel, B.B., Belotto, A., & Meslin, F.X. (2005). Emerging or re-emerging bacterial zoonoses: factors of emergence, surveillance and control. *Veterinary Research*, 36, 507-522.

Farm Animal Welfare Committee (2011). *Economics and Farm Animal Welfare. December 2011*. London: Farm Animal Welfare Committee.

Gouldson, A. & Sullivan, R. (2013). Long-term corporate climate change targets: what could they deliver? *Environmental Science & Policy*, 27, 1-10.

Gouldson, A. & Sullivan, R. (2014). Understanding the governance of corporations: an examination of the factors shaping UK supermarket strategies on climate change. *Environment and Planning A*, 46(12), 2972-2990.

Lemme, C.F., Mauro, P.A., & Ribas, J.C.R. (2014). *Case Study: An Economic Comparison of Group Housing and Individual Sow Stalls*. London: World Animal Protection. Retrieved from https://issuu.com/wspalatam/docs/wspa_folheto_divulgacao_tecnica_ing [accessed October 2016].

Lusk, J.L. & Norwood, F.B. (2011). Animal welfare economics. *Applied Economic Perspectives and Policy*, 33(4), 463-483.

McInerney, J. (2016). In what sense does animal welfare have an economic value? *Veterinary Ireland Journal,* 6(4), 218-220.

Malone, T. & Lusk, J.L. (2016). Putting the chicken before the egg price: An ex post analysis of California's battery cage ban. *Journal of Agricultural and Resource Economics,* 41(3), 518-532.

Menghi, A., de Roest, K., Porcelluzzi, A., Deblitz, C., von Davier, Z., Wildegger, B., de Witte, T., Strohm, K., Garming, H., Dirksmeyer, W., Zimmer, Y., Bölling, D., van Huylenbroek, G., & Mettepenningen, E. (2014). *Assessing Farmers' Costs of Compliance with EU Legislation in the Fields of the Environment, Animal Welfare and Food Safety*. Executive summary commissioned by the European Commission. Retrieved from http://ec.europa.eu/agriculture/sites/agriculture/files/external-studies/2014/farmer-costs/exec_sum_en.pdf

Mullally, C. & Lusk, J.L. (2015). Happy hens, sad consumers? The economic impact of restrictions on farm animal housing in California. Unpublished manuscript. Retrieved from http://agecon.okstate.edu/faculty/publications/5115.pdf [accessed December 2016].

Norgaard, N.H. & Olsen, P. (1995). *Economic Analyses of New Pig Production Systems: Focused on Reduced Capital Input*. Copenhagen: Statens Jordbrugs og Fiskeriokonomiske Institut.

RSPCA (2006). *Everyone's a Winner*. Retrieved from https://science.rspca.org.uk/sciencegroup/farmanimals/reportsandresources [accessed October 2016].

Sullivan, R. & Gouldson, A. (2013). Ten years of corporate action on climate change: what do we have to show for it? *Energy Policy*, 60, 733-740.

Sullivan, R. & Gouldson, A. (2016). Comparing the climate change actions, targets and performance of UK and US retailers. *CSR and Environmental Management*, 23(3), 129-139.

World Animal Protection (2014a). *A Case Study of triple Wins in Milk and Beef Production in Colombia*. Retrieved from https://unfccc.int/files/documentation/submissions_from_non-party_stakeholders/application/pdf/521.pdf [accessed October 2016].

World Animal Protection (2014b). *A Case Study of High Welfare, Large-scale Chicken and Egg Production in Brazil*. Retrieved from https://www.worldanimalprotection.org/sites/default/files/int_files/high-welfare-large-scale-egg-production-brazil.pdf [accessed January 2017].

Part V

Technical briefings

22 An introduction to farm animal production systems[1]

Heather Pickett

PICKETT ANIMAL WELFARE RESEARCH, UK

Inês Ajuda

COMPASSION IN WORLD FARMING, UK

Introduction

The production system in which animals are kept is an important determinant of the delivery of farm animal welfare. Animal welfare refers to the quality of life experienced by the individual animal and encompasses physical and mental wellbeing, as well as the ability to express natural behaviour. The welfare of an animal can be described as good or high if the animal is healthy and has a good quality of life, which encompasses both freedom from suffering and opportunities to experience positive feelings of wellbeing. For farm animals to have a life worth living, positive experiences must outweigh negative ones over the lifetime of the animal.

Welfare can be poor in any system if the feeding, breeding or health status of the animals is poor and/or the stockmanship or management is poor. However, production systems inherently vary in their potential to provide good welfare. This potential is determined by factors built into the system, such as provision of sufficient living space and access to resources that meet the physical and behavioural needs of the animals.

This chapter gives an overview of the main types of commercial production systems for terrestrial farmed animals and highlights key welfare benefits and key welfare concerns for each of these production system types. It also discusses the role that product labelling and assurance schemes can play in differentiating between products by method of production and/or welfare standards.

What are the main types of production system?

From an animal welfare perspective, commercial livestock production systems for terrestrial animals can be broadly categorized as follows (see also Box 22.1):

- Intensive systems:
  - Cages, crates and tethering systems
  - Systems with high stocking densities and minimal or no enrichment

1 This chapter is based on a Briefing Note prepared for the Business Benchmark on Farm Animal Welfare, and funding was provided by Compassion in World Farming.

- Extensive systems:
  - Systems with lower stocking densities and enrichment
  - Free-range systems for pigs, poultry and rabbits
  - Pasture-based systems for ruminants
  - Extensive grazing/foraging systems
  - Organic systems

Globally, an estimated 85% of chicken meat and eggs and over 60% of pig meat is produced in industrial systems (Livestock Global Alliance, 2016). Most rabbits are also reared intensively and many cattle spend at least part of their life in intensive systems. Overall, this means at least 80% of animals farmed for food each year are kept in intensive systems.

Box 22.1 Some definitions

"Intensive" refers to any system that tries to maximize the number of animals produced per unit of space and time. Intensive systems can, but do not necessarily, use close confinement and may be indoors or outdoors (or a combination of the two). These systems may sometimes be described as "factory farming", "industrial" (this term is usually used for large-scale intensive systems but small-scale systems can also be intensive), "landless" (some higher-welfare systems may also be landless), "standard" or "conventional" (for ruminants, systems that involve grazing may also be considered standard/conventional). Intensive systems generally have low welfare potential.

"Extensive" refers to any system that provides significantly more space and enrichment than intensive systems. The term "extensive" is often used specifically for outdoor systems where animals range over large areas but indoor systems with lower stocking densities are sometimes described as "extensive indoor". Extensive systems encompass a wide range of indoor and outdoor systems from those that might be described as "semi-intensive", "extensive indoor", "enriched indoor", "standard-plus" or "alternative" to "free-range", "pasture-based", "extensive grazing", "grass-fed" and "organic". These systems often have higher welfare potential but must be well-managed for this potential to be realized.

"Cage-free" refers to any system that does not involve close confinement in a cage, crate or tether. Cage-free systems can be intensive or extensive.

Intensive systems

Cages, crates and tethering

Close confinement systems maximize the number of animals that can be kept in a given space by using rows, and often multiple tiers, of cages or rows of stalls or tethers, usually within closed or open-sided sheds. These systems simplify management by restricting animal movement and facilitating the separation of animals from their faeces/urine. Usually the systems are barren. Animals bred for rapid growth/high yield are typically used in these systems to maximize the amount of product per unit of feed.

These systems include:

- **Barren cages.** Wire cages are commonly used for housing groups of egg-laying hens, individual rabbits kept for breeding and groups of rabbits reared for meat and, sometimes, for groups of broiler (meat) chickens. The cages are generally barren except for feed and water provision and typically provide less space than the area of a standard A4 sheet of paper per animal: 300–550 cm^2/bird for laying hens, 450–600 cm^2/animal for rabbits reared for meat, and up to 50 kg/m^2 for broiler chickens, which is equivalent to around 450 cm^2/bird at slaughter weight.
- **Enriched cages.** In some cases, cages may be "enriched", for example by the addition of a nesting area, perches mounted a few centimetres above the floor, a scratching area and a little extra space and height for laying hens. This is a legal requirement for cages for laying hens within the European Union (EU), where the minimum space allowance is 600 cm^2/bird usable space (750 cm^2/bird total space). "Enriched" cages for rabbits may provide some combination of platforms raised above the cage floor, hay or straw, items for gnawing, tubes for hiding, a plastic cover over part of the wire floor, and additional space and height; frequently, however, there is only one type of enrichment available.
- **Crates in pig production.** Sows (female breeding pigs) are commonly kept in individual crates constructed of metal bars ("sow stalls" or "gestation crates") during pregnancy and in similar crates with an additional area for the piglets ("farrowing crates") when they are giving birth and nursing their piglets. Sows may also be tethered, i.e. chained in rows by a collar around the neck or body. These systems are typically fully slatted or partly slatted and do not provide comfortable flooring for standing and resting. In countries such as the United Kingdom, sow stalls are prohibited.
- **Tethering and veal crates for cattle and calves.** Cattle may be tethered in "tie-stalls", and calves are often kept in individual wooden or metal crates and may be tethered. Veal crates were banned in the EU, but individual housing is still permitted for the first eight weeks.

Confinement systems were introduced in farm animal production to enable the easier management and handling of animals. Because the animals cannot express natural behaviours—such as contact with other animals (individual cages or tethering), lying down normally (farrowing crates) or freedom of movement (group cages with high stocking density for laying hens)—the risk of injury, fighting, or piglet crushing is reduced. In addition, the risk of exposure to certain diseases may be reduced (due to the possibility of managing biosecurity in closed systems) and the animals are generally protected from predators. Furthermore, lower labour requirements help to reduce the cost of production.

Despite these benefits, individual confinement raises a series of animal welfare concerns. Movement and natural behaviour are severely restricted in confinement systems, resulting in discomfort, boredom and frustration. In turn, these contribute to abnormal behaviours such as repeated biting of the bars or wire. In cages, birds are unable to flap their wings or perform many highly motivated behaviours, such as laying their eggs in a nest (for laying hens in barren cages), roosting on an elevated perch at night, foraging and "dust-bathing" (a maintenance behaviour that helps to keep the plumage in good condition). Rabbits in cages are usually unable to sit up on their hind legs in a species-typical "look-out" posture, lie stretched out in a species-typical resting posture, or move normally by hopping. Animals are generally unable to turn around in individual crates or when tethered, and even the most basic maintenance and comfort behaviours, such as changing position, stretching, grooming and scratching, may be hampered or prevented. Crated sows are unable to perform many highly motivated behaviours, such as rooting or foraging, constructing a nest prior to giving birth, and interacting normally with their piglets and other sows. Deprivation of normal social interaction is also a major issue for tethered cattle and crated/tethered calves.

Physical restrictions due to housing design can also lead to health problems linked to the lack of movement and exercise, such as weaker bone structure or weaker muscles. For example, laying hens and rabbits in cages often suffer from weak bones as a result of lack of space and insufficient exercise.

There are likely to be few positive experiences for closely confined animals and the inherent restrictions of the system mean that the animals are unlikely to have a life worth living.

Intensive systems with high stocking densities and minimal or no enrichment

These intensive systems typically use high stocking densities and relatively barren environments to keep the cost of production to a minimum. Mechanical ventilation systems and/or slatted flooring may be used to maximize the stocking density that can be achieved. Fast-growing/high-yielding breeds are typically used to maximize the amount of product per unit of feed.

The specific systems differ between species. For example:

- **Meat poultry**. Intensively reared meat poultry are typically housed in very large numbers (thousands or tens of thousands of birds) at high stocking densities in closed or open-sided sheds with solid or slatted flooring or, in some countries (e.g. China), they are sometimes kept on suspended nets. Solid flooring may be covered with litter material (e.g. wood shavings). Stocking density for meat chickens is typically 30–45 kg/m^2 (equivalent to around 500–750 cm^2/bird at slaughter weight) but may be lower in hot climates.
- **Laying hens**. Intensive non-cage systems for laying hens may be single-level ("barn") with solid or slatted flooring or have multiple tiers of slatted flooring ("aviaries") without access to litter material or any other type of enrichment. The space allowance per bird is typically a little higher than in cage systems

(9–15 hens/m^2, equivalent to around 670–1,110 cm^2/bird) and the total available space is greater.

- **Pigs.** Breeding sows and pigs reared for meat are often kept in groups in barren indoor pens with solid or slatted flooring at high stocking densities (typically 150 kg/m^2 or 0.65 m^2/animal at slaughter weight). Objects such as footballs, pieces of wood or hanging chains/ropes may sometimes be provided but natural enrichment materials that are rootable, edible, manipulable and chewable are generally absent.
- **Cattle.** Intensive systems for cattle and calves include a range of indoor and outdoor systems with high stocking densities and without access to grazing. Examples include outdoor feedlots, which typically have an earthen or concrete floor and sometimes provide access to housing/shelter, and indoor systems with solid or slatted flooring or free-access cubicles (rows of individual stalls, typically divided by metal bars, with feed provided at the front and a passageway for manure/slurry at the back). The floor of the cubicles may be bare or covered with rubber matting, sand or other materials.

In these systems, the animals are able to move more freely compared with confinement systems and interact socially. Laying hens are usually able to lay their eggs in a nest and dust-bathing may be possible for meat poultry reared on litter (for as long as the litter remains in a friable condition). As with confinement systems, the risk of exposure to certain diseases may be reduced due to the possibility of managing biosecurity in closed systems, and the animals are generally protected from predators.

Despite these relative advantages, there are many welfare issues associated with intensive systems with high stocking densities and minimal or no enrichment. The negative experiences may outweigh positive ones for many intensively reared animals and the animals may not have a life worth living.

High stocking densities and relatively barren environments restrict or prevent many highly motivated behaviours such as foraging and dust-bathing for poultry, rooting and wallowing for pigs, and grazing and browsing for cattle, and limit the opportunity for choice. Meat poultry and laying hens are often kept in very large groups that far exceed their capacity to recognize all individuals, which can result in chronic stress due to the inability to form stable social groups. Breeding sows and pigs reared for meat may be repeatedly mixed with groups of unfamiliar individuals, which can result in aggression and injuries. Frustration of the animals' motivation to forage or explore can lead to damaging behaviours such as feather-pecking and cannibalism in poultry and tail-biting in pigs.

Intensive systems often rely on "mutilations" (removal of sensitive body tissues) to reduce injuries, such as beak-trimming of poultry, tail-docking and teeth-clipping of pigs and dehorning/disbudding (removal of the horn buds) of cattle. Other mutilations may also be carried out to ease management, such as castration of male pigs and cattle and tail-docking of dairy cows. The prevalence of the different mutilations varies according to the country and continent: for example, tail docking of dairy cattle is a very common mutilation in the USA, but less common, although still practised, in Europe.

The fast-growing/high-yielding breeds typically used in intensive systems often have an increased risk of morbidity and mortality. Lameness, cardiovascular problems, sudden death and a range of "production diseases" (conditions related to metabolic problems) are common. Solid concrete and slatted flooring can increase the risk of lameness and injuries. Heat stress can be a problem for densely stocked poultry and pigs and for cattle in feedlots with inadequate shade. Infectious diseases can spread rapidly when large numbers of animals are kept in crowded conditions and intensive systems often rely on routine use of antibiotics to mitigate this risk. Cattle in intensive systems are often fed on diets high in concentrates (e.g. grain and soy) which can cause health problems in ruminants, such as sub-acute ruminal acidosis (SARA), and increase susceptibility to certain infections.

Extensive systems

Higher-welfare indoor and/or outdoor systems with lower stocking densities and enrichment (without access to grazing or other growing vegetation)

These systems provide additional space per animal and a more enriched environment than the intensive systems described above. Slower-growing/more robust breeds are sometimes used in these systems but fast-growing/high-yielding breeds are also commonly used.

The specific systems differ between species. For example:

- **Meat poultry**. Higher-welfare indoor systems for meat poultry may be enriched with some combination of perches, straw bales, pecking objects (e.g. whole brassicas or lengths of rope), scattering of whole grains, regular addition of fresh litter material, natural lighting and additional space (and open water troughs for waterfowl such as ducks). The stocking density in these systems is lower (30 kg/m^2 or less for meat chickens) than in intensive systems.
- **Laying hens**. Higher-welfare indoor systems for laying hens may be single-level ("barn") or have multiple tiers of slatted flooring ("aviaries") with litter material over at least part of the floor area. Additional enrichment may also be provided, similar to that used for meat poultry. In some cases, poultry may have access to a "winter garden" (an enclosed area along the edge of the shed with natural light and enrichment).
- **Rabbits**. Higher-welfare indoor systems for rabbits ("park" or "barn" systems) use floor pens with enrichment such as raised platforms, hay or straw, objects for gnawing, tubes for hiding, natural lighting and additional space, typically 800–1,500 cm^2/rabbit.
- **Pigs**. Gestating sows and pigs reared for meat may be housed in groups in bedded/deep litter systems. In some cases there may be access to an outdoor area, often with additional enrichment. "Free-farrowing" systems have been

developed that allow freedom of movement and provision of nesting material for farrowing sows.

- **Cattle.** Cattle and calves may also be housed in groups in bedded/deep litter systems, with or without access to an outdoor exercise area. Cubicle housing systems for cattle may be enriched with some combination of mechanical brushes for grooming/scratching, access to forage, deep bedding and/or regular addition of fresh bedding material in cubicles, and access to an indoor or outdoor loafing area/exercise yard.

These systems offer greater opportunities for behavioural expression compared with intensive systems. Laying hens are able to lay their eggs in a nest and littered areas encourage dust-bathing and foraging. Enrichment encourages greater activity in meat poultry and rabbits. Sows in free-farrowing systems are able to follow their strong instinct to construct a nest prior to giving birth and interact normally with their piglets. Bedded/deep litter systems provide a more comfortable lying surface for breeding sows, pigs reared for meat, cattle and calves, and encourage rooting and exploratory behaviour in sows and pigs. These systems also encourage play behaviour in pigs and calves. Through careful management, tail-docking and teeth-clipping of pigs, as well as beak trimming of laying hens, can be avoided in these systems.

Increased opportunities to engage in natural behaviours mean that positive experiences are more likely to outweigh negative ones for animals reared in enriched environments and the animals are therefore more likely to have a life worth living or a good life.

Despite these benefits, there are important welfare concerns that need to be addressed. Large group sizes for poultry, mixing of unfamiliar animals for sows and pigs, and the use of fast-growing/high-yielding breeds often remain a concern. Furthermore, it is common to find that many of the mutilations carried out in intensive systems are also carried out in these systems. For example, laying hens are usually (though not always) beak-trimmed in these systems and meat pigs may still be tail-docked because of the multi-factorial origin of these problems.

Free-range, pasture-based and extensive grazing/foraging systems

In free-range and extensive systems the animals are typically kept on, or have some access to, pasture (land with mostly domesticated/sown grasses and/or other forage species), rangelands (land with mostly native grasses, sedges, rushes and/or shrubs), woodlands or other environments with growing vegetation. Slower-growing/more robust breeds are more likely to be used in these systems but fast-growing/high-yielding breeds may also be used.

Again, the specific systems differ between species:

- **Meat poultry, laying hens and rabbits.** Free-range systems for meat poultry, laying hens and rabbits may have small mobile housing units that can be moved periodically to fresh pasture or larger static housing units. The animals may be shut into the housing units at night or may be free to roam at all times.

Access to the range is often through small "pop-holes" but, in some cases, larger doors or the whole side of the shed may be opened. Standards for free-range systems vary widely. In some cases, access to the range may be restricted to a relatively short period of the day and standards do not always require that the outside area is managed to ensure it does not become denuded of vegetation. The best free-range systems provide natural (e.g. trees/hedges) and/or artificial cover to encourage birds to range widely. The range may or may not be surrounded by fencing to deter predators. In some relatively small-scale systems, poultry and rabbits may only have access to a small mobile run, sometimes with a wire mesh floor, which allows the animals to forage/graze but must be moved frequently (often daily) to fresh ground.

- **Pigs.** Breeding sows and pigs reared for meat may be kept in free-range systems on pasture (which may become denuded due to the rooting behaviour of the animals if they are not rotated to new ground regularly). Shelter may be provided, for example by huts, arks, tents or sheds. Some pigs are kept in very extensive systems. For example, Iberian pigs in traditional extensive production systems in Spain and Portugal roam freely in woodlands where they forage for acorns.
- **Cattle.** Cattle grazing on pasture may be provided with some kind of housing or constructed shelter or may rely on shelter provided by natural features, as is usually the case for cattle on rangeland. In dry regions, beef cattle are often kept in very extensive systems, where it may be challenging to provide shelter. Local breeds, adapted to the climate, are often used.

These systems provide much greater opportunities for animals to engage in natural behaviours, including foraging and dust-bathing for poultry, rooting and wallowing for pigs, and grazing and browsing for cattle. Greater space availability and more complex environments facilitate more positive social interactions and provide animals with more opportunities to choose, for example, to lie down in a preferred position and be closer to the animals they prefer. Also, in systems where there is both indoor and outdoor access, animals have the opportunity to choose, for example, to seek cooler or warmer microenvironments.

Some mutilations, such as tail-docking and teeth-clipping of pigs, can often be avoided in free-range systems. Some free-range laying hens are not beak-trimmed, especially those kept in smaller groups/mobile housing units or in systems with good access to the outside and adequate cover on the range to encourage birds out of larger static houses. Where slower-growing/more robust breeds of animals are used, these are likely to have fewer health problems. Lameness and abrasion injuries are much less common in cattle kept on pasture or range and the health of ruminants is improved when grazing forms a major part of the diet.

Increased opportunities to engage in natural behaviours mean that positive experiences are more likely to outweigh negative ones for animals in free-range, pasture-based and extensive grazing/foraging systems and the animals are, therefore, more likely to have a life worth living or a good life.

Although many mutilations are less common in free-range, pasture-based and extensive grazing systems, other mutilations are commonly found in these systems. Breeding sows, and sometimes also pigs reared for meat, may be nose-ringed to reduce damage caused by rooting behaviour. Animals in more extensive systems often take longer to reach slaughter weight so male pigs and cattle may be castrated because they would otherwise reach sexual maturity prior to slaughter. Females may also be sterilized to avoid breeding with males from the same group or, if kept in very extensive systems, to avoid breeding with wild animals, such as sows with wild boars. Animals may be more exposed to certain environmental pathogens in these systems and mortality rates can be higher as a result of predation.

Organic systems

Organic production typically avoids the use of hormones, synthetic feed additives and prophylactic (non-therapeutic) use of antibiotics and other synthetic veterinary medicines, except vaccines. Organic standards vary widely from country to country, and between different certification bodies within a country, but typically prohibit close confinement systems and stipulate requirements for higher space allowances, enrichment and some form of outdoor access (although in some countries organic animals may be housed in conditions similar to conventional farming and be distinguished from conventional products by restrictions on feed ingredients and medicines). Slower-growing/more robust breeds are often, but not always, used in organic systems.

The welfare benefits of organic systems are similar to other higher-welfare/extensive systems. Organic standards often have additional benefits, for example, due to requirements for: the inclusion of grazing/forage in the diet of ruminants, restrictions on mutilations (although there are often exceptions), later weaning ages, humane handling and slaughter practices and restrictions on transport duration, and the avoidance of artificial breeding technologies that are associated with welfare problems (e.g. embryo transfer, cloning and genetic engineering).

The welfare concerns are also similar to other higher-welfare/extensive systems. Restrictions on the routine use of veterinary medicines in organic standards may give rise to potential welfare concerns but this is often mitigated by the use of robust breeds and management practices that promote health and natural immunity. Where high-yielding livestock breeds are used in organic systems, restrictions on feed ingredients may potentially raise issues in terms of meeting their nutritional requirements.

Do animals stay in the same production system throughout their life?

Animals often spend time in more than one production system during their life. They may be moved between systems seasonally or over their life-cycle. Poultry reared for meat are generally reared in the same system from one day of age until slaughter, whereas laying hens are often reared in one system until they are ready to start laying and then moved to another system for the laying period. These systems may be similar (e.g. a cage system during both rearing and laying) or different (e.g. a floor housing system during rearing and a cage system during laying or vice versa). Free-range poultry usually spend an initial rearing period indoors, with free-range access provided for perhaps the latter half of their life.

Breeding sows are often moved between different systems for mating, gestation and farrowing in a repeating pattern (sometimes with separate systems for the early part and the later part of gestation) and may spend some periods closely confined and other periods housed in groups. Pigs reared for meat may be moved between systems at various stages as they grow, often at weaning at two to four weeks of age and again for the final fattening phase prior to slaughter. Cattle reared for beef may be reared in pasture-based or extensive rangeland grazing systems and moved to outdoor feedlots or indoor housing for a final fattening phase prior to slaughter. In temperate regions, cattle may spend part of the year grazing on pasture or range and be housed over winter and/or for calving. For beef cattle, the timing of the final fattening phase may be arranged to coincide with the usual winter housing period. In some cases, beef cattle may be reared entirely on grass/forage.

How are production systems differentiated in the marketplace?

Labelling

Livestock products may be labelled to identify the production system used and/or other aspects of animal welfare standards and production practices. Labelling may be mandatory or voluntary and the labelling terms used may be legally defined or defined by terms agreed and published by industry bodies, or they may be unregulated with no unified definition. In the latter case there is a greater risk that the terms used may be misleading for consumers. Voluntary labelling to identify the production system is often applied only to products from higher-welfare production systems because there is little incentive for producers/retailers of products from intensively reared animals to identify the production system.

An example of a mandatory labelling system with legally defined labelling terms is the labelling of eggs in the EU. Whole eggs produced and sold in the EU must be stamped with a code that identifies the production system and the packaging must carry one of the following labelling terms: "cage", "barn", "free-range" or "organic". Legally defined standards apply to each of these terms.

Labelling terms may apply to the whole of an animal's life or just part of it. For example, a beef product marketed as "grass-fed" may have come from cattle reared on grass/forage throughout their life, poultry meat or eggs marketed as "free-range" may have come from birds provided with free-range access during the latter half of their life, and a pork product marketed as "outdoor-bred" may have come from pigs that spent the first few weeks until weaning in an outdoor system and were then reared indoors for the remainder of their life.

Assurance schemes

Farm assurance schemes are voluntary schemes that apply standards for livestock production and other sectors. Livestock schemes may cover one or more parts of the chain from hatcheries, breeding units and farms, through to transport and slaughter. Assessment audits of scheme members are carried out to check compliance with the standards. Farm assurance schemes for livestock can be broadly categorized as follows:

- Industry-led schemes typically allow intensive production systems but often stipulate standards for higher-welfare/extensive systems as well. The requirements are often based on legal requirements or welfare codes in the country where the scheme operates but may include more detailed standards and sometimes stipulate higher standards for certain aspects. Examples include the Assured Food Standards "Red Tractor" scheme in the UK and the "National Feedlot Accreditation Scheme" in Australia.
- Welfare-based schemes have a specific focus on animal welfare standards (though they may also cover other aspects). These schemes often prohibit certain intensive production systems and typically specify requirements for additional space, enrichment, restrictions on mutilations and transport duration, and humane handling and slaughter practices. In some cases, there may be restrictions on the growth rate/breeds of animals used. Examples of this kind of assurance scheme include "RSPCA Assured" in the UK, "Neuland" in Germany, "Beter Leven" in The Netherlands, "Animal Welfare Approved", "Humane Farm Animal Care" and "American Humane Association" in the USA, and Global Animal Partnership's "5-Step® Animal Welfare Rating Program", which originated in the USA and is used in a number of countries around the world.
- Quality-based schemes focus on the quality of the product rather than animal welfare *per se* but the specifications to achieve the required product standard, for example in relation to the production systems, management practices and animal breeds permitted, may have benefits for animal welfare. An example of quality-based standards with a significant animal welfare component is "Label Rouge" poultry in France.
- Organic schemes typically prohibit close confinement systems and stipulate a range of requirements that can have significant benefits for animal welfare, as summarized earlier in this chapter.

Reference

Livestock Global Alliance (2016). *Livestock for Sustainable Development in the 21st Century*. Retrieved from http://www.livestockdialogue.org/fileadmin/templates/res_livestock/docs/2016/LGA-Brochure-revMay13th.pdf

23 Antibiotic use in animals

Impacts on human health and animal welfare[1]

Inês Ajuda, Vicky Bond[2] and Jemima Jewell

COMPASSION IN WORLD FARMING, UK

What are antibiotics?

Antibiotics are medicines used to control infectious diseases in humans and animals. They are derived originally from natural substances produced as defence systems by microorganisms to inhibit the growth or multiplication (reproduction) of other microorganisms. These microorganisms have then been identified and cultured naturally or synthetically to create the drugs that are used extensively in human and veterinary medicine today. The vast majority of antibiotics are used to kill or inhibit the growth of bacteria. They are not effective against viral infections.

Why is antibiotic resistance so important?

Antibiotics are now widely available and their use has brought significant benefits in terms of fighting once commonplace infections and enabling increasingly complex and invasive surgery. However, every time a dose of antibiotics is given it provides any bacteria present with an opportunity to develop resistance to the drug. The over-use of antibiotics (especially in low doses) and incomplete courses of antibiotics are the main reasons for the increase in antibiotic resistance. This resistance has serious implications: it means that antibiotics can be ineffective when they are most needed, i.e. to treat serious disease. (It is important to note that antibiotic resistance is a different issue from antibiotic residues; see further Box 23.1.)

1 This chapter is based on a 2014 briefing note originally published by the Business Benchmark on Farm Animal Welfare (Bond and Jewell, 2014). The Benchmark is supported by Compassion in World Farming, World Animal Protection and Coller Capital. The views expressed in this chapter are those of the authors and do not necessarily represent those of the Benchmark or its supporting partners. This chapter draws heavily from Alliance to Save Our Antibiotics (2011, 2015) and Compassion in World Farming (2011), which are recommended for further reading.

2 Vicky Bond is now Managing Director, UK, at The Humane League.

Box 23.1 Resistance vs. residues

This chapter does not address residues in food, which is a separate issue from antibiotic resistance. Residues are traces of veterinary drugs including antibiotics that have been given to farm animals, that can remain in food products such as meat, eggs and milk for a certain period after treatment.

In the EU and other countries around the world, regulation is in place to address the issue of residues. These regulations are intended to ensure that traces of drugs ingested by people via their food are kept below a safe limit. A withdrawal period of days, weeks or months may be necessary after the administration of antibiotic veterinary drugs to an animal, during which time the animal or an animal product cannot go into the food chain.

Codex Alimentarius, the international food standards of the Food and Agriculture Organization and the World Health Organization (WHO), publishes the maximum residue limits (MRLs) of certain veterinary drugs that are considered to be safe in food. At the EU and national levels, MRLs are set for drugs that have been approved for use in food animals. Monitoring is carried out under European Directive 96/23/EC by testing samples of meat, imports and other food for residues that exceed the accepted limit.

The over-use and the incomplete use of antibiotics in human medicine is partly responsible for the increase in antibiotic-resistant bacteria. However, for a range of bacteria, farm animal use contributes significantly, and for some infections it is the main source of resistance. This fact has been established by decades of research and is acknowledged by organizations such as the World Health Organization (WHO) and the European Food Safety Authority.

Box 23.2 Critically important antibiotics

The WHO has developed and applied criteria to rank antimicrobials (which include antibiotics*) according to their relative importance in human medicine (WHO, 2011a). The list is designed to help guide usage in farm animals and thus preserve the effectiveness of currently available antimicrobials.

The antimicrobials are classified into three groups: critically important, highly important, and important for human medicine. Critically important antibiotics include cephalosporins and fluoroquinolones; one example of the latter is ciprofloxacin, trusted as a first-line treatment for severe salmonella and campylobacter infections in adults.

* Antibiotics are a type of antimicrobial, but not all antimicrobials are antibiotics. For example, anti-viral drugs and anti-fungal drugs are antimicrobials but they are not antibiotics.

It is also important to note that the efficacy of antibiotics varies; older antibiotics are often less efficacious and require a higher dose or a longer course than modern antibiotics. For example, the newer active ingredient of fluoroquinolone is capable of treating 70 times as many animals as the same weight of active ingredient for tetracycline. These newer drugs are now being utilized by the farming industry as fewer antibiotics can be used for the same effect. However, these antibiotics are also "critically important" drugs for human medicine and are needed in the treatment of bacteria that are resistant to older antibiotics (see Box 23.2).

What is the relationship between antibiotics and farming?

It is believed that farm animals consume nearly half of all the antibiotics produced worldwide (Veterinary Medicines Directorate, 2007). While farm antibiotic use, as is the case with human medicine, is prescription-only in most jurisdictions, no prescription records are collected.

There are four broad categories of antibiotic use on-farm:

- **Therapeutic**. Giving a treatment when clinical disease is identified.
- **Metaphylactic**. Giving treatment to a group of animals when some are showing signs of illness.
- **Prophylactic**. Giving a treatment in anticipation of a disease. On-farm this is often given to a group of animals (typically in close confinement) where there is a perceived risk of infection.
- **Growth promotion**. Giving antibiotics to improve the growth rates of animals. At low doses of particular antibiotics, food conversion rates improve, most likely because the composition of gut microflora is changed, which enables animals to grow faster using less feed. This practice is banned in the EU but is widely practised outside of Europe.

The therapeutic use of antibiotics in farm animals prevents suffering and, as such, the value of antibiotic use to treat disease is not in question. However, the use of antibiotics on-farm is frequently prophylactic (to prevent disease) or to promote animal growth, rather than therapeutic.

Reliance on frequent, prolonged, low-dose use of antibiotics in this way creates ideal conditions for antibiotic-resistant strains of bacteria to develop. Antibiotics are often used prophylactically as animals reared in intensive production systems are at a high risk of infection. This is because they are usually:

- Caged, confined or penned in crowded, often stressful conditions
- Weaned at a very early age
- Pushed to their physiological and metabolic limits to maximize productivity
- Subject to routine mutilations such as castration or tail docking (where antibiotics are used to prevent an infection of the open wound)

These pressures can suppress animals' immune systems and encourage the spread of infection as animals are in close, cramped conditions. Intensive farming therefore often relies on prophylactic use of antibiotics to compensate for an inherently low-welfare environment.

Pigs, poultry and rabbits are the animals most likely to be reared in highly intensive conditions, crowded together in large numbers and kept indoors for most if not all of their lives. It is not surprising therefore that they are also the three species given the most frequent and greatest quantity of antibiotics. Antibiotic use is not confined to intensive systems but the majority of farming systems are intensive and therefore use the majority of antibiotics. Organic farming is subject to specific rules on antibiotic use (see Box 23.3). Prophylactic use is most common in intensive systems for the reasons outlined above.

Outside the EU, antibiotics are routinely used at very low doses as growth promoters. The use of antibiotics as growth promoters in animals pushes them towards their physiological and metabolic limits with negative impacts on welfare. Even within the EU, while growth promoters are officially prohibited, the prophylactic use of antibiotics, particularly at very low doses, has the same effect, exploiting a loophole in the current law.

Where animals are kept in crowded, intensive conditions, resistant strains of bacteria can spread rapidly.

Box 23.3 Organic food

Organic farming regulations typically prohibit the routine use of antibiotics, thus ensuring animals only receive antibiotics when they require them. If an animal receives antibiotics, the legal withdrawal period (the time between the drug being administered and the sale of its meat or milk) must be at least doubled and often tripled before the meat or milk can be sold as organic.

Why does this matter for farm animal welfare?

The direct and indirect impacts of antibiotics on farm animal welfare are summarized in Table 23.1.

There are alternatives—ones that enable a better quality of life for farmed animals and do not present the associated risks for antibiotic resistance. For example, disease outbreaks can be minimized or prevented by good husbandry, hygiene and an improved living environment. Reducing stocking density and using robust breeds also improve the quality of animals' lives and can reduce the need for antibiotics (see Box 23.4).

Table 23.1 Impacts of antibiotics on farm animal welfare

Type of antibiotic use	*Direct impact on animal welfare*	*Indirect impact on animal welfare*	*Indirect impact on human health*
Prophylactic	May be positive in short term as prevents an animal from falling ill	Enables continuation of low-welfare environment	Contributes to risk of antibiotic resistance
Growth promotion	Negative as puts excessive physiological and metabolic strain on the animal		Contributes to risk of antibiotic resistance

Box 23.4 "Antibiotic-free" animal products

There is a growing trend over the past few years, particularly in the United States (Natural Resources Defense Council, 2015), for companies to sell "antibiotic-free meat". This label indicates that the meat has come from animals that were not subject to antibiotic treatments at any point in their life. However, there may be differing interpretations and some companies appear to use it to imply that animals have not been subject to non-therapeutic use.

"No human antibiotics" is a similar label that some companies have adopted. In this case, food businesses are dealing specifically with the use of—and resistance to—antibiotics in animals that are also used in humans.

While it is clear that the over-use of antibiotics in farming must be addressed, to enable a significant reduction in antibiotics the fundamental features of intensive systems must also be addressed. Simply stopping the routine use of antibiotics without also changing the animals' environment could increase the risk of sickness and have a negative impact on animal welfare. In some systems or species, it may also be the case that fewer antibiotics are compensated for with alternative "props" such as a heavy vaccination regime and/or use of prebiotics and probiotics, which does not fundamentally address the conditions in which the animals live.

In accordance with an "antibiotic-free" label, animals that receive therapeutic treatment of antibiotics (in response to a disease episode) are removed from the antibiotic-free supply chain. This runs the risk of sick animals not being treated in a timely fashion. Therapeutic antibiotic treatment is an important component of maintaining good animal welfare. Stopping or delaying therapeutic treatments could cause significant suffering and greatly compromise the welfare of sick animals, who should receive treatment when they need it.

While "antibiotic-free" is easily understood and appealing to the consumer, it is not an easy solution and an "antibiotic-free" approach should only be undertaken responsibly and with due consideration for the conditions in which the animals are reared.

What are the implications for human health?

The implications for human health are serious. The WHO (2011b) describes some antibiotic resistance in humans as being "associated with more frequent and longer hospitalization, longer illness, a higher risk of invasive infection and a twofold increase in the risk of death". The UK's Chief Medical Officer, Professor Dame Sally Davies, has stated that "Antimicrobial resistance poses a catastrophic threat. If we don't act now, any one of us could go into hospital in 20 years for minor surgery and die because of an ordinary infection that can't be treated by antibiotics" (Department of Health, 2013).

The impact of antibiotic use in farm animals on human health occurs because so many of the same or similar antibiotics are used on-farm and in human medicine. The overlap can be explained by looking at the different classes (or families) of antibiotics. Antibiotics in a particular class tend to have similar chemical structures, modes of action and ranges of effectiveness. Bacteria that have a mechanism of resistance to one antibiotic are more likely to develop resistance to a closely related antibiotic. This problem is compounded by the fact that considerable quantities of the same active ingredients are used in farm animal antibiotics and human-related antibiotics.

Although absolute proof of cause and effect in this field can be extremely difficult to identify, scientists have established a clear link between antibiotic use in farm animals and resistance in humans. In particular, the scientific evidence shows that (Alliance to Save Our Antibiotics, 2015):

- For some major human bacterial infections, such as salmonellosis and campylobacteriosis, farm animals are the most important source of antimicrobial resistance.
- For certain other human infections, such as infections caused by *Escherichia coli* and enterococci, there is clear evidence that farm animals are an important source of antibiotic resistance.
- For some infections, such as those caused by MRSA (methicillin-resistant *Staphylococcus aureus*), there is evidence in the UK that on-farm use of antibiotics currently makes a small contribution to treatment problems in human medicine. Moreover, based on the experiences in some other countries (see, for example, Voss *et al.*, 2005), this contribution may increase significantly unless we take urgent decisive action.
- For a further small number of antimicrobial-resistant infections, such as *Neisseria gonorrhoeae* infection, there is as yet no evidence of any link with on-farm antimicrobial use. There is, however, a solid theoretical case that the horizontal transmission of resistance genes of farm-animal origin could contribute to the rise of potentially untreatable cases in humans. This would be such a serious and quite possibly irreversible development that precautionary action is advised, even if the probability of the worst-case scenario is only moderate.
- For many other infections, such as multi-drug resistant tuberculosis and the wide range of infections caused by antibiotic-resistant strains of *Streptococcus pneumoniae*, the use of antibiotics on farms currently appears to play no part in antibiotic resistance in human medicine.

How can food companies address the issue of over-use of antibiotics?

The recognition of antibiotic resistance as a serious risk to human health means that media attention has been increasing and legislative pressure on this issue is likely to grow. Companies seeking to address the use of antibiotics in their supply chains can take a number of steps including the following:

- Understand existing practices and perceptions of antibiotic usage; provide training to key stakeholders on responsible antibiotic usage.
- Actively monitor usage levels of antibiotics and the ingredients used; ensure accurate and complete records are kept.
- Publish a comprehensive policy on responsible antibiotic use, and implement an active programme to significantly reduce antibiotic usage and deliver responsible usage, including absolute targets and/or year-on-year reduction targets.
- Improve animal health and welfare. Key measures to improve animal welfare on farm include: lower stocking densities, environmental enrichment, group housing (even if just in pairs), area(s) for retreat, increased feeding space and feeding availability and early mixing.[3]
- Ensure "critically important" antibiotics are not used. If, however, exceptional circumstances and veterinary sign-off necessitate one-off use, companies should report on this.
- Be transparent about the nature of their antibiotic reduction targets, including:
  - Whether these relate to all geographies/species.
  - Whether these are related to the number of treatments, total volume of antibiotics or volume of active ingredient.
  - Which group of antibiotics the active ingredient targets relate to.
- Report on and provide an explanation for annual progress against targets.
- Evaluate success of efforts to enable responsible antibiotic use, and adjust policies and process accordingly.

References

Alliance to Save Our Antibiotics (2011). *Case Study of a Health Crisis: How Human Health is Under Threat from Over-Use of Antibiotics in Intensive Livestock Farming*. Compassion in World Farming, Sustain and the Soil Association. Retrieved from http://www.saveourantibiotics.org/media/1491/case-study-of-a-health-crisis.pdf

Alliance to Save Our Antibiotics (2015). *Antimicrobial Resistance: Why The Irresponsible Use of Antibiotics in Agriculture Must Stop*. Compassion in World Farming, Sustain and the Soil Association. Retrieved from http://www.saveourantibiotics.org/media/1466/antibiotics-alliance-40pp-report-2015-final-artwork-1.pdf

3 Further guidance on implementation of these measures can be found at www.compassioninfoodbusiness.com/resources

Bond, V. & Jewell, J. (2014). *The Impacts of Antibiotic Use in Animals on Human Health and Animal Welfare. BBFAW Investor Briefing No. 17*. London: Business Benchmark on Farm Animal Welfare.

Compassion in World Farming (2011). *Antibiotics in Animal Farming: Public Health and Animal Welfare*. Godalming, UK: Compassion in World Farming.

Department of Health (2013, March 12). Press release: Antimicrobial resistance poses "catastrophic threat", says Chief Medical Officer. London: Department of Health. Retrieved from https://www.gov.uk/government/news/antimicrobial-resistance-poses-catastrophic-threat-says-chief-medical-officer--2

Natural Resources Defense Council (2015). *Going Mainstream: Meat and Poultry Raised Without Routine Antibiotics Use*. New York: Natural Resources Defense Council.

Veterinary Medicines Directorate (2007). *Overview of Antimicrobial Usage and Bacterial Resistance in Selected Human and Animal Pathogens in the UK*. London: Veterinary Medicines Directorate.

Voss, A., Loeffen, F., Bakker, J., Klaassen, C. & Wulf, M. (2005). Methicillin-resistant *Staphylococcus aureus* in pig farming. *Emerging Infectious Diseases*, 11, 1965-1966.

World Health Organization (2011a). *Critically Important Antimicrobials (CIA) for Human Medicine, 3rd Revision*. Geneva: WHO.

World Health Organization (2011b). *Tackling Antibiotic Resistance from a Food Safety Perspective in Europe*. Geneva: WHO.

24 An introduction to animal welfare issues in aquaculture[1]

Martin Cooke

WORLD ANIMAL PROTECTION, UK[2]

Introduction

Finfish are globally the most numerous farmed animals. They are a major source of affordable protein, especially in developing countries. Finfish are sentient and, therefore, deserve to have equivalent attention paid to their welfare as terrestrial farmed species. This chapter provides an introduction to animal welfare issues in aquaculture, highlighting the most consistently reported issues that affect fish welfare, and offering some practical suggestions to companies on how they should manage finfish health and welfare.

Aquaculture in context

At any given time, the number of finfish—that is, true fish as distinct from shellfish—being farmed in the world exceeds the total number of all terrestrial farm animals. Aquaculture output is almost equivalent on a global scale to that of capture fisheries, and in some regions it is higher. The World Bank estimates that 62% of all food fish will come from aquaculture by 2030 (World Bank, 2013).

According to the Food and Agriculture Organization (FAO, 2015), in 2013 global aquaculture production was in excess of 97 million tonnes. Farmed finfish made up 47 million tonnes of this total (up from 44 million tonnes in 2012), while crustaceans, molluscs and other farmed aquatic food animal species accounted for 23 million tonnes. This compares with an estimated 308 million tonnes of red meat and poultry meat produced in the same year (FAO, 2014a). Finfish aquaculture was worth $94 billion in 2013 and is steadily increasing; between 2003 and 2013, global production doubled in volume and averaged a 9% year-on-year increase in value, in line with the growth over the same period in the global food price index.

China has by far the world's largest finfish aquaculture industry, responsible for over 55% of global output by volume in 2012, with three-quarters of production

1 This chapter is based on a 2016 briefing note originally published by the Business Benchmark on Farm Animal Welfare (Cooke, 2016).

2 The views expressed in this chapter are the author's own and not necessarily those of World Animal Protection.

involving freshwater species. The next largest market is India, which is responsible for 9% of global output. In terms of marine aquaculture, Norway's Atlantic salmon (*Salmo salar*) industry makes it the world's largest marine aquaculture producer, although this accounts for just 3% of total world farmed finfish output (see Table 24.1).

While more than 600 finfish species are farmed worldwide, the majority of global aquaculture relies on a few dozen species. Freshwater species account for 85% of global finfish aquaculture production volume (65% by value). Carp predominates in this group, representing 33% of global production by volume (64% by value). Diadromous species (i.e. species that can have marine and freshwater life-cycle phases, such as salmon and trout) account for only 10% of global production by volume, yet they represent 23% by value. Exclusively marine species, such as seabass and seabream, make up the remainder.

Patterns of production vary with location. For example, carp species are the most numerous farmed finfish in China, while in the USA catfish predominate. In the UK, Atlantic salmon from Norway and Chile is the main aquaculture species. In fact, within the UK retail sector, farmed salmon is the number one fresh fish (by volume and by value); it is also the UK's largest food export (worth over £500 million in 2014) to, principally, the USA, Europe and the Far East.

Table 24.1 Farmed finfish production by country in 2012

Producer	*Inland aquaculture*		*Marine aquaculture*		*Farmed finfish*	*Total*
	tonnes	*%*	*tonnes*	*%*	*tonnes*	*%*
China	23,341,134	60.5	1,028,399	18.5	24,369,533	55.2
India	3,812,420	9.9	84,164	1.5	3,896,584	8.8
Indonesia	2,097,407	5.4	582,077	10.5	2,679,484	6.1
Vietnam	2,091,200	5.4	51,000	0.9	2,142,200	4.9
Bangladesh	1,525,672	4.0	63,220	1.1	1,588,892	3.6
Norway	85	0.0	1,319,033	23.8	1,319,118	3.0
Egypt	1,016,629	2.6	no data	0.0	1,016,629	2.3
Myanmar	822,589	2.1	1,868	0.0	824,457	1.9
Chile	59,527	0.2	758,587	13.7	818,114	1.9
Philippines	310,042	0.8	361,722	6.5	671,764	1.5
Brazil	611,343	1.6	no data	0.0	611,343	1.4
Thailand	380,986	1.0	19,994	0.4	400,980	0.9
Japan	33,957	0.1	250,472	4.5	284,429	0.6
USA	185,598	0.5	21,169	0.4	206,767	0.5
Rep. Korea	14,099	0.0	76,307	1.4	90,406	0.2
Top 15 sub-total	36,302,688	94.1	4,618,012	83.2	40,920,700	92.7
Rest of world	2,296,562	5.9	933,893	16.8	3,230,455	7.3
World	38,599,250	100.0	5,551,905	100.0	44,151,155	100.0

Source: FAO (2015).

Finfish aquaculture (especially inland, fresh water aquaculture of herbivorous and omnivorous finfish species) is the primary source of affordable quality protein food in many developing countries. In 2012, aquaculture provided 9.41 kg of fish and other aquatic animal species for consumption per person in the world (FAO, 2014b).

Fish welfare

There is strong evidence that finfish, like other vertebrate animals, are sentient (see, for example, Chandroo *et al.*, 2004; Kittilsen, 2013). This means that fish have a degree of self-awareness; they can feel pain and distress, they have long-term and short-term memory and, to some extent, they can experience emotions. Consideration of finfish welfare is based on the same principles as for terrestrial vertebrate species.

The World Organisation for Animal Health (OIE) defines animal welfare by the way in which an animal copes with the conditions in which it lives; an animal is in a good state of welfare if, as indicated by scientific evidence, it is healthy, comfortable, well-nourished, safe, able to express innate behaviour, and not suffering from unpleasant states such as pain, fear and distress. Thus, animal welfare refers to the state of the animal. The treatment that an animal receives is covered by other terms, such as animal care, animal husbandry and humane handling.

A briefing paper published by Compassion in World Farming (2009) indicates that intensive aquaculture practices frequently expose fish to a range of stressors (e.g. the stripping of broodfish, handling, vaccinations, crowding, grading, starvation, treatments, loading and transportation) that do not exist for wild fish.

Guidance and standards on finfish welfare

World Organisation for Animal Health (OIE)

The OIE defines the basic principles of animal welfare. The OIE has around180 member countries and is recognized as the reference organization by the World Trade Organization (WTO) for standards relating to animal health and welfare. As such, OIE standards represent internationally agreed guiding principles for animal health and welfare. The OIE's Terrestrial Animal Health Code and Aquatic Animal Health Code exist to ensure the sanitary safety of international trade in terrestrial animals and aquatic animals and their products. Furthermore, its Aquatic Animal Health Code (the "Aquatic Code") sets out standards for the improvement of aquatic animal health and welfare of farmed fish worldwide, including standards for safe international trade in aquatic animals (amphibians, crustaceans, fish and molluscs) and their products (OIE, 2016).

The OIE cites as guiding principles that:

- There is a critical relationship between fish health and fish welfare.

- The use of fish in harvest or capture fisheries, in research, and for recreation (e.g. ornamental and aquaria), is a major contribution to the wellbeing of people.
- The use of fish carries with it an ethical responsibility to ensure the welfare of such animals to the greatest extent practicable.
- Improvements in farmed fish welfare can often improve productivity and hence lead to economic benefits.
- The internationally recognized "Five Freedoms" provide valuable guidance in animal welfare. The OIE defines the Five Freedoms as: 1) Freedom from hunger, thirst and malnutrition; 2) Freedom from fear and distress; 3) Freedom from physical and thermal discomfort; 4) Freedom from pain, injury and disease; and 5) Freedom to express normal patterns of behaviour.
- The scientific assessment of fish welfare involves both scientifically derived data and value-based assumptions that need to be considered together, and the process of making these assessments should be made as explicit as possible.
- Equivalent outcomes based on performance criteria, rather than identical systems based on design criteria, should be the basis for comparison of animal welfare standards and recommendations.

European Food Safety Authority (EFSA)

The European Food Safety Authority (EFSA) Panel on Animal Health and Welfare[3] (AHAW) has issued various opinions on the welfare of fish. The Panel provides independent scientific advice on all aspects of animal diseases and animal welfare. Through its activities on fish welfare, EFSA aims to provide a science-based foundation for European policies and legislation, and to support risk managers in identifying methods to reduce unnecessary pain, distress and suffering for animals and to increase welfare where possible. EFSA is not mandated to give advice on ethical or cultural issues related to animal welfare.

In 2008, the EFSA was asked by the European Commission to assess welfare aspects of husbandry systems for the main farmed fish species within the EU. The AHAW Panel has adopted five species-specific[4] opinions in which potential risks for welfare have been identified across different life stages; these risks include environmental conditions, feeding, husbandry practices, genetic make-up of stocks, disease and disease control measures. Furthermore, in 2009, the AHAW Panel adopted seven species-specific[5] opinions on the welfare aspects of stunning and killing methods for farmed fish.

3 https://www.efsa.europa.eu/en/panels/ahaw

4 Species include: farmed Atlantic salmon, rainbow trout (*Oncorhynchus mykiss*) and brown trout (*Salmo trutta*), European eel (*Anguilla anguilla*), European seabass (*Dicentrarchus labrax*), gilthead seabream (*Sparus aurata*) and common carp (*Cyprinus carpio*).

5 Species include: Atlantic bluefin tuna (*Thunnus thynnus*), common carp, European eel, Atlantic salmon, rainbow trout, European turbot (*Psetta maxima*), European seabass and gilthead seabream.

Aquaculture Stewardship Council (ASC)

Founded in 2010 by WWF and IDH (Dutch Sustainable Trade Initiative), the Aquaculture Stewardship Council[6] (ASC) is an independent, not-for-profit organization, which aims to be the world's leading certification and labelling programme for responsibly farmed seafood. As a consumer-focused organization, products from certified farms may bear the ASC logo. Its standards cover salmon, *Tilapia* spp., *Pangasius* spp. (basa, river cobbler), *Seriola* spp. (amberjack) and cobia (black kingfish, *Rachycentron canadum*) as well as various farmed invertebrate species.

The focus of ASC standards is on the environmental and social impacts of aquaculture. Although animal welfare is not included explicitly, it is addressed indirectly in most of the individual ASC species standards (i.e. through water quality parameters, siting of production facilities, survival performance measures, and procedures for the treatment of sick fish and the use of medicated feed). Since the ASC standards do not effectively cover animal welfare, they cannot give reliable assurance of the welfare status of farmed finfish.

GLOBALG.A.P. *aquaculture standard*

GLOBALG.A.P. is a worldwide, business-to-business standard for safe and sustainable food production. It sets strict criteria for good agricultural practices across a broad range of products, including traceability back to certified farms or production facilities, which farmers must comply with if they wish to sell their products to major retailers around the world.

The GLOBALG.A.P. aquaculture standard[7] covers legal compliance, food safety, worker welfare, environmental care, ecological care and animal welfare. It applies to salmon, trout, *Tilapia* spp. and *Pangasius* spp. as well as various invertebrates. It covers the entire production chain, from broodstock, seedlings and feed suppliers to farming, harvesting and processing. The inspection checklist comprehensively covers more than 100 control points relating to the management of animal welfare, including aspects such as staff training in animal welfare, predator control, biosecurity, transport and slaughter. While the inspection procedure does not include direct assessment of fish welfare (i.e. examination of fish), GLOBALG.A.P. certification provides a reasonable level of assurance of finfish welfare.

Best Aquaculture Practices

A division of the Global Aquaculture Alliance (GAA), Best Aquaculture Practices[8] (BAP) is an international certification programme based on achievable, science-based and continuously improved performance standards for the entire aquaculture supply chain—farms, hatcheries, processing plants and feed mills. BAP certification is based on independent audits, which evaluate compliance with

6 http://www.asc-aqua.org/
7 http://www.globalgap.org/uk_en/for-producers/aquaculture/
8 http://bap.gaalliance.org/

the BAP standards developed by the GAA. The BAP standards currently cover salmon, *Tilapia* spp., *Pangasius* spp. and channel catfish (*Ictalurus punctatus*), as well as carp and various other (primarily marine) species.

Although predominantly focusing on environmental responsibility, BAP certification standards cover the key elements of responsible aquaculture, including social responsibility, food safety, animal health and welfare, and traceability. The animal welfare component is most comprehensively covered in the salmon standard, but it is less well covered in the general Finfish and Crustacean Farms standard, which is applicable to all other species.

RSPCA Assured (Freedom Food)

RSPCA Assured[9] (previously Freedom Food) is the RSPCA's ethical food label dedicated to farm animal welfare. RSPCA Assured has two finfish aquaculture standards, covering Atlantic salmon (*Salmo salar*) and rainbow trout (*Oncorhynchus mykiss*). These are detailed in comprehensive assurance standards, which stipulate a high level of fish welfare. Although not strictly a global standard, RSPCA Assured is important given that farmed European salmon is significant in global trade. RSPCA Assured is recognized as the only scheme in Europe dedicated to farm animal welfare and has been acknowledged as a higher-level scheme by the UK Government. Unlike other schemes, it is completely independent from the food and farming industries. The RSPCA's welfare standards are written by its team of scientific officers in the Farm Animals Department and are based on leading scientific, veterinary and practical industry expertise.

Animal welfare factors

Animal welfare concerns for all species, including finfish, are typically the consequence of a combination of adverse factors. For simplicity, this chapter focuses on the ten most consistently reported issues that affect animal welfare involving commercially important species. Given that signs of poor fish welfare may be the result of several coexisting causal factors, the management of finfish health and welfare should follow a broad approach, taking into account various processes along the value chain.

Factor 1: selection and breeding

Animal welfare can be improved by selecting for characteristics, such as good adaptation to local conditions and disease resistance. Typical practices include:

- Controlling the timing of breeding and egg production by manipulating day length and through the use of hormone treatments.
  - Eggs are normally harvested by manually stripping them from females in most species. Semen (milt) may also be obtained by stripping.

9 https://www.rspcaassured.org.uk/

  - Given that these procedures involve intensive manual handling, are stressful for fish and may result in physical injury, broodfish should be anaesthetised. In species where eggs or milt can only be obtained surgically, fish should first be stunned prior to slaughter.
  - Heat treatment of the eggs of certain fish species (particularly salmon and trout) may be used to induce triploidy—a condition in which the fish has three copies of each chromosome instead of the normal two (diploid). All triploid fish are female and sterile, and they grow to a larger size than diploid fish.
  - Commercial tilapia production generally requires the use of male monosex populations. Male tilapia grow twice as fast as females. Mixed-sex populations develop a large size disparity among harvested fish, which affects marketability. The sex of female fry (i.e. pre-juvenile fish) may be reversed through administering a male sex hormone in their feed. Embryonic fish and fry are particularly sensitive to environmental changes such as temperature, pH and oxygen fluctuation. Consideration of fish welfare should always include aspects of broodfish and hatchery management.
- Eels are a significant farmed fish in Europe, particularly in the Netherlands, Italy and Denmark. Juvenile stock is obtained entirely by capture of eel larvae (glass eels) from the wild during their migration from the Sargasso Sea into European and Mediterranean freshwater systems. Since there is a strong market for the consumption of (dead) glass eels, there is little incentive to have regard for their welfare during capture and in post-capture storage.

Factor 2: feed and nutrition

Larval fish are generally fed on live zooplankton (e.g. rotifers). Larval first feeding is a particularly sensitive stage. Inadequate size or abundance of live feed at this stage can result in metabolic stress and may lead to cannibalism.

- Salmon, trout and other marine species require a significant proportion of fishmeal and fish oil in their diet, originating typically from huge industrial fisheries in South America. Although efforts have been made (for environmental and economic reasons) to reduce fishmeal and fish oil by using other protein sources such as soya, canola and poultry meal, more than 50% of the ration of growing fish may be fish-derived.
- Common carp can be produced in extensive systems in stagnant water ponds, using monoculture (single species) or polyculture (i.e. stocked with other carp species such as tilapia) systems. This enables a natural food and supplementary feed-based production method, in which fish that have different feeding habits and occupy different trophic niches are stocked in the same ponds. Artificial feed-based intensive monoculture production can be carried out in cages, irrigation reservoirs, and running water ponds and tanks, or in recirculation systems. Food supply is the main factor governing stocking density.

- Channel catfish are reared in ponds, cages, and circular tanks or linear raceways in the United States and China. Monoculture dominates in the United States, while in China, both monoculture and polyculture occurs with traditional species, such as carp. Formulated vegetable-based feeds are used. In pond-based systems animal manures provide nutrients that stimulate the growth of protein-rich phytoplankton, which is consumed by filter feeding tilapia. In more intensive cage and raceway systems, supplementary feed, usually containing soybean meal and fish protein, is provided.

In all species, insufficient feed supply or poor quality feed will result in poor growth and low survival. Undernourished fish are stressed and less resilient to other problems, such as infectious disease, which may compromise welfare.

Factor 3: husbandry—water quality

Water quality is arguably one of the most critical factors affecting finfish welfare and should be closely monitored in all aquaculture systems. Some species (e.g. carp) are very tolerant of poor water quality, coping with a wide temperature range, low oxygen levels and high levels of suspended solids. Nevertheless rapid changes in water quality can cause welfare hazards. For example, algal blooms can affect pH balance and toxicity, and collapsed algal blooms can deplete oxygen levels and release ammonia. In marine and river species, poor water flows can result in localized oxygen depletion and carbon dioxide accumulation in sea pens and raceways, causing significant stress. Sea pens and raceways should be sited to ensure optimal water flow. Eutrophication of rivers (e.g. from fertilizer pollution) can reduce oxygen availability.

Factor 4: husbandry—stocking density

Stocking density is a major factor affecting fish welfare and is perhaps the easiest for fish farm managers to control. Stocking density influences fish health and welfare at all life-cycle stages and its effects interact with other aspects of fish welfare. Excessive stocking density can lead to fin damage and other injuries, increased aggression, behaviour alteration (including reduced feed intake) and increased vulnerability to infectious disease. All of these are significant welfare hazards.

Space requirements depend on each species' biology and growth stage. For some species, maximum stocking densities are defined in assurance standards and industry codes of practice. For organic production maximum stocking density may be defined in legislation. Crowding for management purposes, such as transport or vaccination, is stressful for all finfish, particularly so for solitary species. It should be avoided as far as possible and, when necessary, only imposed for the minimum feasible time. Finfish should be given enough space to avoid deterioration of water quality, to avoid aggressive encounters, to allow the expression of normal behaviour and to avoid abnormal behaviours associated with poor welfare.

Factor 5: husbandry—management procedures

Certain routine management procedures, such as size grading and transferring fish between tanks, ponds or cages can cause stress and injury to fish. Size grading is an important management tool that can enable the detection of diseased or injured fish and can be used to ensure correct stocking density. In some systems fin tagging or fin clipping are used to identify broodfish. For example, in the United States, Pacific salmon are reared in commercial hatcheries and released into the wild as young fish (parr or smolts). Virtually all coho salmon (*Oncorhynchus kisutch*) and Chinook salmon (*Oncorhynchus tshawytscha*) produced in Washington state hatcheries are mass-marked by clipping the small adipose fin near their tail. Fishers subsequently catching these species are required to release any unclipped fish.

Wherever possible, the handling of fish should be avoided. Steps should be taken to avoid harm to fish and to reduce the stress caused by management activities.

Factor 6: husbandry—predator control

Finfish in farm pond environments and in sea pens are particularly vulnerable to the effects of predation. As well as the obvious effects of predation, the presence of birds (e.g. cormorants, ospreys and fish-eating eagles) or mammals (e.g. mink, otters and seals) in marine aquaculture can induce significant stress to fish, manifested by behavioural changes and reduction in feeding. Therefore, protection of fish farms from predators can help to safeguard animal welfare and productivity. However, regard should also be given to the welfare of the predatory animals themselves. Shooting seals and seabirds in an attempt to control the problem is unlikely to be very effective and is certainly controversial. In many places these creatures are themselves protected by law. The use of preventive measures is preferred. These include predator netting, both above and in the water, acoustic devices (e.g. bird scarers and seal scrammers) and visual devices (e.g. decoys and flares).

In any aquaculture system where predation is likely to be an issue, risk assessment of the deployment of anti-predator measures should take account of the animal welfare impact on the farmed fish, on the predators themselves, and on any non-target species that may be affected, such as harbour porpoises.

Factor 7: finfish health

Farmed finfish are vulnerable to a range of infectious and non-infectious diseases. The Aquatic Code provides guidance on the control of major infectious diseases (mostly affecting salmon and trout) in international trade in aquatic animal products. In trout and the freshwater phases of salmon, the fungus *Saprolegnia* can be a major problem. Salmon are also vulnerable to a range of viral and bacterial infections and to infestation with sea lice. In some salmon farms Ballan wrasse (*Labrus bergylta*) are used to control sea lice on the growing fish. In carp, environmental pathogens, often with low grade, chronic effects, are the major concern. Many of the most important infectious diseases of finfish may now be controlled by vaccination.

In common with terrestrial farming good practice, all aquaculture facilities should be registered with a suitably experienced veterinarian and should have a veterinary health plan covering the major preventive procedures, such as vaccinations, as well as outlining procedures for dealing with the most important disease risks. Where disease occurs, it must be promptly and appropriately treated to mitigate welfare impact.

Factor 8: antimicrobial agents

The OIE recognizes the need for continued access to antimicrobial agents for treating and controlling infectious diseases in aquatic animals. The Aquatic Code (Section 6) provides guidance for the responsible and prudent use of antimicrobial agents in aquatic animals, with the aim of protecting both animal and human health. The OIE recognizes that antimicrobial resistance is a global public and animal health concern that is influenced by the usage of antimicrobial agents in humans, animals and elsewhere.

Those working in the human, animal and plant sectors have a shared responsibility to address the risk factors for the selection and dissemination of antimicrobial resistance. This includes the responsible use of antimicrobial agents as well as the promotion of sound animal husbandry methods, hygiene procedures, vaccination and other alternative strategies to minimize the need for antimicrobial use in aquatic animals. Some antimicrobial agents (e.g. copper alloys) are used in marine aquaculture systems to control biofouling of nets and maintain good water flow through sea pens. Certain antimicrobial agents, once widely used in aquaculture (e.g. malachite green, chloramphenicol, gentian violet, nitrofurans and fluoroquinolones) are banned in certain jurisdictions, because of concerns about the human health consequences of their use in animals. Antimicrobials and other medicines used in aquaculture should only be used under veterinary supervision, in compliance with legislation and in line with OIE guidance. Veterinarians or other aquatic animal health professionals authorized to prescribe veterinary medicines should prescribe, dispense or administer a specific course of treatment with an antimicrobial agent only for aquatic animals under their care.

Better husbandry techniques coupled with the development of vaccines against some of the major infectious diseases have considerably reduced the use of antimicrobial agents in aquaculture.

Factor 9: transport

The Aquatic Code (Chapter 7.2) describes the general principles for ensuring the welfare of farmed finfish during transport by air, sea or land. It covers the responsibilities of competent authorities (i.e. governments), owners and transporters in ensuring the fitness of the fish for transport; the competence of the personnel responsible for the fish at all stages; the design of vehicles and handling equipment;

the maintenance of suitable water quality during transport; loading, transport and unloading procedures; and contingency planning in the case of emergencies. Food companies should regard the principles contained in the Aquatic Code as a minimum acceptable standard for the transport of farmed finfish.

It is the recommended practice with many species to starve the fish for several days prior to transport. In certain species, this practice can lower metabolic rate and reduce activity and is, therefore, considered to reduce handling stress. However excessive food deprivation can result in depletion of body fat reserves and loss of bodily condition, which is associated with poor welfare. Preparation for transport should include consideration of the fitness of the fish to be transported, the nature and duration of the transport, and the health and welfare implications for the fish being transported and the populations they are to join. Broodfish may be tranquilized prior to transportation. In many aquaculture systems, transport begins by crowding the fish using nets, then pumping them into the transport container or vehicle. Crowding can be particularly stressful for solitary and territorial species (e.g. halibut [*Hippoglossus* spp.]), and it should not be performed to the extent that fish show signs of distress. Pumping and poor handling may result in physical injuries, particularly to the fins. Fish should, therefore, be monitored after pumping for signs of wounds or injuries.

During transport the principal concern is for maintenance of satisfactory water quality (e.g. oxygen, carbon dioxide and ammonia levels, pH, temperature and salinity) appropriate to the species being transported. Deterioration of water quality during transport is the most significant animal welfare issue for transporting live fish, especially the depletion of oxygen or accumulation of carbon dioxide and ammonia. Since this is likely to be related to journey time, some assurance standards specify maximum journey times. Some species are more tolerant of poor water quality than others (e.g. carp are remarkably tolerant of low oxygen levels, which would be fatal to other species). In general, fish fry are more vulnerable to poor water conditions than adult fish. Fish should be unloaded as soon as possible, although it may be necessary to acclimatize fish to new conditions if the water quality at the destination is significantly different (e.g. in terms of salinity, pH or temperature conditions) from that at the start.

Factor 10: humane slaughter

The Aquatic Code (Chapter 7.3) describes general principles that should be applied to ensure the welfare of farmed finfish during stunning and killing for human consumption. It notes that killing without prior stunning results in poor fish welfare and requires that stunning be used wherever feasible. It covers the competence of personnel as well as the design of holding, transfer and slaughtering facilities. Evisceration quickly follows stunning and killing, so it is imperative that fish are dead before this is done.

Since the technology now exists to slaughter all commercially important species in a humane way, food companies should regard the principles contained in the Aquatic Code as a minimum acceptable standard for the slaughter of farmed finfish.

The sale to final consumers of live fish for human consumption is unacceptable. Where local cultural preferences demand that fish are offered for sale alive, competent personnel using recognized methods should conduct humane slaughtering.

The slaughtering process includes pre-slaughter handling, stunning to render the fish rapidly insensible and killing itself. It is common practice with many species to starve the fish for several days prior to slaughter. While the negative welfare effects on finfish are probably smaller than for warm-blooded animals, hunger is a major welfare issue for all animals. The most important animal welfare hazards in the pre-slaughter phase include crowding stress and mechanical injuries resulting from poor handling. In many commercial aquaculture systems, harvesting begins by crowding the fish using nets, then pumping them to the killing point. Crowding can be particularly stressful for solitary and territorial species. Crowding should not be performed to the extent that fish show signs of distress. Pumping and poor handling may result in physical injury to fish, particularly to the fins.

Fish are slaughtered in commercial aquaculture systems by a variety of methods, which, depending on the species and husbandry system, may or may not involve pre-slaughter stunning. In general, the larger species, such as salmon, are stunned, either by a blow to the head sufficient to damage the brain (percussion) or by electrical means. Both percussion and electrical stunning may be done manually or automatically. Welfare hazards associated with percussion stunning include hitting the fish in the wrong place or not hard enough, either because of inexperienced personnel or, in automated systems, because of poor placement of the fish or poor adjustment of equipment. Poor electrical stunning can occur for similar reasons. However the most frequent cause of poor electrical stunning is the use of electrical currents that are too low, resulting in temporary paralysis without complete loss of consciousness. Electrical stunning apparatus is available for group stunning of smaller species, but it is not widely used.

Very large species, such as tuna, are killed by shooting (typically under water) or by coring (i.e. inserting a spike into the brain). In other large species, the major blood vessels in the gill arches are severed. Smaller species tend to be killed without stunning by asphyxia in ice slurry, by live chilling, by exposure to air or by carbon dioxide. These methods may also be used for larger species. Without stunning, all of these killing methods represent a significant welfare hazard.

In some markets the majority of farmed finfish are sold alive in food markets. This is particularly the case with carp, which may be exposed to air for extended periods before sale. This represents a significant animal welfare hazard. Retailers should be discouraged from selling live fish.

Concluding comments: what actions should companies take?

From a management systems perspective, the welfare issues associated with finfish should be managed in a similar manner to the animal welfare issues associated with terrestrial animals. Companies should therefore:

- Explicitly acknowledge the welfare of finfish aquaculture as part of their animal welfare commitments.
- Ensure compliance with the requirements of the OIE's Aquatic Animal Health Code (the "Aquatic Code"), alongside national legislation and voluntary standards relating to animal welfare.
- Formalize their commitment to ensuring the welfare of finfish in a policy statement or other suitable document. Such policies should explicitly acknowledge that finfish are sentient and deserve equivalent welfare considerations throughout their life-cycle to those of terrestrial farmed species.
- Publish their positions on key finfish welfare issues (e.g. close confinement, routine mutilations, genetic modification and cloning, the use of antibiotics, pre-slaughter stunning and transportation).
- Ensure that they have appropriate governance structures and management systems in place to competently manage the welfare of finfish aquaculture internally and through their supply chains.
- Publish information on the proportion of finfish aquaculture that is assured to basic farm assurance and higher welfare assurance standards, and describe their plans for those aquaculture facilities that are not assured to recognized welfare standards.
- Monitor and report on key welfare indicators for finfish.
- Promote welfare aspects of finfish aquaculture to consumers, through labelling and other forms of communication.

References

Chandroo, K.P, Duncan, I.J.H, & Moccia, R.D. (2004). Can fish suffer? Perspectives on sentience, pain, fear and stress. *Applied Animal Behaviour Science*, 86, 225-250.

Compassion in World Farming (2009). *The Welfare of Farmed Fish.* Godalming, UK: Compassion in World Farming. Retrieved from https://www.ciwf.org.uk/media/3818654/farmed-fish-briefing.pdf

Cooke, M. (2016). *Animal Welfare in Farmed Fish. Investor Briefing No. 23.* London: Business Benchmark on Farm Animal Welfare.

Food and Agriculture Organization (FAO) (2014a). *Food Outlook: Biannual Report on Global Food Markets.* Rome: FAO. Retrieved from http://www.fao.org/3/a-i4136e.pdf

FAO (2014b). *Global Aquaculture Production Volume and Value Statistics Database Updated to 2012.* Rome: FAO. Retrieved from ftp://ftp.fao.org/fi/stat/Overviews/Aquaculture Statistics2012.pdf

FAO (2015). *Global Aquaculture Production Statistic Database Updated to 2013.* Rome: FAO. Retrieved from http://www.fao.org/3/a-i4899e.pdf

Kittilsen, S. (2013). Functional aspects of emotions in fish. *Behavioural Processes*, 100, 153-159.

World Bank (2013). *Fish to 2030: Prospects for Fisheries and Aquaculture.* Washington, DC: World Bank. Retrieved from http://documents.worldbank.org/curated/en/2013/12/18882045/fish-2030-prospects-fisheries-aquaculture

Additional reference sources and further reading

FAO Aquaculture resources, http://www.fao.org/fishery/topic/13530/en

FAO Fishery Statistics, http://www.fao.org/fishery/statistics/global-aquaculture-production/query/en

Farm Animal Welfare Committee, Opinion on the Welfare of Farmed Fish (2014) https://www.gov.uk/government/uploads/system/uploads/attachment_data/file/319323/Opinion_on_the_welfare_of_farmed_fish.pdf

Global Animal Network, http://www.globalanimalnetwork.org/

Scientific opinions on fish welfare, European Food Safety Authority (2008–2015) http://www.efsa.europa.eu/en/topics/topic/fishwelfare.htm

The Fish Site, http://www.thefishsite.com

World Organisation for Animal Health (OIE) (2016). *Aquatic Animal Health Code*. Retrieved from http://www.oie.int/en/international-standard-setting/aquatic-code/access-online/

25 Farm animal welfare

Disclosure practices and expectations

Rory Sullivan

UNIVERSITY OF LEEDS AND BUSINESS BENCHMARK ON FARM ANIMAL WELFARE, UK

Nicky Amos

NICKY AMOS CSR SERVICES AND BUSINESS BENCHMARK ON FARM ANIMAL WELFARE, UK

Introduction

Since the first Business Benchmark on Farm Animal Welfare report was released in 2013, there has been a significant increase in the number of companies publishing information on their approach to farm animal welfare. The manner in which this information has been used by investors, by non-governmental organizations (NGOs), by the companies themselves and by their industry peers has provided important insights into how corporate reporting on farm animal welfare might be used to inform and influence internal company practice, into how such reporting might be used to engage key stakeholders on farm animal welfare issues, and into how reporting can provide reassurance that farm animal welfare-related issues are being managed effectively.

This chapter reflects on current reporting practice. It begins with a description of the information that stakeholders—such as investors, NGOs and researchers—generally expect companies to provide on their social and environmental performance. It follows this with a description of the specific information that stakeholders concerned about farm animal welfare expect companies to report. It then takes a closer look at three key issues: animal welfare policies, performance assessment and wider reporting practice. This section includes a number of examples of good corporate practices in these areas.

Disclosure on environmental and social performance

Companies need to provide information on their social and environmental performance that reassures their stakeholders that they are effectively managing these issues. For any particular social or environmental issue (i.e. not just on farm animal welfare), stakeholders generally expect companies to provide the following (Sullivan, 2011):

- Information on the company itself to the extent that such information is necessary to put its social and environmental impacts into context.
- A description of the company's governance and management arrangements for the environmental or social issue or issues in question. Within this,

companies should indicate whether there is a board or senior management committee responsible for oversight of the company's strategy, whether there is a senior manager who is responsible for implementation on a day-to-day basis, and whether the company's management systems have been certified to a recognized standard.
- Details of the business risks and impacts of the issue(s) in question, together with a clear statement on the financial implications—positive or negative—of these issues for the business.
- Details of their policies on the issue(s) in question, including the scope of the policy commitments (i.e. whether or not policy commitments are universally applicable) and a description of how the policies are to be implemented. Policies should also be dated.
- Their objectives, targets and key performance indicators for the issue(s) in question, together with a discussion of how they intend to deliver on these objectives and targets.
- An assessment of their progress towards meeting their objectives and targets, along with a discussion of the factors that have affected their performance.
- An assessment of their performance against their policies and against other commitments (e.g. codes of conduct) that they have made.
- Details of their involvement in collaborative industry initiatives, in policy dialogues and in research programmes aimed at advancing the issue(s) in question.
- Forward-looking information on how performance is expected to evolve over time and of the key factors (e.g. changes in the business environment, public policy and regulation, consumer trends, stakeholder pressures) that may affect performance.

Disclosure on farm animal welfare[1]

In broad terms, the information that companies should provide on their approach to farm animal welfare is similar to that of other environmental and social issues. That is, companies should provide sufficient information to allow stakeholders to understand the importance of farm animals to the business, the company's policies on farm animal welfare, the company's approach to managing farm animal welfare and the company's performance on farm animal welfare.

Stakeholders do, however, expect companies to provide more than a general description of their farm animal welfare-related management systems and processes. Farm animal welfare is a complex management challenge: there are multiple species and production systems involved; the welfare issues differ between species; countries have their own legislation, standards and codes; customers and consumers have different expectations of how companies manage farm animal welfare. Reporting needs to capture these complexities while at the same time remaining accessible and useful for the users of this information.

1 This section is based on Sullivan and Amos (2015a) unless otherwise indicated.

Based on our discussions with stakeholders and our own use of company data in the benchmarking and research that underpins the Business Benchmark on Farm Animal Welfare (see, for example, Amos and Sullivan, 2015, 2016; Sullivan and Amos, 2015a, b; Sullivan *et al.*, 2015), Table A.1 sets out what we see as the core elements of a comprehensive approach to farm animal welfare reporting (see Appendix).

Key reporting issues

The role of formal policy positions

Some companies argue that formal farm animal welfare policies should not be expected for animal welfare-related issues that are already covered by legislation. The rationale is that such policies simply duplicate requirements that are already set out in legislation. While it is possible to have some sympathy with this argument, it ignores the fact that farm animal welfare legislation is not comprehensive across all species or all geographies. For example, while there is legislation for laying hens, pigs and calves within the EU, there is no specific EU legislation relating to species such as finfish, dairy cows, ducks, rabbits or turkeys. Similarly, with the exception of a few states that have legislation relating to barren battery cages for laying hens, there is no US legislation establishing minimum welfare standards for farms animals. Furthermore, even where legislation is in place, the late or inadequate enforcement of legislation can mean that animals are kept in conditions that fail to meet minimum legislative standards. For example, the EU's legislative requirement for the provision of moveable material for pigs is not routinely enforced and such materials are not provided to the majority of pigs in the EU.

Policies are therefore important to ensure that companies manage animal welfare standards within their own operations and, critically, their suppliers' operations. Given that most companies source globally, they therefore need global policies to ensure that their operations and their suppliers' meet minimum standards of performance, irrespective of where they operate. Formal farm animal welfare-related policies also play an important wider role. They signal that companies are committed to action on farm animal welfare and that they expect their suppliers and business partners to adopt similar standards. Examples of company positions on animal welfare issues are set out in Box A.1 (see Appendix).

Given that policies are not only intended to guide internal practices and conduct but also to explain to external stakeholders how the company is managing farm animal welfare-related issues, they should be specific in terms of the commitments being made. It is not uncommon to find that farm animal welfare policies lack specificity in terms of the particular commitments being made or the scope (in terms of products, species and geographies) covered by the policy. For example, companies with commitments to pre-slaughter stunning often do not state whether they adopt different approaches to account for religious concerns (e.g. for halal meat for Muslim communities, kosher or shechita meat for Jewish communities). Similarly, it is common to find that companies with commitments to the avoidance of long-distance transport do not specify the maximum journey times for animals. Finally, most companies are not clear about whether their animal welfare policies apply to finfish.[2]

Performance reporting

Corporate reporting on farm animal welfare performance is relatively underdeveloped. It is also complicated by the fact that companies generally have multiple animal species and production systems, by the reality that companies frequently manage species to different standards, and by the absence of universal performance standards which means that there is no consensus about the specific expectations of companies.

Company standards

Some companies report on the proportion of animals that are managed to particular company-specific standards. While this reporting can allow for trends in an individual company's performance to be assessed, it is frequently difficult to determine how company-specific standards relate to regulatory requirements or to recognized standards such as the RSPCA Assured standard or the Soil Association's organic standard. Companies that report on their performance by reference to their own internal standards should explain precisely how these standards compare with recognized animal welfare assurance standards, and how they compare with prevailing regulatory requirements in relevant countries both in terms of the countries of operation and the countries where the company's products are sold. Box 25.1 sets out McDonald's position on ensuring compliance with its animal welfare standards through supplier auditing.

External assurance

Some companies report on the proportion of animals that are managed to particular external assurance schemes. Farm assurance schemes provide frameworks for managing farm animals, and may cover aspects such as animal health and welfare, traceability, quality and safety, and compliance with animal welfare legislation and regulations.

While farm assurance schemes can play an important role in promoting higher welfare standards, it is important to recognize that basic farm assurance standards typically do not go beyond legislative requirements and so contribute relatively little to enhanced welfare. Examples of standards which provide basic farm assurance (typically within a wider quality context) include the Red Tractor Farm and Supply Chain Assurance Schemes, the British Lion Code of Practice, Viande de Porc Française, Certification de Conformité de Produits, and the American Humane Certified standards. Box 25.2 sets out how The Co-operative Food UK uses Red Tractor Farm Assurance Scheme and equivalent standards as a minimum for all own-brand UK meat and poultry products.

2 For a discussion of the key welfare issues for fish, see Chapter 24 by Martin Cooke. See also Cooke (2016).

Box 25.1 Example of McDonald's position on global animal welfare outcome-based auditing

"To meet our overarching vision of making meaningful and enduring improvement to the health and welfare of animals in our supply chain throughout their lives, McDonald's requires that all facilities providing meat to pass a rigorous animal welfare audit. These audits, developed by leading animal behaviorist, Dr. Temple Grandin, and adopted by the North American Meat Institute (NAMI) in the mid 1990's, now serve as the foundation for beef and pork welfare auditing worldwide; poultry and eggs are audited using the National Chicken Council (NCC) and United Egg Producers (UEP) audit tools, respectively. In 2014, 99.8% of the facilities from which we source beef, poultry and pork passed audits for compliance with our standards. In 2015, 100% of the facilities from which we source beef, poultry and pork passed audits for compliance with our standards.

For beef and pork, using the NAMI objective audit framework as our foundation, we've standardized welfare measurement at slaughter around the following outcomes:

- Vocalization
- Slips and fall
- Prod use
- Stunning efficiency
- Bleed rail insensibility

For poultry, we have a clear line of sight back to the farm through a more vertically integrated supply chain. Using the NCC audit framework, we've standardized welfare measurement at the hatchery, on farm, catching and transport and slaughter."

Source: McDonald's Animal Welfare Auditing Program*

* http://corporate.mcdonalds.com/mcd/sustainability/sourcing/animal-health-and-welfare/issues-we-re-focusing-on/objective-measures.html

Farming systems that provide for behavioural freedom without compromising health can be described as having higher welfare potential. While it is essential to set high standards to ensure livestock production systems have higher welfare potential, it is also important to monitor welfare outcomes (such as mortality, disease, lameness, injuries and the occurrence of normal and abnormal behaviours) to assess the overall performance of the system. In general, schemes with an animal welfare focus require system inputs which offer a higher welfare potential. However, they may also include more detailed welfare outcome measures and require more frequent and/or detailed inspections than basic farm assurance standards. Examples of higher welfare schemes, which offer many welfare advantages relative to standard industry practice for all species, include the Soil Association organic standards, RSPCA Assured standard, Animal Welfare Approved standard, Beter Leven, KRAV, Label Rouge, Neuland and the Global Animal Partnership (GAP) 5-Step® Program. Figure 25.1 provides an example of performance reporting by Waitrose on its farm assurance standards.

Box 25.2 Example of The Co-operative Food UK's position on farm animal welfare assurance*

"All our own brand UK meat and poultry products are produced, as a minimum, to Red Tractor Farm Assurance Scheme standards (or equivalent). All own brand non-UK meat and poultry products are produced, as a minimum, to standards equivalent to Red Tractor. Compliance with our standards is verified through annual Red Tractor Farm Assurance audit or equivalent. All farms supplying us with meat or poultry products may be subject to announced and unannounced audits by either The Co-op or an appointed audit body at any time. To progress the animal welfare standards of all our own brand meat and poultry, we have an in house team of dedicated, trained animal welfare experts. All suppliers must notify us of any audit failures, compliance problems, and proven or investigated breaches in legislation or welfare standards. Once notified we review on a case by case basis and put in place an appropriate management action plan where necessary."

* www.co-operativefood.co.uk/globalassets/policy/pdfs/animal-welfare.ppt

Animal welfare outcomes

In broad terms, animal welfare encompasses physical wellbeing, mental wellbeing and the ability to express important species-specific behaviours. All three aspects must be present for an animal to have a good quality of life. Within this, it is critically important to recognize that animal welfare is about the welfare of the individual animal.

Animal welfare provision is underpinned by good feeding, good housing (including appropriate design and environment provision), good health care, good breeding, and good management and stockmanship on farm, and of course good handling during transportation and at slaughter.

Performance in farm animal welfare is the action or process of achieving an acceptable level of welfare throughout the process of breeding, rearing/finishing, transporting and slaughtering of animals in the food industry. Within this, input-based measures include aspects of the housing (e.g. space allowance, provision of environmental enrichment), treatments and procedures, breed use, feeding and health management (e.g. the use of preventative antibiotics) as well as the

Percentage of livestock reared to Red Tractor Assurance Standards or equivalent

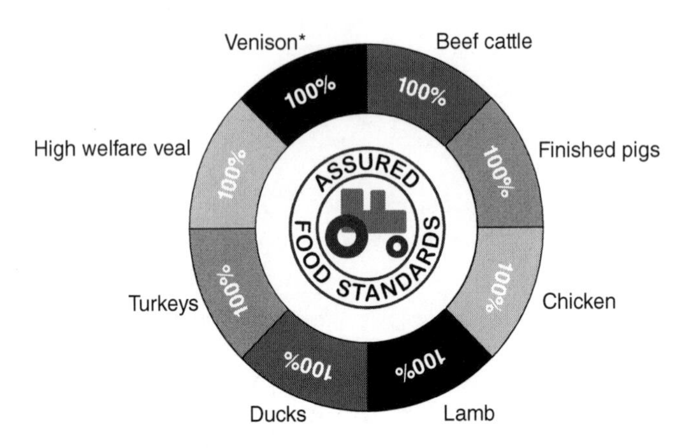

* SAI Global Venison Standard.

Percentage of livestock in higher-welfare systems

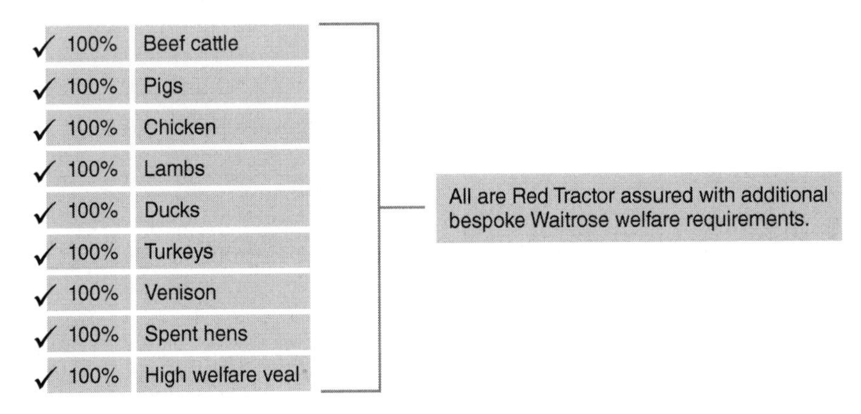

Figure 25.1 Examples of Waitrose's reporting on assurance standards
Source: Waitrose (2016).

practices for transport and slaughter. Outcome-based measures focus on the most important species-specific measures (e.g. lameness and mastitis in dairy cows, gait score and footpad dermatitis in broilers, tail-biting and lameness in pigs, bone breakage and feather coverage in laying hens). Outcome-based measures also include aspects of mental wellbeing (e.g. reaction to humans or novelty, fear, comfort) and behaviour (e.g. time spent lying—resting, ruminating, or being active—foraging, perching, dust-bathing, socializing).

While there is a compelling argument for companies to report on their animal welfare performance, it is important to recognize that performance reporting presents real challenges for companies. These challenges include: the fact that many companies have multiple animal species and production systems across geographies; the fact that companies frequently manage animal species to different standards; the relative difficulties in reporting on ingredients versus fresh produce; and the reality of the absence of universal global performance standards for animal welfare. Furthermore, many companies are concerned about ensuring a level playing field through the accuracy and consistency of reported data; companies are concerned about inappropriate benchmarking and comparisons; and companies are concerned that their ability to deliver competitive advantage through their approach to farm animal welfare may be undermined if they are required to disclose too much information, especially given that some stakeholders (e.g. consumers) may have limited knowledge or awareness of animal husbandry practices. Given these challenges, companies should start by, at least, reporting on (see, for example, Amos and Sullivan, 2016):

- The proportion of animals (or the volume of animal products derived from animals) free from confinement (i.e. those in barn, free-range, indoor group housed, indoor free-farrowing, outdoor bred/reared systems)
- The proportion of animals free from routine mutilations (e.g. beak trimming of laying hens, teeth clipping and tail docking of piglets, and the disbudding of calves)
- The proportion of animals subject to pre-slaughter stunning or (in the case of finfish) rendered insensible
- Average, typical or maximum permitted live transportation times for animals

There are some early signs that companies are starting to provide this sort of information. For example, of the 90 global food companies covered by the 2015 Business Benchmark on Farm Animal Welfare, 30 provided some information on the proportion of animals that are free from close confinement, ten reported on the proportion of animals that are stunned prior to slaughter, eight provided quantitative information on transport times and two reported on farm animal welfare outcomes (Amos and Sullivan, 2016). Box 25.3 provides company examples of performance reporting. In the majority of cases, however, the reporting was limited to selected species or to particular geographies; that is, companies did not provide a comprehensive description of their performance.

The other interesting point to note is that companies do report on a variety of indicators and data points that could form the basis for standardized corporate performance reporting on farm animal welfare (see Table 25.1). The data in Table 25.1 point to the potential to develop a performance reporting framework that captures scale (i.e. the number of animals affected), business relevance (for example, sales), processes (for example, antibiotic usage) and farm animal welfare outcomes (for example, by reference to recognized species-specific standards).

Box 25.3 Examples of performance reporting

Unilever

Unilever was one of the first global companies to work with egg suppliers to provide cage-free eggs for its brands. The corporate website states that: "In Western Europe, our Hellmann's, Amora and Calvé brands have used 100% cage-free eggs since 2009. In the US, we are making significant progress in our commitment to convert 100% of our egg supply to cage-free eggs."

Noble Foods

Noble Foods' Animal Welfare Results document provides an annual update on the company's progress on confinement. For 2015, it reported that: "57% of our birds are free from confinement" and notes that 100% of its "Speciality" eggs are all free-range. The report also confirmed that in the period July 2014 to June 2015 100% of birds were subject to pre-slaughter stunning, and that the average transit time to slaughter was 7.6 hours, with 98% of birds travelling less than 12 hours and 34% travelling less than 4 hours.

Source: Unilever, Farm animal welfare web page;* Noble Foods (2015)

* https://www.unilever.com/sustainable-living/what-matters-to-you/farm-animal-welfare.html

Our discussions with companies point to a number of reasons why the performance reporting scores are relatively low: many companies are still focusing on strengthening their internal management systems and processes; reporting on performance is largely seen as being for internal and supply chain management processes rather than for external audiences; companies generally have multiple animal species; companies frequently manage animal species to different standards. A number of companies commented that, over time, they expect to face greater customer and NGO pressure to report on their performance impact. Some also commented that such reporting will only become standard when there is a consensus on the performance data that needs to be reported and a critical mass of companies are already reporting this information.

Reporting practice

Companies are starting to publish more detail on their farm animal welfare approach on their websites and in their corporate sustainability (or equivalent) reports. However, few companies provide a consolidated account of their farm animal welfare practices (i.e. as an integral part of their sustainability report or as an assigned area of their website dedicated to animal welfare or responsible

Table 25.1 Sample indicators and measures

Indicator/Metric	*Reported by*
Volume and/or proportion of animals sourced by country	Arla Foods, Coop Group (Switzerland), Marfrig
Proportion of products audited to basic and/or higher welfare standards	Ahold, The Co-operative Food (UK), J Sainsbury, Kaufland, Marfrig, Premier Foods, Yum! Brands, Unilever, Waitrose
Volume and/or proportion of eggs sourced that are cage-free	Coop Group (Switzerland), Greggs, Kraft Foods, McDonald's, Marks & Spencer, Noble Foods, Premier Foods, The Co-operative Food (UK), Unilever, Waitrose, Wesfarmers
Proportion of pregnant sows in company-owned farms in US transitioned from gestation crates to group housing systems	WH Group
Levels of antibiotics administered/feed grade antibiotics used per weight of product	WH Group
% products produced free of antibiotics	Compass Group (USA)
Proportion of time animals are allowed outdoors; average space available to animals	Arla Foods, FrieslandCampina
Average transportation time vs. legal limit	The Co-operative Food (UK), Greggs, Noble Foods
Volume or proportion of species involved in transportation accidents/proportion of animal fatalities (by species) in transit	McDonald's, Waitrose, WH Group
Average feather cover score for lay hens	Noble Foods
Proportion of supplier meat processing plants audited and/or proportion of supplier meat processing plants passing audits	McDonald's, Compass Group (USA), Sysco, Tyson Foods
Number of dairy herds (by geography) tested for *Neospora*/cost to average cow herd	Wm Morrison
Proportion of animals processed by species	Marfrig, Tyson Foods, WH Group
Proportion of products bearing Red Tractor (or other) farm assurance labelling	Lidl, Subway, Waitrose
Proportion of revenue/sales of higher welfare products; proportion of sales by welfare system	Coop Group (Switzerland), Migros, The Co-operative Food (UK)
KPIs (e.g. lairage data, farm data and health reports) for all livestock supply chains	Waitrose
Membership voting on farm animal welfare	The Co-operative Food (UK)

Source: adapted from Amos and Sullivan (2016).

sourcing). For the majority of companies, reporting remains piecemeal, with farm animal welfare-related information scattered through CSR reports, press releases and wider discussions about issues such as food and sustainability. For example, we have noted various policy commitments "hidden" in the FAQ sections and in media centres of corporate websites. This creates the impression that the company itself does not have a clear understanding of its approach or of the outcomes that it is trying to achieve, or even that the company is reluctant to draw attention to its animal welfare position. It also means that important information can be overlooked and not reported. For example, the 2015 report from the Business Benchmark on Farm Animal Welfare found a number of companies that had received notable awards from organizations such as Compassion in World Farming and the Humane Society but had not even mentioned these awards on their websites or in their communications (Amos and Sullivan, 2016).

It is therefore important that companies provide a consolidated account of their approach to farm animal welfare, allowing stakeholders to find all of the company's published information on farm animal welfare in a single location on the company's website and/or via links on the company's website to published reports. An increasing number of companies have now established dedicated areas of their websites to provide accessible information about their food policies and sourcing approaches. Notable examples include Coop Group (Switzerland), Cargill, Cranswick, Greggs, Marks & Spencer, McDonald's, Migros, Nestlé, The Co-operative Food (UK), The Wendy's Company, Tesco, Unilever, and Waitrose.

Another criticism that can be levelled at current corporate reporting is that many companies do not provide regular and timely updates on practice and performance. Most companies tend to report selectively on farm animal welfare, presenting case studies and good news stories, rather than structured, quantitative data that enables progress and performance to be tracked over time. This is particularly noticeable in companies that have published strategic commitments to higher welfare practices, such as the phasing out of gestation crates for sows or the elimination of cages for laying hens. Given that the timeframe for such targets and objectives is typically long term (i.e. five years or more), the majority of companies, having put significant effort into publicizing their targets, then fail to provide regular and timely reports on their progress against them.

Finally, despite the progress that has been made in terms of the number of companies that are reporting on their farm animal welfare practices and performance, this reporting is far from institutionalized in many companies. For example, the 2015 report from the Business Benchmark on Farm Animal Welfare (Amos and Sullivan, 2016) noted that a number of companies had seen their overall score decline because they had failed to maintain or update their information on farm animal welfare. The report identified four distinct factors that seemed to be at play. First, some companies had revamped or redesigned their corporate websites, often deleting or reducing the information provided on farm animal welfare-related issues. Second, some had failed to update farm animal welfare-related information; the data provided by some companies was more than five years old (i.e. it had not been updated for at least five years). Third, some had started to produce integrated reports or reports that focused on those issues that were considered financially material to the business. This emphasis meant that these companies paid less attention to reporting on those issues considered to be less financially material, with farm animal welfare often falling into this category. Fourth, although this is a more speculative point, mergers and acquisitions appear to have a detrimental effect—at least temporarily—on the level of attention focused on farm animal welfare, and certainly on the quality of reporting on environmental and social issues more generally. It is not uncommon for the companies that have merged or been taken over to have their sustainability-related reporting subsumed into that of the new merged or the acquiring company, often with the loss of much of the detail on practices and processes on issues such as farm animal welfare. What is not clear is whether this reflects a permanent loss of capacity and expertise or whether, over time, the merged or acquiring company will strengthen its farm animal welfare-related reporting and build on the capacity and expertise of the combined companies.

Appendix

Table A.1 Farm animal welfare disclosure expectations

Specific disclosures	*Comments*
Overview	
General approach to farm animal welfare	*Companies should explain why farm animal welfare is important to their business.* Within this, they may want to discuss issues such as: • Compliance with legislation. • Compliance with relevant voluntary and industry standards. • Food quality and nutrition. • Food security and sustainability of supply. • Productivity. • Waste management and minimization. • Stakeholder/consumer expectations. • Pricing. • Business risk management. • Reputation management. • Market opportunities. *Companies should place farm animal welfare into a wider business context.* They should explain the importance—in financial terms, in brand/reputation terms, and in terms of stakeholder perceptions—of farm animal welfare relative to other social and environmental issues. They should also identify any tensions between higher farm animal welfare standards and the 'business case', and explain how they reconcile these tensions.

Table A.1 continued

Specific disclosures	*Comments*
Policy	
Overarching policy on farm animal welfare	*Companies should publish an overarching farm animal welfare policy.* The policy should set out their core principles and beliefs on farm animal welfare, and should explain how these beliefs are addressed and implemented throughout the business. The policy should: • Explicitly acknowledge that farm animals are sentient beings. • State why farm animal welfare is important to the business (including both the business case and the ethical case for action). • Set out the company's overarching expectations—for its own operations and for those of its suppliers—on farm animal welfare. • Describe how the policy is implemented, including information on senior management oversight processes, performance monitoring, and corrective action processes. • Clearly specify the scope of the policy. If the policy does not apply to all species, geographies and/or products, it should explicitly state the limits to and exceptions from the policy. • Commit the company to reporting on the implementation of the policy and the performance outcomes that result.
Specific policy positions on farm animal welfare issues	*Companies should publish formal policy statements on key farm animal welfare-related issues.* These issues include: • The close confinement of livestock. This should, as relevant, include discussion of their positions on specific close confinement practices such as sow stalls, concentrated animal feeding operations (CAFOs), feedlots, farrowing crates, single penning, battery cages, tethering, veal crates, force feeding, and stocking densities. • The use of genetically modified or cloned animals or their progeny (Stevenson, 2012). • The use of growth-promoting substances. • The use of antibiotics for prophylactic purposes (Bond and Jewell, 2014). • Routine mutilations. This should, as relevant, include discussion of their positions on practices such as teeth clipping, tail docking, dehorning, disbudding, mulesing, beak trimming and fin clipping. • The use of meat from animals that have not been subjected to pre-slaughter stunning or other processes that render them insensible. • Long-distance live transportation. Within this, companies should specify the maximum journey times (from loading to unloading) for animals. Companies should be clear about the scope of their commitments, in relation to the geographies, species and products covered by the policy. Companies should be clear about their aspirations, in particular their plans to reduce or phase out particular controversial practices. As relevant to their activities and operations, companies should set out their positions on the production and/or sale of controversial products such as foie gras, white veal, meat from religious slaughter and eggs from hens confined in barren battery cages.

Governance	
Responsibilities for farm animal welfare	*Companies should specify who is responsible for managing farm animal welfare-related issues on a day-to-day basis.* *Companies should specify who at board or senior management level is responsible for oversight of the implementation of the company's farm animal welfare policy.* This may be through a board-level committee that oversees a range of sustainability or responsible sourcing topics. In these situations, the farm animal welfare strategy should be explicitly identified as falling within the committee's remit.
Implementation	
Internal controls	*Companies should describe their internal systems and controls for farm animal welfare.* This should include discussion of: • Training in farm animal welfare for relevant employees (i.e. those involved in animal handling). • Pre-employment assessments (e.g. the farm animal welfare-related qualifications and experience expected of employees). • Monitoring processes (e.g. remote monitoring, site visits and audits, whistle-blowing mechanisms) in place to ensure compliance with the farm animal welfare policy. • The actions to be taken in the event of non-compliance with the farm animal welfare policy, including remedial action (e.g. follow-up visits or audits, performance monitoring).
Supply chain management	*Companies should describe how they implement their farm animal welfare policy through their supply chains.* This should include discussion of: • How farm animal welfare issues are integrated into supplier contracts, supplier performance reviews, and supplier monitoring and auditing processes. • How supplier performance on farm animal welfare is incentivized. • How they support their suppliers (e.g. through the provision of education, training, supplier briefings and checklists) to achieve higher farm animal welfare standards.
Performance	
Objectives and targets for farm animal welfare	*Companies should publish the specific objectives they have set for farm animal welfare.* Objectives and targets may relate to management processes (e.g. to formalize farm animal welfare management systems, to introduce audits) and/or performance (e.g. to phase out specific non-humane practices, to ensure that specific standards are consistently met for all species and/or geographies). *Companies should explain how their objectives and targets are to be delivered.* Specifically, they should comment on: • The actions that will be taken. • The capital and other costs that are expected to be incurred. • The timeframe for the delivery of their objectives and targets. • Responsibilities for the delivery of the objectives and targets. *Companies should explain how performance against their objectives and targets is to be assessed* (i.e. what indicators are to be used to assess performance).

Table A.1 continued

Specific disclosures	*Comments*
Reporting on farm animal welfare outcomes	*Companies should report on their performance against their farm animal welfare-related policies, and their farm animal welfare-related objectives and targets.* *Companies should report on the welfare outcomes achieved for the animals in their operations and in their supply chains (see further the discussion of performance reporting below).*
Leadership and innovation	
Demonstrating leadership on farm animal welfare	*Companies should report on the efforts that they have made to raise standards of farm animal welfare across the food sector.* This could include discussion of: • Their research and development programmes to advance farm animal welfare. • Their involvement in industry or other initiatives (e.g. working groups, supporting NGO lobbying, responding to government consultations) directed at improving farm animal welfare. • Any notable awards or accreditations they have received for their farm animal welfare performance within the previous two years. • Their engagement with their customers or their clients on farm animal welfare.
Performance reporting	
Reporting on the actions, processes and outcomes linked to the achievement of acceptable levels of welfare	*Companies should report on their farm animal welfare performance, both in terms of input-based measures (i.e. the type of production systems—housing, treatments and procedures, breed use, feeding and health management—used to rear animals as well as the practices for live animal transportation and slaughter) and outcome-based measures (i.e. species-specific measures covering physical and mental wellbeing and behaviour).* The indicators that might be used to structure this reporting could include: Input-based measures such as: • The proportion of animals free from close confinement and intensive feeding systems (e.g. cages for laying hens, sow stalls and gestation crates for pregnant and nursing sows, veal crates for calves, feedlots for cattle, force-feeding of geese, and high stocking densities for poultry, rabbits and finfish). • The proportion of animals free from routine mutilations. • The proportion of animals stunned prior to slaughter. • The average, typical or maximum journey times for animals during live transportation. Output-based measures such as: • Lameness and mastitis in dairy cows. • Gait score and footpad dermatitis in broiler chickens. • Tail-biting and lameness in pigs. • Bone breakage and feather coverage in laying hens. • Time spent resting/ruminating or foraging/socializing.

Box A.1 Examples of company positions on key welfare issues

Avoidance of close confinement

*Cranswick**

"Cranswick closely work with all our global suppliers and we are committed to the avoidance of confinement through all species. For example, in 2015 over 90% of pork processed by our sites was sourced from farms where sows are not confined during the gestation period. All our UK pork comes from Red Tractor approved Farms where it is a requirement not to confine Sows during the gestation period.

We do not source any beef from suppliers who use concentrated animal feeding operations (CAFOs).

Our commitment to avoid close confinement also extends into the ingredients that we purchase, all our egg products are sourced from free range farms.

Many of the pigs supplied to Cranswick are reared to higher welfare standards associated with outdoor bred or outdoor reared production methods. Approximately 50% of those processed by Preston, and 75% by Norfolk come from outdoor systems managed to the exacting requirements of the RSPCA Assured welfare standard, the balance of those processed are reared indoors in full compliance with the Red Tractor/BMPA Quality Assured Pork (BQAP) welfare standards."

Avoidance of genetically modified or cloned animals

Mitchells and Butlers (adapted from Amos and Sullivan, 2016, p. 46)

Mitchells and Butlers' Sourcing Policy specifies that "M&B prohibit the use of genetically engineered or cloned animals in the supply of products to our business and do not sell products made from cloned animals" and that these requirements "...apply to all proteins, including beef, pork, lamb, chicken, turkey and duck".

Avoidance of growth-promoting substances

Migros (adapted from Amos and Sullivan, 2016, p. 41)

Migros has made a formal commitment to the avoidance of all growth-promoting substances for all company branded products. Its Technical Dossier on Animal Welfare includes a zero tolerance policy on the use of growth-promoting substances, including antibiotics and hormones.

* https://cranswick.plc.uk/taking-responsibility/animal-welfare

Reduction or avoidance of routine antibiotics

FrieslandCampina (adapted from Amos and Sullivan, 2016, p. 43)
In 2013, FrieslandCampina developed a Quality and Safety Roadmap, which focused on improving the microbiological quality of its milk and reducing the quantity of antibiotics given to dairy cows. The company is working to reduce antibiotic use to 1999 levels and reports on progress against this target in its annual Sustainability Report.

Avoidance of routine mutilations

Marks & Spencer Plc (adapted from Amos and Sullivan, 2015, p. 43)
Marks & Spencer's Food Animal Welfare Policy specifies that "All livestock used for the production of our foods will be maintained in good health". In particular, it states, "We will not permit the routine mutilation of farm animals."

Requirement for pre-slaughter stunning

Danish Crown (adapted from Amos and Sullivan, 2015, p. 43)
"Danish Crown is keen to meet the slaughtering process requirements of other cultures, but animal welfare comes first. Our cattle slaughterhouses therefore also use the halal method of slaughter, although all animals are stunned before they are slaughtered. Halal slaughtering at our slaughterhouses is approved and monitored by the Danish Food and veterinary authorities. For halal slaughtering to take place, a Muslim must be present, who is authorized to conduct the ritual prayer. Halal slaughtering poses no problems with respect to animal welfare, food safety and the Muslim rituals."

Avoidance of long distance transportation

Greggs (see further Chapter 17 by Copland)
Greggs' live transport policy applies to all purchases of primary source raw pork, raw beef and raw mutton, cooked chicken, and egg laying hens (for whole eggs) at the end of lay. The policy is underpinned with species-specific commitments stating a maximum journey time of eight hours for pigs, cattle, sheep and chickens, from loading to unloading. Greggs will extend its policy to its remaining species according to a published timescale.

References

Amos, N. & Sullivan, R. (2015). *How are Companies Using the Business Benchmark on Farm Animal Welfare? Investor Briefing No. 21*. London: Business Benchmark on Farm Animal Welfare.

Amos, N. & Sullivan, R. (2016). *The Business Benchmark on Farm Animal Welfare: 2015 Report*. London: Business Benchmark on Farm Animal Welfare.

Bond, V. & Jewell, J. (2014). *The Impacts of Antibiotic Use in Animals on Human Health and Animal Welfare. BBFAW Investor Briefing No. 17*. London: Business Benchmark on Farm Animal Welfare.

Cooke, M. (2016). *Animal Welfare in Farmed Fish. BBFAW Investor Briefing No. 23*. London: Business Benchmark on Farm Animal Welfare.

Noble Foods (2015). Animal welfare results. Retrieved from https://www.noblefoods.co.uk/assets/PDFs/ANIMAL-WELFARE-RESULTS-2015.pdf

Stevenson, P. (2012). *Cloning and Genetic Engineering of Farm Animals. BBFAW Investor Briefing No. 6*. London: Business Benchmark on Farm Animal Welfare.

Sullivan, R. (2011). *Valuing Corporate Responsibility: How Do Investors Really Use Corporate Responsibility Information?* Sheffield, UK: Greenleaf Publishing.

Sullivan, R. & Amos, N. (2015a). *Farm Animal Welfare Disclosure Framework. Investor Briefing No. 18*. London: Business Benchmark on Farm Animal Welfare.

Sullivan, R. & Amos, N. (2015b). *How Are Investors Using the Business Benchmark on Farm Animal Welfare? Investor Briefing No. 20*. London: Business Benchmark on Farm Animal Welfare.

Sullivan, R., Amos, N. & Herron, A. (2015). *Engagement on Farm Animal Welfare: A User's Guide. Investor Briefing No. 19*. London: Business Benchmark on Farm Animal Welfare.

Waitrose (2016). *Animal Welfare at Waitrose*. Retrieved from http://www.waitrose.com/content/dam/waitrose/Inspiration/Waitrose%20Way/Animal%20welfare/Waitrose BBFAWVF2.pdf